THE NEW CHINESE CITY

Studies in Urban and Social Change

Published by Blackwell in association with the *International Journal of Urban and Regional Research.* Series editors: Chris Pickvance, Margit Meyer and John Walton.

Published

Fragmented Societies
Enzo Mingione

Free Markets and Food Riots
John Walton and David Seddon

Post-Fordism
Ash Amin (ed.)

The People's Home?
Social Rented Housing in Europe and America
Michael Harloe

Cities After Socialism
Urban and Regional Change and Conflict in Post-Socialist Societies
Gregory Andrusz, Michael Harloe and Ivan Szelenyi (eds)

Urban Poverty and the Underclass: A Reader
Enzo Mingione

Capital Culture
Gender at Work in the City
Linda McDowell

Contemporary Urban Japan
A Sociology of Consumption
John Clammer

Globalizing Cities
A New Spatial Order?
Peter Marcuse and Ronald van Kempen (eds)

The Social Control of Cities?
A Comparative Perspective
Sophie Body-Gendrot

Cinema and the City
Film and Urban Societies in a Global Context
Mark Shiel and Tony Fitzmaurice (eds)

The New Chinese City
Globalization and Market Reform
John R. Logan (ed.)

Forthcoming

European Cities in a Global Age
A Comparative Perspective
Alan Harding (ed.)

Urban South Africa
Alan Mabin and Susan Parnell

Urban Social Movements and the State
Margit Mayer

Urban Studies
Contemporary Perspectives
John Eade and Chris Mele (eds)

The New Chinese City

Globalization and Market Reform

Edited by
John R. Logan

First published 2002

2 4 6 8 10 9 7 5 3 1

Blackwell Publishers Ltd
108 Cowley Road
Oxford OX4 1JF
UK

Blackwell Publishers Inc.
350 Main Street
Malden, Massachusetts 02148
USA

British Library Cataloguing in Publication Data

A CIP catalogue record for this book is available from the British Library.

Library of Congress Cataloging-in-Publication Data

The new Chinese city : globalization and market reform / edited by John R. Logan.
p. cm. — (Studies in urban and social change)
ISBN 0-631-22947-7 (hbk : alk. paper) — ISBN 0-631-22948-5 (pbk : alk. paper)
1. Urbanization—China. 2. Urbanization—Economic aspects—China. I. Logan, John R., 1946– II. Series.
HT147.C6 N483 2002
307.76′0951—dc21

2001002523

Typeset in 10½ on 12 pt Baskerville
by Best-set Typesetter Ltd., Hong Kong

This book is printed on acid-free paper.

Contents

Figures

Tables

Contributors

Dan Abramson is a postdoctoral research fellow at the University of British Columbia's Centre for Human Settlements, with degrees in architecture and city planning. He has conducted urban housing and neighborhood research, planning, design, and development projects in China, Poland, and the United States.

Zhengji Fu is finishing his doctorate in geography at King's College London. He is interested in the urban development of China in the post-reform era, particularly the role of the state and capital in transforming urban patterns in Shanghai.

Chaolin Gu is Professor of Geography and Chair of the Department of Urban and Resource Sciences (Geography), Nanjing University. He has published over 130 papers and ten books about the urban system, planning, and social issues in China.

Li Jia is a postgraduate of regional development and urban planning at Zhongshan University, China. She has published several papers on science parks and population growth in urban China.

Fan Jie is Professor of Geography at the Institute of Geographical Sciences and Resources, Chinese Academy of Sciences, Beijing, and Head of the Department of Geography at the Peking Normal University. He has published many studies of industrial transformation, regional planning, and development in China.

Michael Leaf is an Associate Professor in the UBC School of Community and Regional Planning and a Research Associate of the UBC Centre for Human Settlements, where he is involved in projects on China and elsewhere in Asia. His publications focus on urban change in China, Vietnam, and Indonesia.

Jianping Li is a postgraduate of regional development and urban planning at Zhongshan University, China. He has published several papers on urbanization and commodity housing in urban China.

Taibin Li holds a master's degree in sociology from East China Normal University. He is a member of the faculty of the Department of Social Work, Shanghai Young Administrative Cadres College. His major fields of study are urban sociology and community work in Shanghai.

George C. S. Lin is Associate Professor, Department of Geography, The University of Hong Kong. He is the author of *Red Capitalism in South China* (1997) and many articles. His research interests include urban and regional development in southern China, China's changing land system and land market, transnationalism, and the geography of Chinese diaspora.

Haiyong Liu earned his master's degree at the Chinese Academy of Sciences, and he is currently a doctoral student in the Department of Economics, University of North Carolina at Chapel Hill.

John R. Logan is Distinguished Professsor of Sociology at the University at Albany, SUNY, where he directs the Lewis Mumford Center for Comparative Urban and Regional Research. He has published numerous studies of housing reform, income inequality, and family relations in urban China.

Rachel Murphy completed her doctorate in the Faculty of Social and Political Sciences, University of Cambridge, where she is currently a British Academy Post-doctoral Research Fellow at the Institute of Development Studies and Jesus College. She is the author of *How Migrant Labour Is Changing Rural China* (2001).

Alexius A. Pereira is a Senior Tutor at the Department of Sociology, National University of Singapore. He completed the PhD program in sociology at the London School of Economics and Political Science. His research interests are in the role of foreign direct investment in countries such as Ireland, Singapore, and China.

Alan Smart is Associate Professor and Head of the Department of Anthropology, University of Calgary. He has been conducting field research in Hong Kong and China since 1982, with a focus on urban issues, housing, foreign investment, and social change. He is the author of *Making Room: Squatter Clearance in Hong Kong* and many academic articles and book chapters.

Ngai-Ling Sum is Lecturer in Politics and International Relations at the University of Lancaster. She has research interests in the international political economy of East Asia, global-city strategies, city identities, and transborder regions. She is currently writing a monograph on the "cultural political economy" of globalization and regionalization in East Asia.

Ying Tan received her doctorate at the School of Architecture, Tsinghua University, where she served as Lecturer between 1997 and 2000. She has worked on planning and research projects concerning historic neighborhoods in Beijing and Quanzhou, Fujian, and on related issues of historic conservation, tourism, and participatory urban planning.

Wolfgang Taubmann is Professor of Human Geography at the University of Bremen (Germany). He has been conducting field research in China since 1980 and has published numerous articles and book chapters on migration, and rural and urban development in China.

Jizhuan Weng is a postgraduate of regional development and urban planning at Zhongshan University, China. He has published several papers on the urban modernization of China.

Duo Wu is Professor of Sociology at East China Normal University in Shanghai, where he also serves as director of the Sociology Research Center. He is Vice President of the Sociology Association of China. He has published numerous articles and books on urban sociology and the sociology of community in China.

Fulong Wu is Lecturer in the Department of Geography at the University of Southampton, and previously worked in Cardiff University, the University of Hong Kong, and Nanjing University. He has published papers on housing and land development and urban structures in China. He is currently studying urban governance and social spatial differentiation in Chinese cities.

Weiping Wu teaches urban studies, planning, and geography at Virginia Commonwealth University. Her current research and teaching interests include comparative urban development policy, migrant settlement and adaptation, and urban economic geography. She has published three books and many articles on urban and development issues in China and other developing countries.

Xiaopei Yan is Professor of Urban Geography, the Vice Dean of the College of Earth and Environmental Sciences, and the deputy director of the Center for Urban and Regional Studies at Zhongshan University, China. She has published numerous studies of industrial restructuring and spatial transformation, producer services, urbanization, urban land use, and science parks in urban China.

Min Zhou is Professor of Sociology and Asian American Studies at the University of California, Los Angeles. She has published extensively on immigration and immigrant adaptation, ethnic and racial relations, ethnic entrepreneurship, and the immigrant second generation. She has also done work on housing reform in China and intra-Asian migration.

Yixing Zhou is Professor of Urban Geography and chair of the Department of Geography, Peking University. He has published numerous studies on China's urbanization, urban system, urban policy, statistics, and planning.

Preface

The primary mission of this book is to introduce readers to the far-reaching changes that are now taking place in urban China. The contributors describe cities that are new in many dimensions. They are larger, taller, and more sprawling than those of the socialist era, offering higher standards of housing and consumption, but at the same time more segregated by class and social position and between natives and newcomers. In the best traditions of urban scholarship, these chapters link the visible changes in urban life to changes in the larger political economy of China. Broad notions of the transition from socialism, market reform, and globalization – concepts that are central to understanding this country's re-emergence on the world stage – are given tangible meaning in terms of more mundane questions about people in the city (like how much tenants pay for rent and where migrants can find a protective niche) and about how cities develop (like why local governments have become growth promoters, how profits are reaped from redevelopment, why new skyscrapers stand empty, or how foreign investors make connections in the Chinese market).

This book marks a step in the development of a mature and self-conscious urban research community in China. Just fifteen years ago the few whose writings on these topics were widely available, such as anthropologist G. William Skinner, sociologist William Parish, and geographer Laurence J. C. Ma, were pioneers, working with incomplete data and typically based in universities in the West. Now there is quite a large and diverse array of scholars studying the processes of urbanization, migration, and urban planning and their impacts on Chinese society, many of whom are employed in universities and research institutes on the mainland. Several of the most senior and productive urbanists in China have contributed to this volume, as have some of the most promising in the new generation of scholars. Many have received training in both China and the West. Better data, more advanced techniques, and a wider range of theoretical ideas are being brought to bear now. Readers will find here sophisticated institutional analyses, survey methods, urban applications of geographic information systems, and ethnographic fieldwork.

It is no longer a novelty to find original research on urban China in the major academic journals. International conferences in this field are now held regularly. Indeed, this book itself is the result of such a conference, one that I organized in Shanghai in 1999 with the cooperation of sociologist Lu Hanlong, Director of the Institute of Sociology at the Shanghai Academy of Social Sciences. The initial impetus for the conference came from the Research Committee on Urban and Regional Research, a component of the International Sociological Association, whose founders are also responsible for publishing the *International Journal of Urban and Regional Research*. The post-conference activity that brought this volume to fruition is part of a longer-term effort to strengthen this field through the Urban China Research Network. Based in Albany and supported by the Andrew Mellon Foundation, the Network offers grants for research by graduate students and young Chinese faculty members and fosters new collaborative projects through international working groups.

I wish to acknowledge the many debts that I have accumulated in the years that I have conducted research in China. My deepest gratitude is to Nan Lin, who created opportunities and connections in China for me and for others, and to the Chinese sociologists whom I first knew as my students but whom I now appreciate as collaborators: Min Zhou, Yanjie Bian, and Fuqin Bian. Lu Hanlong (Shanghai Academy of Social Sciences) and Pan Yunkang (Tianjin Academy of Social Sciences) have been long-term partners in data collection and scholarship. For their financial contributions to the Shanghai conference, I thank the Foundation for Urban and Regional Studies and the American Sociological Association, as well as the Vice President for Research, the Center for Social and Demographic Analysis, and the Lewis Mumford Center for Comparative Urban and Regional Research of the University at Albany.

John R. Logan
Albany, New York

Part I
Introduction to the New Chinese City

1
Three Challenges for the Chinese City: Globalization, Migration, and Market Reform

John R. Logan

China has a special place in the sociological imagination, particularly at this juncture of history. As the clock has ticked into a new millennium, China's connections to an ancient past remind us of the continuity of time. Our sense that this civilization is poised for a new leading global role turns our thoughts to the future, to transformations that are barely begun, but to which China now seems irrevocably committed. The weight of tradition and the promise of change combine to make this a remarkable moment. A century from today, we suspect, people will take for granted that this nation was being reshaped at this time, that a new, more dynamic society was being forged in the coastal zones of East Asia.

China has set out on a path whose destination is unknown. We certainly can chart the major changes of the past two decades, when the Cultural Revolution was brought to a close (in 1978) and the revolutionary ideology of Chairman Mao's red book was supplanted by a pragmatic leadership more concerned with economic performance than with political purity. The government's encouragement of joint ventures with foreign investors, combined with the availability of a vast, low-wage, and underutilized labor force, boosted exports of consumer products to the West to phenomenal levels. Work units, even large enterprises in the state sector, were gradually released from central planning controls and given incentives to increase productivity and to seek profitability. Slowly, the workforce began to shift from the traditional state sector to enterprises that mixed private, cooperative, and state ownership in new combinations. Bonuses, which soon became half or more of workers' net wages, were instituted to reward successful work units; the days of a standard, low salary for just about everyone were only a memory. Standards of living rose sharply for both rural and urban residents in the coastal zones. And relaxation of a wide variety of restraints on mobility (from controls on work unit recruitment methods to the end of the system of grain rationing that provided for only authorized city residents) made it possible for large numbers of migrants to move into cities and their surrounding hinterlands. China's cities grew again in tandem with economic expansion: the best estimates show the country evolved from only 12 percent urban in 1950 (and not much more than that at the end of the Cultural Revolution) to close to 30 percent in 1993 (Chen and Parish, 1996).

Something Old, Something New . . .

In fact, the debate over where China is headed – and how fast – is the core question for China scholars. There is no support for the exuberant optimism that led some economists to expect the former socialist countries of the Soviet bloc to be able instantly to create effective market institutions. There is agreement, instead, that China has taken a slower course, that its current status should be called "partial reform" rather than radical marketization. Within this consensus, sociologist Victor Nee (1996) takes the strongest position, predicting a process of displacement of state sector enterprises (representing the centrally planned economy) by the private sector (representing a free market economy). His theoretical imagery envisions these two sectors as remaining separate, one shrinking while the other grows; at the point sometime in the future that the economy becomes predominantly private, reform will have been completed. Nee has been most interested in the ramifications of this process in the stratification system, and especially in the allocation of income. The state sector, he has argued, organizes income inequality mainly along lines of bureaucratic authority. Especially, he emphasizes, it rewards Party membership. The private sector, in contrast, rewards skills, especially education. His model therefore implies that the structure of income inequality will shift over time alongside – and as an indicator of – the shift toward a market economy. Party membership will lose value, while education gains value.

This same logic shows up in other domains. For example, Guthrie (1996) argues that managers with more experience and contact with Western firms, and in more competitive sectors, will be the first to adopt modern industrial management methods, and that these will diffuse throughout the economy as market reform progresses. If we extend this model to the housing sector, we find the current official government view of housing reform: that allocation of housing as a collective good must be replaced by the treatment of housing as a market commodity. In conformity to this principle, apartment rents have been raised from nominal levels to more substantial amounts, and residents have been encouraged to purchase their homes outright (a conversion that now has been extended to more than 50 percent of the housing units in some cities). Housing provision, too, is being marketized. Real estate development firms have been created with the mission of building for a profit; land that was formerly simply allocated for new projects is now bought and sold. The result, potentially, is a new process of urban development and housing allocation, the replacement of a socialist city by a market-driven form.

As always, there is an alternative view. Many China scholars, and perhaps the majority, perceive a strong continuing state presence in what others think of as the market economy. One apt characterization is Zhou's (2000) account of the state and market sectors as two interpenetrated spheres. Work units and other actors in the state sector increasingly find good reasons to take market processes into account – if only, as when the army decides to build and sell trucks as a way to finance arms purchases, to share in the fruits of the private sphere. And at the same time, ostensibly "private" transactions often have a strong public connection, as witnessed by the occasional show trial and punishment of high officials who used their insider status to turn a private profit. It would be a mistake to think of this interpenetration mainly in terms of corruption, however. The fact is, in China it is the state, the Central Committee of the Communist Party, that decided to embark on the path of market reform, and the concrete choices made at every step of the way are marked by the state's continuing intervention. It is the persistence of the Communist Party's rule that naturally implies the persistence of an economy where private interests are interpenetrated with public agencies.

Hence, for example, being a member of the Communist Party, or working for an enterprise with strong connections to the authorities, continued in the early 1990s to be associated with earning more (Bian and Logan, 1996), or with getting allocated a larger or better equipped apartment (Logan et al., 1999). The great transformations of the political economy notwithstanding, traditional ties to influence continued to count.

A central question for research on the new Chinese city is, therefore, how new is it? To be more precise: what aspects of the current explosive urbanization should be interpreted as outgrowths of pre-existing processes of planning, control, and distribution – characteristic of socialist China – and what should be understood as the urban impacts of emerging market processes?

The same question arises in the case of the East European countries that have undergone market transitions in this era. Summarizing research on these changes for the purpose of analyzing their urban impacts, Harloe (1996) emphasizes that the free market was not born whole in 1989. "The transformation now taking place in the former state socialist nations is path-dependent," he writes (1996, p. 10), "it is shaped by cross-nationally (and subnationally) variant historical legacies and current conjunctures. Rather than some simplistic and immediate process of abolition of the economic, political and social structures of state socialism and their replacement by those of an idealized Western capitalism, we see a conflictual and contradictory complex of social actions in which differing groups deploy what resources they have available to secure their position in the new order."

We must be careful not to be misled by use of the term "privatization" to describe the market reforms being undertaken in East Europe or China. As others have emphasized (Walder, 1996), what is at stake is not simply "ownership" but "property rights" over the use of land, the built environment, and future development, a set of social relations involving control, extraction of profit, and investment. China created a very complex system of property rights in the guise of "socialism," and there is an equally complex set of transformations under reform.

Comparison with urban patterns in East Europe also reminds us that we must be cautious in our view of what was specifically "socialist" about the pre-transition situation. Szelenyi (1996) argues that there were distinctively socialist patterns, not necessarily according to the designs of socialist planners, but due broadly to "the consequences of the abolition of private property, of the monopoly of state ownership of the means of production, and of the redistributive, centrally planned character of the economic system" (p. 287). These features included under-urbanization (relative to capitalist systems at the same industrial level), low levels of spatial differentiation, unusually low density in central areas, and few signs of socially marginal groups. Old neighborhoods were allowed to deteriorate, while new construction was focused in high-density blocs in peripheral zones. Similar observations could be made about urban China through the 1970s.

There are, of course, great differences between the Chinese and other socialist experiences. Market reform in China was introduced by newly ascendant members of the old regime, rather than by an entirely new governing coalition, and it was implemented in the context of economic expansion rather than collapse. Szelenyi (1996) believes the economic crisis in East European cities has temporarily blocked some potential effects of privatization. These include new rural–urban movement, and a substantial increase in diversity of use of urban space, with small shops, markets, new marginality, crime, and deviance. Szelenyi envisions also suburbanization and urban decay, as inner city areas suffer crime and environmental problems that render gentrification undesirable. To some extent, the Chinese experience – where the economy has expanded rather than contracted – offers a test of his view. On the other hand, the stability of political control may explain why China has not experienced some of the other expected consequences of the transition, such as the social, ethnic, and nationalistic movements, and collective action

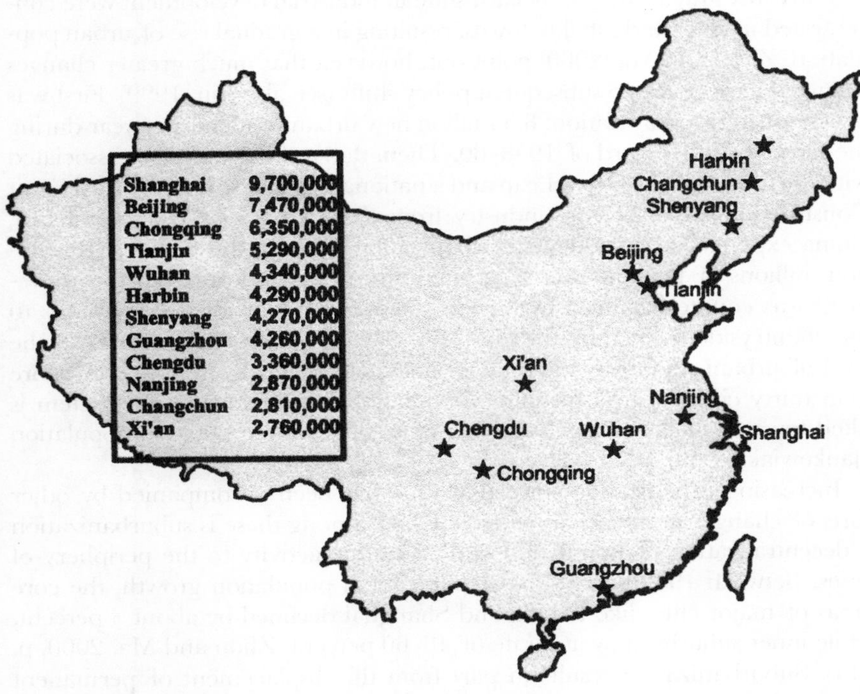

Figure 1.1 Twelve largest Chinese cities (showing non-agricultural population in 1999) (*Source: Statistical Yearbook of China*, 2000)

on issues of housing privatization, that occurred in East Europe. Such mobilization is still under wraps in China.

China's Urban Pattern

China is unusual even in the Third World for its historically lagging level of urbanization. Its older urban centers (like Nanjing and Beijing) used to have a primarily administrative function. A limited number of treaty ports (such as Shanghai, Wuhan, Tianjin, and Guangzhou) became industrial and trade entrepots after the mid-nineteenth century, and these cities grew through large-scale migration through the early twentieth century. A map of China (figure 1.1) shows that the dozen largest cities are highly concentrated along the coast. These are major cities, indeed, with populations in the millions. Still, at the time of establishment of the People's Republic (1949), China was largely a rural nation.

Early investments by the socialist state in industrial development were concentrated in cities and satellite towns, resulting in a gradual rise of urban population. Zhou and Ma (2000) point out, however, that much greater changes occurred in response to subsequent policy shifts (see also Lin, 1999). First was a wave of mass urbanization: 8.3 million new urban residents per year during the Great Leap Forward of 1958–60. Then, due to food shortages associated with the failure of the Great Leap and a national defense strategy (Third Front Construction) of dispersing industry from the coastal cities to the interior, China experienced a sudden de-urbanization. During the Cultural Revolution millions of peasants were recruited into urban industry, but this movement was counterbalanced by "sending down" millions of urban youths to the countryside. Hence by the end of the Cultural Revolution in 1978 the level of urbanization was still only around 17 percent. Even now, with more than thirty cities of over a million population, the nation's urban system is tilted toward smaller places, with 375 cities of less than 200,000 population (Jankowiak, 1999).

Increasing urbanization since that time has been accompanied by other sorts of changes in the urban pattern. Chief among these is suburbanization – decentralization of population and economic activity to the periphery of cities. Between 1982 and 1990, despite overall population growth, the core areas of major cities like Beijing and Shanghai declined by about 3 percent, while inner suburbs grew at a rate of 40–60 percent (Zhou and Ma, 2000, p. 214). Suburbanization results in part from the displacement of permanent city residents out of core areas due to urban renewal activities by the state. Also, work unit investments in new housing vastly increased in the reform era, and these are often located in inner suburbs because of the availability and price of land. Another factor has been the infusion of migrants from the countryside, who are restricted by government policy largely to peripheral zones (a phenomenon discussed in more detail below).

Suburbanization has also been stimulated by changes in the valuation of land. As central locations became more valuable, there were large profits to be reaped from moving out of core areas, especially by large industrial work units that were under pressure to leave the city for environmental reasons and that could take advantage of newly available suburban locations. Suburban land prices, in contrast, were artificially depressed, because land rights were held collectively by villages, and villagers valued not only the cash transaction but also the possibility of gaining urban residency rights and new housing in return for agricultural land.

The trend of urban development can also be seen in the rising levels of investment in the built environment. In Shanghai, for example, Zhu (2000) documents these dramatic changes between the period 1953–78 and 1979–95: investment in fixed assets rose from 8.6 to 40.6 percent of total output, and investment in housing rose from 0.4 to 7.4 percent of total output.

Housing construction soared from 18 million to 86 million square meters in the later period. (For an overview of reforms in the housing sector itself, see: Wang and Murie, 1996; Logan et al., 1999.)

Two chapters in the first section of this book (chapters 2 and 3) summarize and comment on these changes. Duo Wu and Taibin Li describe Shanghai's rapid growth in the 1990s in mostly positive terms, noting the successful redevelopment of the old center alongside the creation of a new and expanded city. They applaud the increasing reliance on market mechanisms and the more limited role of government. Their analysis nonetheless concludes with a number of concerns for planners: the inadequacy of public infrastructure, estranged human relationships, and poor adaptation of migrants to city life. By contrast, Yan, Jia, Li, and Weng emphasize the emerging costs of the metropolitan transition – from new social inequalities to environmental damage. They are especially critical of the lack of coordinated plans on the part of government, and they argue for stronger and more comprehensive social planning mechanisms to counteract these costs. It is important to note that both of these evaluations come from a Chinese perspective, and they reflect a discussion that rages behind closed doors about the character of the new Chinese city. What is at stake is the balance between state planning and market forces, a very sensitive topic given the regime's overall commitment to abandon central controls.

Global Impacts on the Chinese City

As much as in Western market societies, China's urban development depends upon (and its development options are limited by) the country's global connections. This is not a new phenomenon; indeed, most of China's major coastal cities developed under foreign influence after the mid-nineteenth century. Shanghai grew mainly to the north of the confines of its old walled city, with extensive French and English zones that were actually governed by the consuls of those countries. Not until the end of the Second World War, when the Japanese were expelled, was modern Shanghai fully under the control of Chinese authorities. Several of China's major cities therefore always have had both a Chinese side and a global one.

An important indicator of global connections is foreign direct investment, which grew exponentially after 1991 (having recuperated from the effects of the 1989 Tiananmen repression), reaching a total of $16 billion in 1996 (Wu, 2000, p. 1361). Since 1993 foreign investors have been allowed to develop commodity housing for the domestic market, and real estate soon accounted for more than a third of the value of new contracts signed for foreign direct investment. Thus they play a strategic role in urban renewal, replacing older residential neighborhoods with mixed residential/commercial projects. Their chief advantage in this realm is their ability to provide large upfront capital investments, while local government is relatively land-rich and cash-poor. Hence, as in the West, localities have found themselves competing for outside investment.

Foreign investment is one feature of the emerging "global cities" of coastal China. Sprawling Beijing, the nation's capital, lies to the north, with the port city of Tianjin only a short drive away on the new divided highway that connects the two cities. Shanghai, arguably the new economic power center of China, lies near where the Yangtze River completes its journey through such major cities as Wuhan. In the south, where Guangzhou was once the key trading center and Hong Kong was maintained by the British as a kind of international free market city, there is a confusing new lineup. Here within a short distance of one another are Macao (retrieved from Portugal), Zhuhai (a free trade zone created alongside Macao to attract foreign investment), and especially Shenzhen (the newly established city of millions, created as an experiment in international trade and investment). Hong Kong, of course, remains the big city of this Pearl River Delta region. But surprisingly, the bulk of new growth is in the rural towns that lie in the hinterlands of these cities.

Yixing Zhou (chapter 4) proposes that China's first "world city" – a center with the size, economic power, and international weight of cities like New York, London, and Tokyo – will be a regional urban agglomeration of Hong Kong with the Pearl River Delta. This is a very special case, because it involves a very high density of transactions across borders in a relatively limited regional space. The operation of this "Greater China" network (Sum, 1997), involving China, Hong Kong, and Taiwan, hinges on the efficiency of complex transborder networks of actors.

China's Communist Party Central Committee stimulated investments in this region by deciding in 1979 to adopt special policies toward development in Guangdong and Fujian provinces (reforms that were extended later throughout the country). Many enterprises were transferred from central to provincial control, there was a shift from fixed to variable, negotiated prices for products, local governments were allowed to retain 70 percent of surplus foreign currency earnings, and wage reforms were introduced at the enterprise level. Further, Special Economic Zones (SEZs) were established in Shenzhen, Zhuhai, Shantou, and Xiamen. Offering cheap land and labor, common cultural tradition and language (Cantonese and Fujianese), and counting on established personal and kinship connections, officials at the county and township or village level had great success in soliciting investments, first from Hong Kong and later (after 1988) from Taiwan.

Alan Smart (chapter 6) suggests that the *de facto* regional integration that has evolved in this case, despite coexistence of quite different political economic systems on either side of the border, offers new insight about how global connections are carried out. The border itself, he points out, creates opportunities for manipulation of exchange. It now allows unfettered movement from Hong Kong to China, but restricts Chinese access to Hong Kong. The low-wage labor market and ambiguous character of market reform on the Chinese side provides openings for creative opportunism by entrepreneurs with subcontracting ties to Hong Kong. Other mechanisms for taking advantage of the border have even stronger elements of social transgression (from maintaining second wives on the Chinese side to paralegal real estate deals). Up to now, reliance on cooperation and trust, or what Smart refers to as "muddling through" (using informal and under-regulated institutions to manage exchanges), has been successful. But it is unclear whether the real mechanism has been a temporary convergence of interests (allowing outside investors to give up a share of their profits to local Chinese elites in exchange for stable returns). What will be the longer-term relationship between the Pearl River Delta region and the global system?

Part of the answer depends upon Hong Kong itself. Sum (in chapter 5) points out that there have been fierce debates in the past five years about Hong Kong's development strategy, partly inspired by the collapse of Southeast Asian bubble economies in the late 1990s. As textile and other industries were relocated in South China, the performance of Hong Kong's service and property sectors has become more crucial. How can these be sustained? Sum describes two alternatives that have emerged, to develop as an industrial site at high levels of technology, or to aim to be a world service and financial center.

Another part of the answer depends upon competition with other regions. Zhou (chapter 4) suggests that Shanghai will eventually surpass Hong Kong due to its more favorable geographic location with respect to the Chinese hinterland. What could also make a difference, of course, is the central government's willingness to continue to promote Shanghai. It is not simply by chance that the former mayor of Shanghai has now risen to the top of the central government elite. Analyzing the relative success of Hong Kong, Shanghai, Beijing, and other contenders for world city status in China opens a window on the interaction of domestic and global forces in urban development.

More can be learned by exploring these interactions in detail within individual cities. Our interest here is primarily in the impacts of globalization on the process and form of urban development. Thus we highlight the ways in which the locus of decision-making has been altered under these conditions. The key innovation – and one that derives as much from the Beijing-led decentralization of governmental power as from globalization – is the emergence of the municipality as the key player in urban development. And with new priorities: a large share of local government revenues now is drawn from urban renewal and real estate projects in which the municipality (or its district governments) is a partner.

Zhengji Fu (chapter 7) and Alexius Pereira (chapter 8) study these changes in Shanghai and Suzhou. Fu analyzes the specific constellation of local and global forces at work in Shanghai across six historical periods (beginning in the nineteenth century). Like Sum and Smart, he focuses on three categories of actors, representing foreign capital, the national government, and local elites. In the commercial city of the nineteenth century, he suggests, the central government was entirely absent, and development was managed by a dominant foreign faction in alliance with local elites. The socialist era, in turn, was unique in its exclusion of foreign capital and the dominance of national-level planners. In the current reform period, for perhaps the first time, all three play a significant role. There is a convergence of interests in developing the financial and services sectors, as symbolized in the creation of the Pudong development zone. Fu outlines the pattern of deal-making that has taken place around Pudong, and he concludes that the key roles are played by a coalition of local authorities and global capital – both of which seek growth more aggressively than does the central government.

This notion of a shifting triangle of power is illustrated again in Pereira's study of Suzhou. In this city, the national governments of Singapore and China contracted to collaborate in the creation of a vast new industrial zone. The project drew nearly $4 billion in foreign direct investment by 1999, vastly reshaping the character of Suzhou (formerly best known for its gardens and canals). But despite these successes, there were weaknesses in the inter-organizational network through which investment was conducted – in particular, the failure of the Beijing government to involve Suzhou municipal authorities in the project. Indeed, Suzhou initiated its own development zone in 1997. Pereira shows how these strains, combined with the Southeast Asian financial crisis of the late 1990s, led Singapore to withdraw from the project.

Market Reform and the Urban Development Process

Besides opening the country to new international influences, market reform has vastly reorganized the exercise of state power within China. Lin (1999, p. 673) summarizes the changes in terms of decentralization, concluding "that decentralization of decision-making has favored local governments, that the capacity of the central state has been eroded, and that the state system has become increasingly fragile or fragmented such that the central state can no longer monopolize local developmental affairs. . . . The combined result of decentralization, marketization and globalization has been a new central–local relation in which local governments and enterprises no longer play a passive and obedient role." Decentralization was not altogether altruistic: one motive for the national state was to shed its subsidies of local expenditures

(Wu and Yeh, 1999). But soon after giving fiscal responsibility to municipalities, the state also gave increased authority for land use planning. The 1989 City Planning Act made all urban land development subject to the control of the municipal planning authority.

The process of land development within cities has shifted too, including new market features. In the socialist era, development proceeded on a project-specific basis, pursued by a work unit in accordance with its commitments in the overall economic plan. Land was provided without charge (except for the costs of relocation and site preparation), and needed resources were allocated by the state.

There is now a mixed, or dual-price, system. This was first introduced in the SEZs in 1987, when the municipality of Shenzhen sold a 50-year lease to a local public company (though the price was negotiated behind the scenes: Zhu 1994). The notion of paying for use rights was originally applied only to foreign firms. Later, a dual land market emerged, and some land is now leased to users at some version of a market price (based on negotiation, tender, or auction), while other land is administratively allocated at well below market prices. This gap creates incentives for those who control the land to sublet it, as in joint ventures, and there has emerged a black market in leased land. The consequent "unregulated land conversions" take the land development process partly outside of formal channels, into the realm of informal agreements (Wu and Yeh, 1999, p. 379).

As has turned out to be true for many municipalities at the present time, the Shenzhen authorities controlled land, but did not have adequate funds to cover initial infrastructure provision, so they adopted the procedure of displacing land development costs to public building companies or end users. These, in turn, speculated on the value of prepared sites. There have been some spectacular failures, at least in the short term. In 1995, 40 percent of Shanghai's commodity housing was unsold, and vacancy rates remained over 40 percent for class A commodity offices and housing by July 1998 (Zhu, 2000, p. 192). Nonetheless, land development continues to be perceived as a profitable field. Local governments now commonly participate in development projects as partners with domestic or foreign investors, with land provided by the locality and financing by the investor (Zhu, 1996). Municipalities seek new revenues, and state enterprises seek to convert their control of property into income, creating two entirely new kinds of local interest in growth. They, as well as investors, now serve their own interests rather than fulfill national economic plans.

Wu (2000) points out that in the largest cities authority is decentralized to district and suburban county governments. To varying degrees this encompasses planning, financial management, public works maintenance, pricing of staple commodities, foreign trade, and industrial and commercial administration. The fragmentation of governmental authority creates the potential for conflicts between the general citywide plan and detailed district plans. And, as is well known in metropolitan areas in the United States, it has stimulated fiscal competition among urban districts and adjoining counties. Their local development plans typically seek high density commercial and service development, for the sake of the value-added and business income taxes that these would generate. Since the realization of such plans requires external capital, the emerging Chinese system of land development gives great influence to "private" developers (the ambiguity here is in what to consider private, since many of the enterprises and development companies in this system remain formally public work units).

The contributors to this book offer more detailed analyses of how the process of real estate development was changing in the period of market reform. Zhou and Logan (chapter 9) report on fieldwork in the early 1990s in the South China province of Guangdong (adjacent to Hong Kong). As noted above, this is a region in which considerable foreign capital was being invested, much of it by émigrés who had maintained or recreated personal networks within the province. Zhou and Logan ask to what extent the recent introduction of market processes altered previous practices of land development and housing allocation. They emphasize that the introduction of "market" features was only partial. The pricing system, in particular, was arbitrary and subject to political negotiation. In this setting, outcomes were greatly influenced by the perceived interests of local authorities (to pursue revenues from development projects). A favored project would acquire public land at nominal cost; in other cases, land prices could be based on open bidding and approach the levels found in major cities around the world. In the domain of housing, another set of calculations was at work. It had become national policy for work units, which previously often built housing and provided it at low rents to employees, to withdraw from the housing market. Apartments were to be sold to the occupants, and new housing was to be built and sold in a private market. But national policy had not taken into account the interests of work unit leaders: housing was a scarce and valuable resource, and control over its allocation was an important source of power. Zhou and Logan document the creation of a complex system of internal rules and housing subsidies through which work units retained much of their influence over "privatized" housing.

Fulong Wu (chapter 10) offers a similar view of Shanghai. He documents the accelerated and largely speculative investment in commodity housing in the 1990s in Shanghai, of which an increasing share came (surprisingly) not from foreign but from domestic sources. Visitors to this city at the turn of the century witness the results in stark fashion, as blocks of old row housing in the city and formerly cultivated fields in the surrounding suburbs are replaced by modern residential towers, many of which remain unoccupied. Wu provides a detailed analysis of the trends of investment, and he uses his statistical data to develop more fully the notion that a new kind of urban regime is emerging in Chinese cities. In his view, the key features of property-led development in Shanghai are: (a) transferring capital at the enterprise level from production to the consumption sphere; (b) opening the property market to foreign investment; and (c) creating a Chinese version of the growth machine, where the lead actor is the local state apparatus.

Note that in both of these analyses, the residents of the city are a missing actor. There seems to have been a marginalization of grassroots interests, that may have been represented previously, at least indirectly, by their work units (Wu, 2000, p. 1368). There is now an evident lack of representative mechanisms. Thus not only, as Fu points out in Chapter 7, is the central government being squeezed out of participation in the new urban regime, but local residents are not yet finding a place at the table. Is the political marginalization of the public viable in the long term? This is a difficult topic to discuss openly in China, much less to study, but certainly it is at the core of the urban future.

The following chapter of this volume (chapter 11) touches on this question. Abramson, Leaf, and Tan spent considerable time documenting (and trying to influence) the planning process in Quanzhou, China's third most historic city (after Beijing and Xi'an). They encountered the typical post-1989 pattern of growth promotion by district governments to raise revenue for services, with some very large scale projects planned. Yet local planners achieved large-scale urban renewal without destroying the city's historic core. How was this possible?

The authors identify three specific factors that make Quanzhou unique. First is the lack of state investment after 1949, due to the city's vulnerable location directly across the straits from Taiwan, which saved historic districts from redevelopment during the socialist period. Second is an unusual degree of participation by civil society, grounded in the fact that substantial areas of large homes remained under private ownership in the historic urban center. Residents resisted mass redevelopment plans. Third, local government – both planners and the public officials behind them – adopted the role of preserver. The authors believe that the local political elite had a special appreciation of the value of historical preservation. Perhaps also because the locality would not reap the rewards from land leases of privately owned properties, the government showed greater concern with limiting how private households used their own individual land parcels.

Considerable debate has taken place within China about the proper role of urban and regional planning. Early enthusiasm for market reform tended to discredit governmental intervention, but urban problems associated with rapid development have by now begun to stimulate new calls for controls on growth. It is unclear, though, whether the relative success of planning in Quanzhou can be extended to other major cities.

Migration and the Floating Population

In thinking about how urban growth is planned and controlled, it is the complex of elite actors – foreign, national, and local – that we have highlighted. Urbanization is also, however, a demographic phenomenon, and it is based on both rural–urban migration to the major cities and the transformation of smaller towns into sprawling metropolises. Economic expansion since 1979 has inevitably stimulated population movements, as migrants provide the labor force through which growth is possible.

Migration has soared despite legal impediments that have persisted from the socialist period. China's population registration system (the *hukou* system) places limits on movement, with particular emphasis on the distinction between having a rural or urban registration (the latter had the right to live in publicly provided housing, to receive grain rations, and other essential urban services). China has had a fairly stable number of "*hukou*" migrants, who formally change their registration to their new place of residence. These tend to have higher than average occupational standing and education, and they have numbered about 17–20 million migrants per year since 1982. The "floating population," on the other hand, are people with a more fragile (and perhaps temporary) connection to their new homes, reflected in lack of an urban registration. Their number has risen nationally from 20–30 million in 1982 to 80–100 million in 1995 (these estimates are by Chan, 1996a). Although many of these are seasonal migrant laborers in the countryside, a growing number have short-term work contracts in cities of up to 2–3 years, and their presence in the construction and service sectors has an increasingly permanent character. Chen and Parish (1996) estimate the urban "floating population" at from 10 percent in Harbin to 30 percent in Guangzhou in mid-1990s.

The emergence of a private sector economy, particularly in retail trade and personal services, offers job opportunities for undocumented urbanites. Many employers now recruit extensively in rural areas, hiring migrants as temporary contract workers and often providing dormitory housing for them. In sectors with labor shortages, often the process of labor recruitment is well organized and conducted by public agencies. There is much current discussion about reform of the *hukou* system, though up to this moment officials have simply extended mechanisms for temporary migration and housing without basic public entitlements.

Most migrants are concentrated in the urban fringe, where they are able to rent private housing from peasants in outlying towns and villages (though new mechanisms have been developed for the more affluent among them to arrange residence rights in the city proper). Hence, just as in market societies throughout the world, large-scale migration results in new patterns of social inequality and spatial segregation. This is a recent phenomenon in China, though of course it has antecedents in the pre-socialist history of every Chinese city. One aspect of this process that merits more attention is the creation of social networks and boundaries based on people's region of origin (Jankowiak, 1999, p. 376). Emily Honig (1992) argues that migration has historically created the equivalent of ethnic groups within Chinese cities. In the case of Shanghai, she shows, the Subei people who migrated from Jiangsu Province continue to be a despised minority group. Ethnic relations in Western societies are understood to be very intimately tied with migration. In China there is a marked avoidance of the concept of ethnicity, except to refer to certain small minority groups on the periphery of the country. More commonly used is the concept of "native place identity" associated sometimes with language, sometimes with cuisine, and sometimes even with specific sorts of economic activities.

Fan and Taubmann (chapter 12) introduce readers to the scale of rural–urban migration in contemporary China, as well as unique aspects of the marginal legal status of migrants in this society. They provide numerous examples of migrant enclaves in Beijing and Shanghai to show the variety of settlement patterns, as well as common features among them. These "urban villages" illustrate how official state policy (in this case, the *hukou* system and more concretely the security concerns of the police) is reinterpreted in actual practice according to local interests (in this case, the needs of enterprises and the interests of local residents who benefit from migrants' service activities and housing rentals).

Gu and Liu (chapter 13) examine the same phenomenon in post-1984 Beijing, giving greater emphasis to emerging social inequality in the city. They argue that some aspects of the changing occupational structure are attributable to global forces, particularly service sector growth stimulated by foreign investment. But they believe that the new spatial inequalities found in Beijing are more directly linked to migration – to the internal reforms that unleashed the rural exodus and to the open door policy that created a new highly paid professional class, including many foreign managers and people who work for them.

A third perspective on the floating population is provided by Weiping Wu (chapter 14), who uses unique 1997 survey data on the floating population of Shanghai to describe the housing and settlement patterns of migrant households. Excluded from the formal housing distribution system, migrants live predominantly in work unit dormitories and in rented private housing on the fringe of the city. Wu points out that the geographic expansion of the urban area has brought many formerly agricultural villages within the city limits, where former farmers realize large profits by renting space to migrant workers. The strongest determinant of migrants' locational pattern, though, is not housing availability but employment opportunity.

Urbanization of the Countryside

While most scholarly attention is focused on the very visible impacts of new migrant settlements in China's largest cities, another feature of the reform period is a recasting of the relationship between the city and the countryside. Lin (1999) points out that there has been a restructuring of the urban hierarchy, favoring smaller places. People in cities over 500,000 constituted only 50 percent in 1995 of the urban population, down from 63 percent in 1978 (Lin, 1999, p. 685). And studies of population movements showed that towns received a larger share of migrants (40 percent) in 1987 than did cities (37 percent). Lin concludes that "these towns have become the major destinations for most migrants, especially rural–urban migrants" (p. 686).

At the same time, there has been a restructuring of the urban–rural boundary, especially due to the explosion of non-agricultural production in township and village enterprises. New infrastructural investments result in villages that "are becoming more town-like, while regional towns are becoming more city-like" (Jankowiak, 1999, p. 372), changes that Guldin (1996, 1997) describes as deagriculturization, townization, and citization. As awkward as these terms are, they reflect important changes in the meaning of rural or urban residence. "In the words of local people," writes Lin (1999, p. 688), "Chinese peasants are able to 'leave the soil but not the village' and 'enter the factory but not the city.' The spatial consequence of this process . . . has been a new settlement form in which industrial and agricultural or urban and rural activities take place side by side." In the Pearl River Delta, where population growth is largely in formerly agricultural zones, peasants consider a new calculus: is it better to achieve an urban registration status or to take advantage of shared payments for the development of collective farmlands which a rural *hukou* entitles them to?

Murphy (chapter 15 in this volume) analyzes one specific form of this transformation, linked to the substantial return migration to rural counties. In her case study (Jianxi Province), the main consequences are the participation of return migrants as entrepreneurs in the local economy, and the introduction of new technologies and skills in rural towns. Local policy is to promote a permanent shift to an "urban" labor force in the countryside. Officials seek to make connections at Spring Festival (when many emigrants visit their home town) and through networks with migrants still in cities, encouraging their return, and sometimes recruit them to take over (under contract) a state enterprise using "urban" methods. Murphy reports that such return migrants are a potential force for social and political change in the countryside, as they resist the pressure of local cadres for tax payments and donations, and lobby for new methods of raising capital (such as channeling of remittances from cities). Because returnees have their own networks to the outside world, they challenge the established system, though up to now their activities are encouraged by local officials.

Lin (chapter 16) draws our attention back to the Pearl River Delta, where economic and population growth are spread throughout the intermediate zone between metropolitan centers (like Guangzhou, Shenzhen, and Zhongshan). This pattern does not result from urban sprawl, in the sense of people moving out of urban centers. It is more a matter of the destination of migrants within the region and from other provinces. Migrants have settled outside major cities in part due to high housing prices and formal policies restricting residence in officially "urban" settings. Perhaps more important, job development is mainly stimulated by rural industries at the village level, depending on foreign investment and export products. New cities (in the SEZs) and medium-sized cities grew quickly in the past two decades, and formerly rural Baoan and Dongguan Counties themselves took in 45 percent of the total migrant population in the region. Lin's work illuminates the combination of international networks and local growth promotion that make this possible.

Urban China as a Research Frontier

It is easiest to study a country through a single prism. But in the case of China, all observers are aware that the country has been involved in multiple transitions since the 1970s. Each of these is so far-reaching as to merit attention in its own right. One headline, beginning in the midst of the Cultural Revolution, has been China's opening to the world, taking its place in the United Nations Security Council. A second headline, stemming from expansion of the export sector in the post-Mao period, has been explosive economic growth. A third has been a radical restructuring of the economy, sweeping away much of the Soviet-style central planning system. Another, at least as it seemed until mid-1989, was an opening of the political process within and beyond the Communist Party.

These transformations are closely interlocked, in part because they are being managed and coordinated by the central authorities in Beijing and in part because progress in each becomes a condition for advancement in the others. The interconnections, as expressed in China's urban transformation, are extensively documented in this volume. We have least to say about political change. Indeed, uncertainty about the country's political future is an unstated contingency in most current urban research. Discussion of the role of the public, the participation of residents in planning the future city, or emergence of urban social movements is notable by its absence. This does not mean, though, that the issue of political participation is absent. It has an offstage presence, and it has evident links to the other domains.

To begin with, China's opening to international exchange is itself a potential stimulus to political transformation. Open access to information and alternative models from other countries is one source, deepening over time as hundreds of thousands of Chinese – including many from elite families – live and study abroad. Another is information and communication technology, accepted by the regime as necessary to economic growth but at the same time a key new organizational resource for civil society. In other cases (new democracies around the globe, in established zones of Western influence as well as in Eastern Europe) political change has been put on the table as a prerequisite for economic exchange. This is unlikely to occur so overtly in the Chinese case, but the interruption of investment and trade after the events of June 1989 demonstrates that external assessments of China's political situation do have practical consequences.

Economic growth is another stimulus to broader political participation. An urban middle class is being created, based not only in a growing professional and technical category but also in a nascent entrepreneurial elite extending from major cities to town and village enterprises. A new migrant urban working class is also arising, distinct from the established urban population in legal standing and access to collective resources. It is an axiom of political theory that such groups will eventually become aware of their common interests and seek ways to protect them.

Reform of the central planning system is another component with deep political implications. Some of these revolve around the resolution of differences at the highest levels of the Communist Party. Questions about how to organize and control the economy and society have divided the leadership since the 1950s, even though a certain degree of consensus has been imposed by the personal authority of Party heads, first in the radical direction pressed by Mao Tse-Tung and then in the direction of market reform under Deng Xiao-Ping. To achieve his policies, Deng had to work simultaneously to accommodate to, but limit the influence of, Party radicals who outlived Chairman Mao. He and his successors have consolidated what appears to be an unstoppable direction for the country. But divisions about political reform – intermittently intensified in the 1980s when market reformers rallied around issues of freedom of speech and of the press, and subdued since 1989 – have not been settled. Indeed, market reform has introduced new political complications in the form of high-level corruption. Conservatives, who presented themselves as defenders of the Party's leading position in the 1980s, now claim to protect the Party's moral character.

At another level, the reform program is inherently also a political restructuring, because it involves so thorough a decentralization of authority. Enterprises and municipal government have gained much more autonomy of operation, with strong incentives to promote their own local interests. While the Communist Party remains present in both of these arenas, decentralization inevitably loosens the connections across levels of the party hierarchy and limits the reach of the Central Committee in Beijing. Of course, the strategy here may be for the Party leadership to give up responsibility in many domains in order to protect authority on the most essential ones. But the devolution of power is considerable, and it creates new opportunities for expression of interests. Without touching the Communist Party's formal position as a self-perpetuating political elite, it undermines the state authority in Beijing through which the Party previously ruled.

The general processes investigated in this book are not unique to China. Globalization clearly is not a country-specific phenomenon, even if its ramifications vary. Migration is the basis of urbanization everywhere. If it appears to be distinctive in the Chinese case, because of the long history of restrictions on population mobility, China's new "floating population" is nonetheless quite similar to the marginal migrant populations found in much of the Third World, and even in some global cities of the post-industrial world. The issue of market reform arises in China in a unique way, but the transition from socialism to some kind of market society is now a common experience for many countries. And if we conceive of "market reform" in broader terms, the real question is the changing relationship between the state and the economy. At that level there have been changes in the West in a similar direction. In the United States, for example, there has been a remarkable transition from one version of a social welfare state to a new political economy in which the issues of redistribution are much less salient than the promotion of economic development. It cannot be a coincidence that the transition that we describe as market reform in China has such similar results.

Studying China, then, brings into relief comparisons with other countries, and theoretical ideas against which to understand both Chinese cities and cities elsewhere. This is a country where everything is changing before your eyes, and a visitor can return after a year's absence and be surprised at the transformation. It has a kind of frontier character. There has never been such a case, a Third World country propelled so quickly toward the first rank of world powers, at the same time as making a transition from a centrally planned to a market society. And, because urban scholarship in China – by the Chinese as well as by international researchers – is still young, we may also see urban China as a research frontier. The contributions in this volume are a step toward exploring this magnificent territory.

2
The Present Situation and Prospective Development of the Shanghai Urban Community

Duo Wu and Taibin Li

Since 1990, Shanghai has been moving into a phase of accelerated urbanization. Through an exploration of community construction of the Shanghai city proper in the past few years, this chapter investigates and analyzes the primary issues concerning urban community development in the city.

The Basic Trend in Shanghai: Accelerated Urbanization

As a city constructed in modern times, Shanghai has only a century-long history. Prior to 1949, Shanghai had become the financial, trading, and economic center of the Far East. From the viewpoint of social development, however, the city had already experienced a number of complex problems and conflicts. As the social system changed after the liberation, a new chapter was conceived in the urban development of Shanghai, though the manifestation of these changes has only been evidenced in the past few years. Drawing on its own strength and endurance, Shanghai has attempted to overcome these difficulties and, since 1990, has experienced accelerated economic system reform. "Accelerated urbanization," a term that signifies rapid progress in a short period, is evidenced in the expansion of Shanghai's city scale, changes in population structure, improvements in the urban environment, and pronounced progress in municipal administration.

Since the reform, Shanghai's economy has developed substantially, with the gross national product (GNP) per capita having increased precipitously.

Table 2.1 Proportions of industries in Shanghai (percentages)

Industry	*1980*	*1985*	*1990*	*1993*	*1995*	*1997*
Primary	3.2	4.2	4.3	2.5	2.5	2.3
Secondary	75.7	69.7	63.8	59.6	57.3	52.2
Tertiary	21.1	26.1	31.9	37.9	40.2	45.5

Source: *Shanghai Statistical Yearbook* (1998).

Moreover, in the early 1990s, Shanghai's GNP per capita exceeded $1,000, while in 1997 the figure was over $3,000. Statistics show that the proportion of primary and secondary industry in GNP has decreased gradually, while that of tertiary industry has increased. This currently leaves Shanghai in a transitional stage from an industrial economy to a service economy (see table 2.1). Under such circumstances, the acceleration of urbanization in Shanghai is inevitable.

Shanghai's development is evident not only in the change in its industrial structure, but also in changes in city scale, construction, social life, and other urban-related aspects. During the past few years, accelerated urbanization has been manifested in the following ways.

Remarkable expansion of the city

The overall structure of Shanghai's city proper, suburbs, and county remained relatively stagnant from the 1950s to the 1980s. Until 1990, only two districts – Minghang and Baoshan – had been added to the city proper. In 1990, the central government decided to develop Pudong, with the expectation that Shanghai would become an international economic, financial, and trading center, and the leader of Yangtze River commerce. This decision greatly advanced Shanghai's economic development and the economy of both city proper and suburbs advanced side by side. The development of the economy of the outskirts is especially noteworthy, with suburban areas urbanizing quickly. Thus, the existing structure of suburb and county could no longer adapt to development and was, therefore, no longer viable (see table 2.2), and the decision was made to expand the city's territory. In 1990, Shanghai city proper covered 748.71 square kilometers, while the downtown area covered 280.45. By contrast, in 1997 the urban area reached 2,643.06 square kilometers, while the downtown area reached 359.36 square kilometers. These figures represent an increase of 253 and 28 percent, respectively, from 1990 (Shanghai Statistical Bureau, 1990, 1998).

Table 2.2 The adjustment of counties and districts in the 1990s

	1990	*1998*
Districts	Huangpu, Nanshi, Luwan, Xuhui, Changning, Jinag'an, Putuo, Zhabei, Hongkou, Yangpu, Minhang, Baoshan	Huangpu, Nanshi, Luwan, Xuhui, Changning, Jinag'an, Putuo, Zhabei, Hongkou, Yangpu, Minhang, Pudong New District, Jading, Baoshan, Jinshan, Songjiang
Counties	Shanghai, Jiading, Chuanshan, Nanhui, Fengxian, Songjiang, Jinshan, Qingpu, Chongming	Nanhui, Fengxian, Qingpu, Chongming

Source: *Shanghai Statistics Almanac* (1991) *and Report of Shanghai Civil Administration Development* (1998).

Significant changes in the urban population structure

As the economy developed and the city expanded in scale, Shanghai's urban population increased rapidly. In 1990, the urban population in Shanghai was 7.8348 million, although by 1997 that figure had increased to 10.1859 million. At the same time, the population's education also increased. In 1990, there were 94 college students per 10,000 people, while in 1998 the number was 126 per 10,000. Among working people, the percentage of the population that had at least a two-year college education increased from 7.9 percent in 1990 to 11.6 percent in 1997 (Wu, 1999f).

With both the development of Pudong and Shanghai's overall construction, the latter has become a focal point for the flow of migrant labor. In 1997, the accumulated flow into Shanghai was 2.76 million, with those in the city proper amounting to 2.32 million. On the one hand, the floating population flowing from other areas has contributed to economic development and urban construction, thereby promoting Shanghai's urbanization. Yet, on the other hand, a new problem has arisen that asks how the floating population can be assimilated into Shanghai's urban life.

Acceleration of infrastructure construction and rapid investment growth

The most obvious proof of accelerated urbanization is the pronounced improvement of the urban environment and the rapid construction of infrastructure. Prior to its reform, Shanghai's urban infrastructure was underdeveloped due to the scarcity of investment and the high population density. After its reform, especially after 1990, Shanghai has increased its investment in the construction of urban infrastructure. A large number of projects have been integrated, and include the construction of intersects, the south–north viaduct on Chengdu Road, the viaduct on Yan'an Road, the viaduct of the overpass, and the No. 1 and No. 2 subway lines. In 1997, Shanghai invested 41.285 billion yuan, almost eight times as much as the 1990 investment of 4.722 billion yuan. This increasing investment in infrastructure has resulted in remarkable improvements in the urban environment. One example of such improvements is demonstrated in the city's tree planting initiative, which has resulted in a 5 percent increase in grassland coverage. In 1990, grassland covered 12.36 percent of Shanghai's urban area, while by 1997 coverage had increased to 17.8 percent (Shanghai Statistical Bureau, 1998, p. 107).

Progress in municipal administration

In the past few years, to meet the needs of economic development and modernization, the Shanghai municipal government proposed and gradually initiated a new system of municipal administration known as "two levels of government, three levels of administration." This new administrative system, operating on the principle of "maintaining district divisions, cooperation among districts, a stress on function, and coordinated development," will reinforce the connection between districts, and will fulfill and enhance the administrative and financial power of *jiedaos* (neighborhood committees). The new system functions by dividing the following: politics and enterprise (to separate the functions of government bodies from those of enterprise); politics and institutions (to separate the functions of government bodies from those of institutions); and politics and society (to separate the functions of government bodies from those of social organizations). In keeping with the requirements of a socialist market economy, neighborhood committees practice overall governmental administration according to the principle of "small government, big society." This new administrative system and its supplementary mechanisms will be responsible for coping with various problems and improving municipal administration – a prerequisite for urban acceleration.

Since 1990, the city has undergone more rapid construction and a more profound change in its environment than it had since it first opened its ports 150 years ago.

Rebuilding the Old City Proper

Since 1990, and in tandem with rapid economic development, adjustment of the industrial structure, accelerated urbanization, and rising standards of living, Shanghai has accelerated the redevelopment of the inner city. At the peak of this process, slums and dilapidated houses were demolished and new houses were erected in their place, main roads were connected and broadened, and a large number of enterprises shut down.

Shanghai has been redeveloping key areas in the inner city since 1980, when a comprehensive plan was developed to reform 23 neighborhoods. Among these neighborhoods were Tianmuxi Road, Hengfeng Road, Siping Road, Hongqiao Road, and Yaoshui Nong in the Putuo District; Citizen Village in the Xuhui District; Xiling Jiazhai in the Nanshi District; Jiugeng Li in the Hongkou District; and Ruifu Li in the Huangpu District. The urban environment was improved considerably by these initial reforms.

Shanghai initiated urban renewal by addressing the problems of those considered to be "households with difficulties in housing." These households were concentrated in slums and dilapidated buildings where the urban infrastructure was less developed. Because these areas were consistently plagued with traffic jams, inundation in the flood season, unstable voltage, shortage of water, and ineffective telecommunications, all of which affected the city's normal functioning, this site became the focus for redevelopment.

In 1987, the population of Shanghai's urban areas was 6.9 million. The population in the downtown area was approximately 40,000, while the population in the high-density area reached 160,000. However, the housing area was only 7,589,000 square meters – of which the area of slums and dilapidated houses accounted for 370,000 square meters – with the old style neighborhood occupying one-third of the total area. The average housing area of some 216,000 households was less than 4 square meters, and 1.666 million households had less than 2 square meters. In 1987, Shanghai began to accelerate its housing construction to assist those households with 4 square meters or less, especially those with less than 2 square meters. As a result, the city has provided housing for 109,613 such households (Wu and Xu, 1999).

In the early 1990s, there were still 3,632,187 square meters scattered throughout the downtown area occupied by slums and dilapidated houses, with floor space of 6,546,975 square meters (see table 2.3). To resolve the problem of those "households with difficulties in housing" and to accelerate the reconstruction of the old city area, the Sixth Meeting of Party Representatives in Shanghai recommended that, by the end of the twentieth century, 3.65 million square meters of slums and dilapidated houses must be redeveloped, with the living area per person reaching 10 square meters, and the proportion of multi-room housing reaching 70 percent. In 1997, the Seventh Meeting announced that the reform of the old district, in and on both sides of the intersect viaduct, would be completed by the year 2000.

Once this goal was established, the reconstruction of the inner city moved to the next level, with an acceleration in renovation and the removal of slums and dilapidated housing. This activity has been completed in some areas. For

Table 2.3 Slums and dilapidated houses in Shanghai's downtown area

District	*Area (m^2)*	*Floor space (m^2)*	*Dilapidated houses*	*Slums*	*Total number of slums and dilapidated houses*
Yangpu	673,537	1,219,775	5,679	4,629	10,398
Zhabei	407,536	711,965	2,194	4,188	6,382
Hongkou	679,880	1,227,863	1,991	6,499	9,490
Putuo	529,616	963,371	2,259	5,236	7,495
Changning	503,169	897,150	1,675	4,236	5,893
Nanshi	273,337	501,573	926	2,827	3,753
Jing'an	142,024	261,182	1,290	777	2,067
Luwan	119,230	215,329	626	1,700	2,326
Xuhui	303,858	548,767	1,545	2,800	4,345
Total	3,632,187	6,546,975	19,167	32,897	52,059

Source: Application center of remote sense technology, Tongji University: *The Remote Sense Research on Slums and Dilapidated Houses in Shanghai Downtown Area* (1995, p. 7).

example, Luwan district completed the renovation of 337,800 square meters three years earlier than planned. As of mid-1998, there were still 1,250,000 square meters left unfinished, most concentrated in the Putuo, Nanshi, and Yangpu Districts (Ji Wen, 1998).

In August 1998, a reform campaign was initiated for "Two *wan* [bays] and one *zhai* [house]" (Panjia Wan, Tanjia Wan, and Wangjia Zhai in the Putuo district). Located to the south of Zhongshanbei Road, to the west of Hengfengbei Road, to the north of the Suzhou River, and to the east of Guangfu Road, and covering a total area of 49.5 hectares, this area was once the site of 10,500 households. On average, there were once 30 households per mu (1 mu = 0.0667 hectares), and 147 working units, which included 13 city-owned large and medium-sized factories. Although the construction and population densities here were the highest in the city, there were no hospitals, public bathhouses, or well paved roads. Furthermore, the area could not be reached by bus, and there was a shortage of water, electricity, coal, and communication. By the end of May 1999, the project of relocating "two *wan* and one *zhai*" had been completed, and this notoriously poor street disappeared for good (Zhu and Ni, 1999).

To accelerate urban renewal, Shanghai engaged in widespread fundraising. From 1990, the Shanghai government's adoption of the new administrative system of "two governmental levels, three administrative levels" made it possible for the district government in the downtown area to participate in redevelopment activities. Toward this end, the district government invested a large amount of capital, and Shanghai made full use of foreign investment and land leasing. In early 1992, with the approval of the government, the Xiesan Jidi (base) around the Dapu Bridge in the Luwan District became the first site to be reformed by way of land leasing. Both land leasing and foreign investment added incentive to redevelopment, and from 1992 to 1997, 582 pieces of land were leased, more than half of which were located in the old city.

Impressive progress has also been made in new infrastructure. For instance, a large number of residential complexes have been built, such as Mengteli Square in the Nanshi District and Da'an Garden in the Jing'an District. The housing area per capita increased from 6.6 square meters in 1990 to 9.3 square meters in 1997, and grassland areas have also increased. In 1990, there were 1.02 square meters of public grassland per capita, with 12.36 percent of the city covered by trees and grass. By 1997, these numbers increased to 2.41 square meters and 17.8 percent, respectively (Shanghai Statistical Bureau, 1998).

Due to a series of large-scale construction projects, urban renewal, and the construction of residential complexes, the population of the downtown area dispersed to the city's outskirts, leading to a yearly decline in population density. Statistics indicate that this trend of decline is most obvious in downtown areas like Huangpu, Jing'an, Luwan, and the Nanshi districts. To illustrate, the population density in the Huanspu district declined from 70,308 persons per square kilometer in 1993 to 58,964 persons per square kilometer in 1997, indicating a decrease of 16.1 percent. At the same time, the population shift in the high-density areas of Jing'an, Luwan, and the Nanshi districts dropped 10.9, 8.4, and 5.5 percent respectively (Xu, 1997).

As the region's total population has grown, the decrease of population density in the downtown area suggests that the population distribution has become increasingly rationalized. This has reduced the pressure on transportation and housing caused by a high population density in the downtown area. Furthermore, it has helped the population distribution to adapt to an industrial structure, thus becoming conducive to accelerated urbanization.

Certainly, there are still many old neighborhoods where living conditions are poor. In 1990, there were 30.67 million square meters of old neighborhood, and in 1997, 25.82 million square meters still remained (Shanghai Statistical Bureau, 1998, p. 100). The improvement of infrastructure is also an essential component of inner city construction, especially the extension of communication lines and expansion of grassland. The construction of the intersection, the subway No. 1 line, the south–north viaduct on Chengdu Road, the viaduct on Yan'an Road, the subway No. 2 line, and the widening of Wujingnan Road, Changning Road, Xizangnan Road, and Zhoujiazui

Road-Haining Road are all projects which indicate that there is much work yet to be done to reform the old city at the turn of the century.

Construction of the New City Proper

New city construction has become an important facet of community development in Shanghai. Along with the city's increasing expansion and new construction, the "new city proper" was formed. This now accounts for 71.67 percent of Shanghai's total area (Shanghai Statistical Bureau, 1998). The construction of the new village community is also an important facet of the new city proper construction, and complements both the old city reform and the expansion of various districts. From 1980 to 1997, Shanghai had built 16 new villages, including Kangle, Weifang, Liangcheng, Lutai, Leshan, Xinhua, Zhongyuan, Fengzhuan, Quyang, and Jinyang, as well as 115 neighborhoods, including Kangjian Eighteen, Huishan Base, Bamboo Garden B Neighborhood, Meilong Seven Village, and Shuiqing Number One Village (Chen Lingsheng, 1997). These new villages and residential quarters are located especially at the border between city and country, in such areas as the Pudong, Minhang, Jiading, and Baoshan districts, and the perimeters of the Yangpu, Putuo, and Changning districts.

Based on the differences in their community construction, the new villages have been divided into the following three categories:

1 *Common housing.* This type of housing was developed to assist the difficult to house from the old city. Floor space per household is relatively small. Examples of this category of housing are found in Shiguang, Guohe, and Minyuan New Village.
2 *Commercial housing for common people.* The market decides upon allocation of this type of housing. Living conditions are fairly good. An example of such housing is found in Jiande Garden.
3 *High-grade commercial housing.* In comparison to the two former categories of housing, this type offers better living conditions, better access to transportation, more sophisticated architectural styles, more amenities, and standardized management. These houses are mostly sold to foreigners. An example of this form of housing is the Gubei New Complex.

To better identify effective models for future residential complexes, Shanghai has built four prototypical model residential complexes located to the north, south, east, and west of the city: Xinjiangwan City in the Baoshan District; Chunshen City in the Minhang District; Sanlin City in the Pudong New District; and Wanli Quarter in the Putuo District. As time passed, the model residential complexes project progressed, and the number increased to nine. The

Table 2.4 Major economic and technical indicators of model residential quarters

	Unit	Sanlin City						Wanli Residential Complex	Xinjiangwan City	Chunshen City
		Nankuai West District	*Sanlin Yuan*	*Cuizhu Yuan*	*Anju Yuan*	*Nanping No. 2 Neighborhood*	*Zhongxin cooperation*			
Total area	hectare	225.5	11.92	6.6	8.85	8.77	43.56	191	294.3	163.1
Housing	hectare	125.4	7.61	5.23	6.15	4.63	26.54	91.6	190	67.4
Public construction	hectare	43.0	1.87	0.42	0.9	0.82	6.01	35.5	22.3	27.9
Public grassland	hectare	34.1	1.37	0.35	1.0	1.18	6.13	30.3	34	24.8
Road	hectare	23.0	1.07	0.6	0.8	0.75	4.88	33.6	48	17
Total construction area	10,000 m^2	280	18.4	10.6	12.68	9.26	47.1	198.65	285	169.4
Housing	10,000 m^2	245	14.36	9.7	12.15	8.8	42.6	166.95	250	148.2
Public construction	10,000 m^2	35	1.73	0.9	0.53	0.35	4.4	31.7	35	21.2
Planned number of households	House-holds	30,000	2,090	1,480	1,930	530	5,150	19,700	28,000	14,500
Planned population	10,000 persons	9.8	0.67	0.47	0.68	0.17	1.648	6.1	8.2	4.91
Ratio of tall buildings	%	20	0	0	0	38	32	–	20	30
Ratio of grassland	%	33	30	35	33.4	38	40	40	45.3	45.2

Source: *Shanghai Almanac of Economy* (1998).

five new complexes – Fengpuyuan, Pingyang New Village, Tianxin Garden, Jinqiaowan, and Qingshuiyuan and Hongkang Garden – were designed to accommodate 490,000 new residents (Wrnzhong et al., 1999, p. 32), and were expected to occupy nearly 2,000 hectares, more than 15 million square meters of floor space, and more than 12 million square meters of housing space.

Overall, the new villages exhibit the following characteristics:

1 *Better living conditions.* The majority of households have multiple rooms, and the housing area per capita is far above average than that in Shanghai.
2 *Green spaces are emphasized.* The natural environment of the new village is in good condition, with grassland coverage around 40 percent.
3 *Maintenance of property management.* Both property and houses are maintained and operated commercially.

As a result of economic development, the expansion of Shanghai's urban areas, and the urbanization of its suburbs, many new towns have sprung up near the old city, including Xinzhuang, Qibao in the Minhang district, Zhenru in the Putuo district, Jiangqiao in the Jiading district, Yanqiao in the Pudong New district, and Wujiaochang in the Yangpu district (see table 2.4). Xinzhuang is an excellent representative of the newly developed towns. With the Minhang District government located directly in Xinzhuang, the district has become a focal point for commercial housing development (Shanghai Statistical Bureau, 1998, p. 563). Specifically, the Shanghai Xincheng, currently under construction in Xinzhuang, occupies 89.2 hectares, with a planned construction area of 2,040,000 square meters. This modernized complex, accommodating a shopping center, restaurants, a center of business and information, cultural and recreational facilities, and a commercial and financial center, makes Xinzhuang Industrial Park a municipal-level industrial region and burgeoning commercial center (Shanghai Municipal People's Bureau of Civil Affairs, 1999, p. 52). Furthermore, the completion of the subway No. 1 line has greatly improved transportation and connection to the greater urban area. With the establishment of the Xinzhuang Intersection – the largest intersection in Asia – and the Eastern Pearl light rail line, it is expected that transportation will become even more convenient as Xinzhuang continues to develop.

The town of Wujiaochang in the Yangpu district also serves as a good example of the newly developed towns. For example, the construction of the intersection and the Yangpu Overpass has improved transportation, thus bringing about a population increase. Furthermore, these developments have enriched the commercial economy and aided in the development of technology, education, culture, and tourism. In the hope that it would become a subcenter of hotels, finance, and commerce at the municipal level, the Yangpu

Table 2.5 The change in town and county structure in Shanghai

Year	*1990*	*1994*	*1996*	*1998*
Number of urban districts	12	14	14	16
Number of systemized towns	13	60	83	117
Number of systemized counties	13	2	3	3

Note: In 1991, there was one county systemized in Yangpu District, 12 in Baoshan District; in 1994, there were 27 counties systemized in Pudong New District, one in Xuhui District, one in Changing district, and three in Baoshan District; in 1996, there were two counties systemized in Baoshan District and 12 in Xuhui district.
Source: Summarized statistics in *Shanghai Statistics Almanac* (1991, 1995, 1997), and in *The Report of Shanghai Civil Administration Development* (1998).

district announced that the pace of Wujiaochang's construction would be accelerated, thereby extending into the center north of Shanghai.

The development of new towns is apparent in changes to county and town structure. For instance, in 1990, 13 towns and 13 counties in 12 districts were systemized, while in 1998, 117 towns in 16 districts and only three counties were systemized (see table 2.5). This recent increase indicates that Shanghai's outskirts have become primarily urbanized.

To a certain degree, the development of the new village community and initial urbanization in the outskirts took certain functions and pressures from the old city, especially those pertaining to commercial services, cultural and recreational facilities, and industry distribution. As a result, the industrial structure pattern and population distribution in Shanghai has become more rationalized. Undoubtedly, with the expansion of the Shanghai urban area, new city construction will continue to progress.

Analysis and Prospects

Since the 1980s, the simultaneous reform of the old city and construction of the new city proper have constituted the majority of Shanghai's community development. From the start, Shanghai emphasized cooperation between redevelopment and construction. To its credit, the accumulated experience in the development of the city proper has thereby resulted in the formation of a nearly flawless operational mechanism. Since 1990, the overall city construction has been completed, with evidence ranging from the expansion of city limits to the development of new housing complexes and neighborhoods. Analysis of Shanghai's urban community development over the past few years reveals the following operational components:

- *An effective administrative system.* A highly effective city administrative system is the guarantor of success for community construction; therefore, the administrative institutes must be streamlined, rigorous, and effective. Since the April 1996 Meeting of Administration in Shanghai, lower-level administration has gained more power with its acceptance of responsibility for city oversight, and an administrative pattern of "combined strips with stretches as emphasis" was implemented. This pattern has raised administrative efficiency by encouraging the district governments to participate more fully in the construction of their city communities.
- *An efficient differentiation of territory.* In 1990, the State Council decided to turn Shanghai into an international economic, financial, and trading center. To this end, Shanghai reassessed the downtown area inside the outer overpass, and divided the area into six comprehensive districts. (a) The central downtown area, including the area inside the inner intersection, will serve as the locus of tertiary industry, such as finance and trade. Residential, cultural, and recreational facilities will be built accordingly. (b) The North district, including the area inside the inner intersect in Yangpu, Hongkou, in the Zhabei district, will serve as a host for industry, industrialized technology, collection and distribution centers, as well as large, modern residential complexes. (c) The West district, which includes the areas between the inner and outer intersection in Putuo and the Chagnning district, and the areas inside the outer overpass in the Jiading district, will become an important trading, commercial, and export center. (d) The South district, including the areas between the inner and outer interface in Xuhui, Luwan, in the Nanshi district, and the areas inside the Outer Overpass in the Minhang district, will be targeted for trading. Technology and education will also be developed in tandem with an improvement in living conditions. (e) The Southeast district, including the area to the south of Zhagnjiabang between the inner and outer intersection in the Putuo New district, will accommodate the technology industry and will serve as the center for new quality housing. (f) The Northeast district, including the area to the north of Zhagnjiabang between the inner and outer interface in the Putuo New district, will serve as the location for the building of related transportation links, bonded warehouses, and factories dedicated to export (Li, 1998a). The precise allocation of all of these functions clarifies the direction of city development and avoids wasteful duplication of both effort and facilities.
- *Operational construction planning.* Construction planning has been the cornerstone of community development in Shanghai for the past 20 years. In 1979, the city developed The Program for Shanghai City Planning, and in October 1986, the State Council approved The Program for Shanghai Overall City Planning, based on the previous report. Finally, in the early 1990s, the city issued The Program for Pudong New District Overall

Development. Although this development plan is in place, many regional projects have yet to submit their individual operational plans.

- *Clear definition of the government's role in the market economy.* The primary function of the government in the market economy is to create effective systems for economic and social development. In the reform of the old city and construction of the new city, the Shanghai government devolves the implementation of projects to the appropriate enterprises, such as real estate or construction companies. Furthermore, it provides infrastructural support to the implementation of these projects, and practices effective city planning. Yet, in order to guarantee a well funded and dynamic city construction, the government needs to rely more heavily on market forces, rather than administrative decree, to regulate city construction.

When analyzed closely, rapid development also reveals the existence of problems and conflicts in construction. First, because most of the newly built communities are far from the old city, transportation problems have arisen. With a daily commute of one to two hours each way for many of the city's inhabitants, this problem is becoming increasingly common. In addition, the problem of transferring children to new schools remains unsolved, leaving these children to attend schools in their old residential areas. Furthermore, the buses which run from some new villages to the downtown area are grossly inadequate, a problem which negatively affects both the lives of new village dwellers and the construction and development of the new villages themselves.

Second, a more efficient and effective system of real estate development and administration needs to be established. While some new villages have had a comprehensive plan from the beginning, with civil facilities, green spaces, educational facilities, and commercial and cultural services constructed simultaneously with housing construction, other new villages have struggled with their development plans, a problem that was also seen in the days of old city reform. In 1996, essential services and facilities comprised only 10.1 percent of the finished housing area, a shortage that greatly affected the lives of the city's residents. For example, in 1997, there was but one supermarket in Jinyang's new village in the Pudong New district. This and other shortages make it clear that the enhancement of basic living facilities is a priority for new village community construction.

Third, the construction of new village communities puts undue emphasis on material construction, while neglecting the factors of culture, society, and neighborhood. Since most dwellers in the new villages are not from the same working unit or residential quarter, the sense of community is weak at best. The living pattern in the new villages is generally comprised of one suite per household, and there is no contact among neighbors. Such conditions often lead to the "big building pathology," where inhabitants confine themselves to their own quarters. Apart from communicating with family members, they interact only with the technology of televisions and stereos. Given such conditions, each household becomes an isolated island. To amend this growing problem, the enhancement of human relationships and the fostering of a sense of community are of critical importance.

Fourth, with the expansion of the urban area and the increasing number of city residents, the role of new residents needs attention. According to residential registration records, these new city dwellers, many of whom are farmers, have not fully adopted an urban way of thinking and living. An apparent conflict of ideology and habits thereby exists between farmers and city dwellers, and it is feared that some of these differences will negatively impact community development. (For example, new city dwellers in the Jinyang residential complex once unknowingly ruined the grassland by planting a vegetable garden.) It is believed that only when a transformation in the attitudes of new city dwellers is achieved can the urban community begin to develop more healthily.

Based on the long-term development of Shanghai's community construction and especially its social construction, we are still faced with some problems that need further deliberation and straightening out. Specifically for Shanghai, these problems are as follows.

First is the boundaries of government responsibility. As discussed above, the government has clear-cut duties in infrastructure construction in conformity with the requirements of the market economy. However, there is still much government interference in the social environment, which inevitably brings some negative effects that are especially damaging to the enthusiasm of residents, groups, and other community organization. It is undeniable that government interference also has its positive effects on the promotion of community. Presently, it is rather urgent for the municipality to further clarify its own responsibilities and orient itself properly so as to achieve a desirable position in the course of Shanghai's community construction.

Second is the growth and activities of social organizations. Separation between government and community management is one of the aims not only of the reform policy but of community construction as well. To achieve such an aim, focus must be placed on the growth and development of social organizations, a lesson learned from successful foreign countries. Nevertheless, the growth of social organizations, and especially their participation in community development, is not yet satisfactory in Shanghai. There is no precedent to be used for reference or popularization in China regarding the cultivation of social organizations and getting them involved in community development; we still have much to ponder and probe.

Third is the training of social workers. The quality of social workers will have a direct influence on community work. So it is necessary to cultivate high-qualified workers so as to ensure the smooth undertaking of social work.

Though the city has already started training social workers, the following problems still need to be solved. How should professional knowledge and "locality knowledge" be combined? As a career, community work originated in the West. How can the West's work theory be made applicable to Shanghai's situation? Next, how can theory and reality be reconciled? Much professional knowledge is oriented toward communities' future development, in that it cannot be applied to the reality of starting development in a situation which in many aspects is not yet regularized. The third problem is the training of part-time social workers. Much needs to be studied and discussed to pin down training content, time, means, and outlay.

Last but not least is taking advantage of international experience in community construction. In spite of the local specificity of Shanghai's community activities, it is still necessary to promote exchanges with other regions, especially with overseas countries, thus drawing on their successful and unsuccessful experiences. Currently, there is little international interaction on the practical issues of community development, with even less on a theoretical level. It is necessary to increase both governmental and non-governmental exchanges.

3
The Development of the Chinese Metropolis in the Period of Transition

Xiaopei Yan, Li Jia, Jianping Li, and Jizhuan Weng

Although the policy of controlling the development of large cities has been under discussion in China since the 1950s, the number of metropolises with populations over a million has increased rapidly, even more so after economic reform. These metropolitan regions serve not only as national economic and cultural centers, but as sources of socioeconomic development. Furthermore, they reflect the general trend of worldwide urbanization. Currently, China is in a period of systematic transition from an industrial to a service economy. Considering the ongoing penetration of globalization into the economy, the widespread application of information technology, and the increasing participation in international affairs, this chapter explores the following questions. What are the characteristics of metropolitan development? How is development affected by these changes, and what problems are arising in this process?

The Characteristics of Metropolitan Development Since Economic Reform

There has been an obvious process of metropolitanization in China, even though it has been weakening since the 1990s. Due to the speed of economic reform and growth in China's cities, the number and size of its metropolises have developed rapidly. If we define a metropolis as a large city in which the non-agricultural population is above one million, in 1980 there were 15

Table 3.1 The number of cities and the urban population[a] of Chinese cities, 1980–1997

	Very large city			*Large city*			*Medium city*			*Small city*			*Total*		
	No.	*Pop.*	%	*No.*	*Pop.*	%	*No.*	*Pop.*	%	*No.*	*Pop.*	%	*No.*	*Pop.*	%
1980	15	3,511.30	39.0	30	2,231.30	24.8	72	2,128.90	23.7	106	1,126.80	12.5	223	8,998.30	100
1990	31	6,258.24	41.6	28	1,899.40	12.6	117	3,644.39	24.2	291	3,235.74	21.5	467	15,037.77	100
1997	34	7,462.09	34.9	47	3,241.09	15.2	205	6,275.54	29.4	382	4,380.45	20.5	668	21,359.18	100

Note: [a] Non-agricultural population in urban area.
Sources: *The Chinese Population Year Book* (1985), *The Statistics Year Book of Chinese Population* (1989, 1998), *The Statistics Year Book of Chinese Cities* (1991).

metropolises. The number then increased to 31 in 1990, and 34 in 1997 (see table 3.1).

The spatial concentration of metropolises has also been maintained. The line between the Black River in Heilongjiang province and Luxi in Yunnan province divides China into two parts – west and east. In 1980, 14 of the 15 metropolises were located in the eastern region, which accounts for 45 percent of the total area of China. Only one metropolis was in the western half. Similarly, in 1997, 32 of the 34 metropolises were located in the eastern half.

Adjustment of the socioeconomic structure of metropolises

The tertiary sector has developed rapidly and has occupied a leading role in the national economy. All metropolis industrial sectors have experienced unprecedented growth since the economic reform of the late 1970s, with industrial structures having altered accordingly. Regarding employment shares, the proportion of primary sectors has continued to decrease, from 68.7 percent in 1980 to 49.9 percent in 1997 (see table 3.2). Similarly, the relative position of the secondary sector has begun to weaken, though its absolute number of employees has continued to increase. The tertiary sector gradually surpassed the secondary during the 1990s, while the proportion of employment in the secondary sector increased by 5.5 percent from 1980 to 1997. The service sector also developed rapidly, with a 13.3 percent increase in employment in the tertiary sector during the same period. The change in composition of GDP also reflects trends in the industrial structural. The ratio of the three industrial sectors in GDP was 30.1 : 48.5 : 21.4 in 1980; by 1997, this ratio had changed to 18.7 : 49.2 : 32.1. This economic shift toward service industries is similar to those found in other countries. The transformation in Beijing, Shanghai, and Guangzhou is even more notable, with the tertiary sector's share of both GDP and employment having surpassed that of the secondary sector.

The diversity and rapid growth of the service sector

Since economic reform, the metropolitan service sector has undergone considerable development and increased in variety as well as size. On the one hand, the traditional sectors are growing rapidly, while, on the other hand, many new industries in the service sector have developed with comparable speed, especially those related to finance, insurance, real estate, information consulting services, computer application services, and scientific and technical services.

Table 3.2 The change of industrial structure in Chinese metropolises, 1978–1997

Industry	*1980*		*1990*		*1997*	
	Employee	*GDP*	*Employee*	*GDP*	*Employee*	*GDP*
Primary sector	68.7	30.1	60.1	27.1	49.9	18.7
Secondary sector	18.2	48.5	21.4	41.6	23.7	49.2
Service sector	13.1	21.4	18.5	31.3	26.4	32.1

Note: Figures are percentages.
Sources: *The Chinese Statistics Year Book* (1998).

This rapid expansion of producer services has increased the scope of the tertiary sector and has built momentum for continued expansion. For example, in Guangzhou, both the proportion of employment and the increased value of producer services were low in 1984. Compared to the tertiary sector as a whole, they were 4.27 and 12.59 percent, respectively. By 1992, however, those proportions increased to 7.57 and 27.46 percent, respectively. Though traditional service industries still predominate, the development of producer services is notable and reflects the growing importance of technical knowledge and information.

Radical change in social stratification and the development of a "gray-collar" stratum

Given that the service sector plays such a significant role in the metropolitan economy, those employed in the service sector (the white-collar class) have gradually gained in importance. Since the 1990s, due to the rapid development of the information industry, those white-collar professionals (including scientific researchers, technicians and technical administrators, doctors and medical technicians, teachers, and others) and leaders of administrative institutions have increasingly gained in importance, due to their technical skills and the emergence of a post-industrial society. The number of these professionals has expanded rapidly, and a new distinct class has evolved, known as the "gray-collar class." According to census data, in Guangzhou the 1982 employment share for gray-collar workers was 16.76 percent, but in 1990 this proportion changed to 20.53 percent. The gray-collar workers remain essential, though the internal structure of this class is unstable, with the number of leaders disproportionately large compared to the number of high-level professionals (Yan, 1999).

The Spatial Expansion of Metropolitan Regions

The phenomenon of metropolitan suburbanization

Chinese metropolises have shifted from the stage of urbanization (characterized by gathering) to the primary stage of suburbanization (characterized by both gathering and diffusion, centralization and decentralization) (Cao and Yanwei, 1998).

The first aspect of suburbanization is population deconcentration. The population decreases in metropolitan centers, increases rapidly in the closest suburban areas, and increases at a moderate rate in the more distant suburbs. As a whole, however, the population of the metropolises continues to increase. For instance, between 1982 and 1990, population growth rates for the urban center, near suburbs, and far suburbs in Beijing were 3.38, 40.46, and 13.12 percent, respectively. The rates in Shanghai between 1982 and 1993 were 2.26, 55.52, and –1.28 percent, while the rates in Shenyang were 6.73, 31.04, and 3.10 percent. At the same time, the total population of the metropolises of Beijing, Shanghai, and Dalian increased by 17.2, 6.28, and 16.6 percent, respectively (Zhou and Meng, 1998).

The second aspect of suburbanization is industrial deconcentration. While the share of industrial employment and production in the urban central area decreased, the proportion of suburban areas increased. Between 1980 and 1989, the proportion of factories in the old city of Guangzhou decreased from 38.37 to 27.19 percent, and the proportion of employment decreased from 37.51 to 26.21 percent. However, the proportion of factories in near suburban areas increased from 10.29 to 15.29 percent, while employment increased from 13.59 to 18.59 percent. No changes in the intermediate area between the old city and the surrounding suburban areas were noted (Chen and Cai, 1996).

The third aspect of suburbanization is the deconcentration of the service sector. The traditional service sector has grown rapidly in suburban areas (Ning and Deng, 1996). For instance, the traditional sectors of consuming, allocating, and social services have developed rapidly along with population and industry suburbanization. For example, in Guangzhou, the regional quotient of allocating services (transportation, telecommunications, commerce, etc.) in the peripheral area of city is greater than one. However, the same quotient in the center of the city is less than one, indicating a higher concentration of allocating services in the periphery of the city. This contrast is directly related to population migration from the central to the peripheral areas (Yan and Yao, 1997).

The fourth and final aspect of suburbanization is the transformation of land use in suburban areas from a rural to an urban pattern. There is an extension of developed areas of the city, and there is some urban development in areas adjacent to the outer suburbs; however, this is limited by the small number of enterprises willing to locate at such a distance from the center (Ning and Deng, 1996).

Suburbanization of Chinese metropolises is the result of the interaction of several elements, and depends mainly on the involvement of local government and city planning policies. Housing reform and the emergence of a real estate market provide a material base for peripheral development, while modern transportation and information techniques accelerate the process. Specifically, the spatial adjustment of the metropolitan industrial structure accelerates the gathering of industries and population in the periphery of cities (Ning and Deng, 1996; Zhou and Meng, 1998; Cao and Chai, 1998).

For Chinese metropolises, four patterns of spatial change could be identified:

1 Intensive development at the center, i.e. urban renewal.
2 Concentrated outward expansion – the city extends outward incrementally around the core of a developed city center. This is described as "the pattern of making a pancake" and is the typical model of Chinese metropolises.
3 Sectoral development along the major transportation arteries.
4 Jumping and grouping as a discontinuous pattern of city expansion (Zhang and He, 1996; Yao, 1998).

The corridor effect is perhaps the most common pattern, whereby urbanization areas cluster along major transportation routes. Along with major thoroughfares, the built-up areas extend like antennae from the center of city. There is an obvious corridor effect in the "pancake making" pattern which is characteristic of the spatial extension of Chinese metropolises. For example, in 1949, the spatial pattern of the central city of Beijing was a closed toward-center structure, with minimal extension to the northeast and northwest. A similar pattern was found in 1965, with obvious extensions developing eastward and particularly westward. By 1995, even more obvious corridor extensions were prevalent in the east and west (Zong, 1998).

Change to the internal structure of metropolises

The internal structure of Chinese metropolises first developed under a centrally planned economy with mixed patterns of land use and functional differentiation. This situation has changed drastically since reform, especially since the introduction of the self-financing land use system. Commerce, service industries, and especially producer services have been concentrated in the central area of cities, have replaced the original functional areas, and have thereby improved the structure of land use.

Old and new central business districts (CBDs) coexist, with distinct functions. On the one hand, the old CBD developed at the traditional centers of commerce, and was located at the center of the old city. During the economic planning period, the traditional commercial center had a mixed function and a relatively low density. The old CBD is still, to some degree, the retail center of the city. Since the economic reform, the retail business of the traditional commercial center has grown and become the dominant land use. The high-density old CBD has little space for the rapid growth of other industries, especially new producer services. In consequence, they have become distributed on the fringe of CBD or other outlying areas, which have gradually caused the formation of new CBDs.

The composition of the new CBD includes financial insurance, information consultancy, real estate, and other related endeavors. The new CBD also maintains the functions of regional control, management, policy decisions, and regional and international business activities. As a result, the new and old CBDs have become functionally interdependent.

The establishment of new high-technology development zones accelerates the change of the metropolitan regional structure. Facing new global economic competition, each metropolis adjusts its developmental strategy. Many focus on new hi-tech industries and build special areas for this kind of industry, such as Zhongguan Village in Beijing, East Lake district in Wuhan, and Tianhe district in Guangzhou. The establishment of new hi-tech areas has a major effect on the city's function and pattern, and promotes the integration of technology and the economy. It drives industrial development, keeps industry competitive, and accelerates the formation and development of a global CBD. The new hi-tech area needs concentrated modern information services, and tends to centralize and develop such services. It is expected that over time, the new hi-tech areas will become increasingly central to the new economy, and will help determine future trends of socioeconomic development and the regional structure of metropolises (Yan Xiaopei, 1998).

The changing spatial distribution of socioeconomic groups

Since economic reform, especially after 1990s, urban housing has become increasingly commercialized. The original housing allocation policy has changed to one of competitive bidding for purchase, and governmental attitudes have shifted to a market economy stance. Furthermore, the income gap among metropolitan residents has widened. For example, in 1994, households with a family income of 100,000 yuan or more accounted for 7 percent of total urban households, while those with 5,000 yuan or less accounted for 4 percent. The predominant family structure has also changed from an extended family to a nuclear family. Due to a change in the behavior of residents in housing selection, the urban residential areas have been readjusted and reorganized in the following manner: (a) the center of the city is more commercialized, and the high-income residential buildings have increased in number; (b) the residential areas around the center of the city have developed and become gentrified, with neighborhoods of newly built multistory buildings for middle and higher income classes; (c) urban fringe residential areas have been developed for the middle and lower income class residents who relocated from redevelopment zones; (d) apartment areas for the highest income class have emerged on the urban fringe; (e) residential areas where middle and low income classes live have been developed around industrial areas in the nearby suburbs; and (f) migrant areas were developed on the border of urban and rural areas (Li Zhibin, 1997a).

It is obvious that the change in socioeconomic spatial distribution has had a tremendous effect on the urban social economy. First, the original neighborhoods have been destroyed and new neighborhoods have been built. Second, the original heterogeneity has been broken and a new homogeneity has emerged. Third, work areas and residential areas have been separated and the number of commuters has increased. Fourth, retail business has spread to suburban areas. Fifth, residential services and security systems have been shifted to the private market sector. Sixth, the residential problems of the external population have not been considered (Li Zhibin, 1997a).

Sources of Metropolitan Development in the Period of Transition

The information network

The global economy strengthens the relationships among countries in the world and among cities in each country. The new international division changes the nature of urbanization in different countries, making urban functional division clearer, and new technological revolutions change the urban regional factor. The information network among regions, countries, and areas has been built according to techniques that combine computer and electronic communication. On the one hand, a global city system has gradually formed, placing traditional countries, regions, and local urban systems under the direct or indirect control of the global urban system. On the other hand, the cities in the world urban system have become network cities and vital nodal points on various levels of the information network (Yan Xiaopei, 1995).

The Chinese urban system is a product of state policy. Under a planned economy, the structure of the economic plan fits the need of the administrative level of the city's organizational system. The Chinese urban system combines administration and region, and remains close to the central geography theory. Metropolises will influence the economy through the advantages of geographic region, economic activities, and network cluster. However, a few non-hierarchical cities in special zones will develop in the hierarchical urban system. These cities will compete in the nationwide market system, and will maintain close economic relations with other worldwide countries, thereby becoming an important link in the global urban chain (Xu, 1998).

The information network strengthens the status and function of metropolises. There are both centripetal and centrifugal forces at work. The concentrated development of international business activities strengthens the function of CBDs and improves their status and function. The broad development of other social activities and the distribution of population makes the long-distance work pattern an important productive pattern of companies. There are an increasing number of activities based on the family. But the mutual function among sections is closer, and policy plays a greater role in adjustment (Yan, 1998). In the process of informationalization, metropolises increasingly become important places where people interact with each other. The computer cannot replace the pleasure derived from emotional exchange (Ma, 1998). On the other, the need for development of the information industry strengthens the central position in the economy, culture, and information transfer of the metropolises. The information network, as a key factor in spatial economic development, has had an effect on the regional policy toward economic activities, even though it is still at an early stage of development. The role of the information network should be considered in the process of metropolitan development.

The cultural environment

Along with the transition of metropolises from an industrial economy to a service economy, or from economic centers to cultural information centers, the level of civilization and the richness of culture have the potential to further the development of metropolises, even though a strong economy still plays a dominant role. Recently, metropolises around the world have made efforts to establish their reputation, to improve it by developing and diversifying cultural resources and activities in order to attract external economic resources. The effect of culture on the development of metropolises comes through the effects of the cultural environment on the city itself, on neighborhoods, and on individuals. Culture can encourage or discourage the participation of individual citizens in civic life.

Currently, economic factors are still the dominant elements in the development of Chinese metropolises. Many metropolises have lost unique cultural characteristics and competitive potential because they have neglected cultural factors and the crucial role they play in civic life. For example, many objects and sites of great cultural and historical significance have been destroyed or forgotten as the metropolises have evolved (Ma, 1998). So how to construct a city's cultural environment and strengthen citizens' participation in building the city's modernization are core in city development.

Innovation environment

Hi-tech industry has become the new engine of growth for the economy. Two important regional elements of this new industry – the new sources of technology and a highly skilled workforce – are gathering in metropolitan areas. Thus, hi-tech industry has promoted the continued growth of the metropolitan economy and had a major effect on its spatial structure (Yan, 1996). The new technology is reinforced by the concentration of universities and research institutes, a strong industrial base, and the relatively recent development of the service sector. However, the need for diversified economic activities and the global economy require the cities' rapid development on a higher level. In other words, continual and rapid hi-tech development requires a combination of information networks, new environments, and the city space.

Currently there are obstacles to the creation of an innovation environment in Chinese metropolises. The operating system does not interface with the international track. Organizations or companies cannot provide good hardware facilities and work conditions. Living conditions are less than ideal. These shortcomings restrict the transformation of scientific and technological innovation into productivity (Yan Xiaopei, 1999).

An entirely new system is required in order to deal with the macro-environment of social relations, the micro-environment of organizations or companies, and the living environment. Policy-makers, in developing rules and regulations, should follow international practice, e.g. to establish a system of venture capital formation and a new approach to education and recruitment of a skilled workforce, encourage research in the university, promote the working conditions of professionals, and solve the problem of inadequate staffing and funding. Further improvements to the living conditions of skilled personnel would aid in the recruitment of desirable employees. These steps would expedite the transformation of scientific innovation into productivity.

The residential environment

The metropolitan ecological environment is more vulnerable than that of smaller cities. On the one hand, rapid industrialization and urbanization in

China furthered the material interests of cities. On the other hand, there have been many urban problems. First, the concentration of the metropolises' populations has driven population density to become extremely high. Second, the transportation networks in the old cities are insufficient. The cities are also experiencing water shortages. Aquifers are overexploited. In addition, air pollution and noise pollution are getting worse. These problems reduce the quality of the environment, affect people's physical and psychological health, disturb residents' work and life routines, reduce work efficiency, and restrict the development of the economy. Third, the structure of land use is irrational. The proportion of industrial land use is too high relative to residential and services land use. The paucity of public green land is especially problematic. In addition, metropolises continuously expand, absorbing large tracts of arable land. The combination of the rapid speed of urbanization and the backwardness of urban management leads toward a future in which population and economic growth will exceed the carrying capacity of nature and the environment.

Migrant labor force

The immigrant labor force has an important role in and effect on the development of metropolises, guaranteeing that the labor needs of metropolitan industries are met. It accelerates the growth of the cities' service sector, promotes adjustment of the industrial structure, catalyzes the labor market, and strengthens people's sense of competition and innovation. A floating population of highly skilled workers is a sign not only of the expansion of metropolises and internal energy, but also of the human resources necessary for the continued development and transition of the metropolitan economy. However, an external labor force puts heavy pressure on the basic facilities of metropolises, chief among them transportation and security, and unskilled rural workers impede the upgrading of industrial structure and the improvement of the population's skills (*Population Research*, Editorial Department, 1997).

Although the external labor force plays an important role in the development of metropolises, metropolises need highly skilled migrants to adapt and develop the industrial structure. Therefore, metropolises should perfect their labor market, monitor the floating population, strive to attract high-quality talent, and accelerate the formation of a high-quality human resources system of appropriate type and scope. At the same time, during the planning and construction process, metropolises should consider the factor of the external labor force and solve the social problems of transportation, urban aesthetics, and security. The external labor force will become a crucial factor in metropolitan development when it is fully integrated into the metropolitan culture and economy.

Development Problems during the Period of Transition

The core–periphery contrast

There are two patterns in the process of economic development in Chinese metropolises, concentration and expansion, even though concentration is currently the predominant pattern. On the one hand, the economy and population will be further concentrated in metropolises, drawn to them because of advantageous location, better base facilities and investment environments, more opportunities for employment, convenient services and facilities, greater potential for cooperation, and economic and social agglomeration effects. On the other hand, urban centers are overcrowded because of the rapid development of transportation and modern communication and the cost of land, along with the upgrading of the metropolitan industrial structure. Therefore, the metropolis continues to spread spatially, leading to the decline of environmental quality in urban centers and the construction of satellite towns (Hu, 1998). The spatial polarization, to some extent, has resulted in the relative poverty in peripheral areas such as Northwest China, and has become one of the factors causing social uncertainty.

The further restructuring of industry

There is an important trend toward an upgrading of the metropolitan industrial structure. It shows in the shift of dominance from primary to secondary and service sectors, from a labor focus towards a focus on capital and knowledge, from industrial production of primary products to industrial production of intermediate and final products. However, the proportion of the economy occupied by the new hi-tech industry in manufacturing is still relatively low, as is the proportion of the productive services industry in the service sector. Upgrading is retarded by a number of policy choices. Nearly all metropolises have constructed hi-tech parks, resulting in overbuilding, duplication, and wasted resources. The developmental strategies of each park are the same. For example, both Shenzhen and Guangzhou proposed that they will create a "Silicon Valley" for Guangdong Province. Evidently, the construction of two Silicon Valleys 100 miles apart is unnecessary and redundant. An ignorance of regional comparative advantages has resulted in vicious competition among metropolises and hampered the further restructuring of industrial structure.

Population

As metropolises upgrade their industrial structures and become more fully merged with the international economy, a highly skilled metropolitan population is needed. There are some problems in the current Chinese metropolitan population. First, education is low and varies considerably among cities. Although the cultural level of the Chinese metropolitan populations is higher than in other Chinese cities, the population's cultural and technological sophistication lags far behind that of the major modern international cities. In addition, the talent structure is unbalanced. There is a general dearth of workers with high qualifications in critical areas, especially science, international business and finance, and modern management. Both the low quality of the labor force and the unbalanced structure of available expertise impede the improvement of the industrial structure.

Second, the metropolitan population is aging. The working population is in decline, and retirement is becoming a serious problem. In Shanghai in 1993, the rate of natural population increase was –0.78 per 1,000, and the rate of general population increase was 4.32 per 1,000. The general fertility rate in urban areas is 0.95. This will result in age insufficiency and structural unemployment in the urban labor force. The fostered population will increase and the demands of the aging population for more medical services and service facilities will increase as well. This will alter the structure of consumer goods, further affecting the metropolitan industrial and spatial structure (Shuai, 1997). In addition, many new service industries are in sectors in which high levels of expertise are concentrated.

Third, the cultural and skill levels of the external labor force are too low to meet the needs of the metropolitan industrial structure as it upgrades and modernizes. The external labor force will cause structural unemployment in metropolises and destabilize society if its quality structure is unchanged.

Social inequality

Although metropolitan residents' incomes have increased and their lives have improved since the reform, the income difference among different areas and social strata is growing. For example, household income inequality has increased in both city and town. The difference in income between households in the top 20 percent of the income spectrum and those in the bottom 20 percent has increased from 2.9 times as much per person in 1990 to 4.2 times as much in 1994. The pay differential between different professions has also increased. Salaries in sectors such as agriculture, forestry, husbandry, fishery, industry, and geological prospecting are relatively low, but those in service sectors, such as transportation, telecommunications, finance, insurance, real estate, and foreign investment, are relatively high. In 1994, for example, the average salary in industry was 4,961 yuan/year, and 7,101 yuan/year in finance and insurance. This has polarized the metropolitan income structure. There are large numbers of people in high-income brackets, and the same holds true for the lower-income brackets. The middle-income bracket, however, is relatively small, creating an instability in social development.

There is also social inequality between the external population and local residents. The external workers are not guaranteed legal rights. The income of external workers is low. The children of external workers cannot go to school. In addition to this, they have different backgrounds than the urban population, and they are hardly acknowledged by urban society. Therefore, the crime rate of the external population is relatively high and this jeopardizes social public security. These phenomena result in sharp conflicts between the external population and local residents on issues of politics, economy, and society. Obviously, social equality is related to societal stability and cohesion. It is also related to sound, efficient, and sustainable metropolitan development.

Urban and regional planning for sustainable development

The rapid economic growth of Chinese cities has other costs, although the people's living standard has been greatly improved. First, it has a big effect on the environment. The rapid increase in production has been achieved with low productivity and a high level of consumption of material resources. Second, adjustments to the industrial structure have not kept pace with the rapid increase of production, and the regional industrial structure exhibits similar tendencies (Yao, 1997a). As sustainable development becomes a worldwide trend, it has also been put on the agenda in Chinese cities. Land conservation, stabilizing the supply of water sources, and preventing pollution could be considered the first focus.

Although China has abundant water resources, they are unequally distributed. Some cities lack for water due to water pollution resulting from the rapid growth of the economy. The average water resource per person in the Pearl River Delta Region is 6.63 times higher than the nationwide average (25,000 cubic meters). Serious water pollution, however, has affected the water supply to Guangzhou, Foshan, and Shenzhen (Yao Shimo, 1997a). In China, the average cultivated land amounts to 1.2 mu/person. This is less than one-third of the world average, which is 3.7 mu/person. But from 1992 to 1994, the development zone absorbed a large amount of cultivated land. The land is only "open," not "developed." It is not producing what it could and should produce. At the same time, the efficiency of land use across China is very low, and the functional structure is irrational. The flow of capital and material is concentrated mostly on basic facilities. Therefore, the operating benefits of the economic system have been affected and the cities' vitality has declined. In addition, the structure of land use in Chinese metropolises is also irrational. The amount of land used for residences, for green space, or for roads, plazas, and international transportation is lower than that for industry, municipal, and public facilities. For example, at the end of 1990s, in Beijing the former proportions were 26.3, 9.5, and 12.1 percent, respectively. And the latter proportions were 23.2, 4.2, and 15.2 percent, respectively (Deng, 1997). This situation is nearly opposite to that in many Western cities. This situation is related to urban planning in China.

Urban planning is always affected by state politics and the economy. The current Chinese system was devised under the economic, social, and technical parameters of an earlier era and is now outdated. Every metropolis has developed a general urban plan, revolving around the notions of development around a single center, which degrades the environmental quality of the central area. However, it is hard to change this pattern. The damage that it creates has not been considered seriously, because the interests of developers and businessmen are stronger than the interest of environmentalists. Also, the shortage of cultivated land around the metropolis is often a factor in raising the density of inner city development. Although the new direction of urban planning now contemplates a more decentralized city structure, not enough attention has been given to creating independent residential areas that are protected from other urban land uses (Xu, 1998). There needs to be greater recognition of the interplay between material elements and social, economic and political elements in the planning process. Certainly the planning, construction, and maintenance of basic facilities should be conducted with a due emphasis on efficiency. We urge consideration of new approaches, grounded in a correct understanding of metropolitan structural transition. The focus should be shifted from physical planning to a more integrated and comprehensive planning system.

Policy Implications

All the problems mentioned above will influence the sustainable development of metropolises and even the whole country. Thus, suitable measures should be put forward.

The tradition of the centrally planned economy in China still has advantages over the market-oriented economy in alleviating the problem of core–periphery contrast or spatial polarization. This is because the centrally planned economy has a stronger power to adjust the macroeconomy, which has been proved by the history of the centrally planned economy during the 30 years after the foundation of People's Republic of China and the practice of economic reform shifting from the planned economy toward the socialist market economy and paying more attention to development in the coastal areas since the late 1970s. But in the market economic environment, the economic interest is the top priority. Thus, a strategic adjustment to paying more attention to the periphery areas in policies and capital is needed in order to narrow the great difference between the core and periphery areas. The recent national strategy of developing Western China is a significant one in narrowing the strong regional disparity. However, although many forums for developing the western area, sponsored by the national and local governments, have been held, effective actions have not yet been seen. The development of western areas faces many barriers, such as less capital, fewer high-quality professionals, outmoded notions, obsolete equipment and industrial plant, big urban–rural disparity, and bad transport services, but these areas do have relatively rich natural resources. It seems that the role of the central government will be to improve the investment environment in western areas by putting huge amounts of capital into infrastructure construction, to give favorable policies to attract investors, and to encourage local people and enterprises to face the coming economic transformation actively. The development projects and process should be determined by the market mechanism. The development of Western China will be a long-term task and therefore the goal of narrowing the core–periphery contrast will be a long-term one as well.

Especially in the coastal areas of China, the upgrading of the industrial structure is under way, i.e. shifting from the primary toward the secondary sector, from the secondary to the tertiary, but for a given area (a county, a city, or a province) the current or the upgrading industrial structure cannot be considered an optimal one, and regional development cannot be considered integrated either, which is unfavorable for development. It is the administrative divisions that are the largest obstacle to the optimal industrial structures and regional integration. For a long time, the regional economies in China have been the administrative area economies. Each administrative area has only paid attention to the development of its own area and has not considered the regional comparative advantages and regional integration and mutual complementarity, so that many administrative areas have the same industrial structure and the same products, which has resulted in a regrettable competition between the areas, such as marketing at a low price. Thus, breaking the administrative barrier among areas is the key to promoting the formation of an optimal industrial structure and regional integration and development. The way of breaking the administrative barrier is to organize economic activities based on functional areas, extending across administrative areas, in which close economic and social links exist, rather than changing the administrative divisions definitely. Unfortunately, although governments at different levels have realized the impacts of the current administrative divisions on economic development and have considered breaking the administrative barrier, the lack of a clear recognition of the problem has resulted in superficial action, e.g. changing the administrative designation of some areas (e.g. Panyu City, at the county level, bordering Guangzhou became the Panyu district of

Guangzhou recently, and now the Guangzhou municipal government has the power to determine the development of Panyu, whereas before its power was very limited). This action in fact only changes the territorial extent of the administrative area economy and does not resolve the problem of the administrative barrier. On the other hand, it has caused new problems, like losing the tradition and history of some areas. Obviously, greater regional planning is needed to guide the development of regional economies. Some regions have started to carry out this kind of planning in order to integrate the economic development of cities and counties. The regional planning of the economic zone of the Pearl River Delta in Guangdong province is a good example. The first consideration of regional planning is to break the administrative barrier and organize economic activities based on the functional area. However, although some actions have been taken according to regional planning, new actions are taken, against the aims of the planning, due to changes in the leaders of the province. This point is discussed further below.

In the long term, more attention will need to be paid to education in order to raise the population's abilities. On the one hand, the Chinese government has increased education input, which is central to the goal of making primary and secondary education universal and expanding higher education. On the other hand, the central government has imposed a strict family planning policy, so that the natural growth rate of the population could be at a low level and total population growth could be controlled at a low rate. These policies undoubtedly have been effective (e.g. total population growth has been successfully maintained at a low level) but the policies have been differently carried out in rural and urban areas. For example, in urban areas, the "one family, one child" policy is strictly carried out, but in most rural areas one family is permitted to have two children and in some developed rural areas one family is permitted to have one and half children (i.e. if the family has a son, it is only permitted to have one child, but if the family has a daughter, it is allowed to have another child; this is because the daughter will become one of the members of her husband's family when she is married). This policy has a potentially harmful influence on the population in the near future. Generally speaking, urban people are well educated compared with rural people, and therefore urban people have better skills than rural people. Because the rural population is still greater than the urban population in China, the policy of "one family, one child" in urban areas and "one family, two children" in rural areas means that the poorly educated rural population will increase more rapidly than the well educated urban population, and the quality of the working population in the country will decline. This will influence economic growth and social progress. The government must pay more attention to this problem and adjust the current family planning policy, transforming it toward raising population quality as well as controlling the size of the population.

The problem of social unfairness has been caused, on the one hand, by the rapid economic growth itself, and on the other hand by the incomplete legal system. For example, due to the incomplete income tax system, some people with high incomes evade taxes. In many areas, the rights and interests of the migrant labor force have not been guaranteed. Amplification of the legal system is the key to solving the problem of social unfairness. In recent years the government has issued many rules and regulations, but it still shoulders heavy responsibilities in the solution to the problem.

In China, urban and regional planning have lagged behind economic development. In recent years, urban and regional planning have been paid great attention, especially in the developed coastal areas, but the plans have tended to be unrealistic so that they could not be carried out effectively. This phenomenon has many sources:

1 The impact of decision-makers. Urban planning should be scientific and authoritative. But in China, urban planning has been heavily influenced by decision-makers. The ideas and strategies of decision-makers often guide the content and pattern of urban planning. To some extent, urban planning becomes the blueprint for displaying the ideas of decision-makers and, even more, the decision-makers can revise the planning, which weakens the authority of urban planning. The other aspect of the impact of decision-makers is that they tend to be keen on quick success and instant benefits, so that some irrational behavior by developers is allowed, which prevents the enforcement of urban planning.
2 Level of planners. For a long time, urban planning education in China has been deeply influenced by the zoning system, based on the physical planning of the industrialization period of Western countries. Thus Chinese planners have paid more attention to physical planning and are skillful in drawing, but they pay less attention to the socioeconomic factors of urban planning. Urban planning of China is only physical planning, not socioeconomic planning, so that the enforcement of urban planning is not satisfactory.
3 Lack of public participation. Urban planning in China seems to be the task of decision-makers and planners and the public have no right to speak, so that urban planning often deviates from the demands of the public.

Fortunately many urban planning bureaus and urban governments have noticed these problems in urban planning and are trying to find ways to solve them. For example, the Construction Commission of China has begun to implement a system of registered planners in order to raise the quality of planners and manage the planning market. In Shenzhen City, the urban planning committee, consisting of decision-makers, planners, experts, and representatives of the public, has been founded. This committee has absolute power in urban planning and no one can change its decision, which avoids interruptions from decision-makers, developers, and other interests, and can guarantee the rationality and authority of urban planning. In addition, public participation has been addressed. In Shenzhen and Guangzhou, urban plans have been announced to the public and the suggestions of the public have been considered in readjustment of the plans. Furthermore, urban planning courses in universities often cover socioeconomic development. The government has taken the first step in making urban and regional planning more scientific and authoritative, although the situation is still far from ideal.

Part II
Globalization and Urban Development

4
The Prospect of International Cities in China

Yi-Xing Zhou

Since the 1980s, two obvious trends have been developing throughout the world: economic globalization, and urban internationalization. China, with its reform, opening-up policy, and rapid economic growth, has kept pace with these two trends.

"International city" is a far-ranging term that has no international putative standard or definition to date. However, the conception of "the world cities" appeared early, and can be traced back to Patrick Geddes's 1915 book *Cities in Evolution*. Years later, in 1966, Peter Hall analyzed the characteristics, regional structure, and city planning of seven world cities. Invoking wide debate and adoption, the "world city" was first advanced by John Friedmann in the early 1980s to the backdrop of economic globalization. Compared with the old conception, it involved some new content (Friedmann and Wolff, 1982; Friedmann, 1986, 1998; Sassen, 1994; Knox and Taylor, 1995; Lo and Yeung, 1996). "International city" and "global city" are often confused with "world city" in usage. Despite the different academic definitions of these terms, there should not be any dispute about the fact that they are all conceptions of urban functions.

If we make an analogy of urban functional hierarchy in the world with a pyramid, the international cities are the few elite at the top. It is suggested that the highest level of international cities should be called "world city" or "global city." These are comprehensive key cities, such as New York, London, and Tokyo, with global control and coordination functions in the new international division of labor. The second-class international cities are either key cities with international comprehensive functions across different countries, or cities with important international functions specialized in politics, economics, culture, etc. This class of cities, including most of the important cities except the above three, has been referred to in the research of Friedmann (1986, 1998), Sassen (1991), and Shachar (1994).

Many scholars have presented similar opinions on what characteristics or conditions an international city or a world city should have (Friedmann and Wolff, 1982; Hall, 1998). "International city" is still a term of academic discussion whose quantitative criteria have not been defined by any authorized international organization. What kinds of cities can be called international cities is still empirically oriented and qualitative. Even the same writer can put forward a different list of world cities during different periods. The purpose of this chapter is to discuss China's international cities against such a background.

International Cities: The Necessity and Possibility in China

Many scholars who studied the "world city" in the 1980s paid little attention to former socialist countries such as China. As a matter of fact, no city in China can be called an international city with the exception of Hong Kong. Hong Kong was returned to China in 1997, and can be regarded as a second-class international city. However, in the 1990s, China began a period of "international city craze." Nearly 50 cities set their development goal as becoming an "international city" in one or two decades (Xu, 1995). Although this "craze" is a little dramatic, to some extent, it reflects China's strong desire to create the "international city." One reason for this is based on the desire for rapid economic development driven by international cities; in the meantime, international cities represent the comprehensive economic power of China and enable it to take part in international production division and competition. As a result of developing the international city, China has experienced some advantages.

Increasing economic scale and comprehensive power since reform

Excluding Singapore and Hong Kong, the 28 world cities identified by Friedmann (1995a, p. 24) are located in the world's 17 largest economic powers (see table 4.1). This indicates that an international city is related to the economic scale of its country. Only China, Russia, and India have no international cities in Friedmann's scheme. It is roughly estimated that China maintained an average economic growth of more than 10 percent per year for 13 years after 1983. Although influenced by the Asian financial crisis in

Table 4.1 National economic scale of countries (1997) and their world cities

Country	*GNP (US$ billion)*	*Rank*	*PPP estimates of GNP (US$ billion)*	*Rank*	*World cities*
USA	7,690.1	1	7,690.1	1	New York, Miami, Los Angeles, San Francisco, Seattle, Houston, Chicago, Boston
Japan	4,772.3	2	2,950.7	3	Tokyo, Osaka–Kobe
Germany	2,319.5	3	1,748.3	4	Frankfurt, Munich, Rhine–Ruhr
France	1,526.0	4	1,280.3	6	Paris, Lyon
UK	1,220.2	5	1,208.9	7	London
Italy	1,155.4	6	1,152.1	8	Milan
China	1,055.4	7	4,382.5	2	(Hong Kong)
Brazil	773.4	8	1,019.9	9	São Paulo
Canada	583.9	9	661.6	12	Vancouver, Toronto, Montreal
Spain	570.1	10	617.6	15	Madrid, Barcelona
Korea, Rep. of	485.2	11	621.1	13	Seoul
Russian Fed.	403.5	12	618.4	14	
Netherlands	402.7	13	332.8	20	Amsterdam
Australia	380.0	14	373.2	18	Sydney
India	373.9	15	1,587.0	5	
Mexico	348.6	16	770.3	10	Mexico City
Switzerland	313.5	17	186.2	29	Zurich

Note: The GNP of China does not include that of Hong Kong, Macao, and Taiwan.
Source: World Bank (1998), Friedmann (1995).

recent years, it still maintains a rather high growth rate. According to the World Bank (1999), China's annual average GDP growth rate was 10.2 percent from 1980 to 1990, and 11.9 percent from 1990 to 1997, ranking top in the world during those periods. In 1997, China became the seventh largest economic entity. If GNP is calculated in purchasing power parity (PPP) terms, China is the second largest economic entity in the world. Recent research (Liu, 1999) shows that there is little possibility of China reaching an annual growth rate of over 10 percent again. It is expected that the national economy will enter a long period of the second highest growth rate, ranging from 6 to 10 percent. The increase in China's economic power provides the foundation for its forming international cities.

Rapid integration with the world economy

A country's proportion of imports and exports to its GDP can roughly reflect its degree of openness to international markets. Compared to the rapid growth of China's GDP, the foreign trade value has increased even more quickly. The proportion of imports and exports to GDP was 43.6 percent in 1994, which is much higher than that of the USA. China is now making an effort to join the World Trade Organization. It is believed that once China joins, the openness of China's economy and its role in the world economy will be further increased.

The great unevenness of China's economy: international cities in the coastal region

China is a country with some of the greatest regional differences in natural, social, and economic conditions in the world. China's coastal region possesses better physical and human resources than the interior. Historically, Chinese regional development has been extremely uneven. Although there exists disputation about whether regional inequality in post-Mao China has been decreasing or increasing since the launch of the economic reform in 1978 (Wei, 1999), the unarguable fact is that China's regional economic inequality is still great (see figure 4.1). According to World Bank statistic criteria, China's GNP per capita in 1997 was US$860. But if viewed from the province level, there are ten provinces in the eastern coastal region whose GDP per capita exceeds $1,000, with Beijing over $2,000 and Shanghai over $3,000 – ten times more than the lowest GDP per capita, in Guizhou Province. The economic inequality between China's urban and rural areas is also great, with the GDP per capita of metropolises much higher than the average level in rural areas and provinces. Because of the greatly uneven economy, the coastal region and several coastal metropolises can reach rather high development levels, and on the whole become international cities with low economic development levels.

China's Future: International Cities Will Emerge in the Eastern Coastal Provinces

International cities will first appear on the eastern coast, not only because the economic development level of the coastal areas is much higher than that of the interior, but also because they keep the closest contact with the world economic system. Friedmann and Wolff (1982) divided the spatial system of the world economy into three levels: (a) core; (b) semi-periphery; and (c) periphery. China, or at least China's eastern coastal region, is now entering the level of semi-periphery.

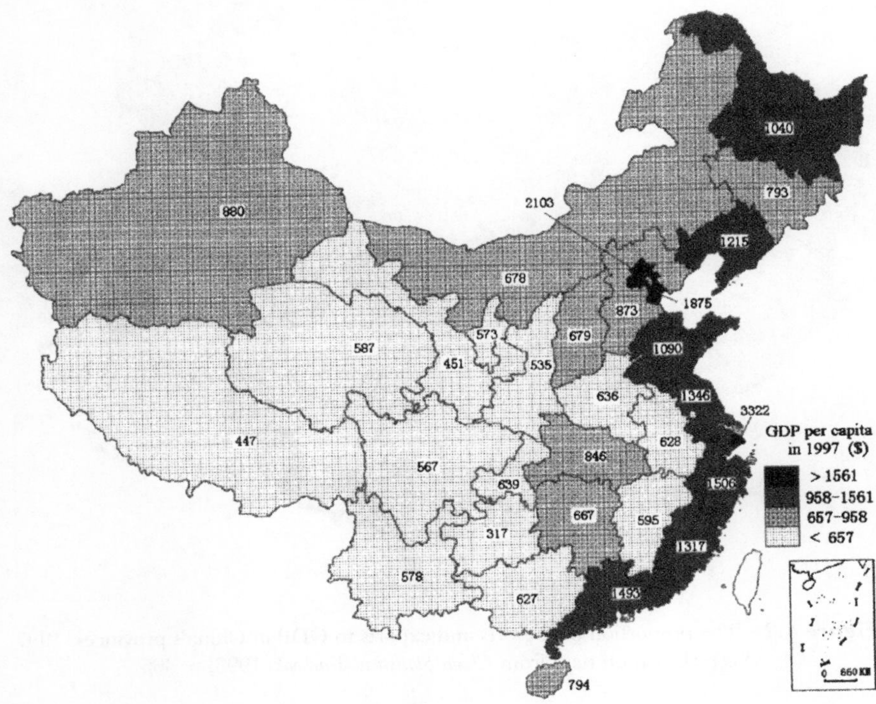

Figure 4.1 The GDP per capita of each province in China, 1997

Figure 4.2 shows the proportion of imports and exports to each province's GDP in 1997, which reflects the degree of openness of their economy. Obviously, Guangdong (150 percent), Shanghai (75 percent), Beijing (72 percent), Tianjin (72 percent), and Fujian (53 percent) take the first five places, with proportions much higher than the average value of other provinces. The next five provinces are Hainan (39 percent), Liaoning (35 percent), Jiangsu (31 percent), Zhejiang (29 percent), and Shandong (24 percent). All ten of these provinces are located in the eastern coastal region. With the exception of Hainan, newly established in 1988 at a relatively low economic development level, the other nine coastal provinces are those regions with the highest GDP per capita and with the most advanced economic levels in China.

Under the reform and opening-up policies, foreign capital is the main driving force of China's economic development. The growth of local economies, as well as that of trade in coastal provinces, is directly related to the advantages of absorbing foreign capital. With respect to the proportion of imports and exports created by foreign-funded enterprises to the whole

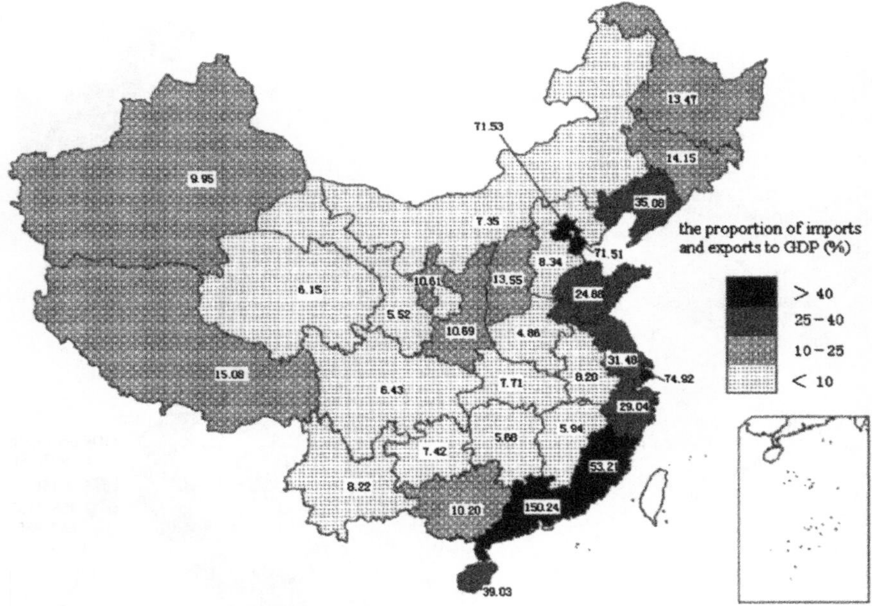

Figure 4.2 The proportion of imports and exports to GDP in China's provinces, 1997 (*Source:* based on data from *China Statistical Yearbook*, 1998, p. 365)

province's foreign trade value, it is clear that more than half of the foreign trade is created by foreign-funded enterprises in provinces such as Tianjin (73.69 percent), Jiangsu (55.39 percent), Shanghai (54.65 percent), Fujian (54.75 percent), and Guangdong (52.43 percent). This kind of trade in the coastal provinces occupies 96 percent of total trade value created by all foreign-funded enterprises in China and accounts for 45 percent of the whole country's foreign trade value. It can be concluded that the foreign-funded enterprises in coastal regions serve as the bridge to integrate China's economy with the world system. Given this, China's first group of future international cities will certainly emerge from the eastern coastal region.

Which Cities in China Will Become International?

As Friedmann and Wolff (1982) point out, for a world city,

> a more fundamental question is in what specific ways these urban regions are becoming integrated with the global system of economy relations. Two aspects need to be considered: (1) the form and strength of the city's integration (e.g.

Table 4.2 The distribution of the 500 largest foreign-funded industrial corporations in Chinese cities, 1995

Rank	*City*	*Number*	*Rank*	*City*	*Number*	*Rank*	*City*	*Number*
1	Shanghai	69	9	Xiamen	14	17	Jiangmen	10
2	Tianjin	35	10	Fuzhou	13	18	Zhongshan	7
3	Guangzhou	26	11	Dalian	12	19	Zhaoqin	7
4	Beijing	23	12	Hangzhou	12	20	Qingdao	7
5	Shenzhen	23	13	Shuzhou	12	21	Nanjing	6
6	Zhuhai	20	14	Nantong	10	22	Weihai	5
7	Foshan	18	15	Dongguan	10	23	Shantou	4
8	Wuxi	16	16	Huizhou	10	24	Loyang	4

Source: Compiled by the Foreign Capital Department of the Ministry of Foreign Economic Relations and Trade and the *International Commercial Newspaper* (1996) The 500 largest foreign-funded industrial corporations in China. Beijing: Publishing House of Economic Daily.

to what extent it serves as a headquarters location for transnational corporations; the extent to which it has become a safe place for the investment of "surplus" capital, as in real estate; its importance as a producer of commodities for the world market; its role as an ideological center; or its relatives strength as a world market); and (2) the spatial dominance assigned by capital to the city (e.g. whether its financial and/or market control is primarily global in scope, or whether it is less than global, extending over a multinational region of the world, or articulating a national economy with the world system).

Friedmann and Wolff point out that "the question is an empirical one: how and to what extent are China's major cities tied into the international capitalist economy and therefore subject to its influence? Only further research can provide answers to this question." Although the relevant data fully fit for Friedmann's indexes cannot currently be found, some similar indexes are sufficient to be used in judging which cities in China will first become international.

Distribution of the 500 largest foreign-funded industrial corporations

China's 500 largest foreign-funded industrial corporations in 1995 located in the eastern, middle, and western regions are 443, 46, and 11, respectively. The cities where these corporations are located reflect to a certain degree their relationship to the world capital market and commodity production market. Shanghai takes first place (69 corporations), then Tianjin (35), Guangzhou (26), Beijing (23), and Shenzhen (23) follow. The first 23 cities are all found in coastal regions, such as Pearl River Delta, Yangtze Delta, Beijing–Tianjin, Fujian, Shandong, and Liaoning (see table 4.2).

Table 4.3 The distribution of the 500 largest import and export value corporations in Chinese cities, 1995

Rank	*City*	*Number*	*Rank*	*City*	*Number*	*Rank*	*City*	*Number*
1	Beijing	73	9	Ningbo	14	17	Chengdu	8
2	Shanghai	44	10	Changsha	13	18	Harbin	7
3	Guangzhou	41	11	Fuzhou	12	19	Chongqing	7
4	Qingdao	23	12	Wuhan	10	20	Nanning	7
5	Nanjing	20	13	Hefei	10	21	Suzhou	7
6	Hangzhou	20	14	Shenzhen	9	22	Shantou	6
7	Dalian	19	15	Shijiazhuang	9	23	Kunming	6
8	Tianjin	14	16	Xiamen	9	24	Changchun	6

Source: Compiled by the Foreign Capital Department of the Ministry of Foreign Economic Relations and Trade and the *International Commercial Newspaper* (1996) The 500 corporations with the largest imports and exports value in China. Beijing: the Publishing House of Economic Daily.

Distribution of the 500 corporations with the largest imports and exports

The 500 corporations with the largest imports and exports in 1995 have the closest relationship with the world market. They also have the best prospect of growing into transnational corporations. Table 4.3, summarizing the distribution of the headquarters of these corporations, shows Beijing (73), Shanghai (44), and Guangzhou (41) in the top three. The numbers in the eastern, middle, and western regions are 389, 74, and 32, respectively (five corporations' data are missing).

Distribution of foreign telecom and computer companies

It is reported that 151 of the 500 largest transnational corporations in the world had invested and set up factories in Beijing by the end of 1998 (*Beijing Youth Daily*, February 4, 1999). In the first half of 1998, the headquarters of the Northern Asian Center of Motorola Company were established in Beijing. Furthermore, Chevron, one of the ten largest oil enterprises, moved its Asian headquarters from California to Beijing at the beginning of 1999. The Beijing government has implemented various policies to encourage transnational corporations to set up their regional headquarters in Beijing (*Beijing Youth Daily*, March 15, 1999). Similar reports can often be found in Shanghai and Guangdong, displaying the obvious trend that more and more transnational corporations are coming to China to expand their businesses. Beijing has offices of 43 foreign telecommunications companies and 62 foreign computer companies, far above Shanghai (9 and 18, respectively), Guangzhou (4 and 18), or any other city.

Table 4.4 Amount of foreign capital actually used by city, 1985–1996 (US$ million)

Rank	*City*	*Amount*	*Rank*	*City*	*Amount*	*Rank*	*City*	*Amount*
1	Shanghai	26052	9	Dongguan	3898	17	Foshan	2357
2	Shenzhen	10654	10	Shenyang	3436	18	Huizhou	2221
3	Tianjin	9265	11	Shantou	3258	19	Zhongshan	2218
4	Beijing	7920	12	Zhuhai	3214	20	Chongqing	2171
5	Guangzhou	7655	13	Haikou	3150	21	Daqing	1938
6	Xiamen	6156	14	Fuzhou	3005	22	Wuxi	1914
7	Dalian	5699	15	Wuhan	2935	23	Yantai	1855
8	Suzhou	3938	16	Qingdao	2692	24	Nanjing	1855

Sources: Based on data from *Urban Statistical Yearbook of China* (1985–1997).

Distribution of foreign-funded financial institutions

In the process of establishing international cities, an advanced financial system is a decisive link. In order to promote the openness of finance actively and safely, in 1999 the president of the People's Bank of China announced a cancellation of the restriction on regions where foreign-funded banks may set up their business branches. He also guaranteed continuous improvement of regulations on foreign-funded banks managing Chinese yuan. By the end of 1997, there were 731 foreign-funded financial institutions (representatives and branches) located in 29 cities. Among them, 700 were in the eastern coastal regions. Beijing (243) and Shanghai (215) hosted 63 percent; the next highest shares were in Guangzhou (61) and Shenzhen (54). Clearly Beijing has the strongest attraction for foreign-funded companies and banks, as international economic activities tend to gather in the political center in developing countries (Browning, 1958; Friedmann and Wolff, 1978). At the same time, however, foreign direct investment is more heavily directed toward productive centers: as shown in table 4.4, Beijing ranks fourth in this dimension, following Shanghai, Shenzhen, and Tianjin. These cities, as well as Guangzhou, are undoubtedly advantaged over Beijing by their predominant role in foreign trade. Table 4.5 summarizes not only the volume of trade for major customs offices of China, but also the principal sources of imports and destinations of exports for each one.

Cities with the largest number of international flights and foreign tourists

International airlines' network with the global urban system plays an important role in personnel exchange. International cities are the hinges of the network. Beijing and Shanghai not only have the most frequent, but also the most widespread, worldwide connections. Guangzhou and Xiamen are

Table 4.5 Import and export values of China's main customs and their main contact directions, 1997 (100 million US$)

Customs	*Total imports and exports*	*As % of whole country*	*Major directions of imports*	*Major directions of exports*
Shanghai	586.82	18.05	Japan, EU, North America	Japan, North America, EU
Shenzhen	564.13	17.36	Japan, Taiwan, Southeast Asia	Hong Kong, North America, EU, Japan
Guangzhou	543.06	16.71	Taiwan, Japan, EU, North America	Hong Kong, North America, EU, Japan
Tianjin	214.03	6.58	Japan, North America, Korea, EU	Japan, EU, North America, Korea
Qingdao	207.32	6.41	Korea, North America, Japan	Japan, Korea, North America, EU
Dalian	170.16	5.23	Japan, North America, Korea, EU	Japan, Korea, EU, North America
Shantou	134.54	4.14	Korea, Japan, Southeast Asia, Taiwan	Hong Kong
Nanjing	131.82	4.06	Japan, EU, North America, Korea	Japan, EU, North America, Hong Kong
Xiamen	122.79	3.38	Taiwan, Korea, Japan, Southeast Asia, EU	Hong Kong, Japan, North America, EU
Gongbei	99.07	3.05	Japan, Hong Kong-Macao, Taiwan	Hong Kong, North America, Japan, EU

Source: Data collected from China customs.

Table 4.6 Rankings of Chinese cities on various indexes of internationalization

Dimension	*Ranking of the top six cities*
Foreign-funded industrial enterprises	1 Shanghai, 2 Tianjin, 3 Guangzhou, 4 Beijing, 5 Shenzhen, 6 Zhuhai
Enterprises with largest import and export value	1 Beijing, 2 Shanghai, 3 Guangzhou, 4 Qingdao, 5 Nanjing, 6 Hangzhou
Offices of foreign-funded telecom enterprises	1 Beijing, 2 Shanghai, 3 Guangzhou, 4 Nanjing
Offices of foreign-funded computer enterprises	1 Beijing, 2 Shanghai, 3 Guangzhou, 4 Chendu, 5 Shenzhen
Foreign-funded financial institutions	1 Beijing, 2 Shanghai, 3 Guangzhou, 4 Shenzhen, 5 Dalian, 6 Tianjin
Foreign capital actually used	1 Shanghai, 2 Shenzhen, 3 Tianjin, 4 Beijing, 5 Guangzhou, 6 Qingdao
Imports and exports through custom	1 Shanghai, 2 Shenzhen, 3 Guangzhou, 4 Tianjin, 5 Qingdao, 6 Dalian
International flights	1 Beijing, 2 Shanghai, 3 Guangzhou, 4 Dalian, 5 Qingdao, 6 Xiamen
Foreign travelers	1 Beijing, 2 Shanghai, 3 Guangzhou, 4 Xi'an, 5 Shenzhen, 6 Kunming

primarily linked with Southeastern Asia and Japan; Dalian and Qingdao with Northeastern Asia; Shenyang and Tianjin with Northeastern Asia and Russia; Kunming with Southeastern Asia; and Xi'an with Japan. Beijing and Shanghai are also in the lead in terms of foreign tourism.

Rankings on all of these indexes are summarized in table 4.6. It is easy to find the top cities in China's urban system. Beijing, Shanghai, and Guangzhou, whose internationalization degree is far higher than other cities in China, are ranked in the first level. These are the key cities with the greatest possibility of becoming international cities in the future. Shenzhen, Tianjin, Qingdao, Dalian, and Nanjing are the other large cities with high degrees of internationalization.

Some Spatial Relationships in the Formation of China's International Cities

Friedmann has discussed the spatial dynamics of world city formation in the Asia–Pacific region (Friedmann, 1998). The four main characteristics he mentioned that influence the future of world cities exist to a greater or lesser extent in China. The following are some applications of these characteristics to the formation of China's international cities.

First, China's international cities cannot form without the surrounding metropolitan interlocking region (MIR). I initially explored the concept of MIR while discussing urban China and the statistical standards of the urban population (Zhou, 1986). In response to the notion of the Desakota region, which was advanced by McGee in an international conference in Hawaii in 1988, I further clarified the prospects for MIRs for Hong Kong–Guangzhou–Macao in the Pearl River Delta, Nanjing–Shanghai–Hangzhou in the Yangtze Delta, the Beijing–Tianjin–Tangshan region, and Shenyang–Dalian in central and southern Liaoning (Zhou, 1991a). In the mid-1990s, China's urban geographers reached the following conclusions about the four regions (Hu et al., 2000).

The MIR is China's core economic area and is equivalent to the megalopolis with Chinese characteristics. It must meet five conditions: (a) two or more especially large cities with a population of over one million as growth poles, at least one of them with a relatively high opening-up and with the main characteristics of international cities; (b) large seaports with handled freight of over 100 million tonnes per year, and international airports; (c) a development corridor formed by various modern transportation methods (furthermore, the growth poles at various levels in the region must have convenient road communications with the corridor); (d) several middle and small cities in the region, metropolitan areas connected by the development corridor with a total population of 25 million, and population density of up to 700 persons per square kilometer; and (e) close social and economic interactions among the metropolitan areas, central cities, and outlying counties that make up the MIR.

In the Pearl River Delta and Yangtze Delta of southern China, metropolitan areas are already mature. They are connected to each other and combine spatial formation on an enormous MIR scale. The Pearl River Delta, including Hong Kong and Macao, is the MIR with the highest economic development level at present in China, whle the Yangtze Delta is the largest. In contrast, the Beijing–Tianjin–Tangshan and Shenyang–Dalian regions possess the basic conditions necessary to develop the MIR, but the connections among urban centers in these regions are still weak.

As mentioned above, Beijing, Shanghai, Guangzhou, Shenzhen, Tianjin, Dalian, and Nanjing are the core cities, or the second or third most important cities, in the MIR; therefore, future international cities in China will be urban agglomerations represented by core metropolises in the MIR – somewhat similar to Rhine–Ruhr and Randstad.

A second general theme is that China's international cities will develop from south to north. Guangzhou is the only foreign trading port that has remained prosperous for 2000 years (Li and Xu, 1994). As the primary city in the south of China, it has never been challenged. Before the reform and opening-up, China's foreign trade volume was very small. Guangzhou was the important economic gateway for China. After the reform and opening-up, Shenzhen was specified as a Special Economic Zone. With the political nature of the border between Hong Kong and Shenzhen changing from hostile to friendly, Shenzhen became the largest gateway city, establishing the economic relationship between China and Hong Kong, as well as other countries, and replacing Guangzhou's international functions. After Hong Kong was returned to China in 1997, it became the largest gateway city in the Chinese economic system.

In the future, it is predicted that the international functions of Shenzhen and Guangzhou will be somewhat weakened (Zhou, 1998). With Hong Kong's built-up area developing toward Shenzhen, and the strengthening of the supplementary relationship between Hong Kong and Shenzhen, the latter will become a component of Hong Kong's urban area. Furthermore, 90 percent of cargo exported from Guangzhou and Shenzhen is from Guangdong, and its largest export direction is Hong Kong. With the existence of these spatial relationships, Guangzhou and Shenzhen will not become international cities independently. They must seek support from Hong Kong to go to the world. Hong Kong–Guangzhou–Shenzhen should realize the plethora of advantages in joining forces with each other, and with other cities in the Pearl River Delta, such as Macao and Zhuhai. If this is done, the influence of this area will far exceed that of present-day Hong Kong.

A third general point is that Shanghai must deal with issues of cooperation and competition with Hong Kong as it contends for international city status. Shanghai was the financial center of the Far East before the Second World War and had a splendid history as the third largest financial center in the world (Pang, 1996). After the war, Shanghai lagged behind in comparison with the developing pace of the world. Since 1990, with the development of the Pudong New Region, Shanghai has begun its process of becoming an international city once again, and has become a strategic and international economic, financial, and trading center. Facing severe challenges from international cities of the Far East such as Tokyo, Seoul, Singapore, Hong Kong, and Taipei, Shanghai's development space remains limited. From my point of view, the first challenge is not from abroad, but from Hong Kong. There is a large gap in the economic level between Shanghai and Hong Kong (Yao, 1995; Deng and Jiang, 1998). In 1997, Hong Kong's economic scale ($164.4 billion) was 16 percent of that of the mainland, and 3.3 times as much as that of Shanghai ($49.5 billion). Furthermore, the GNP per capita of Hong Kong ($25,280) was 7.6 times that of Shanghai ($3,322), while bank savings and loan values of Hong Kong ($770 billion) were ten times those of Shanghai ($77.2 billion). The two cities also had opposing policies on cargo, traveler, air, and sea transportation. Supported by its unique advantages in macroeconomic location, Shanghai certainly has a higher economic growth rate and a higher opening-up speed than Hong Kong. If the country's rate of development is low, the rapid increase in Shanghai must restrict Hong Kong's development, since both have the same hinterland. To maintain Hong Kong's continuous prosperity, and at the same time not affect Shanghai's development, it will be necessary for the entire country to develop rapidly and maintain its cooperation and coordination with Hong Kong.

Another general point is that Beijing's international future depends on cooperation with Tianjin. Beijing has many advantages. First, it is the political and cultural center of the country, and the center of Chinese culture more generally. Second, it has good international links on multinational political affairs and business in the Asia–Pacific Region. Third, it is the largest international tourism center in China. Fourth, it is the city with the highest educational, scientific, and technological talents in China, and has the greatest potential for developing high-technology industries. However, there are still many factors that impede Beijing from becoming an international city, including relatively low comprehensive economic power, infrastructure far behind needs, scarce water resources, poor urban environmental quality, no seacoast, and a lack of large-volume sea transportation facilities.

Prior to 1980, Beijing developed in an unusual manner. Its overall economic power was stronger than that of Tianjin, and it became China's second largest industrial city and economic center. After 1980, under the market economy system, Tianjin's location and resource advantages became more fully apparent. In a short period of time, many of Tianjin's indexes, such as gross industrial output, industrial benefits, foreign capital, and foreign-funded industrial enterprises, exceeded Beijing's. Tianjin has historically served as Beijing's outside port and North China's economic center. It is very important that each city maintains its unique urban functions. At present, Tianjin's seaport, gateway location for North and Northwest China, cheap land and sea coast, and long history of industrial and commercial tradition are the very qualities that Beijing lacks for developing as an international city. Only when Beijing and Tianjin realize the importance of coordination will it be possible for them to accomplish their own development goals. The coordination between Beijing and Tianjin will also involve coordination with Hebei province. The unification of Beijing, Tianjin, and Hebei has been proposed for many years, but it is difficult to realize, since every province-level unit has its own plans, goals, and interests. For the good of the whole, this kind of transprovince development problem should be recognized and solved by a higher authority, the State Council.

Finally, it will be a long time before Shenyang and Dalian jointly build an international city. The middle southern portion of the Liaoning province is the metropolitan interlocking region in North China. Its present development is relatively grim, in that although Dalian is outstanding in its urban construction and rate of growth, its overall urban scale and power remain relatively small. Furthermore, the structural transformation of heavy industries and the systematic transformation of state-owned large and middle-sized enterprises are still far from complete in Dalian and its economic hinterland. Since the spatial relationship between Shenyang and Dalian is somewhat like that between Beijing and Tianjin, it is necessary that the two cities realize the mutual benefit of separation of urban functions, and make joint efforts toward the development of an international city. However, the distance between Shenyang and Dalian is 375 kilometers, over twice the distance between Beijing and Tanggu Port in Tianjin; therefore, it will be more difficult for Shenyang and Dalian to jointly maintain the functions of international city.

Conclusions

China's reform and opening-up policies will not change. The trend of strengthening economic power and bettering the people's living conditions will not reverse. Under the impetus of economic globalization, it should not be long before several cities or MIRs in China's eastern coastal areas become international cities. It is surmised that the formation order will be as follows: Hong Kong–Shenzhen–Guangzhou (Pearl River Delta), Shanghai (Yangtze Delta), Beijing–Tianjin, and Dalian–Shenyang.

Although the suggestion of building international or world cities in China is an exciting concept with potentially positive effects, an international city is not formed artificially, but spontaneously driven by social and economic forces. Its formation not only faces competition from surrounding international cities, but also needs to be recognized by the international society (Xu, 1995).

For China, the most important concerns are: to deal effectively with the relationship between reform, development, and stabilization, and maintain the rapid growth of the social economy; to solve reform problems regarding state-owned enterprises; to build China's own transnational corporations and join the world market; to upgrade the technological level and add to the value of commodity exports; to continue opening up and reform, and to strive for more investment from developed countries at higher technological levels; to improve the urban environmental quality and investment environments; to expedite the political system reform, punish corruption, and improve the legal system; and to improve the natural environment while improving the built environment.

5

Globalization and Hong Kong's Entrepreneurial City Strategies: Contested Visions and the Remaking of City Governance in (Post-)Crisis Hong Kong

Ngai-Ling Sum

This chapter contextualizes the emergence of Hong Kong's entrepreneurial city strategies in relation to globalization. The latter is linked to the rise of information and communication technologies that facilitate increased movements of goods, services, finance, and people across borders and enable multinational firms to intensify their sourcing of cheap (un-)skilled labor, component parts and raw materials around the world. For our purposes these changes can also be linked to the opening of China from 1978 onwards and the resulting opportunities for globally and locally managed subcontracting firms to move their labor-intensive production processes to different parts of China. For Hong Kong, this "northward match" led to the so-called 'hollowing out' of its industrial sectors. This gap was "filled in" as Hong Kong became a global-gateway city (Sum, 1999) that served as: (a) a regional hub to provide producer services mediating between China and global markets; and (b) a regional financial centre for global–regional capital seeking potential fields for investment in the region. Growing wealth and inflows of finance promoted the rise of property investment and speculation not just as a form of business but as a way of life. In response to this "hollowing out" and its compensatory processes, governmental and quasi-governmental agencies as well as private economic actors began a dialogue on how best to promote Hong Kong's "economic future" and "competitiveness." While industrial interests preferred a reinvigorated manufacturing strategy, service interests supported the development of a producer/trade service role in a changing regional–global economy. Reflecting this basic division, my chapter critically examines the specific proposals and broader significance of two consultancy reports commissioned around 1996 by industrial and service interests, respectively. These reports develop two alternative entrepreneurial city strategies, each concerned in its own way to remap Hong Kong's "competitiveness" and to insert the Hong Kong economy to best advantage into a changing global–regional–national division of labor (Jessop and Sum, 2000).

The emergence of these two strategies coincided with two major events. First came the long-expected political transition of Hong Kong from British colony to Special Administration Region in July 1997; second, Hong Kong underwent the unexpected economic onslaught of the "Asian crisis" in 1997–9. Together these events undermined the city's political economy both politically and economically. Nonetheless, this chapter examines only the economic aspects of Hong Kong's changing governance regimes and practices in the (post-)crisis period. It adopts a material-discursive (or "cultural political economy") approach (Jessop and Sum, 2001) to the remaking of Hong Kong's entrepreneurial city strategy/urban governance and highlights the importance of discourse in mediating these changes. As the crisis unfolded, private and public actors were urgently seeking to define new visions and projects that might guide the rebuilding of the crisis-ridden economy as well as realign and consolidate key economic forces behind these new images and initiatives. Between 1998 and 2000, different private and public actors have reimagined Hong Kong's future in terms of "technology," a "knowledge-based economy," a "cyberport" or "Silicon Valley," and, more recently, a "world(-class) city," and have proposed forms of governance to realize these objects/projects. As these images, visions, and projects circulated among the leading private and public actors, an inter-discursive space was formed in which actors renegotiated their identities and interests. An important feature of this space is the polyvalence of "technology" discourses and the resulting opportunities for redefining the service sector's interests and reorienting Hong Kong's urban identity.

Competing Entrepreneurial City Visions/Strategies: Service versus Manufacturing, Harvard versus MIT

Hong Kong's competing entrepreneurial city visions/strategies can be fruitfully related to its experience of "hollowing out"/"filling in" (Jessop and Sum, 2000). This prompted the manufacturing and service fractions to initiate discussions about the city's "economic future" and "competitiveness." First, worries about rising costs in southern China and the lack of industrial and high-tech support in Hong Kong were voiced by industrialists, especially major manufacturers (e.g. the Federation of Hong Kong Industries and the Hong Kong Electronic Industries Association). Second, hit by rising residential and office rental costs, the service sector (e.g. the Hong Kong Chamber of Commerce and its think tank, the Hong Kong Coalition of Service Industries) was wondering how best to enhance its service-based competitive advantages. These worries triggered debates in the Legislative Council, advisory bodies, professional meetings, and the mass media. Around 1996, these concerns were reflected in the concurrent commissioning of two consultancy reports that were sponsored and/or supported by different factions of capital, public organizations (e.g. the Trade Development Council and Hong Kong Productivity Centre), and government departments (e.g. the Trade and Industry Departments). Published in 1997, they represented alternative entrepreneurial city strategies to insert Hong Kong into a changing global–regional division of labor. This involved redefining the object(ive)s of Hong Kong's entrepreneurialism, the bases of its future economic advantages, and the 'new combinations' required to create and sustain its structural and systemic competitiveness. The contested nature of these strategies emerges clearly from the two reports (as summarized in table 5.1).

The first study, by Harvard Business School consultants, was *The Hong Kong Advantage* (Enright et al., 1997). This Porterian-inspired report was officially sponsored by the "Vision 2047 Foundation," which combined commercial and financial capital interests. This group promoted a revisioning of Hong Kong's future time and space, favoring service and multinational interests. The report noted Hong Kong's manufacturing decline and the challenge of interurban competition from Shanghai, Singapore, Taipei, and Sydney. It promoted a market-oriented vision of the city's new identity as a "business/service/financial centre" with "hub" functions. In entrepreneurial terms, it portrayed Hong Kong as a type of urban economic space that would manage ever-expanding global–regional–local flows of production and exchange. In this regard, its entrepreneurial ambition was to establish a "beyond-the-gateway" image, or, more specifically, to offer a "new combination" of "hub" functions around a "knowledge–information-based" economy with access to mainland China, Asia, and the Asia–Pacific region (pp. 25, 167–87).

This urban entrepreneurialism recalibrated not only Hong Kong's spatial horizons but also its temporal horizons of action. Thus, as a cluster-based global–regional "hub," it would capture and manage "flows" rather than continue to serve as a manufacturing platform. The aim was to rearticulate relations among global, regional, and local traders/investors by: (a) organizing internationally located systems of production; (b) combining inputs from a diversity of sources in many different countries; (c) managing a diversity of supply outlets; and (d) furnishing the required capital, technical support (design, construction, engineering, legal, financial), and infrastructural provisions (particularly real and virtual port and transport facilities in southern China and Asia). This central logistical role would enable Hong Kong to

Table 5.1 Two contested entrepreneurial city strategies for Hong Kong in 1997: services versus manufacturing

	"The Hong Kong Advantage"	*"Made by Hong Kong"*
Object(s) of entrepreneurial intervention	Decline of manufacturing: promote trade, finance, and high technology industry	From "Made by Hong Kong" to "Made in Hong Kong"
City identity	Business/service/finance center Information hub Logistic hub (Metropolitan economy)	Hi-tech manufacturing center: brand-name production original design manufacture
Innovative practices		
Purpose	Manage the flows	Fix capital/technology in place
New scales of activities	Global-regional-local (re-)articulation	Regional-local technology diffusion (with hints of global)
New temporal horizons	Re-articulating factory pipeline/logistic time Importance of electronic time	Research and training time for higher-value products Development of electronic time
New governance capacities	Dynamic clusters and linkages Property, construction, finance and business	R&D base
	Input to all industries: location (promixity to China) infrastructure (airport, port, telecom) capital and finance capital goods and components human resources regional and international specialists	Input to technology: government fundings private R&D investment incentives for research information services and technologies
Form of competitiveness	Space-based form of trading competitiveness	Place-based form of industrial competitiveness
Fraction(s) of capital	Commercial and financial capital (and its associated networks)	Industrial capital (and its associated networks)

Source: Author's own compilation.

coordinate new temporal horizons that promote new ways to link: (a) factory and pipeline/logistic time crucial to time-bound and compressed-time projects; and (b) electronic time to tame the flow of financial, logistical information and service-based knowledge across borders as well as across the private–public divide.

These new time–space horizons of action should, the report continued, be facilitated and mediated by new urban-based institutional arrangements and practices. Here it referred to certain features of Hong Kong's entrepreneurial and/or governance capacities that were embedded at the interpersonal, institutional, and societal levels. Thus the "hustle and commitment strategies" of Hong Kong's "merchant manufacturers" should be combined with the institutions of "government as referee" and the activities of "entrepreneurial and managerial firms" from Hong Kong and abroad (pp. 45–6, 127, 34–40). These networks would clearly be supported by an existing societal ethos of "hard-working people," but this entrepreneurial culture must nonetheless be assisted in its striving for greater competitiveness. This was to be achieved through the provision of "inputs to industry" (p. 85) and by promoting strategic clusters such as property, construction, infrastructure, business and financial services, transport and logistics, light manufacturing and trading, and tourism. Interlinkages among such clusters had enabled them to "draw upon common skill bases or inputs and reinforce each other's competitive positions through dynamic interaction" (p. 95). In short, this competition-based Porterian construction of Hong Kong's trading advantages promoted a space-based and global–regional city strategy to reinsert it favorably into changing flows produced by regional and global restructuring.

The MIT report, entitled *Made by Hong Kong* (Berger and Lester, 1997), offered a more place-based account of Hong Kong's entrepreneurial future. This report was sponsored by manufacturing/industrial capital and supported by parts of the bureaucracy (most notably the Hong Kong Government Industry Department and the Hong Kong Productivity Council). It portrayed Hong Kong as locked into a *Made by Hong Kong* manufacturing trajectory, i.e. as organizing the low-cost manufacture of "Hong Kong" goods in offshore locations such as southern China and other parts of Asia. This trajectory would allegedly prove "unsustainable" due to rising labor and land costs in Guangdong province, the "craze for property" in the region, and competition from Japan's successful organization of its own regional networks in the area (pp. 52–7).

The "best" response to such uncertainties for Hong Kong was to "climb the technology ladder" by producing higher value-added goods in Hong Kong itself. The report deployed the symbols of *Made by Hong Kong* and Hong Kong as a "high-tech manufacturing centre" to reorient its future competitiveness and urban character. Seen in entrepreneurial terms, this reconstruction sought to narrate Hong Kong as a new type of urban economic space that could 'refix' its role as a base for production. "Technology" was the key symbol here in building "Hong Kong's new engine for growth." And this would involve a different temporal–spatial fix from that involved in the previous *Made by Hong Kong* mode of growth. It involved new methods of producing and organizing socioeconomic space and would require the support of government.

Spatially, the team envisioned a global–regional–local diffusion of technology that could launch Hong Kong on the path to its own brand-name production and original design manufacturing. This place-based competitiveness involved intensifying (including compressing) research and training time as well as exploiting possibilities in electronic time. This remixing of time–space horizons required flows of information conducive to the development of an R&D base crucial to Hong Kong's competitiveness. This in turn required new urban-based institutional arrangements and practices. Accordingly, the report concentrated on the institutional changes required to boost the entrepreneurial and self-governance capacities of Hong Kong's technological base. These included: (a) acquiring technical knowledge from the PRC, diasporic Chinese, international experts, and multinational corporations; (b) promoting R&D agglomeration economies based on universities, technology-based enterprises, education institutes, (virtual) science parks, and private firms; (c) acquiring new inputs such as government funding, human resources, and information technology; and (d) strengthening the technological capabilities of government by injecting more technical expertise and raising the profile of technology-related policies. In short, this construction of Hong Kong's structural competitiveness is clearly based on a place-based account.

The Asian Crisis and the Contested Visions of Hong Kong's City Governance

These entrepreneurial city visions revealed the contested nature of Hong Kong's economic restructuring and its implications for social and political relations. Matters were further complicated by the transition from British colony to Special Administrative Region in 1997 and the unexpected outbreak of the Asian crisis.

The Asian crisis

In February 1997, speculators first attacked the Thai bhat, and the Bank of Thailand allowed the bhat to float on July 2, 1997. This triggered a financial contagion that spread from Thailand to Indonesia, Malaysia, South Korea, Philippines, and then Hong Kong (Sum, 2001a). In Hong Kong, the dollar came under speculative pressure on several occasions in July, August, and October 1997. These currency attacks forced the government into short-term crisis management. It intervened in the money market initially by pushing up interest rates in the inter-banking sector and later by imposing penalty interest on borrowing of the Hong Kong dollar. The government maintained the pegged exchange rate under conditions of high interest rates, capital flight from the Hong Kong dollar, and reduced external demand. These pushed the local stock index and residential property prices down by over 50 percent between October 1997 and June 1998. This asset depreciation, especially in the property sector, cut at the heart of Hong Kong's internal "growth" dynamics as this had developed since the opening of China. This bursting of the "property bubble" gave rise to fears of further asset depreciation. In order to prevent the asset from further depreciating, the government's short-term strategies were: (a) to freeze land sales (until April 1999); (b) to allocate HK$1,390 million for home buyer loans; and (c) to grant tax rebates to property owners.

The Hong Kong dollar was attacked again in August 1998 when the yen depreciated against the US dollar and hedge funds sold the Hong Kong stock market short in the expectation that the index would fall as interest rates rose. Speculative attacks triggered significant capital outflows in the belief that this might also force a yuan devaluation. The government reacted with further short-term measures. These included: (a) drawing on its reserves to buy US$15 billion worth of selected Hong Kong shares (60 percent of these were property related – higher than this sector's weight in the stock market); and (b) introducing a package of technical measures to strengthen the transparency and operation of the linked exchange rate system (e.g. a rediscount facility to reduce interest rate volatility). The pegged system was rescued at the expense of high interest rates, weak domestic demand, and rising unemployment. Hong Kong's GDP fell 5 percent and the unemployment rate had reached 5 percent by 1999, but this did not lead to a dramatic reduction in wages and rents, which remained high (Sum, 2001a, c). As the crisis subsided, the debate over Hong Kong's future economic strategies resurfaced.

Contested visions of Hong Kong's city governance in the (post-)crisis period

The discussions between the service and manufacturing (or Harvard versus MIT) visions of Hong Kong's future and their associated strategies reappeared. The crisis prised open Hong Kong's political economy and exposed it to several challenges: (a) the erosion of Hong Kong's role as agent for China's exports as trade declined and new Chinese seaports emerged; (b) overdependence on the property sector; (c) the vulnerability of financial and related services; (d) the effects of recession (e.g. negative growth rate, fall in asset values, 6 percent unemployment rate); (e) the fall in tourist earnings; (f) competition from other regional cities, especially Shanghai and Singapore; and (g) the rising "tide of the information revolution." Faced with this declining "competitiveness" and lacking a general vision for post-transitional development, public and private actors began to seek means and trajectories to rebuild and/or reposition Hong Kong, and, if possible, to bridge this service–manufacturing divide.

In his first policy address, delivered in October 1997, the Chief Executive established the Commission on Strategic Development under the Central Policy Unit to advise him on Hong Kong's long-term development. This search for a long-term strategy was overshadowed at times over the next year by short-term attempts to "contain" the "financial contagion" (see above). But the search for new ways to thematize the problems and to realign the two fractions continued. On the service front, the Financial Secretary spearheaded service promotion as early as May 1997 by forming the Business and Services Promotion Unit under his office. Its tasks included forming a "partnership with the business community," and, at the initiative of the Hong Kong Coalition of Service Industries, a private–public discussion network – known as the "Tripartite Forum" – was formed. It comprised the Business and Service Promotion Unit, the Hong Kong Coalition of Service Industries, and the School of Business of Hong Kong University, where Michael Enright (a co-author of *The Hong Kong Advantage*) is the Sun Hung Kai Professor of Business. This forum aimed "to engage top business leaders, senior officials and leading academics in discussion, debate and brainstorming of ideas for promotion of the service sector" (Services Promotion Strategy Group, 1998). A private–public Services Promotion Strategy Group was also formed in April 1998 to enhance communication, generate "mutual" discourse, and remake service-oriented "common sense" through committee meetings, annual forums, keynote speeches, and moderators' summaries.

Concurrent with the engagement/consolidation of the service interests, the Chief Executive, backed by two industrial-oriented Executive Councillors (Raymond Chien, Chairman of the Industrial and Technology Development Council, and Henry Tang, Chairman of the Federation of Hong Kong Industries), sought to surf the "high technology" tide. In March 1998, the Chief Executive appointed Chang-Lin Tien (Chancellor of University of California, Berkeley and a member of President Clinton's National Science Board) to chair the Commission on Innovation and Technology. Its remit was to explore the chances of Hong Kong becoming a "technology-intensive economy in the twenty-first century." This study was undertaken in a period when the service faction still opposed an MIT-type industrial/interventionist policy of picking "winners." This opposition was voiced by Enright, one of the architects of the service discourse, in a public seminar hosted by the Central Policy Unit on Hong Kong's competitiveness in April 1998. He claimed: "Technology is over-rated and the biggest challenge facing Hong Kong will be the Managerial Revolution" (Professor Michael Enright's transcript, public conference organized by Central Policy Unit on "Hong Kong's Competitiveness," April 22, 1998).

Nonetheless, the first report of the Commission was published in September 1998. It envisioned Hong Kong's future role as a "centre of innovation and technology" that would "serve the region not only as a business and financial centre, but also as a centre for development and commercialization of innovative ideas and technology" (Hong Kong SAR, 1998a, p. 13). This vision could be realized through a strategy that focused on: (a) strengthening technological infrastructure and promote technological entrepreneurship; (b) building human capital to meet the needs of a knowledge-based economy; (c) enhancing technological collaboration with the mainland; (d) fostering university–industry partnership; and (e) lowering information, financing, and regulatory barriers. This strategy could be implemented by setting up the Innovation and Technology Fund of HK$5 billion and an Applied Science and Technology Institute Research Institute (Hong Kong SAR, 1998a, pp. vi–vii). These recommendations were endorsed by the Chief Executive in his second policy speech in October (Hong Kong SAR, 1998b, pp. 8–11). He also injected a sense of urgency by suggesting that the "Asian crisis" had underlined the need to develop "high technology" in Hong Kong. In his speech, he remarked, "To help our economy respond to the changes [related to the Asian crisis], our strategy will be to focus on increasing the diversity of the economy by creating conditions for growth in sectors with a high value-added element, in particular in those industries which place importance on high technology and multi-media applications" (Hong Kong SAR, 1998b, p. 8).

Such official support/endorsement for the building of a high technology regime in the wake of the crisis coexisted with continuing advocacy of a 'traditional' role by spokesmen for the service fraction. This can be seen from a new report written by two of the three authors of *The Hong Kong Advantage*. Entitled *Hong Kong's Competitiveness Beyond the Asian Crisis*, this was commissioned by the Trade Development Council and appeared in February 1999. Its authors reiterated the importance of the "service economy" in Hong Kong and argued that the city was increasingly acting as a major metropolitan management and coordination center for local firms, for business activities in the Chinese mainland, and for multinational companies. Given its "metropolitan" nature, it would remain competitive beyond the Asian Crisis. As for government policy, it could sustain "competitiveness" by building on "traditional strengths, such as market-oriented economic policies, rule of law, efficient and clean government, low and simple tax regimes, equal treatment of local and overseas companies, non-intrusive but effective regulatory regimes, and a liberal policy toward the employment of foreign professionals" (Hong Kong TDC, 1999, p. vii).

Surfing the High Technology Tide

While the service sector was still calling for continuation of the "traditional" regime in early 1999, other private actors were surfing the high technology tide and proposed new hi-tech/IT urban object(ive)s/projects. One high-profile project is the "Cyberport" (see table 5.2), which was originally the brain child of "Hong Kong's Bill Gates" (Richard Li) and his Singapore-based corporation called Pacific Century. Li's (and Pacific Century's) idea was to create "a comprehensive facility designed to foster the development of Hong Kong's information services sector and to enhance Hong Kong's position as the premier information and telecommunications hub in Asia." In addition, "the Cyberport is meant to attract, nurture and retain the relevant innovative talent necessary to build a cyber-culture critical mass in Hong Kong." In this regard, Li's (and Pacific Century's) vision was interesting in two aspects.

First, it could be seen as a reworking of the Harvard report, which was based on Hong Kong's pre-existing niche as a "metropolitan economy." The Cyberport project aimed to push Hong Kong's service-based cluster into the "information age." However, its conception was narrated less in positive Porterian (1990) terms than in the more metaphorical terms of a "Silicon Valley" type "incubator." Compared with Porter's conception of "cluster" development rooted primarily in competition, the incubator depends more on collaboration – "decentralized networks" of firms collaborating flexibly and adaptably with local universities and financial systems (Saxenian, 1994). For Pacific Century, the building of an incubator-type multimedia service cluster could help Hong Kong to "catch up" in the information age. Hong Kong's competitiveness would thereby be extended in the following ways: (a) capturing global "information flows" and managing them within the service-space of Hong Kong and its broader region (e.g. as an IT hub); (b) connecting Hong Kong's services to a fast cybertime and the knowledge-based economy; (c) consolidating a social space in which to build a "cyber culture critical mass" that links the global, regional, and local; and (d) developing decentralized collaborative networks that reach out beyond trading/financial services.

Second, given that the Cyberport was a new imagined service cluster intended to capture the information technology flows, it could symbolically (and, perhaps, materially) bridge the traditional city–university and technology–service divides in the cityspace of Hong Kong. The project highlighted the role of (information) technology in expanding the activities of traditional service clusters – a critical mass could be (partly) nurtured by the physical/social form of the built environment that would be modeled on "Silicon Valley."

Table 5.2 New "IT" object of city governance: the Cyberport

Cost	HK$13 billion (US$1.68 billion)
Size	64 acres (25.6 hectares)
Location	Telegraph Bay, Pokfulam
Aims	"To create a world class location for the conduct of a variety of activities which through the use of information technologies, can leverage Hong Kong existing strengths in the service sector (e.g., in financial, media, retail, transportation, education, and tourism services)" (Pacific Century, 1999, p. 1).
Built environment I	Cyber facilities (2/3 of the site) • fiberoptic wiring • satellite signal senders • built-in high-speed modems • cyberlibrary • media laboratories and studio facilities
Built environment II	Real estate (1/3 of the site) • houses and apartments • hotel • retail
Completion date	2007 (commencing from 2002)
Job creation	4,000 during construction 12,000 professional jobs on completion (10% from outside Hong Kong)
Partners	Pacific Century CyberWorks (HK$7 billion equity capital) Government (land worth HK$6 billion)
Cluster of tenants	Multinational corporations (Microsoft, IBM, Oracles, HP, Softbank, Yahoo!, Hua Wei, Sybase) Local tenants of small to medium-size information technology companies
Metaphors/images used	"Silicon Valley," "incubator," and "catching up"

Source: Author's own compilation.

The government quickly seized on the bridge-building potential of this project and integrated it into its emerging strategy for urban governance. This involved remaking Hong Kong as a "city going into the twenty-first century" that would derive its competitiveness from riding the speed-time of the information age (Sum, 2001b). This symbolic appropriation of the project received material backing when the Financial Secretary unveiled a HK$6 billion land grant for the Cyberport in his March 1999 budget speech. Nonetheless, some market analysts criticized the Cyberport as comprising little more than "Cyber villas by sea" (i.e., a real estate project as opposed to a high-tech project) and claimed that it "is no 'Silicon Valley'" (Webb, 1999). Excluded from such an important strategic project, ten real estate developers jointly denounced the government's decision-making process as being "not open for bidding," and accused it of using residential land to subsidize the Cyberport project. The Democratic Party, for different reasons, challenged the government for lack of transparency, creating "favoritism/cronyism," and departing from its *laissez-faire* policy.

The Remaking of Service Interests Mediated in and through Discourses on Technology

The discourses on technology, which had been encouraged by the US Internet boom as well as the first Commission report and were later reinforced by the Cyberport project, began to circulate within and beyond the service sector. They provided an intersubjective space in which actors could reinterpret their strategic interests and reorient their activities. This is illustrated by one of the important actors in Hong Kong's service sector – the Hong Kong General Chamber of Commerce. In response to the first Commission report and its discourse of technology, in March 1999 the Chamber submitted a (re-)position paper entitled *Industry and Technology – A Constructive Role for the Chamber*. It began by selecting and reinterpreting two specific paragraphs from the 92-page first Commission report. It acknowledged that the Commission was "right" in three ways: (a) the importance of technology and industrial policy in promoting technological upgrading; (b) the possible contributions of technology/industrial policy to the competitiveness of all sectors (meaning both manufacturing and service); and (c) the blurring of the service–manufacturing divide and their interdependence. More specifically, the following remarks demonstrate how the first Commission report structured the Chamber's attempts to reposition itself:

> One misunderstanding about industrial policy is that it is pictured as a one-sided promotion of "high technology." However, as pointed out in the Commission report, "improved technology is important not only to the 'high tech' segments of the economy; but to all sectors" (para 3.6). The Chamber believes that it is right. The right approach to Hong Kong industries should be that of technological upgrading and application, not high technology per se. This applies to both manufacturing and services.

> Another misunderstanding about industrial policy is that it advocates manufacturing in opposition to the service sectors. The division between manufacturing and services tends to overlook the fact that many services are related to manufacturing. In fact, one of the main features of the Commission's report is precisely to highlight the relationship between the manufacturing and the associated service industries (for example, para 3.9). (Hong Kong GCC, 1999a)

The Chamber's new stance was reinforced in a follow-up press release in the same month (Hong Kong GCC, 1999b). This affirmed the boundary-crossing potential of technology and/or industrial policy in bridging the service–manufacturing divide. This account not only reflected its new view of the service–manufacturing question, but also created new areas in which the interests of the two sectors might coincide, e.g. "e-commerce" and "virtual research centers." These changes can be seen in the following quotation:

> The Chamber advocates an industrial policy that focuses on the integration between manufacturing and services, rather than division of the two. In fact, there are areas where integration can be found, such as in electronic commerce and the application of information infrastructure, as well as the development of "virtual" research centres that integrate individuals, government, industry, and academia online. (Hong Kong GCC, 1999b)

This shift, which was mediated by the technology discourses, was reflected in new activities corresponding to the Chamber's newly redefined identity and interests. For example, in 1999, the Chamber, together with the Hong Kong Polytechnic, started to co-host a series of high technology "mixer" gatherings that aimed to provide an informal platform for networking among university graduates, entrepreneurs, industrialists, venture capitalists, and professionals. As for the manufacturing fraction, the Chairman of the Federation of Hong Kong Industries in its thirty-ninth Annual General Meeting in June 1999 openly supported the Commission's report, especially the establishment of the Innovation and Technology Fund for new technology, the promotion of industry–university collaboration, and the Growth Enterprises Market for new innovative firms to acquire capital. The Federation even came to adopt the slogan of "Working Together with Industry and Business" on its homepage to echo, at least discursively, the new service–manufacturing partnership. The emergence of a common framework for the service versus manufacturing controversy provided a more favorable environment for the publication of the Second and Final Report of the Commission in July 1999.

Exploiting the symbolism of "technology," the report reiterated its integrative potential in realigning manufacturing and service interests (Hong

Table 5.3 Major recommendations in the Second and Final Report of the Commission on Innovation and Technology 1999

A New institutional arrangements

- Set up a standing advisory body reporting to the Chief Executive to succeed the Commission (later known as the Chief Executive's Council of Advisors on Innovation and Technology).
- Establish a high-level policy group headed by the Financial Secretary and comprising relevant bureau secretaries.
- Merge the Hong Kong Science Park, Hong Kong Estates Corporation, and Hong Kong Industrial Technology Centre Corporation.

B Building up human capital

- Continue to invest heavily in education.
- Increase overseas liaison and promotion efforts in major technology centers such as Silicon Valley.
- Relax immigration restrictions on mainland talents.

C Fostering an innovation and technology culture

- Expand the incubator program.
- Organize sector-specific events involving industry and academia to develop industrial clusters.

D Creating an enabling business environment

- Consider setting up a co-investment scheme with matching government and private venture capital funding.

Source: Author's own compilation from the Report.

Kong SAR, 1999a, pp. 6–8) and proposed new practices to build a new "techno-economic" regime. These include: (a) establishing institutional/organizational arrangements for coordination and leadership; (b) building up human capital to enhance science and technology; (c) fostering innovation and technology culture; and (d) creating an enabling business environment (see table 5.3).

The Reinvention of Technology Discourses and World-Class City Positioning

"Technology" certainly seemed to offer a common discursive framework for resolving the conflicting economic–corporate interests of the manufacturing and service sectors. But this framework still lacked broad appeal and did not provide a positive symbolic reference that might change the public mindset and appeal to global-regional investors. In this regard, "technology" provided the space for another round of discursive reworking that would link technological innovation (in the guise of information and communication technologies) to the question of economic restructuring and the transformation of Hong Kong into a knowledge-based economy to everyone's benefit. This reworking of technology begged for a city identity to be portrayed in a "flattering" light (Short and Kim, 1999, p. 97). The issue of city identity was not new. Various city signifiers were used in official and unofficial reports/discussions in the (post-)crisis period. These ranged from "information hub," "leading city in the world," "digital city," and "regional centre," to "world city." They all proposed slightly different urban images/identities for Hong Kong.

By mid-1999, the idea of Hong Kong as a "world(-class) city" emerged in various discussion sessions and informal reports promoted by the service sector (e.g. the report *Hong Kong's Future – Working Together to Create the World City of Asia*, submitted by the Business and Professionals Federation of Hong Kong in 1999). These ideas circulated in various public–private meetings and were also stressed in interviews conducted by Tung's advisory body, the Commission of Strategic Development of the Central Policy Unit; and they eventually found their way into the Chief Executive's Policy Address in October 1999. Noting Hong Kong's need for "clear positioning" in the contexts of globalization and rapid development in China, the Chief Executive called for Hong Kong to become a "world-class city." In his speech, he remarked:

> I have on many occasions during the past two years spelled out our long term developmental objectives, the purpose of which was to establish a clear positioning for Hong Kong. Drawing upon the advice of the Commission on Strategic Development, I said in last year's Policy Address that I firmly believed that Hong Kong should not only be a major Chinese city, but could become the most cosmopolitan city in Asia, enjoying a status comparable to that of New York in North America and London in Europe. . . .
>
> Hong Kong already possesses many of the key features common to New York and London. For example, we are already an international centre of finance and a popular tourist destination, and holding leading positions in trade and transportation. These are all pillars of our economy. If we can consolidate our existing economic pillars and continue to build on our strengths, we should be able to become world-class. Then like New York and London, we will play a pivotal role in the global economy, be home to a host of multi-national companies, and provide services to the entire region. (Hong Kong SAR, 1999b, pp. 15–16)

This address promoted the image of a "world-class city" by: (a) drawing the analogy between Hong Kong, New York, and London; (b) reinterpreting Hong Kong's main economic sectors as "pillars" that could be strengthened to attain world-class status; and (c) assigning Hong Kong global and regional roles (e.g. serving multinationals). This positive status (and its related roles) was possible/sustainable because Hong Kong could build "quality people" (cultivating talents for a knowledge-based economy/society) and a "quality home" (cleaning up the environment to make Hong Kong an ideal home) (Hong Kong SAR, 1999, pp. 52–140). This "world-class city" discourse was further developed by the Commission on Strategic Development, which published a report in February 2000 entitled *Bringing the Vision to Life: Hong Kong's Long-term Development Needs and Goals.* This report demonstrated a further round of creative reinvention of Hong Kong's future that combined and articulated elements and symbols from pre-existing discourses to produce an equivocal narration of Hong Kong.

First, it deployed some spatial symbols now favored by management and geography gurus. Given that a number of cities (e.g. Singapore) also claimed to be versions of world/global cities, Tung's world-class city was respecified as "Asia's World City, A Major City in China." To ascertain that Hong Kong deserved these positive statuses, it was benchmarked against major cities in terms of: (a) its "hard" and "soft" infrastructures, such as transportation, telecommunication, education, and rule of law; (b) its relationship with the Chinese hinterland as a "multi-centered city region"; (c) its capacity to embrace new technologies to support its position as gateway to China; and (d) its strengthening linkages with China and the new opportunities therein (Hong Kong SAR, 2000a, pp. 6–8).

Second, it deployed some popular political symbols invented by social science gurus. It sought to jump on the "Third Way" bandwagon but gave it a Hong Kong inflection. It adopted Blairite language to connect the city's pursuit of competitiveness with notions of community (but without the embedded social democracy typical of Western discourses and practices). In this regard, competitiveness was defined in and through an eclectic combination of elements drawn from the Harvard, MIT, Trade Development Council, and Commission on Innovation and Technology reports. These included often-repeated triggering symbols (e.g. highest quality human resources, most supportive environment for innovation and technology, best physical infrastructure, freest and most open economy, most favorable business environment, and most respected and effective public administration) and well known strategic sectors that cut across the service–manufacturing divide (e.g. financial and business services, tourism, information services and telecommunication, innovation and technology, trade, transportation, and logistics). To further enhance a broad-based and positive understanding, the report added a "human face" to this competitiveness rhetoric by introducing a dash of community-oriented discourses that ranged from "sense of civic pride," "better environment," "housing," "welfare," "art and culture," to "community-wide responsibility" for making this vision work.

In short, this rearticulation/recombination of symbols could provide diverse actors and social forces in both the private and public sectors with a set of symbolic references indicative of an economic commonsensical understanding of what seems to be at stake in a (post-)crisis and post-transition Hong Kong. At the time of writing, the symbolism of "technology" and "world-class city" created by this private–public (communicative) network seems quite successful in quietening opposition from the service and manufacturing sectors and within the economic power bloc. Paradoxically, its "acceptability" to these groups owes much to its equivocal nature – which enables forces with quite different or at best partially overlapping perceptions and understandings of Hong Kong's future to believe that they have a stake in this new project. The scant attention that this project gives to "community" has not gone uncriticized by more grassroots-oriented groups such as the Frontline.

Conclusions

This chapter has adopted a discursive-material approach to the (re-)making of enterpreneurial city strategies (Jessop, 1997, 1998a; Clarke and Gaile, 1998; Short and Kim, 1999) in Hong Kong. It has focused on discursive aspects of these developments and struggles around the reworking of identities and visions around how city governance should be organized. This leaves unanswered key questions about how the architecture and practices of city governance are being refashioned to enhance economic restructuring. Nonetheless, it is worth noting that the Financial Secretary in his 2000–1 Policy Speech started to redefine Hong Kong's economic policy approach away from the much celebrated tradition of "positive non-intervention" to one of "maximum support, minimum intervention" (Hong Kong SAR, 2000b, paras 23–8). This new self-identity is matched by several institutional changes introduced since April 2000. These include the setting up of: (a) the Chief Executive's Council of Advisors on Innovation and Technology; (b) an inter-bureau committee to work with this Council; and (c) the Innovation and Technology Commission. In addition, this new Commission and the existing Business and Service Promotion Unit were placed under a rebranded Commerce and Industry Bureau. These new institutional arrangements "to provide maximum support for Hong Kong's manufacturing and service industries" mark a new step in the realignment of policy concerns and the attempt to bring greater coherence to individual policies and the overall governance of Hong Kong as a world-class, knowledge-based economy (Commerce and Industry Bureau, 2000). At the time of writing, it is too early to say whether these new (inter-)organizational arrangements can coordinate activities well enough to enhance the reflexive, deliberative, self-organizing governance structure appropriate to a learning-oriented, complex, networked, knowledge-driven economy (Storper, 1997; Jessop, 1998b).

6

The Hong Kong/Pearl River Delta Urban Region: An Emerging Transnational Mode of Regulation or Just Muddling Through?

Alan Smart

Two decades of integration between Hong Kong and the adjacent parts of Guangdong province have produced an urban region that encompasses two radically different systems and has drawn on their complementary advantages to generate rapid economic growth. In this chapter, I examine the processes that have made this integration possible, and the challenges that remain. Some efforts have been made to theorize these processes as an emerging regime of flexible accumulation or flexible specialization (e.g. Leung, 1993; Christerson and Lever-Tracy, 1997). However, the regime of accumulation is only one of a pair of central concepts involved in regulation theory, the second being the mode of regulation: "a coherent set of mechanisms for social mediation that guide the accumulation of capital in the direction of social progress" (Aglietta, 1998, p. 62). Interdependence of the Hong Kong Special Administrative Region (SAR) and the Guangdong portions of the Hong Kong/Pearl River Delta urban region (hereafter HK/PRD) means that such a mode of regulation must include mechanisms, practices, and institutions operating under distinct systems of governance. Effective regulation of the transborder region is far from assured in such a situation.

The emergence of the HK/PRD urban region has been the outcome of simultaneous processes of territorial integration and separation. To some extent, the effectiveness of economic integration has been dependent on the maintenance of separation. The selectively permeable barrier of the Hong Kong SAR border allows easy movement by Hong Kong people and capital into the rest of China, but the reverse flow of people into Hong Kong is sharply controlled. By contrast, rapid integration made it much harder for Germany to take advantage of factor complementarities while integrating the former East Germany. Separation avoids such costs as expanding citizenship rights to equal those across the border or removing differentials in environmental regulations. Maintenance of separations in an otherwise closely integrated urban region creates a kind of "osmotic pressure," which encourages transgressions by people whose movement is restricted. Transgressions that are almost inevitably generated by regulation (Moore, 1978; Heyman and Smart, 1999) have been largely absent from regulation theory.

Accumulation, Regulation, and Governance

For Michael Aglietta (1998, p. 62), the basic premise of regulation theory is that: "capitalism is a force for change which has no inherent regulatory principle; this principle is provided by a coherent set of mechanisms for social mediation that guide the accumulation of capital." Capitalism generates crises which cannot be resolved by purely economic mechanisms. The most fundamental among these crises for Aglietta is that the imbalance of power between capitalists and employees may result in insufficient demand for expanded production. Overproduction leads to profit declines and recessions. Mechanisms which overcome these conflicts, and preserve continued accumulation and profit, are referred to as a mode of regulation: mediations which ensure that "distortions created by the accumulation of capital are kept within limits which are compatible with social cohesion" (Aglietta, 1998, p. 44). Boyer (1990) calls the broader system that contains a regime of accumulation and a mode of social regulation a mode of development.

Modes of regulation build up their own pressures which lead to new crises. The post-Second World War period of sustained growth in North America, Australia, and Europe has been labelled the Fordist regime of accumulation (Boyer, 1990). Its mode of social regulation was characterized by highly profitable large corporations, collective bargaining, and the development of a unionized working class with middle-class powers of consumption, and fine-tuned through Keynesian macroeconomic management and redistribution. By the mid-1970s, this mode of regulation had exhausted its capacity to increase profit, and began systemic collapse. New regimes of flexible accumulation still lack modes of social regulation able to provide stable underpinnings (Tickell and Peck, 1992). During the crisis after Fordism, the flexible firm "survives through perpetual adaptability rather than perpetual cost reduction" (Lovering, 1990, p. 161). The result is a tendency toward disintegration into divisions of labor which are widely distributed through space.

Tickell and Peck (1995, p. 358) argue that we cannot yet refer to a post-Fordist regime of accumulation because "the establishment of a broadly functional coupling between the accumulation system and the MSR [mode of social regulation] is . . . a prerequisite for the formation of a regime of accumulation" (p. 361). For them, we are indeed in a situation of crisis resulting from the collapse of Fordist social regulation, but since a new compromise or institutional fix has not yet emerged, we cannot refer to the new production patterns as involving a regime of flexible accumulation.

I find this identification of the regime of accumulation with the mode of development problematic. Clearly a mode of development, in this sense, must have both a regime of accumulation and a mode of social regulation consistent with it in order to be identified as a distinct pattern. But there is no inherent reason why a regime of accumulation might not develop for a period without a suitable mode of social regulation. Such a regime would undoubtedly be more than usually prone to crises and disorder, but this seems a fair description of the current era. It might only be after a prolonged period of disorder that necessary compromises are achieved.

Tickell and Peck assume that since regimes of accumulation had "broadly functional" couplings with modes of social regulation in the past, this is a necessary outcome of any post-Fordist regime of accumulation. It may be an implication of the theory, but will it hold in practice? It may instead be that the conditions of economies decoupled from nation-states, a more multi-centered world, and information-intensive communication systems have made the prospect of a global compromise that would serve as a replacement for national Fordisms only a utopian wish. The advantages of hierarchical coordination may be "lost in a world that is characterized by increasingly dense, extended, and rapidly changing patterns of reciprocal interdependence" (Scharpf, quoted in Jessop, 1998b, p. 32). Can a new regime of accumulation persist despite a background of disorder? Something comparable to what Tickell and Peck (1992, p. 194) described as the competitive mode of social regulation that prevailed before the First World War may have re-emerged. Perhaps the "new world disorder" is as much as we can reasonably expect, and after all it does still continue to muddle through its periodic crises. The longevity of the pre-Fordist regime suggests that we cannot deny the emergence of a regime of flexible accumulation simply because a mode of social regulation equivalent to that described under Fordism has yet to appear. Perhaps governance, in the form of attempts to steer autonomous systems that cannot be directly controlled (Jessop, 1998b, p. 33), rather than regulation in a strong sense, is the most that can be hoped for in attempting to stabilize the contemporary crisis.

An additional problem is that regulation theory begins from the analysis of national economies (Fagan and Le Heron, 1994, p. 275). Discussions of transnational linkages are jury-rigged on top of theoretical apparatuses that were developed for making sense of nations. Post-Fordist theory pays substantially more attention to global chains of production and distribution.

Nevertheless, the tendency to begin with national economies is still predominant, and raises difficulties in making sense of cross-border urban regions.

Another problem is that approaches have "tended to be statist in their approach, thereby neglecting many of the important non-state dynamics" (Smith and Swain, 1998, p. 29). Regulatory processes involve a wide variety of distinct relations and practices, and in early stages, new regimes commonly involve social responses rather than state interventions. In the HK/PRD region, continued absence of coordinating agencies highlights the centrality of informal social regulation.

Accumulation and regulation in Hong Kong

Hong Kong was a major beneficiary not just of the post-war Fordist boom, but also of its post-1973 crisis of profitability. The industrial structure that developed consisted of thousands of small and medium-sized enterprises characterized by high levels of flexibility and responsiveness to world market opportunities (Smart, 1999a). Social regulation was accomplished through minimal economic controls combined with intense involvement in property development (generating a large stream of revenues for the government and allowing a low level of taxation) and the provision of large amounts of low-income housing, now sheltering about half of the total population (Smart, 1992).

Success, in the form of higher wages and rents, by the mid-1970s undermined this pattern of industrialization. Restructuring into higher value-added products or a crisis of profitability seemed the likely outcomes at that time. The opening of China to foreign investment in 1979 provided an alternative. The majority of manufacturing was transferred across the border. The dominance of neoliberal ideas of non-interventionism resulted in weak institutional support for technological upgrading in Hong Kong (Yeung, 2000), due partly to the greater influence of commercial rather than industrial interests in the political system (Chiu, 1996). Yeung (2000, p. 157) argues that an appropriate "institutional fix" for Hong Kong's industrial accumulation crisis "should include more involvement of the state in enhancing the competitiveness of the economy" in order to facilitate long-term investment. One limitation of Yeung's analysis is that it takes for granted an analysis focused on national economies. From the perspective of the HK/PRD region as a whole, rather than deindustrializing, manufacturing production has expanded (Berger and Lester, 1997).

The return of Hong Kong to Chinese sovereignty has not transformed the local regime of accumulation, although there have been a variety of policy interventions intended to promote a more knowledge-intensive economy. Financial crises throughout Pacific Asia resulted in a sharp downturn until

2000 and substantial increases in unemployment. As economic growth continued in China, its importance to Hong Kong's prosperity has increased further. Economic integration between Hong Kong and the Pearl River Delta has been accompanied by multifarious forms of social and cultural interaction, producing a complicated regional web. But modes of social regulation adequate to the new demands have not been developed. Indeed, it is unclear how this could be accomplished, given starkly different forms of governance. Governments and individuals have been opportunistically taking advantage of possibilities raised by the integration of a region encompassing such differences in prices and rules, and this has often led to competition rather than cooperation, contradiction rather than mutuality.

Accumulation and regulation in the People's Republic of China

Katherine Verdery (1996, p. 36) has argued that the collapse of socialism in Eastern Europe "came in part from the massive rupture produced by its collision with capitalism's speedup" under flexible postmodernity. Since the most important remaining communist state has achieved among the highest recorded rates of economic growth over the past two decades, it would seem important to ask why China has so far managed to survive its collision with flexible capitalism rather well.

Verdery's argument begins from the claim that the "inner drive" of socialism is very different than that of capitalism because it strives to accumulate "distributable resources" rather than profits, and that it does so to "increase dependency of those within" (Verdery, 1993, p. 7). From this perspective:

> markets create problems because they move goods horizontally rather than vertically towards the center, as all redistributive systems require. . . . Because these horizontal movements and individualizing premises subverted socialism's hierarchical organization, market mechanisms had been suppressed. Reformers introducing them were opening Pandora's box. (Verdery, 1993, pp. 12–13)

The internal tensions that developed in socialist societies were managed so that they "involved decisions that to a greater or lesser degree opened socialist political economies to western capital" (Verdery, 1993, p. 13). The resulting disruptions were intensified by changes in the world economy to post-Fordism, which created a context "even more inimical to socialism than was the earlier 'Fordist' variant" (Verdery, 1993, p. 16). Similarly, Altvater (1993, p. 23) argues that European socialism "collapsed not because of shortcomings in material welfare, but because the institutions of society were insufficiently flexible in adjusting to crisis tendencies that had been concealed for too long." How has China coped with this situation?

Perhaps the reforms have had the effect of producing a capitalist economy with only a superficial coating of socialist ideology. Evidence does not support this. State-owned enterprises generated 34 percent of China's total industrial output in 1995, and collective enterprises produced another 36.6 percent, while private enterprises and joint ventures accounted for only 29.4 percent (Gore, 1999, p. 27). While the regime of accumulation in China is still clearly extensive, the shift appears to be toward greater intensivity overall. The biggest increase in productivity clearly involved sectoral shifts: the transfer of tens of millions of farmers out of agriculture. Rural industry concentrated on light manufacturing of consumer goods, helping to redress state sector overemphasis on producer goods and heavy industry. In the state sector, rural migrants became incorporated in a secondary labor market, hired on a contract basis without security or benefits.

Woo (1999) suggests that there are two schools of thought about how to explain China's successes. The experimental school focuses on a gradualist strategy of enabling economic experimentation which "has fostered the emergence of new, non-capitalist institutions that have fostered growth" (p. 116). By contrast, the convergence school attributes China's economic performance "to the same factors that promoted the fast growth of the East and Southeast Asian economies: the increasing liberalization, internationalization, and privatization of economic activities" (p. 116). While both schools agree that China has many features that differ sharply from standard capitalist patterns, the convergence school argues that rapid growth has occurred *despite* these deviations rather than because of them. The main factor has simply been "the quick absorption of surplus agricultural labor" in an underdeveloped economy (p. 137). Looking for lessons from experimentation simply encourages political interference that may choke off the accomplishments so far achieved. The policy prescription deriving from these analyses is that China should liberalize as quickly as possible and "implement a Meiji-style wholesale adoption of key market institutions from abroad" (p. 136).

While the convergence school may be right that the standardization of economic regulation and the clarification of property rights would now be useful for continued expansion, it is not clear that the adoption of such policies in 1978 would have been successful, since they have been tried with little success elsewhere. The decentralization of planning and the authorization of local innovation has generated a diverse set of local efforts to develop in a context of "hard budget constraints" so that failed efforts at least were not further subsidized, at least outside the state sector (Rawski, 1999). A market orientation emerged even in the largest state enterprises (Naughton, 1995).

Woo's account of the "experimental school" places too little emphasis on the impact of local diversity and competition between local innovations as opposed to the non-capitalist nature of the patterns. This lack of attention to variation can also be found among opponents of the convergence approach.

Processes of development under the Chinese variety of socialism have left different regions with widely varying sets of economic, spatial, and social resources, and taking advantage of these can encourage distinct organizational forms and practices.

Whereas, in some regions, collectives controlled by local governments have been the most dynamic economic sector (Walder, 1995), in the Pearl River Delta experimental reform has allowed the emergence of many more capitalist enterprises and practices. The region has been characterized by economic integration with Hong Kong, decentralized growth in a large number of formerly rural townships rather than the growth of existing urban areas, and considerable success at producing consumer manufactured goods for the advanced capitalist economies (Smart and Smart, 1991; Lin, 1997a; Hsing, 1998). Rather than being either disadvantaged by government intervention or directly controlled by local governments, the small and medium-sized foreign-invested enterprises that have been at the heart of this process have benefited from ambiguity in their legal status/regulation and the political support of local officials in overcoming the many conflicts that arise (Smart and Smart, 1993). The enterprises that have prospered have been able to build up sufficient trust and capacity to cooperate in order to overcome the incompatibilities between the PRC and Hong Kong capitalism (Smart, 2000).

Christerson and Lever-Tracy (1997) found that districts of integrated producers, thought characteristic by some of flexible specialization, are not common in China's rural exporting regions. They suggest that if we accept the claim that

> the primary advantage of spatial concentration is the creation of trust through repeated interaction and personal contact, then it may be possible that other social structures which increase trust and interaction could serve as a substitute for the spatial proximity of suppliers, producers and buyers. We will argue that ethnic and family ties in Chinese production possibly provide such a substitute. (Christerson and Lever-Tracy, 1997, p. 571)

These advantages are related to complementarities between cheaper land and labor within China, and the entrepreneurial skills and knowledge of the world market of the Hong Kong investors. By taking advantage of opportunities created by China's reform process, coalitions of Hong Kong entrepreneurs and Chinese local officials have succeeded in producing a very dynamic analogue of the industrial district of the Third Italy.

The effective harnessing of these potential complementarities was hardly inevitable, however. The potential for mutually destructive exploitation and rent-seeking in this context of underspecified rules and property rights was considerable (Smart, 1998). What were the regulatory processes that made profitable accumulation possible?

Neither markets nor hierarchies have been adequate to the task. Markets provided the hard budget constraints that helped to limit the extraction of resources from investors. Local governments have often been effective at providing the necessary infrastructure to allow the expansion of export-oriented production (Lin, 1997a; Hsing, 1998). Despite these contributions, without other regulatory processes based on social networks crossing the Hong Kong border (Smart and Smart, 1998) and an interactional culture that has made possible effective economic cooperation in a climate of considerable risk and chaos (Smart, 1999b), market and hierarchical coordination would have failed to tap into the potential of this region. The unruly transactional environment has been partially tamed through the interactions between government policy, market constraints and inducements, and network processes.

The cooperative arrangements that have been achieved may not be sustainable. There are certainly many features of this creative managing of the "edge of order and chaos" (Jin and Haynes, 1997) that generate instabilities. The lack of match, in the low-wage, labor-intensive economy of the PRD, between consumption and productive capacities has created a variety of problems, including trade disputes with the United States resulting from the massive level of exports and deflation in the domestic economy. Whether or not the domestic market can take over from the role of export markets is also uncertain, particularly since the workers in the foreign-invested factories of the Pearl River Delta are unlikely to be able to afford the goods that are being produced. It is very easy to be pessimistic about the future. Yet it would have been equally easy to have been pessimistic about the prospect of these relationships, and Hong Kong's prospects more generally, in the past. In fact, most non-Chinese foreign investors were indeed pessimistic about the short-term potential for profitable investment when China first opened up. How long can muddling through continue to support profitable accumulation in this region? Based on the past, I hesitate to make any firm predictions, but my inclination is not to discount the viability of muddling through, using informal and underregulated institutions, as a coping mechanism.

A Transnational Mode of Regulation?

The differences between the PRC and Hong Kong are still extreme, though less so than they were two decades ago, but neither can be understood without a consideration of the economic and social ties that connect them. Understanding these interactions within a regulationist framework is a considerable challenge, and one that requires questioning of the state-centric nature of regulation theory. Particularly for the parts of China that can be considered to have been incorporated into an extended Hong Kong urban region, a mode of regulation that provides some degree of stabilization cannot be associated with a single territorial state, nor is there a category of citizenship that encompasses all of those involved in the regional economy. Inter-governmental cooperation has not been adequate to the task either, although certainly it has made some contributions. Instead, governance through informal processes of regulation and "muddling through" based on negotiations that serve mutual interests seems to have been of greater importance. Describing the nature of this informal mode of social regulation, and its impact on the characteristics of the emerging cross-border urban region, is the goal of this section.

The Open Policy of the PRC since 1979 and the 1984 Sino-British Agreement to transfer sovereignty of Hong Kong back to China in 1997 set off an explosive economic and social integration of Hong Kong and its border region. However, a sharply discontinuous and policed border still separates the Special Administrative Region of Hong Kong from the rest of China. Hong Kong people's movement into China is largely unimpeded, but movement from China to Hong Kong is almost as difficult as it was when Hong Kong was still a colony. The denial of citizenship rights of entitlement and mobility are crucial to the nature of the urban region that has arisen.

These disjunctions and problems are found in all of the urban regions that have sprung up across national boundaries. The problems, but also the opportunities, seem to be greatest when the national boundary separates sharply different societies. The similarities between Canada and the United States create border regions that are very different from those on the border between the more sharply distinguished United States and Mexico. The intense differences in average wage rates, costs of land, environmental regulations, and so on produce considerable potential for heightened profits for investors, while also creating potential risks and management problems. Differences in legal and political institutions produce governance challenges that dwarf those of the politically fragmented metropolitan regions within the borders of the United States.

Formal systems of governance do not operate which would be adequate to the task of intentionally regulating accumulation and administering the total population of the HK/PRD region. They have allowed social networks and practices to cross the border and transform social life and the economy on both sides of the divide. While government to government interactions have determined the nature of the formal governmental institutions for Hong Kong's historically unprecedented form of existence, they have not been the main actors in producing regional integration. Individuals and enterprises have taken advantage of the opening to transfer or start up businesses, purchase homes across the border for investment or retirement, and participate in a variety of other practices. On the other side, local governments have been particularly active in attracting investment from Hong Kong, frequently renewing or mobilizing social ties with Hong Kong residents who emigrated from these areas and encouraging forms of local patriotism and obligation (Smart and Smart, 1998).

Smith (1998, p. 13) indicates that the three main elements of a regime of accumulation concern social relations involving "the production and extraction of surplus, ownership and property relations; a particular pattern of sectoral organization; and a certain relationship and co-ordination between production and consumption." In the Hong Kong region, multiple sets of relations of production co-mingle. In the Hong Kong SAR itself, capitalist relations of production based on secure private property rights predominate. In the Pearl River Delta counties, state socialist relations persist, particularly for state-owned enterprises, but capitalist relations have emerged in the context of less secure property rights. While it is the capitalist relations that cross the SAR border that are of greatest interest here, they cannot be seen in isolation. Hong Kong investors have relied on tactical alliances with local officials to provide support for their enterprises, and thus the development of capitalist relations of profit production are dependent on what has been described as "local corporatism." At the same time that Hong Kong investors obtain access to land and labor for export-oriented manufacturing, local officials extract a variety of forms of rent from these capitalist enterprises (Smart, 1998). I have suggested elsewhere that the dependent nature of such capitalist activities can be seen as representing "local capitalisms" which are subordinate to the political and social tactical alliances which make them possible (Smart, 2000). At present, increasing pressure by the United States on China to liberalize rapidly and more completely in order to gain membership in the World Trade Organization is helping to shift the balance of power toward more routine varieties of capitalism.

In terms of sectoral organization, the crucial issues revolve around the transfer of workers from very labor-intensive agricultural activities to industry and services. From the perspective of Hong Kong, the freeing of Chinese peasants from the land has permitted the continuation of an extensive regime of accumulation that takes advantage of cheap labor and land instead of continually transforming productive technologies. Accomplishing this has been dependent on success in exporting to the consumers of the advanced capitalist nations. While high levels of consumption have emerged among the elite of the Pearl River Delta counties, this has been based more on the extraction of rent generated through facilitating foreign investment than on the expansion of consumption capacity through the wage fund. Instead, factory workers have severely restricted capacities to consume, as in pre-Fordist Europe. Collective bargaining is severely limited by governmental distrust of independent labor movements and by the existence of large pools of cheap labor.

In order to maintain the dynamism of this region, a variety of challenges must be dealt with. Infrastructural development must cope with increasing traffic and trade. Workers must be housed, and their dependents fed and educated. A minimum of civic order must be achieved. Revenues must flow to governments to provide many of these necessary services. At the same time, taxation, corruption, and rent-seeking must be kept below levels that would drive investment into other localities. Regulatory conflicts, such as labor or environmental rules, between the distinct systems of the two sides of the Hong Kong border must be dealt with. Integration means that no state can deal with these challenges by itself. Can the region's governments continue to provide at least the minimum requirements for an increasingly sophisticated and interdependent transborder economy? I would suggest that we cannot begin to answer such questions unless we start to think about processes that act against it, and not just in the form of endogenously generated crises.

The word "regulation" implies the likelihood of processes that operate in opposition to the stabilizing forces. Yet regulation theory has paid little attention to the obverse, transgression. Without the danger of transgression, regulation would occur naturally. In the case of the HK/PRD region, transgression has been as influential as has regulation. Indeed, some transgressive actions have paradoxically served to generate informal governance; for example, where deals made between investors and local officials "pushed the envelope" of what formal legislation allowed and resolved some of the incompatibilities that discouraged and delayed American and European investment.

While informal processes that have facilitated the emergence of capitalist enterprises within the Pearl River Delta are almost certainly the most important pattern of transgression, there are many other significant challenges to governmental regulation. Cross-border integration and the extension of activities and networks into a transnational social field almost invariably create a variety of transgressive movements, including sex tourism, second wives, illegal immigration, smuggling, and quasi-legal real estate development practices.

Extension of activities outside of their territory of origin does not create a deterritorialized world (Brenner, 1999). Instead, borders remain crucial in structuring activities which transgress them. Indeed, many such activities are actually impelled by the existence of the border. The potential implications of separation/integration, mobility controls, and citizenship issues for regimes of accumulation can be seen in the right of abode issue. The decision by Hong Kong's Final Court of Appeal that the Basic Law granted the right to enter and reside in Hong Kong to all children of Hong Kong residents set off a serious constitutional debate. The estimated 1.67 million PRC residents who would have been entitled at present (692,000 of the total) or in the second generation (983,000 of the total) are accused of posing apocalyptic threats for Hong Kong's economy, environment, and society. The issue also raises crucial questions about both the social and political regulation of the HK/PRD urban region. The large number of those who would be entitled to the right of abode under this ruling is a result of past integration of the region, until 1978 primarily through illegal immigration from China to Hong Kong, and subsequently through migrants' return to China to find spouses and establish households, supplemented by substantial numbers of Hong Kong born men taking second wives or mistresses in China.

Hong Kong's Chief Executive asked the Standing Committee of China's National People's Congress to reinterpret the right of abode ruling, and as a result the numbers qualified were reduced sharply. This request was widely seen as threatening the rule of law in Hong Kong and the integrity of the "one country, two systems" formula. Hong Kong's Chief Executive argued that "Hong Kong cannot afford the influx of mainlanders expected to take up residence here under the right of abode court ruling," since "the government had to balance the need to respect the rule of law and the independence of the judiciary with the projected financial strain," which his government estimated at up to HK$710 billion "to pay for homes, hospitals and schools for the 1.67 million new arrivals" (SCMP Internet Edition, May 17, 1999). The continuing controversy about this ruling, and the conditions under which mainland residents can enter Hong Kong, is a clear illustration of the dual movements toward integration and the preservation of separation in the transborder region. While low-wage labor forces are very important for the accumulation process in the region, their utility is thought to be predicated on their continued residence across the Hong Kong border. An influx is seen not only as increasing costs in a dense urban space with one of the world's highest costs of living, but also as potentially discouraging the movement toward higher value-added production in a more knowledge-intensive economy. It would do this by providing workers whose low wages might reinvigorate labor-intensive production with Hong Kong's territory.

While keeping low-skilled mainlanders out of Hong Kong might be seen as offering various advantages for capitalist accumulation (although this has been debated), the way in which exclusion has been accomplished seems to show more evidence of "muddling through" than it does of the constitution of a "broadly functional" mode of regulation to support the accumulation process. While the region has prospered, and even the recent financial crises have been relatively short in duration, there has been little indication of creative and imaginative resolutions of the conflict caused by cross-border kinship networks and the sharp differential in accommodating people in Hong Kong as opposed to the Pearl River Delta. The tactics adopted by the SAR government have raised international concern over the rule of law in Hong Kong, generated substantial social conflict in Hong Kong, including exacerbating discrimination against recent arrivals from the mainland, provided precedents for Beijing's intervention into Hong Kong affairs, and failed to adopt any of the creative proposals suggested for more effective integration of the region in order to resolve the problem.

For transborder cities, much of the effort to assert control and promote accumulation is related to promoting or coordinating activities in complex and discontinuous spatial circumstances. Sum (1999, p. 130) refers to this as "time–space governance" and defines it as: "the strategic networks of trans-border actors (both public and private) involved in coordinating and stabilising divergent trans-border modes of growth and their capacities to manage self-reflexively the material, social, discursive, and time-space dimensions of these modes of growth." Reshaping and disciplining time (for example, by reducing regulatory delays or providing more effective communications infrastructure) and space (for example, by reclaiming land or relocating polluting and space-intensive land uses across the border) are thought to be increasingly crucial for territories endeavoring to heighten their competitiveness.

In the HK/PRD region, interventions have facilitated production that integrates the region, while maintaining strong dis-integrations in the form of controls on border crossing that even keep apart separated nuclear families. The right of abode issue is only one illustration of the complexity of governmental management of the opportunities and dangers posed by an integrated but disjunctive urban field. Other crucial issues include the lack of integration of the construction of infrastructure such as freeways and airports (Ng and Tang, 1997), the lack of control over industrial development in the Pearl River Delta that is endangering the quality of Hong Kong's air and water supply, and competition rather than cooperation in the endeavor to develop and attract high technology industries in the region.

Conclusions

We live in a world where the technological and institutional compression of time and space makes living lives across borders increasingly feasible. As a result, "urban research needs to be literally 're-placed' from the local to the trans-local and transnational scales" (Smith, 1999, p. 134). Cities, and non-urban localities, are becoming simply the visible tip of icebergs of social networks that extend around the world. For cosmopolitan elites telecommunication makes possible daily interactions that span the globe. Border cities suggest possible futures in which translocal and transnational linkages become even more important in everyday life and in framing expectations about future possibilities.

Governing localities that are ever more tightly bound into transnational spaces is certain to become more difficult. Regulating capitalist accumulation and urban places may need to be superseded by accepting that governance is the most that can be achieved without undermining the very technologies, networks, and innovations that fuel accumulation. While we continue to need institutional fixes, they may need to be less like the grand compromises of Fordism and more like haphazard patches as we muddle through increasingly uncontrollable complex transnational webs.

Acknowledgments

Part of the research reported here was conducted with the support of a Social Sciences and Humanities Research Council Standard Research Grant (1999–2001). This chapter has benefited from discussions and suggestions from a wide variety of colleagues, including George Lin, Tang Wing-shing, Roger Chan, Toshio Mizuuchi, Kris Olds, Henry Yeung, Katharyne Mitchell, Chan Kam Wing, Josephine Smart, Siu Yat-ming, Lui Tai-lok, Sum Ngai-ling, Gaby Vargas-Cetina, and Michael Blim. An earlier version of this chapter was presented at the Osaka Workshop for Frontiers of Asian Geographies, August 16–17, 1999.

7

The State, Capital, and Urban Restructuring in Post-reform Shanghai

Zhengji Fu

The rapid and even startling development of the Chinese economy has had profound effects on China's urban development since the Chinese government adopted its reform policy in 1978. Whereas it may be principally correct that urban development in China is largely occurring from within as a consequence of the adjustment from a rigid and traditionally repressive rural subsistence to a more open and liberal service-based urban economy (Clark, 1996), some scholars (Olds, 1995; Wu, 1995, 1997, 1998a; Eng, 1997) have started to look at some urban issues from without, i.e. to interpret the urban restructuring in some Chinese cities in the context of globalization.

Among those cities in the coastal region where international capital first affected China, Shanghai, as the biggest city in China, has recently attracted increasing interest regarding its rapid economic, social, and spatial transition in both English and Chinese literature (Xu, 1993; Olds, 1995; Wu, 1996; Yao, 1997b). However, the cause of Shanghai's rapid urban changes seems somewhat bewildering. On the one hand, any change in Shanghai, a city viewed as a model of state socialist cities and tightly supervised by the central government for three decades, would be incredible without a "first push" from the central government. In other words, without the change occurring internally in the first instance, there would have been no place for external forces to have effects on any Chinese city. On the other hand, since the door opened and international capital came in, the dynamics of urbanization have been changing step by step, and to such a point that any understanding of Shanghai's urban restructuring without consideration of international capitalist forces would be incomplete. Take foreign direct investment (FDI), for example. China started to accept FDI from 1978 on. In 1994, China in general received US$82.68 billion, which accounted for 17 percent of global FDI, of which Shanghai accounted for 12.13 percent. That meant Shanghai took around 2.1 percent of global FDI in 1994. How can one understand urban changes in a city which accounted for 2.1 percent of global FDI, while ignoring the effects of transnational capital?

In this chapter, Shanghai's urban restructuring is seen neither as internally induced as it was in the pre-reform era nor as solely externally produced by global capital, but the outcome of the interaction of the global and the local. This local–global interaction is examined from the perspective of the state–capital relationship. While acknowledging that the state, at both central and local levels, still controls Shanghai's urbanizing processes, this chapter explores how the mechanisms of Shanghai's urban development have been changed by the market-oriented reform as well as the introduction of international capital since 1978, and how the three main actors, namely the central government, the municipal government, and international capital, have changed their roles in the shaping of urban patterns. It is argued that Shanghai's urban restructuring in the post-reform era has been driven by a project-based, implicitly pro-growth coalition between the local state and international capital. The argument is further illustrated in the case of development of the Lujiazui Central Financial District (LCFD).

Theoretical Framework

Compared with other megacities in developing countries, Shanghai's speciality is reflected historically in three aspects. First, modern Shanghai is a direct outcome of the expansion of the world capitalist system in the nineteenth century. In other words, the transformation of Shanghai from a feudal commercial town to a capitalist city is the outcome of the incursion of external forces rather than a natural evolution from within. Second, the development of capitalism in Shanghai was interrupted by the victory of the communist revolution in 1949. Through the civil war, a capitalist Shanghai was revolutionalized into a socialist city. Third, unlike urban restructuring in capitalist countries, which results from the natural evolution of capitalist economic development, the present Shanghai's urban change is based on the state socialist system. And unlike urban restructuring in the East European countries, where the political economy was drastically changed into a capitalist system through "shock therapy," Shanghai's urban transformation is occurring as China reforms its state socialism toward a market-oriented economic system in a gradual way. It is a post-socialist urban restructuring in nature. Thus, from feudalism to capitalism to socialism to post-socialism, Shanghai has experienced a distinctive path in urban development. It is in such a historical context that Shanghai's urban restructuring should be understood.

An understanding of Shanghai's current urban restructuring should also be approached in a broad geographical context. It is not possible to understand a city's change by looking only at the city itself. Contemporary urban restructuring is the outcome of an interplay of forces at work on regional, national, and global scales. Any adequate explanation has to set the city in its wider geographical context (Massey, 1993). In Shanghai's case, two scales have to be taken into account as well as the local: the national and the global. Shanghai's urban changes in the post-reform era should and could be traced to changes of the whole political economy in China since the Chinese government adopted the reform policy in late 1978. After the Communist Party took power in 1949, it established a centrally authoritarian socialist system in which the vertically controlled Party system penetrated every corner of society and local government had little power over local things. It was also a system that was fundamentally isolated from the world capitalist system, and this did not change until 1978. Under such a political economy, it would have been impossible for Shanghai to make any significant change without a tremendous shift in the central government's policy (more precisely, the Communist Party's political line). Therefore, understanding the development of China's reform policy becomes the first step in an approach to Shanghai's urban change.

Meanwhile, China's "door" was opened at a time when the process of globalization speeded up at all levels in the world. Therefore, while the state retreated intentionally step by step, international capital stepped in and penetrated the society. In many ways, Shanghai's urban restructuring has been and is shaped by the dynamic interplay of the state and international capital over the control of production and markets.

Despite the complexity of Shanghai's urban development, which ranges from colonial capitalism to socialism and to the current post-socialist urban restructuring, and which has involved a variety of forces at work on different geographical levels, the key state–capital relationship is the main theme which cuts across all different periods. I divide the modern history of Shanghai's urban development into six periods. In each period, we can find the key relation of the state and capital which underlies Shanghai's urban development.

Six Periods of Shanghai's Urban Development: The State and Capital

The formation of modern Shanghai (1842–1895)

Modern capitalist Shanghai was not born from within, but in effect superimposed by the Western powers on a peasant civilization. Defeated in the

Opium War in 1842, the Qing dynasty was forced to open Shanghai to Western trade and residence. Within the international settlement and later the French Concession, both set beside the Chinese walled city, Westerners enjoyed the extraterritoriality which protected them from the Chinese jurisdiction. While the whole country was still under feudal control, the international settlements were an enclave that provided a secure place for capitalism to prosper. It was in this enclave that the capitalist economy, its institutions, and its way of life were implanted directly from the West, almost without any intervention from the Chinese government. It was in this enclave that a modern Shanghai was born, distinctive from its preceding form as a feudal commercial town.

In this period, the Chinese central government was fended off from the international settlements. There were three local authorities, each with its own laws and officials: the Chinese Shanghai Municipality in the Chinese walled city, the Shanghai Municipal Council in the international settlement (SMC), and the French Municipality in the French Concession. The French municipality was a "bureaucratic autocracy" (Bergere, 1981, p. 7), subject to the authority of the consulate and thence to the government in Paris. The Shanghai Municipal Council of the international settlement, however, was a typical local growth coalition, consisting mainly of the Western elite, who had strong local business interests and enjoyed relative autonomy from the local consulate body. Both authorities managed to provide Shanghai with public infrastructure such as gas street lighting, telephone wires, railways, and the public tram service, most of which made their debut in China in Shanghai.

Given the fact that national capital was still in an inchoate state at the beginning of the opening-up and started to grow in the late nineteenth century (the first Chinese textile mill was established in 1890), transnational commercial capital played the major role in Shanghai's economic development in this period. Therefore, if we were to diagram the key actors in the early development of modern Shanghai, we would find that one level of the state (the local state) and one level of capital (international capital) were especially critical from 1842 to 1895. The formation of modern Shanghai was mainly determined by international capital, and the role of the state was subdued.

The golden age of Shanghai (1895–1927)

Shanghai remained almost exclusively a trading city until China signed the Treaty of Shiminoseki with Japan in 1895. The treaty, which ended the war of 1894–5 between China and Japan over Korea, first granted foreigners the right to establish factories in the treaty ports of China. The consequent investment of transnational capital together with rapidly growing local capital led to the industrialization of Shanghai, by which a capitalist mercantile Shanghai was transformed into a highly centralized industrial capitalist city.

After over fifty years of transnational capitalist-led development, the local capitalist emerged as an important player in Shanghai's urban restructuring. The upsurge of local capital came in the First World War and its aftermath, when the presence of the old imperial powers in Shanghai began to decline. The establishment of local professional associations, the Shanghai Banker's Association in 1917 and the Chinese Millowner's Association in 1918, reflected this tendency.

Following the Xing Hang Revolution led by the Nationalist Party (known as Kuomingtang in Chinese) on October 10, 1910, the last emperor of the Qing dynasty abdicated and the Republic of China was established in Nanjing on January 1, 1911. However, China was still in political chaos, with warlords in the north and the Nationalist Party in the south, until 1927 when the Nationalist Party finally unified China and set up the central government in Nanjing. In this period of political turmoil, Shanghai, under the protection of extraterritoritality, enjoyed rapid industrialization and rapid growth and expansion of the city. The population of the city increased from one million inhabitants in 1910 to nearly two and a half million in 1920 (Bergere, 1981, pp. 4–6). International capital poured into this "paradise of venture," and Chinese national capital flourished. At the turn of the twentieth century, Shanghai was known as the Paris of the East, where sojourners from all corners of the globe converged to created one of the most dynamic and sophisticated capitalist entrepôts the world had ever seen (Perry, 1993). It was "as crowded as Calcutta, as decadent as Berlin, as snooty as Paris, as jazzy as New York" (cited in Yeung, 1996, p. 2).

Therefore, in the golden age of Shanghai, the capital-dominated state–capital relationship remained strong. If there was any difference from the previous period, we see the emergence of a new member on the capital side – Chinese local capital. Chinese local capital together with international capital and the local state brought in Shanghai's golden age.

Nationalist Shanghai (1927–1937)

With the victory of the Northern Expedition in 1927, the Nationalist Party led by Chiang Kai-shek unified China and established the central government in Nanjing. Although the establishment of the national government did not lead to a change in Shanghai's legal status, the Kuomingtang regime started to penetrate into the international settlements and managed to regain part of the rights of which China had been deprived. First, it established the Greater Shanghai Municipality in July 1927, which brought together under its authority the different Chinese parts of Shanghai and its outskirts. The previous Chinese City Council, which was a representative municipal government established in 1905, was replaced by the Municipality of Great Shanghai, whose mayor was named by the central government. Second, the Kuomingtang regime pursued a series of policies that returned to the imperial tradition of bureaucratic capitalism and consequently resulted in the decline of the bourgeoisie in Shanghai. Thus, the General Chamber of Commerce, which gathered together the most influential businessmen within the international settlement and which has often displayed political independence, was taken over by a government-appointed committee in April 1927, and was placed under the direct control of the Kuomingtang in March 1929. The "coup" of March 1935, which brought the Bank of China and the Communications Bank under the direct control of the government, put an end to the financial power and independence of the Chekiang banking group. In a few years, the old business middle class had been replaced by a class of officials/capitalists working privately or publicly with their own capital or funds from the state (Bergere, 1981, p. 18).

In this period, although the international status of Shanghai remained, the Kuomingtang regime started to tighten its economic control of the international settlements by using state capital. So, apart from the local state, international capital, and local capital, Shanghai, for the first time since 1842, started to be affected by another key actor – the central state, which appeared in the state–capital relation by bringing in bureaucratic capital. However, the penetration of the central state was indirect given the fact that the international settlements were still politically controlled by Westerners. Shanghai's remaining international status meant that although the state–capital relationship started to tilt toward the state side, Shanghai's urban development was still basically determined by capitalist logic.

The end of Shanghai's international status (1937–1949)

After the outbreak of Sino-Japanese War in July 1937, Japan occupied the Chinese part of Shanghai, and on December 8, the day following the attack on Pearl Harbor, Japanese troops entered the international settlement. In January, 1943, a hundred years after the Nanjing Treaty was signed, the Western powers renounced their treaty rights, although Shanghai was still occupied by the Japanese.

It was a period of political and economic chaos. The eight years of Japanese occupation were followed by the civil war between the Nationalist Party and the Communist Party. For Shanghai, the years of civil war were years of wild inflation. Prices increased by 33.7 percent a month during the 1945–8 period (Bergere, 1981, p. 27). Shanghai's economic activity was only maintained thanks to help from abroad. Shanghai was returned to the national government, but it had no time to rebuild it.

The Japanese occupation and later the renouncement of treaty rights by Western powers put an end to Shanghai's century-length international settlements and together with them the Shanghai Municipal Council. International capital fled the war-plagued country, and its impacts on Shanghai's urban development faded away. Therefore, in this period (more precisely the period 1945–9), key actors that determined Shanghai's urbanization processes can be identified as: the central state, the local state, and national and local capital.

Socialist Shanghai (1949–1979)

The victory of the Communist Party in the civil war in 1949 is a watershed in the history of Shanghai's urban development. Before 1949, Shanghai's changing urban pattern was dominated by capitalist logic, despite the increasing challenge from the Chinese state. This capital-dominated relationship of the state and capital was fundamentally changed by the communist revolution, which brought about a socialist Shanghai. Under the direct control of the central government and the Central Committee of the Communist Party in Beijing, Shanghai lost its position as an independent economic unit. The relationship with the West, which had been so critical for Shanghai's successful economic development after 1842, was completely cut off. International capital no longer existed. Most national capital fled to Taiwan, Hong Kong, and overseas, where it rose again; the remaining capital was nationalized. Private capital was then eliminated as required by the socialist ideology. A capitalist cosmopolitan Shanghai was transformed into a socialist "productive city" based on the centrally planned economic system. Although it still played a very important role in national industrialization, Shanghai was isolated from the world economy, and lost its role as the financial and trade center in the Far East.

In socialist Shanghai, the state, particularly the central state, was the dominant force that decided Shanghai's fate. The key actors in Shanghai's urban development, therefore, were the predominant central state and much less the local state, and the role of capital disappeared in the state–capital relation that underlay Shanghai's urban development.

Post-socialist Shanghai (1979 to the present)

The reform policy adopted by the Chinese government in December 1978 started a new era for Shanghai. Shanghai's relation to the central government as well as the world economy has since been dramatically changed. With the marketization and decentralization introduced by reform, the municipal government regained relatively significant autonomy from the central state. With its opening up to the world economy, transnational capital came back to Shanghai again.

China's reform led by the central government unfolded gradually, however. Shanghai's urban development did not speed up drastically until 1990, when the central government launched the development of Pudong (East Shanghai), demonstrating its determination to revitalize Shanghai into a world class city as it was in 1920s and 1930s. Seeing Shanghai as the gateway to the huge Chinese market, as it always is, foreign direct investment poured in and greatly changed Shanghai's urban structure, economically, spatially, and to a lesser extent socially. In 1996, the share of foreign-funded enterprises' gross output value in Shanghai's industry reached 34.8 percent of the total, while the share of the state-owned enterprises which once dominated Shanghai's industry dropped drastically to 38.8 percent (State Statistical Bureau, 1997). Compared with international capital, which has become a major player in Shanghai's urban development, internal private capital, although unleashed gradually by the government, still plays a minor role. So, in this period, we see the emergence of the local state as a key player, and on the side of capital, we see the comeback of international capital as an important actor in the shaping of Shanghai's urban patterns.

The State, Capital, and Urban Restructuring in Post-reform Shanghai

China's reform has been mainly understood as a gradual process of marketization and decentralization. However, it can be also seen as a process of redefining the Chinese state (White, 1993). In the process, the role of the Chinese state, both central and local, has changed dramatically in its relation to the economy as well as to society as a whole. With the changing role of the Chinese state and the opening-up to the world capitalist economy, international capital has gradually penetrated into China and played an increasingly important role in China's urban restructuring.

The role of the central government

The central government still has a strong presence and decisive influence in Shanghai. Take industry, for example. In 1996, there were 248 central-run industrial enterprises in Shanghai, employing 279,100 workers, which accounted for 9.2 percent of total industrial workers, producing 80.1 billion yuan gross output value, which accounted for 18.5 percent of the total (State

Statistical Bureau, 1997). Most importantly, the central government has the final say in crucial decision-making by means of the Party and administrative system. First, although the municipal government is nominally accountable to the local assembly, the Shanghai Party committee is still the top decision-maker. While the mayor, who is nominated by the Central Committee of the Chinese Communist Party (CCCCP) and elected by the local assembly, is usually the vice-secretary in the municipal party committee, the secretary, who is appointed by the CCCCP and usually a member of the Political Bureau, which is the paramount decision-maker in China, is the *de facto* boss. Whenever there is a conflict between the central and the local, which has become frequent since decentralization, the secretary is supposed to speak out in favor of central government. Through this political arrangement, central government is still in control of Shanghai's urban development. Some critical development projects, such as the development of Pudong, would be impossible without the support of central government. Second, the so-called "approval economy" remains pervasive. Any important project whose investment exceeds a certain threshold set by the central government has to be approved by the ministry concerned in the center. For example, any FDI venture whose investment surpasses US$30 million has to be submitted to the central planning commission for approval.

Formation of the pro-growth coalition of the municipal government and international capital

After reform, the priority facing the municipality has shifted from the implementation of production plans made by the central government to the development of the local economy. Somewhat surprisingly, it seems that all Chinese cities suddenly changed from being "factories" of the central government to being "firms" of their own, immersed in "growth machines" politics (Logan and Molotch, 1987). Just like their capitalist counterpart, the defining character of municipal government in post-reform Chinese cities is what Harvey (1989) called entrepreneurialism. However, the formation of entrepreneurialism in Chinese cities is quite different from that in Western cities. Whereas in the West the political parties, labor organizations, local chambers of commerce, and the like play the crucial role in the formation of entrepreneurialism, in China, due to the immaturity of civic society and the lack of party politics, entrepreneurialism is usually the consequence of decentralization, and of intercity competition for external capital.

With the introduction of marketization and the opening-up of the Chinese market to international capital, Shanghai's structure of ownership of enterprises changed dramatically. Take industry, for example. When the government introduced the reform policy in 1978, there were only two kinds of ownership in Shanghai: state-owned and collective-owned which were run by the local government. In 1996, although these two kinds of enterprises still accounted for 72 percent of enterprises, their share of the total gross output value dropped drastically to 38.8 and 12.3 percent respectively, while the share of foreign-funded enterprises reached 34.8 percent (State Statistical Bureau, 1997). From the point of view of ownership, Shanghai has become a mixed economy with foreign-funded enterprises the most rapidly growing sector. FDI has become an increasingly important factor in the restructuring of Shanghai's economy.

The introduction of FDI is the epochal event in Shanghai's urban development, which not only altered the economic structure as mentioned, but also, perhaps more importantly, changed the attitude and behavior of the municipal government. Nowadays, international capital has an unprecedented mobility that is completely beyond the control of the Chinese government. To attract this scarce resource, Shanghai has to compete with other cities in China and even with those in other countries. To prevail over other competitors, a so-called "good business climate" became crucial. Based on this perception, which is now prevalent in all Chinese cities, the municipality tried to do its best to cater for the needs of international capital. As a result, "to act in accordance with international rules" became a popular slogan in government documents and the mass media. Thus, the importance of FDI from inside and the intercity competition for FDI from outside strongly drove the municipal government toward entrepreneurialism.

On the other hand, from the standpoint of international capital, Shanghai is the gateway to what is potentially the world's biggest market. The product that catches Shanghai catches China, it is said. Multinational corporations tend to view Shanghai as key to the Chinese market, a place to set up their affiliates. Researchers (e.g. Nyaw, 1996) have shown that the huge market potential in China is the primary motivating factor for FDI in Shanghai.

So, both the municipal government and international capital have a great interest in promoting Shanghai's economic growth. In pursuing this common interest, the capital-thirsty municipal and the profit-motivated international capital formed a pro-growth coalition in the process of Shanghai's urban development. However, as is shown in the next section, this pro-growth coalition has distinctive Chinese characteristics. It is a project-based, implicit, and informal one, differing from the American-style growth machine politics.

The Development of Lujiazui Central Finance District (LCFD): The Project-based Pro-growth Coalition

The Lujiazui Central Finance District is a sub-zone in the Pudong New Area – China's most famous development zone, which was launched by the Chinese government in 1990. Immediately opposite the colonial-era Bund, the LCFD covers an area of 1.7 square kilometers, with a planned total floor space of 4.2 million square meters. LCFD is the SMG's pet project and is intended to become the symbol of twenty-first century Shanghai – the Chinese equivalent of Manhattan in New York, Shinjuku in Tokyo, and La Défense in Paris. As the most elaborately planned area in China, it is divided into 68 parcels of land, prefixed with Roman letters, where dozens of super high-rise buildings will be located.

With direct and strong intervention by the SMG and the Pudong New Area Administration (PNAA) and the inflow of international capital, the development of the LCFD was swift, and even astonishing to foreigners. Prior to the development of Pudong, there were 595 enterprises in total, some of which were run directly by central ministries, and 27,300 households, in the LCFD. By the time I did my final fieldwork in summer 2000, only ten enterprises and 1,100 households, located in the N sites, were left in the LCFD. Meanwhile, on the cleared land, 31 projects (buildings) had been contracted, among which 18 buildings had been completed in accordance with the master plan (my interviews in 1999 and 2000).

Among these 31 high-rises, 23 buildings involved investment from Hong Kong, Taiwan, and other countries (ten buildings were wholly foreign-invested). In the design of buildings, the involvement of foreign and Hong Kong architects was even more significant. Twenty-six buildings were designed or jointly designed by foreign or Hong Kong architects. All the buildings were built for the purpose of office or hotel with luxurious facilities. With the selling price ranging from US$1,800 to 3,500 per square meter, it may be still relatively cheaper compared with the real estate market in London, New York, or Hong Kong, but it is expensive enough to scare away most Chinese companies. Multinational corporations, foreign banks, and large Chinese companies are the targeted occupants for these luxurious buildings.

Ten years on, a brand new financial district has emerged in a place that used to be a mixture of industrial and residential areas. Such a rapid development would have been impossible without great efforts from an implicit pro-growth coalition between the local government and international capital which was formed in the process of development. The following case of the would-be world tallest building at site Z 4-1 of the LCFD is illustrative of the formation of this pro-growth coalition.

During my fieldwork in July 2000, the general manager of SLDC, Kang Huijun, gave me an account of investment by Forest Overseas Co. Ltd in sites D 1-1 and site Z 4-1, which, for him, demonstrated the achievement of SLDC in attracting foreign investors, but, for me, reflected the interaction between the Chinese state and international capital.

The mother company of the Forest Overseas Co. Ltd, Forest Building Co. Ltd, is the largest real estate company in Japan. The owner of the company,

Minoru Mori, was named in 1992 as "the richest man in the world" by *Fortune* for his personal fortune of US$14.8 billion. The development of Pudong caught the attention of Mr Mori, who was considering a new strategy of overseas investment in the wake of the collapse of the Japanese real estate market in the early 1990s. In his first visit to Pudong in November 1993, he expressed strong interest in site D 1-1 and particularly site Z 4-1, which would be the tallest building (96-story) in the LCFD according to the plan. Realizing that Minoru Mori would be a heavyweight figure in the development of the LCFD, leaders of the Shanghai government were keen to promote these two sites. On his second visit to Shanghai in February 1994, Mr Mori was met by the vice mayor of Shanghai, Zhao Qizhen, who was concurrently the Director of the PNAA, the standing vice mayor of Shanghai, Xu Kuangdi, and mayor Wong Ju. When Xu Kangdi was promoted to mayor of Shanghai in the spring of 1994, his first letter was sent to Minoru Mori. In the letter, Xu expressed the hope that the SMG would fully support and cooperate with Mr Mori in making the projects in sites D 1-1 and Z 4-1 successful.

In September 1994, SLDC and Forest Overseas Co. Ltd, which was financed by Forest Building Co. Ltd and dozens of Japanese financial institutions signed a contract of land lease for sites D 1-1 and Z 4-1. According to the contract, Forest Overseas Co. Ltd got 50 years' use of sites D 1-1 and Z 4-1 at the price of US$500 per square meter and US$540 per square meter of the buildable area, respectively. Ten percent of the cost was paid upon signing of the contract. The rest would be paid in September 1995 for site D 1-1 and at the end of 1995 for site Z 4-1 on the condition that the land would be cleared on time. As foreign investment, the projects would enjoy all preferential policies given by the Chinese government, among which was the tariff waiver for materials imported for the purpose of building construction. Since these two projects were two super high-rise buildings, this policy of tariff waiver was very significant in the company's budget plan. In addition, the SMG pledged a reduced rate of 15 percent income tax for the projects. Income tax at a reduced rate of 15 percent was one of the preferential policies given to foreign invested enterprises in Pudong by the central government, but this was for enterprises in the manufacturing sector only. Obviously, as an important international real estate company, Forest Overseas Co. Ltd obtained a major concession from the SMG.

According to the contract, SLDC would make these two pieces of land ready for use by September 1995 and by the year end of 1995, respectively, providing the land with "seven connections and one clearance." "Seven connections and one clearance," the usual standard for land leasing in China, means that the land is connected with "running water pipes, drainage, sewage, electricity, gas, telephone lines, and roads," and all attachments to the land are cleared, with existing residents relocated. The most difficult job involved was the relocation of residents. In an interview with Yang Chuancai, the general manager of Pudong Lujiazui Urban Construction Company, a subsidiary of SLDC which is in charge of land clearance, he outlined the relocation of site Z 4-1.

On site Z 4-1, there were 834 households and 41 work units. In October 1997, Minoru Mori came to see the progress of land clearance, which had just started a month ago. He doubted very much that SLDC would complete in three months what would take years (even decades) in Japan. In company with Minoru Mori, the then general manager of SLDC Wang Ande assured Mr Mori that the land clearance would be finished as scheduled or SLDC would pay RMB 380,000 for each day delayed in accordance with the contract. The majority of residents were very cooperative, except one man who was forced out by the court on December 10, 1995. A miracle perhaps in Mori's eye, the clearance of site Z 4-1 was completed on December 22, 1995.

Starting in the mid-1990s, there was an objective that the special treatment of foreign investment would be gradually replaced by policies that treat national enterprises and foreign-invested enterprises equally. In September 1995, the Chinese Customs Authority issued a statement that the old policy that foreign-invested enterprises could import self-use materials with zero tariff would end by the end of 1995. This meant a huge increase in the cost of construction of the super high-rise building on site Z 4-1, which would rely heavily on imported materials and facilities. Forest Overseas Co. Ltd immediately sent a letter to the SMG asking that the project could enjoy the tariff-waiver policy until the completion of building as written in the contract between Forest Overseas Co. Ltd and SLDC. Considering the importance of this 96-story building, the SMG tried its best to cooperate with the company. Because it was beyond the power of the SMG, the SMG made a direct request to the State Council asking for a special consideration. Finally, Premier Zhu Rongji, who was the mayor of Shanghai before being promoted to the central government, gave a personal instruction allowing Forest Overseas Co. Ltd to continue enjoying the tariff waiver policy. Meanwhile, the PNAA signed another agreement with Forest Overseas Co. Ltd assuring that the project would enjoy the preferential policies pledged by the SMG.

In the development of the LCFD, we have seen that there is a convergence of interests between the local government and international capital. The SMG is keen to revitalize Shanghai as China's major financial center by launching the development of the LCFD, and international developers such as the Japanese Forest Building Company, attracted by China's potential market, switch their capital into property development in the LCFD. Both interests rely on the growth of the LCFD. In pursuing this common objective, they form what can be called a project-based, implicitly pro-growth coalition.

This Chinese-style "interest coalition" of local government and international capital is different from American-style "growth machine" politics. In

America, local business communities are well organized. They are "mobilized interests" (Fainstein et al., 1983, p. 214). Local business people are the major participants in urban politics, particularly business people in property investment, development, and real estate financing (Logan and Molotch, 1987). Through continuous interaction with local politicians, including substantial political campaign contributions, their interests are well integrated in the decision-making procedure of urban development. Often, the leading politicians come from the local business community (ibid.). In China, politics are still monopolized by the Communist Party. Local social organizations independent from the Communist Party are barely allowed. International capital, although very influential, is not institutionalized into China's urban politics. Therefore, unlike the American-style pro-growth coalition that is formal, official, and well integrated, the interest coalition found in the LCFD is project-based, informal, and temporary.

However, this implicit coalition, once formed, is very powerful and even more so than its American counterpart. In the case of the LCFD, we have seen that this coalition demonstrated its formidable ability and performed very well in transforming the urban form of the LCFD. The SMG organized the planning consultation process, which involved four internationally renowned firms with "global vision" in mind. To implement the plan, the SMG and the PNAA managed to raze the whole area, relocate hundreds of enterprises and tens of thousands of households, clear the land, and provide a modern infrastructure. International investors, attracted by China's huge market potential, stepped in. Dozens of international standard office buildings, which are mainly funded by Hong Kong, Taiwanese, and foreign developers and designed by internationally renowned architects, have sprung up in the LCFD. This model of urban redevelopment, exemplified by the case of the LCFD, is illustrative of a general pattern of interaction between the state and capital which underlay hundreds of redevelopment projects across Shanghai in the 1990s. It is this project-based pro-growth coalition that has been rapidly and relentlessly transforming Shanghai's urban form.

Conclusions

Shanghai's development can be ultimately attributed to two factors: state activities and capital dynamics. These two factors have for more than a century been inextricably interrelated in shaping Shanghai's urban patterns. This chapter identifies six key relationships of the state and capital which have underlain Shanghai's urban development in six historical periods.

International capital has been always important to Shanghai's development. Shanghai's two most thriving periods – the early and the late twentieth century – are times when international capital has been most deeply and actively involved in Shanghai's development, although the kinds of involvement have differed because of different political situations.

Shanghai's current urban restructuring has been driven by a unique pro-growth coalition between the municipality and international capital. It is a pro-growth coalition with Chinese characteristics: implicit, informal, and project-based, differing from the American-style growth machine politics. The formation of this pro-growth coalition is mainly attributed to China's asymmetrical reform – while the developmental aspect of the state has changed, the political aspect of the state remains intact. This political situation, however, makes this Chinese-style growth coalition extraordinary strong. It is this pro-growth coalition that has been rapidly and relentlessly reshaping Shanghai's urban pattern.

Acknowledgments

I would like to thank my supervisor, Professor Chris Hamnett, for his invaluable guidance and inspirational encouragement. Without his kind support and help, this chapter would have been impossible. A travel grant from the RC21 enabled me to attend the international conference in Shanghai in 1999, at which an early version of this chapter was presented.

8

The Transformation of Suzhou: The Case of the Collaboration between the China and Singapore Governments and Transnational Corporations (1992–1999)

Alexius Pereira

The year 1992 marked the launch of the China–Singapore Suzhou Industrial Park (CSSIP). This park, a self-contained industrial estate located in Jiangsu province, was a formal joint venture between a Chinese consortium and a Singapore consortium. However, at another level, it was also a unique case of complementary collaboration between the China and Singapore governments. In the years since then, the CSSIP has experienced over US$3.76 billion in foreign direct investments, almost entirely by transnational corporations, in addition to over $155 million directly invested by the Singapore consortium, accounting for nearly two-thirds of all investments in Suzhou city (Chan, 1999). By 1999, 91 enterprises had begun operations in the CSSIP, employing around 14,000 employees. The growth of the industrial park has also affected Suzhou city. By 1997, it ranked fourth among all Chinese cities for foreign direct investment. The city's per capita income has risen from $100 to $450 in six years to become the sixth highest in China. During this same period, economic growth averaged over 15 percent per annum (Suzhou Municipal Statistical Bureau, 1999). However, in June 1999, the Singapore government, citing "frustrations with the venture," announced that it was disengaging from the CSSIP at the beginning of the year 2001 (Chan, 1999).

This chapter argues that the Singapore and China governments jointly collaborated in the CSSIP project as part of their own economic development strategies. Through an analysis of the CSSIP between 1992 and 1999, this chapter will explain the park's initial competitiveness, and its later weaknesses. Finally, the chapter will evaluate whether this form of intergovernmental collaboration is a viable strategy for economic growth and industrial transformation. Research for this chapter was conducted in Suzhou and Shanghai between July and September 1999, consisting of interviews with managers of companies located in the CSSIP, officials of the CSSIP, officials of the neighboring Wuxi Singapore Industrial Park (WSIP) and Suzhou New District (SND), and economists and academics based in China. In total, 102 respondents were interviewed. In addition, secondary data, such as newspaper and media reports that covered the period 1992–9, were also surveyed.

The Expansion of Industrial Transnational Corporations

This chapter argues that the China–Singapore Suzhou Industrial Park was designed by the Singapore and China governments to take advantage of one aspect of global capitalism: the capitalist expansion of industrial transnational corporations (TNCs). For the purposes of this chapter, a TNC has the ability to coordinate and control the various stages of its individual production chains within and between different countries. It has the ability to take advantage of geographic differences in the distribution of factors of production (natural resources, capital, labor) and in state policies (taxes, trade barriers, subsidies, etc.). It also has geographic flexibility, defined an ability to switch and to reswitch its resources and operations between locations at an international or even a global scale (Dicken, 1998, p. 177).

Despite TNCs being very diverse in terms of their actual composition and the nature of their business, one common feature is their capitalist motivation for profit maximization (Sklair, 1998). Within this larger group of TNCs are those that are involved in industrial production. This sub-group will engage in cross-border industrial production to reduce transaction costs, and gain economic and strategic advantage by exploiting their distinctive proprietary assets in several markets (Dobson, 1997, p. 9). Operationally, this involves establishing production units in various locations to source for the most cost-effective primary factors of production, such as raw materials, labor, land, and technological capabilities, as well as the most conducive secondary factors of production, such as fiscal incentives, financial inducements, tariffs, availability of infrastructure, and political stability (Henderson, 1989). Industrial TNCs seek to maximize profits through expansion, which entails establishing additional units in order to increase capacity. In this manner, industrial TNCs generate a demand for primary and secondary factors of production.

In the global economy, certain groups attempt to supply these factors in exchange for essential resources. These groups include not just local enterprises, but local labor and governments as well. In this sense, the demand and the supply of factors of production creates a system of exchange within the global economy. There is competition on both sides of the exchange process;

on the demand side, industrial TNCs are competing with each other in their drive toward profit maximization. On the supply side, various groups are also competing for the opportunities to supply these industrial TNCs with factors of production. This leads to a situation where actors in this global exchange system have to constantly negotiate, bargain, and compete with others (Dunning, 1997). It is of particular relevance to this chapter that certain governments are interested in participating in this exchange system as part of their economic development strategies. For instance, certain states may welcome foreign direct investment (FDI) from TNCs, offering their own population's labor, raw materials, and lands, in exchange for developmental processes such as employment creation, technological and managerial knowledge transfer, and income generation. This can be seen in the policies of governments that have established "export processing zones" (see Sklair, 1993; Chen, 1995). Such governments usually choose "FDI-led" development because of "market failures" within their own national economies (often as a result of inefficient local industrial enterprises), or because the country can take advantage of certain comparative and competitive advantages. Two such cases were the development strategies of the Singapore and China governments, converging at the beginning of the 1990s.

Singapore's Development Strategies, 1965–1990

It is widely accepted that Singapore's rapid industrial transformation and economic growth was mainly due to the government's FDI-led development strategies (see Mirza, 1986; Lim et al., 1988; van Ekland, 1995). Unlike many other Asian governments, the Singapore government did not choose import substitution industrialization (ISI) as the national development strategy because the majority of local Singaporean enterprises were small and technologically backward (Huff, 1994). Instead, as TNCs had the most modern technologies, pre-existing markets for the products, and financial capital for industrial transformation, the Singapore state targeted them as the engines for economic growth. The developmental benefits from the location of TNCs would include employment creation, capital investment, and technology transfer.

To attract industrial TNCs, the Singapore government had to offer competitive factors of production in exchange. As the country lacked raw materials and land, the government was aware that its main competitive advantage was the abundant but relatively cheap Singaporean labor force. Advised by the Singapore Economic Development Board, it also offered secondary factors of production, such as "pro-business" financial incentives, in order to attract industrial TNCs (Mirza, 1986). In addition, the Singapore government invested international aid and World Bank loans in developing industrial infrastructure and communications. Finally, the state controlled labor unions tightly, ensuring first that the cost of labor in the country remained globally competitive and second that labor itself remained "disciplined" and did not threaten social and political stability (Pereira, 2000). With these incentives, the Singapore government targeted industrial TNCs that were looking to expand operations in the Asia-Pacific region.

By 1980, many such corporations had chosen to locate in Singapore, in turn driving rapid industrialization. By 1985, TNCs employed over 75 percent of the industrial workforce in Singapore (see Mirza 1986; Lim et al., 1988). By the early 1980s, labor was so scarce that the government eased restrictions on foreign workers. Between 1972 and 1978, the total investment in Singapore was US$2,600.7 million, of which 84 percent was "foreign" (Lim et al., 1988, p. 255). In the mid-1980s, foreign companies accounted for 70 percent of the gross output in the manufacturing sector and 82 percent of exports (Bello and Rosenfeld, 1990, p. 293). Singapore's per capita gross domestic product increased from US$500 to 15,000 or S$1,330 to 22,587 (see Lim et al., 1988). The country had grown from being a "hopeless third world country" to "being on the edge of the rich industrial world" in only 20 years (Schein, 1996, p. vi). More importantly, during the period 1965–80, the relationship between the Singapore government and the TNCs had improved significantly. Starting as virtual strangers, by the 1980s, the Singapore government – through proving itself as an effective industrial infrastructure developer and administrator as well as conducting itself as an honest and efficient government – had earned the trust of transnational corporations (Schein, 1996; Pereira, 2000).

However, by the mid-1980s Singapore's niche as a location for low-cost manufacturing had become economically uncompetitive. This was in part due to rising wages and costs in Singapore and in part due to the emergence of new industrial regions and zones in Asia, many of which had abandoned import substitution industrialization strategies. Now receptive to transnational capital, many were hoping to supply primary factors of production (Krause, 1987). In most of these areas, raw materials, wages, and land costs were only a fraction of those in Singapore. In response, in 1990, the Singapore government unveiled a new national development which included the "regional industrialization" programme (see Wong and Ng, 1997). This marked the Singapore government's evolution into an entrepreneurial state. An entrepreneurial state is not only concerned about achieving economic growth and development; its main objective is to generate financial surpluses (see Eisinger, 1988; Yu, 1997). The Singapore entrepreneurial state was aware that despite the extremely low cost of primary factors of production in the emerging industrial regions in Asia, the lack of available secondary factors of production – particularly high quality industrial infrastructure and administration – would increase risks and transaction costs for industrial transnational corporations. Thus, the Singapore government devised a strategy of acting as an industrial broker in the region for the clients (expanding industrial TNCs) on behalf of the landlord (host country). It sought to capitalize on the TNCs' trust by establishing industrial estates developed and managed by the Singapore government at various strategic sites in the Asia-Pacific region (see Perry and Yeoh, 2000). However, as an entrepreneurial actor, the Singapore government was hoping that its brokerage role in the region could generate financial surpluses that would eventually supplement Singapore's national economy.

China's Developmental Strategies, 1979–1990

By 1978, China's "closed door" economy was facing several economic problems that were hindering growth, including poor production from state-owned enterprises, lack of capital, and technological stagnation (Naughton, 1995; Park, 1997). In 1979, the Deng Xiaoping-led government reformed the national economic policy and ideology. Essentially, it chose to open the country to global capitalism, albeit in a limited and gradual manner. Pursuing employment creation, technology and management expertise transfer, and capital investment, China's government began its reform policy with the Special Economic Zones (SEZs) program (Chu, 1986; Philips, 1989). The aim was to attract industrial TNCs looking to expand operations by offering extremely competitive primary factors of production such as labor, raw materials, and land. The China government initially targeted industrial enterprises from Hong Kong, Macao, and Taiwan (Huang, 1998). Not only were enterprises from these areas geographically close to China, Beijing was also hoping to take advantage of the "overseas Chinese" links, as kinship and village ties remained extremely pervasive (see Lever-Tracy et al., 1996, p. 6).

The SEZs program led to a flood of investments mainly from overseas Chinese industrialists. To illustrate, although more than 40 countries from all over the world have direct investments in China, by 1995 almost three-quarters (73.29 percent) of the total FDI came from the Chinese "commonwealth," which consisted of investors from Hong Kong and Macao (59.75 percent), Taiwan (10.04 percent), and Singapore (3.49 percent) (Luo, 1998, p. 179). This was because overseas Chinese industrialists had three advantages: they understood Chinese business institutions, language, and culture. Conversely, to the non-Chinese, China was an extremely "uncertain" and risk-laden location for investment.

> The problems that non-Chinese investors face have frequently been noted: the language barrier, the incompatibility of Western and Japanese management styles with Chinese practices, the distinctive bureaucratic organization of the

> workplace, the difficulties of hiring and firing workers and of eliminating inefficient work practices, low labor productivity, poor quality control, differences in negotiating practices and the long time-frame needed for their completion and most of all the lack of an established legal framework. (Lever-Tracy et al., 1996, p. 67)

> To non-Chinese businesses, China's weak property rights were compounded by the relatively unstable geo-political status of the state itself and the prevalence of corruption at most levels in the Chinese state bureaucracy. (Wong, 1999)

By 1990, despite these problems, from an economic perspective the SEZs program was a success. They had the effect of expanding employment opportunities, increasing workers' income, raising living standards, and most importantly increasing foreign currency earnings (see Chu, 1986; Park, 1997). Encouraged by this, the Beijing government began to expand the zoning programme. By 1995, there were 422 zones in China that permitted transnational capital (Yang, 1997, p. 30). However, from the perspective of the Chinese government, this programme also had unintended and undesirable consequences. The most serious problems in the zones were the formation of slums and shanty towns, a consequence of drastic increases of temporary farmers, individual stores, and temporary laborers (Park, 1997, p. 197). Also by 1991, Beijing found that crime was rising in these zones (Park, 1997, pp. 6–7). Therefore, although the Chinese government was satisfied with the economic performance of the zones program, it hoped that the economy could engage with global capital without these unintended and undesirable consequences. In 1978, on his first visit to Singapore, China's Premier Deng Xiaoping said that Singapore's economic development was something that China ought to learn from (Wong, 1999). He was particularly interested in exploring whether China could replicate Singapore's rapid industrial transformation and economic growth without the "negative" aspects of capitalism, such as crime and loss of central political control (Clemens, 1999; Wong, 1999).

Complementary Collaboration in Suzhou

At the beginning of the 1990s, the Singapore entrepreneurial state – led by former Prime Minister Lee Kuan Yew – had identified China as a location where expanding industrial TNCs wanted to penetrate because of its highly competitive primary factors of production. However, its existing secondary factors of production – particularly its quality of industrial infrastructure and bureaucratic administration – were problematic to certain industrial TNCs. Larger industrial TNCs had the resources and expertise to deal with local Chinese authorities themselves. Others opted to establish strategic joint ventures with local Chinese enterprises. However, for those that lacked these resources, China was a location that carried many uncertainties and risks. It was because of this that the Singapore entrepreneurial state identified a specific niche in China. The Singapore government believed that Singaporeans embodied the best of both business worlds. As the majority of the Singapore population were of overseas Chinese descent – indeed, the majority of Singapore's governmental leaders were ethnic Chinese – they would be familiar with Chinese business institutions and practices. However, because of Singapore's British colonial history and recent industrialization process, Singaporeans were also familiar with so-called "Western" business institutions and practices. In this way, the Singapore government believed that Singaporeans could effectively act as the industrial broker for the industrial TNCs on the one hand and Chinese authorities and local labor on the other.

After several fact-finding missions in China, the Singapore entrepreneurial state chose to establish two Singaporean industrial estates in the Jiangsu province. The two main reasons behind Jiangsu's selection was its the relatively high quality of human resources and its proximity to Shanghai. Also, there were factors such as the relative industrial saturation of the southern provinces and the Beijing–Tianjin corridor, while the northern provinces were considered too remote. Within Jiangsu, Lee Kuan Yew decided that the Singapore government's major industrial park would be located in Suzhou, whereas the minor one would be at Wuxi. The first difference between these two parks was that the Singapore government would be directly responsible for the development, marketing, and management of the China–Singapore Suzhou Industrial Park (CSSIP), whereas a government-linked company (Sembawang Corporation) would be responsible for the Wuxi–Singapore Industrial Park (WSIP). The second difference was that the CSSIP would be 70 square kilometers in size, whereas the WSIP would only be one square kilometer large. The Singapore entrepreneurial state projected that in 20 years, a total of US$20 billion could be invested in the CSSIP, providing over 360,000 jobs for the population of Suzhou (Singapore Economic Development Board, 1995, p. 5). Thus, the CSSIP was clearly the Singapore government's flagship project, not just when compared to the WSIP but even when compared to all the other Singaporean industrial parks in Asia.

Synergy strengths

As mentioned at the beginning of the this chapter, between 1992 and early 1997 the CSSIP was one of the fastest growing industrial estates in China (Tanzer, 1997). Its growth can be explained by the synergy strengths of the collaborating Singapore and China governments. Synergy refers to the positive combination of different inputs (Evans, 1996). Thus, the collaborators contributed critical elements that allowed the CSSIP to gain competitive advantages over other economic zones in China.

The Singapore government's input was industrial infrastructure development and administration to establish an industrial estate that was of "international standards" (Tanzer, 1997). This was operationalized to mean that the industrial facilities would be technologically advanced and of the highest standards. Furthermore, the Singapore government invested in building a power substation and water treatment plant specifically for the CSSIP. In addition to the large financial investments made by the Singapore government, it introduced Singaporean institutions and practices at the CSSIP. This was done through the official "Software Transfer" program:

> "Software" transfer refers to the sharing of Singapore's successful public administration and economic management experience with the Chinese authorities so that they can formulate *pro-business policies* in the CS-SIP, and govern with *transparency* and *efficiency*. . . . SIPAC together with the SSPO will identify the relevant type of "software" to be shared. Mutual visits and training attachments help Suzhou officials understand the Singapore way as well as international practices. Together with Singapore government officials, Suzhou officials decide how best to adapt Singapore's practices to suit local circumstance by selecting and modifying appropriate elements. Singapore sends its government officials to Suzhou to assist in this adaptational process. (CSSIP Prospectus, 1999, p. 10; original emphasis).

The Singapore entrepreneurial state gave this programme high priority. By 1996, nearly 50 Singaporean government bodies were involved in conducting courses for 200 Chinese officials in both Singapore and Suzhou (Koh, 1996). Singapore's Ministries of Labor, Trade and Industry, and National Development, the Housing Development Board, the Central Provident Fund Board, the National Trades Union Congress, the Trade Development Board, and the Urban Redevelopment Authority were among those involved. The courses covered three areas: economic management, encompassing marketing, registration of companies, and incentive programs for investors; urban management, which includes environmental protection, building control, and town planning; and labor management, which includes employment contracts, health care, and labor insurance. In addition, specialized courses on customs clearance, waste management, workers' provident fund, human resource matters, and real estate management were also organized. To industrial TNCs that were already familiar with the "Singaporean or international practices" from the earlier era, these institutions and practices were highly desirable as they had a transaction cost reducing function.

On its part, the China government invested political and social rather than economic capital in the CSSIP. In terms of political capital, CSSIP was granted a national status that was on par with the five SEZs and Pudong

(Shanghai). Also, senior leaders in Beijing regularly endorsed the CSSIP in public. For example, in 1992, President Jiang Zemin of China and President Ong Teng Cheong of Singapore jointly presided at the signing of the agreement to develop the CSSIP. In 1994, Vice-Premier Li Nanqing of China and Lee Kuan Yew, who was appointed Singapore's Senior Minister, signed a supplementary agreement to transfer the "software." At the same time, Li was appointed co-chairman of the Joint Steering Committee of the CSSIP. In addition, President Jiang was quoted as having said that the CSSIP was the "priorities of all priorities in China, and must not be allowed to fail." By supporting and endorsing the CSSIP, Beijing gave the park high importance and prestige. These measures were important in acting as a form of social guarantee to industrial TNCs.

The response from investors has been positive. In 1994, at the CSSIP's formal opening ceremony, it had already secured the investments of 14 enterprises (Tan, 1994a). By June 7, 1996, two years after the park began operations, 62 transnational corporations had signed up at the CSSIP, pledging US$2 billion in investments, exceeding the Singapore government's initial expectations (Tanzer, 1997). Also, up to July 1999, every industrial tenant in the CSSIP was a foreign enterprise (either wholly foreign owned or a Sino-foreign joint venture). This indicated that the high occupancy rates were not buffered by relocating Chinese enterprises to the estate but reflected the high demand from industrial TNCs. Interestingly, this high demand for space was despite the fact that the operating costs in the CSSIP were higher than in any other SEZ in China. For example, in 1998 land costs were US$65 per square meter, almost 20 percent higher than the next most expensive zone, Shenzhen. Labor costs within the park were also higher as the Singaporean park management company imposed a mandatory provident fund for all workers, which added nearly 66 percent to salary costs (Seidlitz, 1998).

The intergovernmental collaboration had enhanced the competitiveness of the CSSIP in China. This was also validated by research conducted by the author as well as by the public testimonies of several of the investors. Three themes were recurrent: industrial TNCs located in the CSSIP because of (a) the "trust" they had in the Singapore government, (b) the high importance and prestige placed by the two governments on the project, and (c) the (promised) high quality infrastructure and administration. The trust that industrial TNCs had in the Singapore government was based on the credibility that the Singapore government had developed in its earlier industrial transformation program between 1965 and 1980. For example, Kentaro Hirata, Vice-Chairman of Board and General Manager of Suzhou Towa Electron, was quoted as saying: "We chose Suzhou [Industrial Park] because we are confident of Singapore's involvement in the Park, the successful software transfer and customer satisfaction service provided by the Chinese government" (CSSIP Prospectus, 1999).

The "prestige" of the Suzhou Industrial Park referred to the top-level intergovernmental (Singapore–Beijing) desire to ensure that the park was successful, not just at an economic but also at a diplomatic and bilateral level. To illustrate, some managers of industrial transnational corporations were quoted thus:

> Singapore and China have put so much prestige in the project that we can only benefit from it. Our start-up was smoother and faster than expected. (Reimer Friedrich, Managing Director, Siemens Rexton Hearing Systems, in Tanzer, 1997)

> We chose Suzhou [for our first China plant] because of our working relationship with the Singapore Economic Development Board and because we thought it's a much safer bet with government support from both sides. Multinationals want a comfort zone. If they have a problem, they need somebody to talk to. (Yap Chew Loong, General Manager, Becton Dickinson, in Tanzer, 1997)

Having high-quality industrial infrastructure and administration also contributed to the industrial TNCs' locational choices. The Asia-Pacific Production Manager for Black and Decker, Ian Walker, went on record to say that he visited 16 industrial zones in China before deciding on the CSSIP. His reasons were, as told to the *Singapore Business Times*, that land rights in Suzhou were set by the Singapore management team for 50 years from 1992. He claimed that this immediately robbed Chinese officials of the common trick of "renegotiating" such fees upwards after the factory has been built. Also, tenants could choose their own construction supervisors and were not forced to use local contractors with ties to the authorities. Walker also stated that his company preferred to do "hard-nosed business with the Singaporeans, rather than the grey business of the Chinese" (Seidlitz, 1998).

This demonstrated that the intergovernmental collaboration had enhanced the competitiveness of the CSSIP *vis-à-vis* other industrial estates in China. The park's competitiveness encouraged the location of many industrial transnational corporations, which in turn generated developmental effects in Suzhou, particularly in employment creation, technology transfer, and foreign investment.

Synergy weaknesses

On June 29, 1999, the Singapore entrepreneurial state announced that it was disengaging from the CSSIP project, relinquishing management of the industrial park and reducing its shareholding from 65 to 35 percent on January 1, 2001 (Loh, 1999). It would only develop a total of eight square kilometers instead of the 70 that it originally planned. After 2001, with the Chinese government at the helm of the CSSIP, the Singapore government would remain only as a minority financial stakeholder. This section examines the factors that had led the Singapore entrepreneurial state to withdraw from a project that it initially believed could not fail.

The Singapore government's "official" reason for disengaging was because of unfair competition from one particular industrial estate, the Suzhou New District (SND), which was managed by the local Suzhou municipal authorities. Located to the east of Suzhou, by 1998 the SND had grown to cover 25 square kilometers, already larger than the CSSIP. This industrial estate, established in 1990, was awarded "economic development zone" status, which allowed for foreign investment. It was in fact offered to the Singapore government during the fact finding missions in 1991. However, the Singapore government chose to develop the CSSIP on the west of Suzhou rather than locate it either within or beside the SND. By the end of 1998, there were over 1,500 enterprises operating in the SND, with total investments pledged at US$2.5 billion. According to the information provided by the SND:

> Over 340 foreign funded enterprises from 30 countries, including MNCs, such as DuPont, Motorola, Siemens, Philips, Sony, Panasonic, Mitsubishi, are investing in SND. 13 of the World Top 100 and 5 of the World Top 5 are investing here. There are 12 projects whose total investment is no less than US$100 million each. (SND Investors Guide, 1999, p. 5)

However, the Singapore government was not "upset" because the SND was a direct competitor to the CSSIP; instead, it accused the SND of "bureaucratic shenanigans" (Lague, 1998). Lee Kuan Yew, a key figure within the Singapore entrepreneurial state, accused the SND of stealing potential clients away from the CSSIP through undercutting industrial unit prices. Also, he claimed that the Suzhou local municipal authorities and the Suzhou Mayor appeared to be more interested in the SND than the CSSIP (*Economist*, 1998). In response, Suzhou's Mayor Chen Deming insisted that his government had behaved honorably in its dealings with Singapore. He told the *International Herald Tribune*, "We have followed every step according to the contract" (Lague, 1998). He said that it would have been a mistake for the municipal authorities to give "50–50" treatment to the two parks, as the CSSIP has the backing of two national governments while the SND "must fend for itself" (Kwang, 1998). He also emphasized that tax revenues that accrue to the CSSIP go straight to Beijing rather than to Suzhou city. In his own manner, Chen was outlining his priorities.

By 1997, the SND had become an effective competitor to the CSSIP. Economically, it could afford to offer lower industrial land prices in comparison to the CSSIP because the latter's prices reflected a value-added mark-up that was supposed to bring financial profits for the Singapore government to supplement its home economy. The Singapore government was initially confident that TNCs would be willing to pay this premium in order to gain access to high quality industrial infrastructure and administration. However, it was clear that some expanding industrial TNCs were extremely cost conscious and opted for cheaper facilities. Furthermore, the SND was replicating some of the Singaporean institutions and practices, especially infrastructure provision and administration. The lack of support from the Suzhou municipal authorities could be explained by the Singapore government's strategic oversight in not cultivating the support and trust of local (Suzhou) authorities. In this sense, it was understandable that the Suzhou authorities would put their efforts behind their own estate rather than support one that already had Beijing's backing. Still, it was incredible that the CSSIP – which was for a short time the fastest growing zone in China and one with huge financial and political clout – would "fall" to competition from a municipal industrial estate. The Singapore government claimed that its decision to disengage was based on the CSSIP's future lack of profitability. In reality, the CSSIP was severely affected by the Asian financial crisis as well.

Although the Asian financial crisis did not severely affect either China or Singapore, when it began in the middle of 1997, the repercussions were felt at the CSSIP. The crisis had the effect of drastically reducing consumer demand for a wide range of products (see Wade, 1998; Henderson, 1999). As such, industrial producers were suddenly faced with overcapacity. Under such circumstances, transnational industrial producers had to consolidate production and focus on key markets. As a direct consequence, all expansion activities would be halted or postponed. This dramatically reduced the number of the CSSIP's potential customers:

> You can say that business at the office has been slow since 1997. The new companies that started between 1998–99 were those that were signed up before or during the early months of the Crisis. Yes, we have had some business, but definitely not of the size and the scale we got in the early days, and mostly smaller than we hoped for. (CSSIP Executive, interviewed in Suzhou, July 1999)

With the intensifying competition from other Chinese industrial estates and other zones in the Asian region, the prospects for filling the remainder of the CSSIP's 60-odd square kilometers made the venture economically non-viable, especially when the Singapore government was the main financier. In addition, because of the lack of support from the Suzhou authorities, the prospect of generating financial surpluses was poor. Despite the CSSIP's huge amounts of foreign direct investment, very little of it actually supplemented Singapore's economy. Instead, the only income generated came through the selling or subleasing of industrial units to TNCs, and was very small compared to the Singapore government's large financial investments made in industrial infrastructure development, power substation, and water treatment plant. Under these circumstances, the Singapore government announced the disengagement, blamed it on the Suzhou municipal authorities, and sold 30 percent of the shareholding of the CSSIP to the Chinese partner in order to recoup some of its investments.

Assessing Intergovernmental Collaboration as a Developmental Strategy

The case of the CSSIP is unique. Indeed, comparative evaluation is almost impossible because of the lack of similar cases. The other Singaporean regional industrial parks, including the other one in Wuxi, appear to be progressing steadily. All of them are formally joint ventures between a Singaporean company and a local development agency. In those ventures, the governments played a facilitative rather than directive role. However, comparison is problematic because of the large difference in scale and scope. In this sense, questions such as "was the CSSIP project too huge (70 square kilometers) or was its downfall down to bad luck (Asian financial crisis)?" remain open. Yet there are lessons that can be drawn from this project. First, the CSSIP had demonstrated that "FDI-led development" was possible, even despite the temporary weakness caused by the Asian financial crisis. Although the Singapore government may not have financially benefited from the venture, the city of Suzhou has undoubtedly benefited from the many industrial TNCs that have located at the CSSIP, particularly from the employment created and the large levels of foreign direct investments. Second, the CSSIP has validated the Singapore government's vision that secondary factors of production, such as high quality industrial infrastructure and administration, are important factors that encourage the location of industrial TNCs. Indeed, this was reinforced with the emergence of the SND, after it adopted many of the CSSIP's institutions and practices. However, whether the future Chinese administrators of the CSSIP can continue to attract new industrial TNCs remains to be seen.

Questions also remain open about the viability of intergovernmental collaboration as a developmental strategy. On the one hand, it is clear that the close government-to-government collaboration was one of the CSSIP's most effective competitive advantages. On the other hand, the evidence from the case of the CSSIP indicates that top-level collaboration alone is insufficient in ensuring that the competitive advantage could be maintained over long periods of time. This could be because of the potentially conflicting interests of the two governments. Although the China government was interested in developmental effects, the Singapore government was hoping to benefit from the venture in an entrepreneurial manner (through generating financial surpluses). The initial hope was that the two separate interests could be complementary; however, after it was evident that one partner was not benefiting, the collaboration began to weaken. Even though it cannot be concluded that "top-level" intergovernmental collaboration pursued by the Singapore government either enhanced or hindered the CSSIP's competitiveness, the case has demonstrated the strengths and weaknesses of such a strategy.

Part III
Market Reform and the New Processes of Urban Development

9
Market Transition and the Commodification of Housing in Urban China

Min Zhou and John R. Logan

China in the 1990s continued on a course pioneered a decade or more before in Eastern Europe to introduce market mechanisms into a socialist economy. Important structural changes in the economy occurred – the relaxation of central planning controls over investment, production, and distribution of goods, the emergence of a small private sector, and the promotion of a much larger collective sector that behaves much like private enterprise. We analyze this reform process and its consequences from the standpoint of housing and real estate development in urban centers.

Under socialism, housing was treated as a welfare provision to which everybody was entitled and was ideally intended to be distributed according to a formal definition of a minimum requirement and a maximum entitlement of space per person (Andrusz, 1984, p. 15). The Chinese norm was the assignment of two persons to a one-room unit, three to five persons to a two-room unit and six to eight persons to a three-room unit (Friedman, 1983). But in reality the supply was not sufficient for such a distribution.

Since housing was a very scarce resource, its access was highly unequal, as in other socialist countries (Szelenyi, 1978, 1983; Hegedus, 1987). Housing authorities could use housing and other welfare benefits to institute cadre privileges and to reward politically loyal and disciplined workers (Whyte and Parish, 1984; Walder, 1986). According to a 1985 survey by the China State Statistical Bureau (cited in World Bank, 1992), about 40 percent of the households were in crowded housing (per capita dwelling space less than four square meters) or inconvenienced housing (married couples sharing a room with parents and or teenage children). Sixty percent of the households were in housing without exclusive use of running water, 72 percent without sanitary facilities, and 71 percent without own kitchens. The same survey showed that households with higher income had more housing space and were more likely to have apartment units with running water, separate kitchens, and sanitary facilities than other households, and that no higher ranking cadres lived in crowded housing (defined as less than four square meters per person).

Most theoretical and empirical work on the effects of market reform has focused on income inequality rather than housing. Szelenyi (1978) had initially expected that market reform would actually result in an overall decline of inequality in socialist countries. Even under partial reform, he had anticipated an expansion of the private economy that would benefit those without redistributive power and ties with it (Szelenyi and Manchin, 1987). In examining the process of market reform in China, Nee (1989) put forward the model of market transition. He argued that, as power – control over resources – shifted progressively from political disposition to market institutions, there would be a change in the distribution of rewards, favoring those who held market rather than redistributive power. Privilege based in party membership and the old planning bureaucracy would be undermined, and new lines of stratification based on economic principles would replace it. Human capital and productivity, as measured by such variables as education and years of experience, would become chief predictors of income. Nee emphasized, however, that most sectors of the Chinese economy remain dominated by redistributive coordination even where elements of the market have been introduced (Nee, 1991, 1992). He suggested that, without extensive political change, a more decisive shift to market processes would be unlikely (Nee, 1989, pp. 678–9). Consistent with this reasoning, many observers have pointed to ways in which the gradual and partial reforms made by Chinese authorities have been absorbed into the existing institutional framework (Walder, 1992; Shirk, 1993).

Less has been written about how market reform has affected the housing sector. We would expect some of the same characteristics of "partial reform" to apply here. To the extent that housing is becoming a commodity, inequalities in housing should increasingly coincide with inequalities in personal income and less to position in the socialist order. Most relevant in the case of housing is the hierarchy of work units (Bian et al., 1997b). In urban China as a whole in 1990, 59 percent of housing space was in housing owned and managed by work units (Yang and Wang, 1992). Prior to 1978, such housing resulted directly from central government planning decisions. A portion of the state's budget allocation to municipal governments and to work units was designated for social service provision, including housing. However, work units were not equal. State-owned work units were treated according to their administrative rank, their size, and their economic sector (productive or nonproductive). As a result, larger and higher ranking work units, especially those in the productive sector that provided crucial products for the state, provincial, or municipal plans, had larger welfare funds and were able to build housing directly for their employees. Furthermore, large work units could exercise influence with municipal housing bureaus to procure apartments for their workers (Walder, 1986, p. 67). Most of the work units that owned housing were state-owned enterprises. Few collectives could provide fringe benefits as in the state sector (Whyte and Parish, 1984), and their employees had to depend almost entirely on private or municipal housing (Walder, 1986, p. 43).

Some commentators consider the goal of housing reform since 1978 to be to separate work units from their direct role in housing provision (Tolley, 1991). Nevertheless, Bian and his associates (1997b) find that, even in Shanghai, the Chinese city with the lowest proportion of housing owned and managed by work units (12 percent in 1990), work units increased their participation in the housing sector during the reform period. In 1990, 86 percent of new investment capital for public housing construction in Shanghai was raised by work units, increased sharply from 55 percent in 1980. Further, they show that the ability to provide housing through the work unit continues to be highly correlated with the rank and size of the work unit – the traditional indicators of the institutional hierarchy – and state enterprises are more likely than collectives to provide such housing.

Market Reform in Housing

Many of our historical and contemporary observations are grounded in the experience of the city of Zhongshan in southern Guangdong Province, not far from Hong Kong. We believe that this case reveals the main features of China's system of building and allocating housing, the characteristic inequalities that it fomented, the new institutions and processes that are being introduced, and – at least for the present – their outcomes. But conditions may vary greatly from city to city (Wang, 1990), and Zhongshan is somewhat unusual. First, because of its distance from Beijing and the multiple layers of government that insulate it from the central government, it enjoyed a relatively high degree of autonomy. Second, compared to cities like Beijing and Shanghai, this is a small city. We suspect that its local institutions are therefore more malleable. Perhaps also because of its proximity to Macao and the development zone of Zhuhai, Zhongshan has undergone more rapid institutional change – and certainly more speculative land development – than much of the rest of China. Finally, like Guangdong province as a whole, Zhongshan has historically been the origin of large-scale emigration to Southeast Asia and North America and has thus benefited from financial remittances from abroad. More recently it has attracted much direct investment by overseas Chinese with local connections. For all of these reasons, we would expect to find greater possibilities for market reform to affect housing development in this city than in larger cities, even other southern cities like Guangzhou. Since our analysis emphasizes the continuities between the old system and the new, our findings may be more surprising in a case that is near the leading edge of change.

The new approach to housing policy was initiated by the government under Deng Xiao-Ping in the early 1980s, consistent with the broader market reforms that had already taken place. Reformers began from the assumption that housing shortages were caused by the welfare character of housing. They argued that the only effective way to solve the urban housing problem was to increase rents and to encourage urban dwellers to buy houses from the government or their work units or to build their own housing. Four cities (later extended to 80 other cities and towns in 23 provinces) were designated to experiment with housing reform, including subsidized sales of existing or newly built public housing and increase of rent rates on new public housing (Zhou, 1991b, p. 184). At the same time, the state began a process of confirming and registering ownership titles to properties that had been seized during the Cultural Revolution. In Zhongshan, by 1990, about 85 percent of these units had reverted to private rental housing.

As we address the impacts of market reform on the housing sector, we emphasize that more is happening than a simple process of privatization. The creation of a market system for housing is institutionally complex, involving an interconnected set of policies, procedures, and institutions extending well beyond the work unit. The "commodification" of housing requires broader institutional reforms in the pricing of land, in the financing of construction, and in the mechanisms of distributing housing (this is the official position of the World Bank, as reflected in Dowall, 1993). We consider each of these three areas in turn to show that housing remains under the control of government and as contingent on the economic and political resources of work units as ever. As it moves from a rigidly central planned economy, close observers describe China's housing and real estate development as "anarchic and chaotic" (Tang 1994c, p. 412). What is most interesting about the changes that have been instituted is that they have succeeded in attracting investment (even private investment) into real estate, but with a very limited market foundation.

The Land Market

Before economic reform, there was no land market at all. Land requisition for development projects was handled through the central planning process. The central, provincial, and municipal governments had the power to appropriate urban land *gratis*, to acquire buildings with minimum payment to owners, and to acquire rural land with payment for just compensation to owners (the people's communes) for government-approved development projects. Despite economic reform, state appropriation of urban real properties for urban development continued in the same fashion until 1988, when the Chinese National People's Congress amended the Constitution, stipulating for the first time that land-use rights can be transferred.

The government – particularly the municipal government – now participates in various ways in the state-controlled market (or the primary market) and an "emerging" price-making market (or the secondary market).

The primary market is unilaterally controlled by the state. It is here that land-use rights of undeveloped land, or properties designated to be redeveloped by the municipal government, are exchanged. The absence of laws governing land use and of local government experience in land-use planning, control, and management places authorities in a vulnerable position, however. They must respond to demands for land by profitable state enterprises, enterprises directly under ownership of the municipal government, and private firms which have direct access to *guanxi* (connections to those with redistributive power or with political capital) networks. Some firms are even provided with free land. The transfer of land-use rights from the state to potential land users is mainly through direct negotiation. Municipal government continues to have the right to take over undeveloped or agricultural land from rural collectives (with minimum cash compensation), and it can lease these parcels to other land users. It can also designate urban parcels on which structures are to be torn down for new development and lease these parcels to other users. Leases specify the land use (commercial, industrial, or residential) and lease period. Once land-use rights are transferred, the land user will have the right to either develop the land or sell it to other users in the secondary market.

Local government is often a participant in development projects in this primary market, seeking profits much like any other investor, even in luxury housing. For example, the municipal government of Zhongshan endorsed the Fuhao Estate project in 1992. This project is the biggest development in the urban center, occupying 40 hectares of land with a total investment of US$103 million. Most of this capital was raised from overseas investors. Initially, the municipal government intended to lease the site to two real estate companies at a rent of 180 yuan per square meter. Later, it decided to open the site for competitive bidding. The bidding was presided over by the Municipal Bureau of State Land and included three real estate companies, one from Zhongshan, another one from Hong Kong, and a third one from Macau. The highest bidder was the company from Macau, which offered 285 yuan per square meter. This land deal yielded a total profit of 114 million yuan (US$20 million) for the municipal government.

Although competitive bidding enables the state to gain greater returns from land transfer, Zhongshan municipal government does not favor the extensive use of this method for fear that it may result in excessive fluctuations in price. One reason is the lack of experience in making a reasonable bid. Another is the tendency of state-owned real estate development companies to push prices to unrealistically high levels just to get hold of a particular piece of real estate, anticipating that the price could go even higher in the secondary market. Land speculation by public agencies and state enterprises, even from distant regions, is a common phenomenon, reinforced by the fact that only public funds are at risk.

The secondary market involves the exchange of land-use rights of semi-developed or developed properties between the state and land users and also among users. It is potentially very profitable, because there are few restrictions on the resale of developed or semi-developed land or commodified housing. As a result, land speculation is rampant. Land in valuable locations is often underutilized or vacant purely for speculative purposes. Fortunes are being made through what appear to be market transactions, buying low and selling high. We believe a market interpretation would be a serious error in this case, primarily because prices are determined in large part by non-market considerations. In both the primary and secondary tiers of the land market, there is a complex array of market and discount prices.

In Zhongshan, there are three common pricing procedures. The first is arbitrary pricing. The price of land can be as low as 10 yuan per square meter or as high as 1,500 yuan per square meter, and the price of commodified housing can be as low as 500 yuan per square meter or as high as 3,000 yuan per square meter. The actual price in the primary market depends on the nature of the development project and the relationship between the owners and the prospective users. For example, the development of Baiyuan Village in 1986 required the requisition of 122,000 square meters of agricultural land to the east of the city. The municipal government obtained the land through routine negotiation with the collective owner, paying a small compensation fee approximating only 60 yuan per square meter, a fifth of the market value. Another example involves a Hong Kong industrialist who purchased a large piece of land totaling 220,000 square meters to build an electronics industrial park at about 75 yuan per square meter, one quarter of the market rate. This was largely due to the fact that the investor was kin to the villagers who collectively held the land and that he promised the municipal government to create 3,500 jobs from the project.

Arbitrary pricing is also common in the secondary market. For example, the municipal government set three different prices for housing units of equal quality after completion of Baiyuan Village in 1987. About 70 percent of the 1,887 housing units were sold at the government-set discount price, at 500 yuan per square meter, which was applied to households designated as lacking adequate housing. About 25 percent were sold to work units at full standard prices, at 850 yuan per square meter. The rest of the units were sold at a "market" price of 1,200 yuan per square meter. In sum, arbitrary pricing depends on policy rather than on the market, and it usually is underpricing.

Another method is comparative pricing, which is more common in the secondary than in the primary market. Contacts with other market-oriented economies in Chinese-speaking Asia such as Hong Kong, Taiwan, and Singapore provide pricing standards. Pricing takes into account a city's position in the national economy. If the city benefits from special development policies made by the central government, such as Shenzhen and Zhuhai, or is located in a strategic location with strong development potential, such as cities along the south and southeast coast, the price of real estate tends to be set high. For example, in the central government designated Special Economic Zones (i.e. Shenzhen and Zhuhai), downtown land and commodified housing are priced at a level that matches the prices in downtown Kowloon, Hong Kong. In Shenzhen, the price of commodified housing for internal sales was at 905 yuan per square meter in the mid-1980s. It went up to 3,640 yuan per square meter in 1991. In Zhongshan, the price was at 1,200 yuan per square meter in 1988, and it inflated to about 2,500 yuan per square meter in 1991. Comparative pricing often results in overpricing, because land markets in Hong Kong or Taiwan have proved to be unstable.

A third method is the expenditure approach. Here the government plays the central vital role. According to "The Temporary Measure for Pricing Commodified Housing," the price of commodified housing (i.e. housing for sale on the market) takes into account several components. The first component includes actual costs incurred, including direct costs, such as building materials and labor, and indirect costs, such as design and architects' fees and interest. The second component is a fixed rate of profit. However, this "fixed" rate actually varies according to the general political climate and shifting orientation of national economic policy. The third component is taxes. The fourth component is a locational differential designed to reflect land value. The government-set "discount standard price" of housing is based solely on the first component, while the "full standard price" is based all four components.

Consequently, various prices are floating in the emerging real estate market. "Market" prices are mostly applied to houses sold to foreign buyers and to urban residents who have no connection to either state or collective work units, such as private business owners and workers in foreign-owned enterprises. Discounts of varying levels are applied to houses sold by the municipality to urban workers classified as lacking adequate housing or to work units that are unable to build by themselves, and by work units to their own employees. Discount prices are applied at the discretion of the municipal government and work units. In sum, the pricing mechanisms are operating within the institutional constraint of the socialist state and depend largely on government policies, especially on interpretation of these policies by municipal authorities and officials at lower levels of government.

The Financing of New Housing Construction

Before the housing reform, financing of new housing construction depended solely on state budget allocations. The state now encourages a wider range of sources. In light of the high rate of housing construction in the past decade, it is clear that this sector has been attractive to capital. The principal sources include: (a) bank loans; (b) funds collected by the municipal government from transfer of land-use rights and proceeds from the sale of existing municipal housing; (c) retained profits of work units and proceeds from the sale of work-unit housing; (d) savings of individual workers; and (e) foreign investment.

Bank loans

Bank loans are one of the major sources of real estate financing in market economies. However, like prices, they are not based on an open market. The People's Construction Bank of China (PCBC) is authorized to be the primary specialized housing finance bank (World Bank, 1992). The PCBC is also authorized to set up a special housing account, providing interest rates higher than the usual state rate to encourage savings from work units and individuals. The difference between the lower interest rates charged on mortgage loans and the higher rates paid on savings deposits in the housing account is made up by the state budget (Ma, 1993).

In Zhongshan, bank loans for residential housing, if available, are mostly short-term (five years maximum) collateral mortgage loans. The annual interest rates of these loans are set arbitrarily, ranging from 12 to 15 percent. These loans are mostly made to municipal housing projects and a few higher ranking work units with sufficient collateral and "credit" (or *guanxi*). As borrowers, municipal government and higher ranking state work units have the advantage of backing by the state.

The PCBC officials are extremely reluctant to make loans to individuals. Those with proper political connections, or with collateral or asset holdings (real property, own business, or sizable savings or deposits in the housing account), or whose work unit is able to guarantee a loan for its workers, have a higher probability of obtaining a bank loan. In Zhongshan, mortgage loans made to individuals are extremely rare and are usually limited to three to six months. Individuals who do obtain bank loans often have the resources for self-financing, but a bank loan at below-market interest rates allows them to invest their funds in other higher yielding short-term media.

Proceeds from land transactions

Land and real estate transactions by government agencies are another source of development capital. A key goal of housing reform is to transfer ownership of housing to residents, and even at discounted prices these sales result in substantial one-time revenues to the municipality. According to state regulations, funds generated from municipal land transactions must go into the development account of the PCBC to be used for either public infrastructure or housing. Funds generated from the sale of existing rental housing are also required to be deposited into the PCBC for the same purposes.

In Zhongshan between 1983 and 1990, the municipal government invested 60.97 million yuan (US$16 million) in urban housing. During this period, two million square meters of floor space of new residential housing was constructed by the municipal government, six times what had been built between 1949 and 1978. Municipal housing projects and some joint projects between the government and work units were mostly financed by land and real estate transactions.

Municipalities have become entrepreneurs to meet social needs; but they have an eye to profitability. Even the Baiyuan Village project, which was supposedly intended for urban workers in difficult housing situations, had a certain portion of housing set aside for the open market. The Fuhao real estate development project mentioned above is another example. This project tore down a forested area, blocked the view of the city's largest natural park, and forced a local university to look elsewhere for land. But it generated immediate profits and promoted economic growth.

Since the most valuable land in the city was reserved for profitable development, in what might be called "public–private partnerships," affordable housing projects were pushed outside the urban center where land was cheaper. One worker in a firm near Fuhao Estate pointed to buildings under construction and complained, "When it becomes my turn to buy an apartment unit, it will probably be far away from the city. I will probably have to pass many of these empty houses everyday on my way to work." A city official commented from a different perspective, "this is how we get money to build housing, roads, and public facilities. We have to be willing to give capitalists something they want in exchange for something we lack."

Retained profits

A third source of housing finance is from retained profits of work units. In the previous centralized economy, state enterprises had to depend on the central government's allocation of funds and building materials for housing. The allocation was a fixed amount, so the work unit's profit or loss did not affect its housing allocation. Since the economic reform, state enterprises have been given some market or market-like incentives. They are now allowed to make their own production decisions rather than following quotas from central planning; to sell and buy (at least in part) in free markets rather than selling and producing everything at a state-controlled price; and to retain a substantial fraction of their profits beyond the fixed amount required to be remitted to the state (McMillan and Naughton, 1992).

The Zhongshan Sugar Refinery, about 20 miles from downtown Zhongshan, provides an example. The enterprise is a state division-ranked work unit and was a profitable state enterprise even during the Cultural Revolution. It added 320 new apartment units between 1978 and 1985 to ease the housing shortage for its growing work force (around 2,000). Between 1985 and 1993, the enterprise built another 800 units which were larger and of better quality. More than 90 percent of financing for this construction came from retained profits. When asked whether such a practice was legal, one of the managers in the enterprise said, "by law, it is forbidden to spend all retained profits on bonuses and housing. In reality, this is a common practice that nobody seems to question. You may say it's illegal, but I say it's legitimate."

Work units' investment in housing has been a key element in housing provision. In the long run, the currently wealthier work units, those engaged in highly profitable activities and with substantial land holdings, may over-invest in housing, while smaller and less profitable work units may not be able to do much to improve the housing situation for their own workers. Wealthy work units tend to focus on quality of housing. For example, Zhongshan Washing Machine Corporation, highly profitable in its production of washing machines and other popular home appliances, built a fenced, high-quality residential complex of 400 spacious apartment units (75 percent of them 80-square-meter units and 25 percent of them 130-square-meter units) in 1989 at a net cost of nearly 800 yuan per square meter, compared to around 400 yuan per square meter in Baiyuan Village. These apartment units had granite floors, tiled or well painted walls, built-in cabinets, one and a half or two baths, two or three spacious balconies, and a fully equipped kitchen. Consequently, inequality based on the work unit has become more related to profit than to bureaucratic ranking. In this respect it is more like a "market" phenomenon. But we emphasize that investments in housing are partly due to restrictions on other uses of profit.

Private savings

Private funds, including personal or family savings and loans made by families and friends, are another important source of housing capital. For individuals, private savings are the single most important source. Between 1985 and 1991, the average increase in personal income was 17.7 percent annually. In 1991, average annual income for urban workers was 4,229 yuan. Although average wage levels are about the same as those in other southern cities, personal savings in Zhongshan are substantially higher. In 1991, the average savings deposit was measured at 4,358 yuan per capita, about the equivalent of a year's income. One explanation for such a high savings rate is income from overseas remittances. Unlike urban households in other areas, whose sole source of incomes are wages, over 60 percent of Zhongshan's households have some sort of remittance from family members abroad (Jian, 1989).

Foreign investment

Funds from overseas are another important source of real estate development capital. Between 1979 and 1981, foreign investors were not allowed to invest in real estate because land sales were prohibited. Foreign capital could participate in joint ventures with municipal governments (who owned land) to develop luxurious commodified housing intended for overseas markets, mostly to expatriate Chinese who wanted to purchase a second home in their homeland and who could afford the prices. Profits generated from such developments were split between the foreign investor and the municipal government (Zhou et al., 1992).

Since 1982, when the land market was opened up, foreign capital has increased its share in the real estate market. Although foreign capital as a proportion of total investment in real estate remains relatively small, only about 5 percent nationwide, it made up between 25 and 55 percent of the total investments in profit-oriented and foreign-market-oriented real estate and commodified housing development in the coastal areas in China (Zhou, 1993; Zhou et al., 1992, pp. 46–7). In Zhongshan, foreign capital investment totaled US$300 million between 1978 and 1988, about one-fifth invested directly in real estate, including 11 hotels, an amusement park, two golf courses, and an entertainment complex (Jian, 1989). The Fuhao Project described above is an example of such investment.

The Distribution of Commodified Housing

Investments in work unit housing were considered a transitional step in housing reform. The next phase was to press for the creation of a private housing market. This was a politically difficult move. It faced potential resistance from all social strata: officials and workers who already enjoyed free or low-rent housing might object to higher costs; those on waiting lists might object that the list had been a sham. Thus commodification had to appear to be egalitarian (satisfying the latter group) while favoring the privileged (appeasing the former group). As a result, although overall housing conditions for urban workers have been significantly improved by increased investment, the distribution of commodified housing is similar to the old system except that housing is no longer "free."

In an entirely private housing market, only a small number of urban residents could afford housing at current construction costs. The rent required to recover fully the costs of investment in new housing could surpass 70 percent of the average household income monthly (World Bank, 1992). Thus the actual pricing scheme for commodified housing is complex. It can be sold to work units or directly to urban workers at either the government-set discount standard price or the full standard price. Housing built or purchased by work units is usually sold to workers at further discounted prices. Note, however, that persons buying at discounted prices typically do not receive full title to their properties; the work unit retains an interest. The most commonly used discounts by work units include: (a) one-time discount, 20 percent off the discount standard price in return for cancellation of the purchasers' monthly cash subsidies from the work unit; (b) seniority discount, 0.3 percent off the discount standard price for each year of service; (c) pay-up discount, 10–20 percent off if paid in full at the time of purchase; and (d) waiver of property taxes and land-use fees.

The most visible continuity in the current approach to housing distribution is the level of institutional control, especially the work unit, in deciding who gets what. Before the economic reform in 1978 the role of the work unit in housing construction was limited because work units were not allowed to retain profits for welfare provision. However, larger and higher ranking work units were better able to squeeze funds for provision of housing and other welfare benefits than smaller and lower ranking work units. Under market reform, work units continue to be the focus point of housing and welfare provisions. Higher ranking and profitable work units are able either to build new housing or to purchase commodified housing (or to do both) for their workers. The type, size, quality, and quantity of housing available to a worker – and its price – are largely determined by the work unit.

Workers whose employers have both land and substantial retained profits are especially privileged, as they were before. What has changed is the resource: previously, it was easy access to free rental housing, while now it is subsidized purchase of their own apartments. For example, since 1991 the Zhongshan Sugar Refinery has purchased commodified housing units near the city center at the market rate (about 1,100 yuan per square meter) to sell them to model workers approaching retirement. The workers only paid 30 percent of what the enterprise had paid in the market. Younger workers complained, however: "This is not fair. These old guys have the privilege of buying a second home at discount price simply because they are lucky enough to still share the rice from the big pot [the socialist system]. By the time we get old, there will be nothing left. We will have to live with our children and grandchildren."

School teachers are a typical example of the opposite situation. Schools are smaller, non-profit state work units that cannot build housing. Except for a tiny fraction of the faculty who are able to obtain housing from their spouse's work units or who have sufficient savings for purchase from the market, most teachers depend on the municipal government for housing provision. They are on a much longer waiting list for housing allocation. Moreover, their purchasing power is weaker since their salaries are relatively low and sources of other incomes are limited. In Zhongshan, the municipal government set aside 100 apartment units in Baiyuan Village at deeply discounted prices for distinguished teachers as a symbolic gesture of support. Again, because there were more deserving teachers than apartments available, connections to the government became a criterion in combination with merit.

Conclusions

Housing has gradually been changed from a public good to something approaching a commodity. The life-long welfare right to housing has been replaced by one-time purchase subsidies. Housing can be bought and sold in a controlled real estate market. Another significant outcome is that housing investment is no longer constrained by rigid state budget allocations. Municipal governments, work units, and individuals are allowed to raise housing funds through different sources to build new housing. A more open market on the supply side of the system has begun to take form.

Access to housing has been broadened. The reform has undoubtedly resulted in significant improvement of the overall housing conditions among urban residents. The average per capita dwelling space in cities nationwide increased from 3.6 square meters in 1978 to 6.9 square meters in 1991 (China State Statistical Bureau, 1993, p. 279). In Zhongshan, the average per capita dwelling space increased from 6 square meters in 1978 to 13 square meters in 1991 (Zhongshan Planning Bureau, 1993). There is some evidence to show that some individuals without redistributive power and *guanxi* connections were able to gain access to housing through the market, suggested by Szelenyi (1983).

Despite these changes, which are consistent with the expectations of the market transition model, other outcomes demonstrate the partial character of market reform. First, except for a tiny fraction of housing that is being sold or bought in the open market, a disproportionate amount of housing in the reform system remains a redistributive good rather than a commodity. Although the welfare nature of housing has been gradually transformed, housing has to be heavily subsidized by public institutions – municipal governments or work units, or both. Given the current wage structure that has changed very slowly, workers' incomes continue to be highly socialized, creating a significant financial constraint on affordability. Commodified housing in the true market sense is simply outside the price ranges affordable to most urban workers without substantial state subsidies.

Second, although control has been progressively decentralized down to the local level and the work unit level, the construction of housing continues to be determined by institutional mechanisms embedded in the housing system prior to market reforms. The housing market that is being created is at best a quasi-market controlled by such old institutions as the local government and the work unit. Work units have emerged as a powerful and autonomous actor not only in the allocation of housing but also in its production. Unlike Western systems, where investors are primarily oriented toward profit, the chief investors of housing in China – the municipal government or the work unit – are now oriented toward two ends: to broaden access and to control who gets it. Profits are made. But property rights, as Walder (1992) has emphasized, are dispersed across a hierarchy of municipalities and work units and exercised through multiple channels, such as access to bank loans, ability to engage in land transactions, and rights to use retained operating profits. Property rights are poorly defined and have no clear legal apparatus to enforce them. Transactions and prices are still subject to severe restrictions and institutional constraints. The quasi-market therefore reinforces rather than weakens the position of those who held redistributive power prior to market reforms.

Third, the new financial mechanisms reproduce the inequalities created under socialism because they are susceptible to manipulation by the same privileged groups, especially powerful work units and persons with strong political connections. What is unique about housing financing in China is the weakness of the banking system (its undercapitalization and inability to make long-term loans) and the extent to which frankly political factors determine its interest rates and access to loans. Work units with sizable holdings of land and housing have superior access to credit and to capital from the sale of existing housing to the tenants. Individual savings have become an important factor for people of higher social status, in more profitable work units, or with family remittances from overseas. "Market reform" in this case allocates resources to the same privileged groups in new but familiar ways.

Finally, the mechanism by which housing is distributed to workers has changed very little under market reforms. Since affordable housing at discount prices is available only in the highly controlled quasi-market and is scarce, its access is structured by the hierarchy of municipalities and work units, which is deeply embedded in Chinese society. Distribution follows criteria similar to those before market reforms, such as rank, seniority, merit, loyalty, and *guanxi* connections. Consequently, access to subsidized commodified housing was at least as unequal as before. Meanwhile, a new segment of the workforce that first grew to significant numbers under market reforms has created a new source of housing inequality. Workers in joint-venture firms and temporary contract workers are not eligible for work unit housing. Thus housing inequality is linked to the new class divisions (temporary versus permanent workers, joint-ventured versus state workers) rather than simply to income inequality.

We are unable to estimate the degree to which housing inequality may have increased under market reforms. What we see here is that inequalities have been maintained in a remarkably familiar way. The more general phenomenon described here – the complex interaction between institutional inertia and change – is relevant to the process of market reform of the economy as a whole. Our research supports and adds to the "partial reform" model of socialist transition. At the current stage, market mechanisms have not replaced the existing institutional mechanisms to determine land development and housing allocation. We might ask, indeed, whether they ever will. Influenced by Polanyi (1957), sociologists have begun to think of urban development in capitalist societies as a hybrid system, based on a real estate market whose operation is subject to political influence and monopolistic behaviors. There is growing interest in analyzing the organizations and institutions that have stakes in urban growth and examining how their activities shape market processes (Cox, 1981; Mollenkopf, 1983; Logan and Molotch, 1987; Fainstein, 1994). Seeing formerly socialist countries as another form of hybrid system offers new possibilities for comparative research on what these organizations and institutions are, how they operate, and in what direction they move the urban future.

Acknowledgments

This is a condensed version of a previously published article (Min Zhou and John R. Logan (1996) Market transition and the commodification of housing in urban China. *International Journal of Urban and Regional Research*, 20, 400–21: © 1996 Blackwell Publishers, reproduced with permission). The research on which it is based was supported by the Committee on Scholarly Communication with China (grant for the 1993–4 National Program for Advanced Study and Research in China). The final version of the manuscript was written while one of the authors was in residence at the Russell Sage Foundation, whose support is also gratefully acknowledged. We thank the municipal government of Zhongshan, Leiming Zhou of the Zhongshan Construction Committee, Min Fang of the Zhongshan Planning Bureau, Yin Liang of the Zhongshan Bureau of State Land, and numerous interviewees from various government agencies and work units in Zhongshan for their assistance in completing this research. We also thank Victor Nee and two anonymous reviewers for their helpful comments.

10
Real Estate Development and the Transformation of Urban Space in China's Transitional Economy, with Special Reference to Shanghai

Fulong Wu

Property-led urban development has become a major feature of Chinese cities since the 1990s. Numerous efforts have been made to document policy and institutional changes in China. Less understood is the investment structure. The aim of this chapter is thus to examine the dynamics of real estate investment and its impact on urban space.

In the next section, three hypotheses about real estate development are developed. The changing investment structure related to the hypotheses is examined in the second section. Then, the impact of real estate development on urban space is discussed. In the conclusion, the complexity of Chinese cities and the significance of urban China studies are highlighted.

Hypotheses of Real Estate Development

In this chapter I develop three hypotheses regarding real estate dynamics and urban transformation in China. The first hypothesis is derived from Bian and Logan's thesis of "power persistence" in the transitional economy (Bian and Logan, 1996). The thesis suggests that in a transitional economy the newly introduced market mechanism does not replace the mechanism of a redistributive economy, but is grafted on to the existing institutional framework. In essence, the market and non-market elements are mixed and coexist. An outstanding feature of the socialist city is the organization of economic and urban development on the basis of state work units. The reform did not break this basic form of organization but introduced incentives to state work units to increase productivity. The second and third hypotheses are developed with understandings, respectively, of the increasing importance of globalization and of proactive local governance. Each hypothesis is discussed below.

The first hypothesis states that in the new urban development process capital is transferred from the production to consumption sphere at the enterprise level. Due to the introduction of real estate markets through housing and land reforms, the preserved institutional form – the state work unit – has a wide range of opportunities to "capitalize" state properties. Because of the dual effect of marketization and decentralization, the thrust of seeking local interests is no longer constrained by conventional planning. This on the one hand created new incentives to increase investment in housing production but on the other hand hurt production by diverting capital away from more productive areas. The use of productive funds in collective consumption embodies not only "irregular" or illegal behavior such as corruption but also "normal" institutional behavior such as the allocation of commodity housing to employees at discount prices. As a result, at the microscopic level (i.e. state-owned enterprises), the shift of capital from the productive area to real estate development occurred. The expansion of in-kind benefits provided by state work units is a primary source of capital transference into the built environment. Capital transference could also take other routes; for example, the setting up of a development company or a joint venture in which capital is contributed by the state firm.

The second hypothesis states that foreign capital has been making significant contribution to real estate development, along with globalization and the continuity of China's open-door policy. The hypothesis, derived from a wider understanding of globalization, emphasizes the exogenous factor of Chinese urban development. For example, Wu (1997a) pointed out that foreign capital plays a role in linking the global and local spheres. In the Pearl River Delta, Sit and Yang (1997) argued that urbanization is mainly induced by investment from Hong Kong and Macao and specialized in export processing and manufacturing sectors. Small and medium-sized towns created in this externally driven industrialization process are "industrial towns" purely for the making of a profit rather than integrated urban communities (Eng, 1997). Regarding the large cities, Jiang et al. (1998) suggested that foreign investment led to the sustained increase in the real estate price against the tightening of macroeconomic control over real estate investment. The literature highlights the importance of foreign capital in China's recent urban development. This is evidenced by the impressive growth of FDI in China. Only Lardy (1996) has argued that the contribution of foreign capital to capital formation might be overestimated.

The third hypothesis is a step forward from the thesis of "power persistence" (Bian and Logan, 1996), suggesting the more proactive role of the local government. In particular, the role in the transference of capital to the built environment is achieved through the city government's entrepreneurial behavior in land revenue generation. The power persistence thesis only points out the continuance of the state in development organization. In a transitional economy, however, reshuffling resource control creates new interests and power. The local (territorial) government has emerged as a powerful regulator and land supplier in real estate development. This power is newly created rather than persisting. Active involvement in the promotion of urban development is not unique here. Place promotion is becoming the key feature of urban governance in the contemporary post-Fordist society (Short et al., 1993). The global city such as London and New York in the 1980s relied on the property industry as a vehicle for local development (Fainstein, 1994). In China the land leasing system provides a unique mechanism for the local state to intervene in the real estate sector. The consequence of the local state's involvement is capital injection in the built environment through the extraction and reinvestment functions of the state. In the East and West, the need for entrepreneurial governance is justified by the discourse about the increasing mobility of capital and hence intercity competition.

To test these hypotheses we need to investigate in detail capital investment by both enterprises and local governments. This is a challenging task, as land revenue and income are sensitive issues. It is possible, however, to identify the trend of capital shift through the publicly available data, though the detailed routes and concrete forms of capital transference are still subject to further investigation. A caveat is needed about the accuracy of official information about investment in real estate. But we understand through observation that the inaccuracy may underestimate rather than overestimate the trend – this is because real estate investment may be disguised under industrial development but there is no reason for a genuine industrial project to register as a property development company.

Dynamics of Real Estate Development

The growth of real estate investment

Contrary to common wisdom, the housing reform was not intended to develop a market-oriented housing provision system at the beginning. Instead, it aimed to increase the housing stock by whatever means possible to ease the problem of housing shortages. The policy required local governments, state-owned enterprises, and individuals to make contributions to housing investment. This is essentially a resource decentralization process. While the increase in wages was subject to state control, work units were allowed to use

Table 10.1 Annual housing completion in Shanghai, 1990–1996 (floor space in 1,000 m^2)

	Total housing	*Capital construction*		*Update and renewal*		*Collective housing*		*Commodity housing*	
	Floor space	*Floor space*	*%*	*Floor space*	*%*	*Floor space*	*%*	*Floor space*	*%*
1990	4,219	1,537	36.4	1,715	40.6	128	3.0	739	17.5
1991	4,777	1,578	33.0	2,133	44.7	96	2.0	970	20.3
1992	5,435	2,268	41.7	1,950	35.9	112	2.1	1,134	20.9
1993	6,165	2,201	35.7	2,332	37.8	272	4.4	1,360	22.1
1994	8,736	2,258	25.8	3,058	35.0	222	2.5	3,199	36.6
1995	12,689	3,175	25.0	3,847	30.3	369	2.9	5,298	41.8
1996	15,095	2,002	13.3	2,795	18.5	375	2.5	9,923	65.7

Source: Shanghai Statistical Bureau (1997).

retained profits to invest in housing development and subsequently to relocate subsidized housing to their employees.

Various studies have already suggested that, while the production of commodity housing is gradually undertaken by real estate companies, the allocation of housing is still mediated through the state work unit system (Wang and Murie, 1996; Wu, 1996; Zhou and Logan, 1996). For example, in Beijing, the annual completion of housing floor space averaged about eight million square meters in the mid-1990s. About half was constructed through self-build and joint-build by work units. Commodity housing produced by the real estate companies accounts for the other half. But among the housing developed by real estate companies about half was used for compensation and the municipal government. The floor space sold in the market was only two million square meters, accounting for no more than one-quarter of the total housing produced (Deng, 1998).

The role of real estate development, however, varies from city to city and has been strengthened by further housing reform policies. In Shanghai, commodity housing accounted for 65.7 percent of the total housing completed in 1996. Table 10.1 represents the changing structure of housing production in Shanghai. It can be seen that the share of market-based production increased from about 20 percent in 1990 to about 65 percent in 1996. Among commodity housing, sales to individuals at market prices also increased. In southern China – for example, Shenzhen and Guangzhou – housing sold to individual buyers was as high as, respectively, 91 and 87 percent in 1997. In Shanghai, about 79 percent of commodity housing was sold to individuals in 1997, whereas the figure was only 40 percent in Beijing.

Because various actors are involved (including state-owned enterprises and foreign investors), housing investment in Shanghai increased from 0.2 billion yuan in 1978 to 43.4 billion yuan in 1996. The rate of growth is unprecedented in history. If we calculate the rate of growth as the difference between two consecutive years divided by the value of the previous year, the velocity of change is striking. At the peak of the building boom (1994), the growth rate of housing investment reached 333 percent. Fixed investment has also seen a dramatic increase. Between 1992 and 1993, the annual growth rate was about 80 percent. The completion of housing space is less remarkable but still obvious at a growth rate of 14 percent. Nonetheless, the supply of housing increased to 15 million square meters in 1995. And the annual growth rate reached 45 percent.

The boom in real estate development is clearly reflected by the increase of real estate investment in the share of investment in fixed assets, which refers to the amount of work done in construction and purchase of fixed assets, each expressed in monetary terms (Shanghai Statistical Bureau, 1997). The components of investment in fixed assets include capital construction investment (referring to the new construction), technical updating and transformation (referring to the additional investment in existing assets), other investment by state-owned enterprises, investment by urban collective enterprises, and a separate item called "investment in real estate." Investment in real estate has been separated from the first two items since 1990. It mainly refers to investment in the development of properties that can be sold in markets (commodity housing and offices). Capital construction investment can also be used for housing production, but housing produced cannot be sold in the market. The proportion of capital construction investment in housing, however, is decreasing. In 1996, only 13 percent of housing floor space completed was invested by capital construction investment. Figure 10.1 shows the frenetic growth in real estate investment between 1993 and 1994. The annual growth rate reached 433 percent in 1994. In the same year, the central government tightened the macroeconomic policy to control real estate investment. Consequently, the rate of growth dropped to 297 percent in 1995 and down to 41 percent in 1996.

Investment structure

Investment in real estate has increased at an unprecedented pace during the building boom. But where did capital come from? The question seems difficult to answer without tracing the movement of capital. However, examining the changes in the structure of investment can reveal the shift of capital from one area to another. Indeed, urban China has experienced a series of structural changes. With reference to Shanghai, these structural tendencies are summarized as follows:

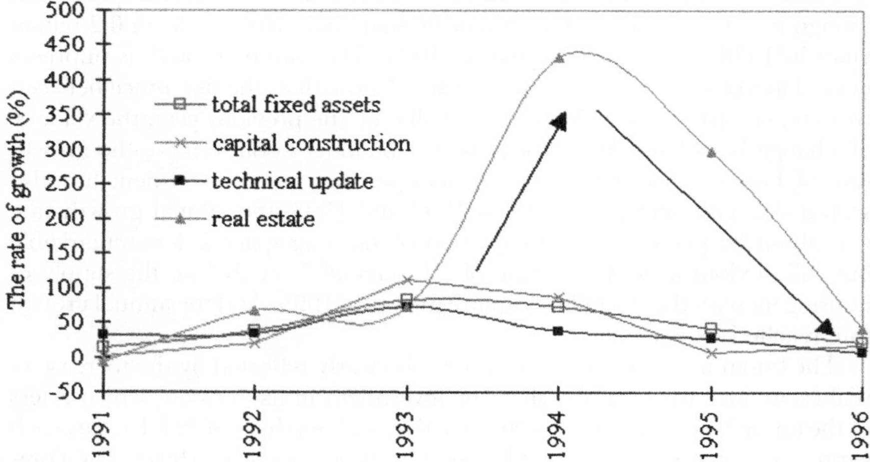

Figure 10.1 The growth rate of the total investment in fixed assets and its composition between 1991 and 1996

- Intensification of investment in fixed assets, infrastructure, and housing in relation to GDP. For example, investment in fixed assets increased from 29 to 67 percent of GDP from 1992 to 1996.
- An increase in the share of wages in GDP and thus accumulated savings deposits. However, an increase in the latter is much higher than in the former, suggesting an increase in grey income and in-kind benefits. The banks under the high saving rate need to find an outlet for loans.
- An increasing disparity between housing investment and housing affordability supported by wages. Because of the lack of measures to secure loans to individuals – for example, repossession of property – housing mortgages are underdeveloped. Instead, banks lend capital to various development companies.
- An increase in the share of housing investment in fixed assets: the share increased from 8.4 percent in 1979 to 13.6 percent in 1990, to the peak of 28.2 percent in 1995, and back to 24.1 percent in 1997. In the booming years, the falling profit rate in manufacturing industries made a sharp contrast with the windfall profit in real estate.
- An increase in housing prices before 1995. The above logic cannot stand unless there is some support/demand for housing, thus sustaining the price. Here the logic closed its loop – the deep involvement of state work units in housing consumption. In other words, the in-kind distribution of housing had sustained strong demand until it was abolished in late 1998.

To put various clues together, we can piece out a wide picture of urban dynamics in the post-reform era. The key mechanism of the reform is the redefinition of the right to derive economic benefits. The right is redistributed to the basic units of the economy so as to raise the incentive for production. Rapid urban development is not based on the end consumer demand but is instead a result of the pumping of investment into previously constrained "non-productive" areas. The gap between nominal income and the increasing housing consumption is filled by the persistent role of the work unit. The involvement is logical, at least from the viewpoint of relative profitability: the declining profit rate in the production sphere in the transition from the shortage economy to the over-accumulated economy has driven both the banks and enterprises to seek other outlets for a higher profit. Quasi-market development companies emerged and fulfilled this function.

Contribution of foreign investment

The contribution of foreign investment to the development of coastal cities in China is undeniable. Particularly for the small cities in South China, investment from Hong Kong and Taiwan has become an important source of capital. The influence of foreign investment is related to its mobility and its nature as an external source outside the control of the state. Despite being a late comer, Shanghai has seen significant growth of foreign investment. Foreign capital utilized grew from US$2.24 billion in 1992 to US$7.51 billion in 1996, and foreign direct investment (FDI) increased from US$1.26 billion to 4.72 billion in the same period. The structure of foreign investment also saw some changes. Investment in real estate increased. In 1996, real estate attracted about 22.3 percent of FDI and became the second largest sector to absorb foreign capital. In comparison, the primary sector accounted for 0.07 percent of the total foreign capital utilized, and the secondary sector for 53.4 percent.

In terms of the contribution of foreign investment to capital formation in real estate, in 1996 about US$1.05 billion of foreign investment was in the real estate sector. The total investment in real estate was, however, 65.78 billion yuan. Then, the ratio of foreign capital in real estate to the total real estate investment was 13.4 percent, assuming an exchange rate of US$1 = 8.4 yuan. The figure is relatively low, considering the rapid growth of foreign investment. If we calculate the ratio of foreign investment to investment in fixed assets, we find that the ratio has been in general increasing since the mid-1980s. However, the ratio decreased in the period of building boom; that is, from 1992 to 1995, the ratio decreased from 0.47 to 0.21. Similarly, comparing foreign investment in real estate and the total investment in housing, we find the ratio of the former to the later decreased from 0.60 to 0.14. What these figures suggest is that the growth of foreign investment is outstripped by domestic investment in both fixed assets and housing. The change further suggests that measured by quantity foreign investment did not form the dominant source of capital in the real estate market. Or, to put it differently, in terms of capital formation, real estate development was not driven directly by foreign investment. Evidence suggests that real estate development involved mainly overseas Chinese developers and, to a less extent, Japanese developers rather than developers from Europe and North America.

Local economic development and place promotion

Foreign investment may not directly contribute to capital formation in real estate development. But, as an important source of capital, foreign investment does raise the need to enhance city competitiveness. As a result, local governments began to inject capital to improve urban infrastructure. In Shanghai, investment in infrastructure grew from 3.6 billion in 1990 to 37.8 billion in 1996. In the same period, the ratio of infrastructure investment to GDP increased from 5.2 to 13.0 percent. The municipality, in charge of land leasing, benefited from land revenue, thus creating the incentive to investment in land development. The local governments began to use the land leasing instrument to promote local economic growth, which now became the key theme in urban management. The designation of the Pudong New Area and the remaking of Shanghai as a financial and trade center in China provide a lot of investment opportunities. In the Eighth Five Year Plan and Ninth Five Year Plan key infrastructure projects were developed, which greatly improved the investment environment.

Summary

To summarize the findings in relation to the hypotheses raised in the first section, we see that the formation of real estate markets involves a historical process of institutional change. Starting from power decentralization and redistribution of economic benefits, the process has been characterized by two major changes. First, some resources have been transferred outside state control. Private investment and foreign investment emerged. Second, some resources have been decentralized from the central to local governments. For example, the municipality began to control state land, thus gaining interests in land development. As a result, multiple channels of investment have been opened up. As a progressive experiment rather than a coherent social engineering project, the economic reform in China adopted a pragmatic and gradualist approach. The policy aimed to encourage multiple actors – the central state, the local government, state work units, and individuals – to participate in housing development. To achieve this purpose, the "partial and gradual" reform implanted economic incentives in urban development processes by redefining and redistributing property rights among these actors. For example, the state-owned enterprises are allowed to retain the part of their profit to improve housing conditions.

Relating to the first hypothesis, we have seen the persistence of state work units in the urban development process and the shift of investment from production to the built environment. This is evidenced by the structural change in investment and the burgeoning quasi-development companies set up by various state-owned enterprises. The second hypothesis is, however, less supported by the data. In terms of the structure of foreign investment, real estate has become an important sector. Foreign investment in real estate did increase over the period of rapid real estate development. However, foreign investment accounted for only 13 percent of direct capital formation in real estate, even in cities such as Shanghai. This suggests that the influence of foreign investment in real estate did not lie in the quantity of capital it provides. Related to this understanding is the third hypothesis that the local state apparatus is deeply involved in place promotion. Real estate development is becoming an important arena for massive domestic investment and is used as a key vehicle for city promotional policies.

The Chinese economy has transformed from a shortage to an over-accumulation regime. In the 1990s, the excess capacity of industries became a major problem. Faced with the lack of effective demand, profits and capacity utilization began to fall. The Asian financial crisis in 1997 further exacerbated the problem, as the strong currency compared with other Asian currencies began to hurt the export sector. As a result, real estate development is chosen as a new growth pole. Housing consumption was hoped to stimulate domestic demand, thus supporting the economic growth target. In 1998, the central bank supported the increase in housing credit and encouraged commercial banks to release mortgages to households. Under the new mortgage scheme about 100 billion yuan was prepared.

In the light of the complex objectives behind real estate development, we should not expect that urban transformation in China can be summarized by a single notion of the "market transition." For example, so-called commodity housing in fact varies widely and has different types of property rights. The complexity in spatial terms is even less understood.

Transformation of Urban Space

Statistical data about investment in housing are now available for us to understand the temporal changes in investment structure. However, due to the lack of spatially disaggregated data at the intraurban scale, understanding of the implication of real estate investment for urban spatial structure is limited. Empirical studies are yet to be developed so as to shed light on the (intra-urban) distribution of population, land use, economic activities, and developments in the transition to a market economy.

The impacts of real estate development on urban space, however, are obvious. Szelenyi (1996, pp. 310–15) discussed three dimensions of the spatial consequence of post-communist transformation, namely the possible end of under-urbanism, increasing diversity, and suburbanization and inner urban decay. Bertaud and Renaud (1997) observed the problem of the suburban residential areas developed in the era of state socialism in the former Soviet Union. Andrusz et al. (1996) examined the changes in urban space in East European cities, in particular the modification of the "socialist city" model proposed by French and Hamilton (1979). For Chinese cities, Dowall (1994) suggested that the introduction of land prices would provide capital for relocation of factories and thus redevelopment of industrial land. Yeh and Wu (1996) examined the impacts of the establishment of a new land leasing system on the organizational forms of land development. Evidence suggests that Chinese cities are now witnessing accelerated urban land restructuring and suburban land expansion (Ning and Tang, 1996; Wu and Yeh, 1999). As a result, urban space in China is now being remodeled.

Urban space was characterized by "cellular structure" in the socialist era. Through work unit based housing provision, the workplace and residence maintained a strong link. This led to the differentiation of urban space according to land use rather than social stratification. Yeh et al. (1995) studied social areas in Guangzhou and found that unlike social spatial structure in Western cities, which commonly differentiated by socioeconomic status, family status, and ethnicity, the main components of social space in Guangzhou are population density, education, employment, house quality, and household composition. Accordingly, five types of social areas have been identified: (a) high-density, mixed function areas; (b) cadre areas; (c) worker areas; (d) intellectual areas; and (e) scattered agricultural areas. Wu (1992) pointed out the complexity of urban space in China and classified residential areas into four major types: (a) traditional neighborhoods in the old city area, mainly developed in the pre-1949 period; (b) single work unit living quarters, largely associated with industrial development, with clear boundaries (walls) defining land uses, and mainly developed in the period from 1949 to 1978; (c) mixed comprehensive communities, in the suburban areas, jointly developed by work units or through comprehensive development by the municipality, and developed since the late 1970s; (d) rural–urban fringe villages, related to urban encroachment on rural villages, developed spontaneously and sometimes "illegally" since the late 1970s. In fact, because of the "thick" layer of the pre-socialist legacy, especially in cities like Shanghai, urban space had not been thoroughly reshaped according to the socialist ideology. Rather, the old city area still saw high density, mixed land uses, and residential communities managed by "street offices" (*jiedao banshichu*), while in the suburban areas the living quarters of state workers were developed and often managed by work units themselves.

The introduction of real estate development has produced a number of impacts on urban space. Studies on urban space have so far been confined to a few large cities such as Shanghai, Guangzhou, and Beijing and mainly by the use of land data (Wu and Yeh, 1997, 2000; Wu, 1998a, b), by characterizing urban landscapes (Wu, 1998c; Gaubatz, 1999), or by identifying the implication of institutional changes such as housing reform (Wang and Murie, 2000). These studies suggested the transformation of urban space under real estate development. First, housing and land reforms have accelerated land-use conversions. In the central area, urban redevelopment occurred at an unprecedented scale, leading to the reshaping of urban skylines (Wu, 2000).

Second, because of the revenue generated by real estate development, the enthusiasm of local governments, including county and district governments, for the promotion of land development is also unprecedented. More importantly, by real estate development the local governments have gained the instrument on the basis of land leasing to stimulate local economic growth. This has led to a local development approach, which stimulates the dispersal of development. The increasing land rent gradient has also driven industrial land uses to the suburban areas. The urban space has been transformed from a compact to a dispersed metropolis. Related to the dispersal of land use is the polycentric development. Economic and Technological Development Zones (ETDZs) have formed subcenters. The Guagnzhou ETDZ is mainly based on industrial and export-oriented activities, while the Pudong New Area in Shanghai has taken over certain downtown and central business district functions. Competition is intensified between the old city districts and newly merged subcenters. For example, new developments in the form of skyscrapers in the Dongshang District and Tianhe District undertake service functions in Guagnzhou. The Lujiazui Finance and Trade Zone is becoming a strong competitor of the Bund in Shanghai.

Third, real estate development has produced various forms and typologies of residential space. The tight relationship between the workspace and residence has been broken, though the influence of work units may continue. Wang and Murie (2000) observed that developers adopted different design standards to target different "consumer" groups. For ordinary and affordable housing projects, multistory buildings plus a few high-rise tower blocks are common building forms. For the rich, standards vary from the cottage and detached houses to expensive apartments. The inequality of housing conditions between work units is likely to persist (Logan et al., 1999), but this may be complicated by the changing social structure. For example, private

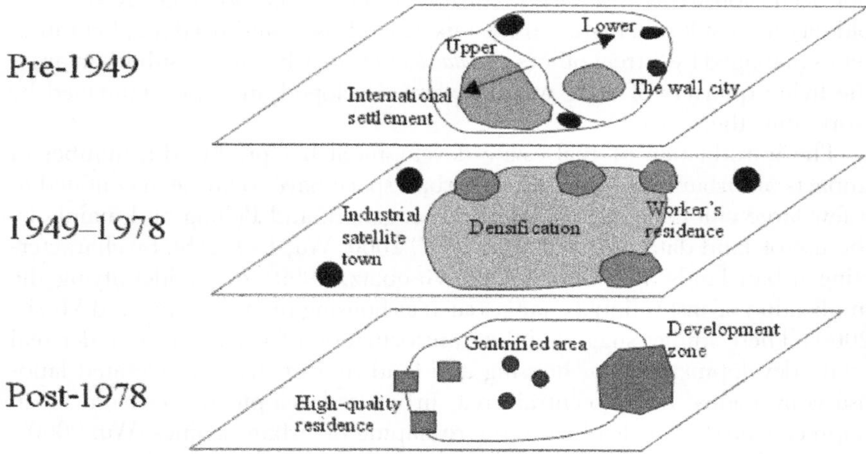

Figure 10.2 The urban spatial structure in three historical periods in China

businessmen, managers of joint ventures, and expatriates of multinationals can afford luxury and exclusive housing. While the overall housing condition has been improved, the contrast between high quality housing and housing in dilapidated areas is increasing.

The urban space post-reform has been transformed by real estate development. But as discussed above the transition is not simply the establishment of the market logic. Instead, the institutional arrangement is involved. As a result, the urban space is mixed with different layers of urban spatial structure produced in different periods (see figure 10.2). In the pre-1949 period, the coexistence of the Walled City with international settlements presented a distinctive feature. The urban space was differentiated into the "upper" and "lower" end in Shanghai. Rural migrants flooded into the city after the collapse of the rural agricultural economy, forming shanty towns along the fringe areas and the river. The differentiation of urban space was strengthened by the sharp land price difference in different areas.

In the period from 1949 to 1978, the differentiation of urban space began to change. The People's government was faced with the urgent tasks of eliminating the extreme poverty and improving living conditions. Starting from the 1950s, workers' villages have been developed according to the principle of maximizing access to workplaces. However, due to strict control over nonproductive investment, such a "planned" development could not be implemented citywide. Instead, population growth was largely accommodated through densification of existing urban areas. Some inner urban areas saw extreme high density, even measured by the standard of the Chinese cities. In Shanghai, the government did formulate a population decentralization strategy. However, the strategy was doomed, simply because of the lack of the mechanisms and necessary resources to redistribute population. Instead, the effect of population decentralization, mainly achieved through the setting up of industrial satellite towns, was limited.

In the third period of urban development starting from 1978, new elements emerged. The precise form of new development varies from city to city, depending on the location of the city and the progress in land and housing reform. With reference to Shanghai, the new pattern includes the establishment of development zones and the emergence of selective gentrified areas and high-quality residences. The opening up of a real estate market re-established the land rent gradient. Factories are relocated to the periphery and so are the residents on redevelopment sites. However, redevelopment through real estate is selective. In part, this is related to the fact that the distribution of FDI is more selective than that of domestic firms (Wu, 1999a). The location of redevelopment projects is also conditioned by the dynamics of the real estate market itself. The dilapidated areas with extremely high density and poor infrastructure have been left out in the commercial redevelopment projects. In fact, it becomes more and more difficult for remaining areas of shack dwellers to attract commercial projects if the compensation standard is maintained. In some places, residents are relocated to the peripheral areas. With the emergence of development zones, the distribution of economic activities is more decentralized and polycentric in the metropolitan areas. One additional element, which is not portrayed in this proposed layer structure model, is rural migrant communities. This is because the concentration of rural migrants varies widely from city to city. In Beijing, for example, migrants from the same rural areas tend to cluster into "migrant enclaves," while in other cities like Shanghai the distribution of rural migrants is more dispersed, perhaps due to tighter controls.

The evolution of urban space has its historical continuity, which means that the new layer is built upon the existing urban fabric. As a result, the urban space in post-reform China is composed of overlapped layers built in different historical periods. Empirical studies have so far been limited to Guangzhou, Shanghai, Beijing, and a few other cities. Moreover, comparative studies are scarce to provide an answer as to whether the transformation of Chinese cities is unique in the post-socialist transition (Andrusz et al., 1996; Bertaud and Renaud, 1997). In the study of urban spatial structures, attention has been paid to the change in land uses rather than population distribution and social differentiation. The transformation of urban space is not only of theoretical significance but also of profound welfare implication. Will Chinese cities continue to see social polarization? With the rising unemployment rate, the retreat of state welfare provision, and the increasing number of rural migrants, will the social differentiation be projected into urban spatial inequality?

Conclusions

Real estate development in China has always juggled with different objectives. At the beginning of the reform it was the overwhelming necessity to ease housing shortages. Now it is chosen as a new growth pole of the economy. Throughout, market-oriented institutional reform is *not* the priority. After all, the reform is not a social engineering project. It is thus important to analyze the political economy of real estate development. The notion of the "transition from the planned to market economy" might be popular owing to its simplicity but cannot summarize the complexity of the change.

Equally simplistic is to see the development of Chinese cities as solely driven by globalization and foreign investment. There has been a strong local dimension to real estate development, though foreign capital helped to fuel the building boom in the 1990s. The thesis of "power persistence" of Bian and Logan (1996) correctly captured such a local dimension. The studies on the production of landed property production and place promotional activities show that a new version of the urban growth machine based on real estate development is under formation in China (Wu, 1999b, 2000). This chapter further analyzed in detail the structure of investment related to real estate development and largely confirmed the shifted capital movement, a hypothesis derived from the thesis of power persistence.

The findings further highlight the complexity of real estate development in China and suggest the need for empirical research on the spatial transformation of Chinese cities. The changes in real estate development have enormous implications for urban spatial structures. However, so far our understanding of spatial aspects of Chinese cities has been very crude. To enhance our knowledge, new databases at a finer spatial resolution (such as 2000 Population Census and property data) are needed to identify more precisely the trend of changes in land uses, population, property, and economic activities. Second, it would be fruitful to develop some empirical models to describe spatial distribution. In the previous section, a conceptual model of layered urban space was used to discuss its transformation. However, it is necessary to develop more quantifiable measures to pave a way for comparative studies.

11
Social Research and the Localization of Chinese Urban Planning Practice: Some Ideas from Quanzhou, Fujian

Daniel B. Abramson, Michael Leaf, and Tan Ying

In early 1984, the Chinese State Council issued the "City Planning Ordinance." Through this state directive, all municipal and county governments were required to develop master plans to guide their physical development in accordance with existing practices of local economic planning. By establishing the basic norms for urban spatial planning practice throughout the country, the promulgation of this ordinance in effect designated the official starting date for the rise or, more properly, resurrection of the field of urban planning after decades of dissolution.

In this respect the urban planning profession was not unique. The Maoist state's attack on this field was only one part of a broad dismantlement of professions that ostensibly served to elevate "common knowledge" (*chang shi*) in their place, but which in fact established the party-state's hegemony over societal information. The resurrection of professional fields in the 1980s can be interpreted as an official recognition that modernization through market reform depends on the technical knowledge of elite groups. Urban planning in its first manifestation following reform and opening was thus driven by the goals of modernization and economic growth. However, since under "socialism with Chinese characteristics" economic opening must be accompanied by maintenance of statist social and political controls, the revival of professions poses a problem for the state. What exactly is the relation of professions to the state, and how their activities are to be kept strictly "technical," are still open questions.

We emphasize here both the newness of the field of urban planning and its initial focus on supporting economic growth objectives in order to draw out some critical differences between the current state of Chinese urban planning practice and the norms of practice which have become established over time in the developed countries of the West. The field of planning in the West is often described as being derived from two streams or traditions, a rationalist stream flowing from the design professions (architecture, engineering, systems theory) and shaped by positivist scientific thought, and a critique coming from the social sciences that posits the lack of a true, coherent "social welfare function," stressing instead the need for articulating and negotiating trade-offs between social and institutional forces in the allocation of public or collective goods. Differences between these two intellectual traditions of Western planning have prompted spirited debate over the epistemology of planning. At root is the recognition that planning problems, being socially embedded, are fundamentally "wicked problems" (to use the terminology of one early expression of this), in that social context creates a shifting milieu which cannot properly be anticipated in either problem definition or planning implementation (Rittel and Webber, 1973). The implications of such debate are not merely academic; processes of public participation, stakeholder analysis and negotiation, and social empowerment became central to local planning practice in the 1990s (Innes, 1995).

In contrast, urban planning practice in China has so far followed a much narrower mandate. It is a profession with a single tradition, derived virtually in its entirety from the design professions, and especially the socialist Soviet one. In Chinese, urban planning (*guihua*) is clearly distinguished from economic planning (*jihua*). Over the history of the People's Republic, *jihua*, "the setting of economic targets," has been a fundamental role of the state and was an important function of the government even during periods when *guihua* was utterly discredited as Soviet elitism. Under the centrally planned economy, therefore, urban planners have had little opportunity or reason to include economic or social analysis in their activities (with the occasional exception of user needs analysis), and, unlike in the West, neither theory nor practice has been fundamentally influenced by the social science critique. This is attributable in part to constraints on social discourse in the Chinese polity, but as well to the very newness of the field. For example, Burgess and Park's classic work on urban social ecology was not even available in Chinese translation until the late 1980s.

As a consequence, Chinese urban planning during both the period of Soviet influence in the 1950s and the current reform era has exhibited some of the worst traits of professional elitism: an exclusive, paternalistic attitude toward determining the needs of urban dwellers, combined with a lack of real experience with average living conditions and a tendency to focus on future visions and end products rather than on processes and implementation. Of course, these traits went hand-in-hand with the entire command economy. The fact that social analysis and critique have recently made their way into urban planning discourse in China at all is really a reflection of the extent to which markets, and particularly urban spatial markets, have eroded the planned economic system (Abramson, 1997a).

A second critical concern in the comparison between Chinese and Western planning arises from the problematic question of administrative or political decentralization. In the liberal democratic polities of the West, planning as a social endeavor originated perforce as a vehicle for the articulation of local needs. In contrast, the socialist Chinese state in the pre-reform period was notable for its emphasis on democratic centralism and the strength of its centralized planned economy. The historic Chinese political culture of local autonomy, as expressed in the oft-quoted aphorism "the sky is high and the emperor is far away," was largely kept in check throughout this period by the machinery of state in Beijing. In administrative terms, decentralization has been the most profound impact of the reform period, although there is a good case built for this being a transition to a "decentralized command economy" when looked at nationally. Reforms have greatly strengthened the local state and prompted the articulation of regional and subregional differences throughout China.

The diversification which is inherent in China's momentous changes since the early 1980s is expressed not only in the varied practices at the level of the local state, but also in the broad opening up of roles for new social and economic actors. In consideration of the historically unprecedented waves of growth and change that are now shaping China's cities, it is becoming clear to practicing planners and local officials that new processes of urbanization and development have emerged. These are processes that have different correspondences to state policies and actions than in the past, and therefore new strategies or new modes of planning thought are necessary in response. Our argument here is that these changes occasion the introduction and promotion of a second stream of thought for Chinese urban planning practice, a stream derived from social science research and analysis. In developing a research agenda for the twenty-first century, Chinese social scientists can play a major role by taking an explicit orientation toward applied research in support of the evolving field of urban planning.

In this chapter we examine the trends of urbanization and urban planning in the city of Quanzhou, a medium-sized city in Fujian province, in order to explore the potential for using social science research practices in support of urban planning in China. In the following sections, we review the characteristics of Quanzhou's urbanization processes and examine how the city's approach to urban planning changed over the course of the 1990s. Finally, we discuss our recent research exercise in three neighborhoods of the city, looking in particular at the trend toward localization of planning practice.

Our point here is that the articulation of the diversity of development processes that are now shaping the city of Quanzhou can help to inform the city government's approach to planning.

Urban Change in Quanzhou

Like every city, Quanzhou is a unique place, with its uniqueness growing out of its historic and geographic roots and intertwining with the complex patterns of present-day change. As with other cities in China today, there is a great deal of ambiguity around the concept of urban in Quanzhou. The Quanzhou municipality, first of all, has been administratively defined to include the surrounding six-county region, roughly equivalent to the prefecture that Quanzhou administered under previous regimes. In 1997 it had a total population of 6.5 million and a total area of 10,865 square kilometers, although the registered non-agricultural population of the municipality – an alternative way of thinking about "urban" – was only about 850,000. Moreover, many of the built-up areas that accommodate the municipality's urban population are not continuous with the administrative center. This historic and administrative core is comprised of the Old City district of Licheng and its adjacent suburbs, which in 1994 had a population of over 185,000 (Quanzhou Municipal Government, 1995). In addition to these official numbers, one must also consider the sizable population of rural migrants from elsewhere, which is estimated to be around 200,000 people within the built-up areas of the municipality. With all these qualifications and approximations, it is reasonable to think of the urban core of Quanzhou municipality – Licheng and its surroundings – as containing around 300,000 people, about one-third of whom are categorized as "temporary" migrants.

The flow of rural migrants into cities is only one of a number of defining characteristics of China's reform period (Davis et al., 1995; Leaf, 1998). Other major urban changes of this period are also evident in Quanzhou. The rapidly developing market economy has prompted accelerated economic growth, as indicated by a 22-fold increase in municipal GDP between 1980 and 1997 (Quanzhou Municipal Statistics Bureau, 1998). Also, as elsewhere in the coastal regions of China, the bulk of economic growth has been in the township and village enterprises (TVEs); total production value of TVEs increased 368 times during this same period. This wealth has accrued both to the local government and to the citizenry. Devolution of fiscal responsibility from the central government since the late 1980s has allowed for a greater proportion of locally retained revenues. When coupled with the introduction of new municipal financing techniques that make use of land market value, this has resulted in greatly improved municipal budgets in recent years, with the budget deficit in Quanzhou dropping from 16 percent in the mid-1980s to 2 percent in 1990. Following the land market boom of the early 1990s, the municipality had achieved a 1997 budget surplus of 44 percent. At the same time, the municipality has typically been able to rely on developers to include infrastructure upgrading in project costs as a kind of tax in kind. Thus the economic boom underlies ongoing investments in physical modernization, with major programs of inner city redevelopment and rapid suburbanization.

This is not to say that municipal governments have been unhampered in achieving their development goals. Administrative and fiscal decentralization in the early 1990s extended lower than the municipal level, down to the district and subdistrict governments as well, and created sharp internal rivalries. The object of large-scale redevelopment, for example, was understood differently at different levels of local government. Municipalities, empowered with control over enormous rural hinterlands and an array of new revenue sources outside the traditional urban center, saw redevelopment primarily as a means to achieve major infrastructure goals, particularly street-widening and traffic improvement. Inner-city district-level governments, however, which were burdened with the responsibility of maintaining other urban services without the benefits of a mature tax collection system, have viewed redevelopment more as an opportunity to raise badly needed revenue. Consequently, the scale of urban redevelopment orchestrated by district governments quickly outgrew municipal master plans (Tan, 1994b; Dong, 1997; Wu, 1999c). In Quanzhou, as much as 56 percent of the city center was slated for redevelopment by the year 2000 according to the Old City District Plan of 1992 (Quanzhou Municipal Government, 1992), and further planning pushed by the Licheng District in 1993 revised this amount up to 65 percent or about 420 hectares (Tao, 1995). As of the end of 1999, approximately 17 percent had actually been rebuilt. While this is far below the original goal, it still represents a significant portion of the Old City.

What we see to be the most significant aspect of current urbanization trends in China has been the rapid diversification of city-building processes, arising from the growing role of new social actors in contrast to the near-monopoly position of the state in the past. When looked at in these terms, Quanzhou can be understood to be a typical Chinese city, yet a consideration of the specific mix of new actors and new processes affecting change in Quanzhou emphasizes how exceptional the city is. Three basic factors, derived from the city's specific historic and geographic circumstances, underlie the uniqueness of Quanzhou in this regard:

1 Southern Fujian is notable in China for its relative lack of state investment during the period of the centralized command economy, due to what was seen to be its vulnerable position on the Taiwan Straits.
2 Quanzhou is famous both locally and internationally for its extensive *huaqiao* (overseas Chinese) connections, as it has been a place of tremendous out-migration since the late nineteenth century.

3 A high degree of private property control has been maintained in the city, even during the most radically collective periods of China's recent past.

These three factors are tightly interlinked, forming the basis of a particular political economy of development which differs from what might be considered to be the Chinese urban norm. As one example, the low level of central state investment in the area translates in practical terms into a relatively smaller proportion of state sector involvement in the local economy. In 1993, only 6.78 percent of production was state-owned, and 53 percent of retail was private. The "front line" position of Quanzhou on the Taiwan Straits is thus a contributory factor to the persistence of the private economy throughout the period of state socialism.

The persistence of private ownership at the household level is linked not only to the lack of central government investment in the region, but also to the influence of *huaqiao* ties. City officials have always worked to maintain good relations with overseas expatriates, being careful not to implement policies which might disenfranchise those members of the local community who have external connections. The investment and development implications of the *huaqiao* connection are historically rooted (Dai, 1996; Zhuang, 1996), with major initiatives for development and change originating from returned expatriates in the 1920s and 1930s, and a special district for elegant mansions (the Huaqiao Xincun) set aside in 1954 to reward the wealthiest overseas supporters of the Revolution. Indeed, this *xincun* ("new village") was only the first of many planned housing areas laid out during the 1950s and 1960s for returning overseas Chinese; the more typical socialist apartment-style housing estates for local workers did not appear in Quanzhou until after 1978 (Quanzhou Municipal Construction Commission, 1995). The continuing importance of the overseas Chinese connection is reflected in the fact that the city's most recent master plan states the number of overseas Chinese who can trace their roots to Quanzhou – estimated at more than six million, including up to 45 percent of the Han population of Taiwan – even before it mentions the current population of the municipality itself (Quanzhou Municipal Government, 1995, p. 2; see also Zhuang et al., 1991).

Unlike most of urban China, the Quanzhou government never carried out a program of housing collectivization, even during the Cultural Revolution. By the end of the 1970s, more than 90 percent of Licheng District's housing stock was still in private hands, and during the first decade of economic reform in the 1980s, individual households carried out the bulk of new housing construction in Licheng District. By contrast, in Beijing's Old City, private housing ownership even now does not exceed 10 percent, and most of this is still rented out to government-designated families at government-controlled rents. Overall, it can be seen that Quanzhou's *huaqiao* connections have long been crucial to the local economy and the provision of essential public services and housing. In the context of low levels of central state spending, this factor has provided the local government with a significant degree of leverage *vis-à-vis* the Beijing leadership. It may have also provided individual households with an equally significant degree of leverage *vis-à-vis* the local government.

These three deeply rooted factors – low state sector investment, strong *huaqiao* connections, and high levels of private ownership – intersect with the new pressures arising from the reintroduction of market forces in China to shape a locally defined new political economy of urbanization in Quanzhou. This is most clearly evident in the ongoing conflict between Quanzhou's position as a city of historic importance and the city's rapidly expanding urban land market. Quanzhou is officially designated as China's third most historic city (after Beijing and Xi'an), based on the number of registered historic structures in the city and the recognition that it was China's major seaport during the Song and Yuan dynasties (Schinz, 1989; Liu, 1997a). In 1982, Quanzhou was included in China's first lot of officially listed "Famous Historic and Cultural Cities," and in 1991, UNESCO included the city in its study tour of the Silk Road, giving it widespread international recognition as "the origin of the maritime Silk Road," thus linking it with a chain of historic sites stretching across South Asia and the Arab world (Liu, 1997a). Encouraged by this recognition, city conservation and tourism officials have actively courted the support of Arab states and Islamic leaders, and are pursuing UNESCO designation as a "World Heritage Site." Planning for redevelopment and modernization has thus proceeded with an emphasis on contextual sensitivity and historic conservation. The attempt to marry conservation and modernization, however, has met with many false starts, dead ends, and detours. Conventional urban planning and development standards and practices have more often hindered than helped this enterprise, and after the experiences so far, local planners are now developing local solutions that in many instances challenge the urban planning regulations promulgated from the central government.

Planning in Quanzhou

The initial listing of historic cities in 1982 and the resumption of master planning in 1984 can be seen as parts of the same resurgence of professionalism arising from the central government's overall attitude toward the urban environment and its development. Yet there was very little coordination of the new standards and methods that conservation and planning each demanded of local governments. Master planning, and its correlate, the more detailed district regulatory, or "control," planning, uniformly entailed the division of urban land parcels into standard use categories, separated by roads of standard widths deemed appropriate for any "modern" city, and occupied by buildings that are to be spaced according to detailed standards for sunlight access and the layout of typical infrastructure lines. These national standards were developed essentially for new settlements on "greenfield" sites, with no regard for the complexities of existing urban fabric or land-use rights (Abramson, 1997b; Dong, 1997; Liu, 1997b; Tan, 1997).

Even in the case of designated historic cities, regulatory and development planning tends to produce a literal blueprint of the future urban environment, with most existing buildings and land use boundaries wiped away and replaced by vaguely Corbusian landscapes. Such visions also tend to be only partially, if nevertheless destructively, realized. In any city, an entire host of institutions, excluded or ignored by the planning process, can ultimately subvert the master plan as they attempt to lease out the land they occupy or otherwise use their land to satisfy immediate development needs.

This is evident in Quanzhou in the many multistory buildings built by individual households, work units, and even local government agencies, despite a general planning policy to limit new buildings to three stories throughout the Old City center. The most prominent transgressors in the early 1990s were the major extensions of two hotels owned respectively by the Municipal Government and the Licheng District Government, and the offices of the Public Security Bureau, all of which exceed nine stories. Even the Municipal Planning Institute and Planning Bureau built a five-story office building in a poorly accessed, crowded old neighborhood of vernacular houses. Meanwhile, during the critical two years or so that the Old City's environment began to suffer most sharply from increasingly dense construction, large tracts of well serviced open land outside the urban core were being kept from development by speculators waiting for the market to ripen even further.

The inability of conventional urban planning to consider and influence the development activities of individual land holders was one factor that pushed local governments to adopt a large-scale, clean-sweep approach to redevelopment; if one development agency or company took responsibility for a large parcel of the Old City, then it would be easier to provide adequate services and to control building density and appearance, at least within that parcel. Redevelopment projects then became largely the result of a compromise between those factions in the government that on one side favored increased density in the interest of economic development, and those that on the other side favored lower densities in the interests of the public environment and/or historic conservation. The logic inherent in developer-provided infrastructure, however, tended to favor sharp increases in density; the more public infrastructure developers were required to include in their projects, the more existing buildings they would have to demolish, and the more buildings they demolished, the more new floor space they would have to build to cover the costs of relocation and compensation of existing residents and work units.

In all of these respects, Quanzhou's experience is not unlike that of the rest of urban China. What is unusual about Quanzhou's experience in the Chinese context is the extent to which redevelopment projects in the Old City ultimately strove to respect the projects' historic and environmental context despite their large scale and drastic levels of demolition. The current national trend of inner-city redevelopment in China is to replace old, dense low-rise urban fabric with isolated single-use blocks in an open matrix of green space and separated by broad automobile-oriented avenues (Lu, 1997; Wu, 1999c). The three major redevelopment projects to date in Quanzhou, however, have taken the form of more modestly widened streets and squares, continuously lined by new apartment buildings with arcaded shops on the ground floors. Densities have increased significantly, from an original gross floor area ratio generally not exceeding 1 : 1 to a new gross density of over 1 : 1.6, with nearly all original buildings demolished (Lin, 1997a). Nevertheless, the style and materials of the new buildings have adopted elements of the local building traditions to an almost carnival extent, competing with each other in the local press for recognition as being the "most Minnan" (see, for example, Huang, 1997 – "Minnan" refers to the southern Fujian linguistic and cultural region of which Quanzhou is a center). References to local style in Quanzhou's new buildings are seen at many scales, from the employment of traditional crafts in the finish work, all the way up to the choice of building for the articulation of public urban spaces.

This kind of architectural contextualism in Quanzhou's redevelopment derives partly from the growing professionalism of urban planning in China. Since Quanzhou is a relatively small but recently wealthy city, its planning authorities have been able to hire from prestigious units elsewhere in the country the planning expertise they lack in-house. Designers from Tianjin University, the Jiangsu Provincial Planning Institute, Dongnan University in Nanjing, and Tsinghua University in Beijing have all contributed to the city's redevelopment planning. These outside professionals, impressed by what they recognize as Quanzhou's strong local character, have more enthusiastically attempted to work that character into their new designs than they might have done in projects closer to home. Moreover, just as "the monk from far away knows better how to read the scriptures," the advice of planners from nationally renowned institutions has carried more weight in the debates over planning policy than similar viewpoints expressed by local factions. In the case of Quanzhou, it so happened that the contextualism advocated by outside consultants met with unusual sympathy among many influential local leaders.

Even before the completion of the city's two initial large redevelopment projects, Quanzhou's planning authorities began to look for alternatives to the unified, large-scale approach to redevelopment. Not only was this approach seen as too destructive of the Old City fabric, more importantly it was proving too expensive given the Licheng District's property structure. As a rule in China, most city center residents wish very much to remain in their central location due to the proximity of urban services. However, a major factor in the ability of most Chinese cities to redevelop inner city neighborhoods is the high proportion of government-owned housing and thus the weakness of existing residents' rights to occupy their current housing site. Typically, such residents are entitled to new housing, but only in very distant locations. Since housing in Licheng District is nearly entirely private, and has been continuously so since before 1949, nearly all residents have the right to return to their original neighborhood after redevelopment and to purchase at cost the same amount of space in the new housing that they had previously occupied. Moreover, since residents of Licheng District also tend to have rather spacious houses by Chinese urban standards (14 square meters per person on average), redevelopment projects in this city must include large amounts of unprofitable space for returning residents.

After the softening of the luxury-end real estate market in 1994, speculators who had allowed suburban land to lie fallow began to release these tracts for development. Dense new housing estates began to spring up, taking some of the pressure off the Old City. The municipal planning authorities, more concerned now than before about the conservation of the Old City, were therefore unable to justify raising densities to the necessary level to offset the high costs of on-site relocation in redevelopment projects. Quanzhou's planners ceased using the term "old [i.e. obsolete] city redevelopment" (*jiucheng gaizao*) and instead spoke of "old [i.e. historic] city preservation and construction" (*gucheng baohu jianshe*). Treating the Old City as a unique but integral core for the entire municipality, rather than as a self-contained district that had to cover its own modernization costs, the municipal government essentially passed a moratorium on further large-scale neighborhood redevelopment. Additional street widening might be carried out, but as a public infrastructure project rather than a money-making venture.

A number of factors – the continuity of traditional cultural and social activities within the community, the persistence of private property at the household level, the collapse of a nationwide boom in luxury real estate, cosmopolitan professionalism among both local and outside planners, and a locally rooted but globally sophisticated political leadership – have combined to create a powerful constituency in favor of a form of redevelopment that respects local environmental conditions, and, by extension, local cultural and social conditions. Contextualism in the rebuilding of urban space in Quanzhou over the course of the 1990s was an expression of an emerging localization of the entire planning process, even though it required the engagement of national-level professionals and international exchanges to give it official momentum. Ultimately, the entire large-scale approach to redevelopment had to be reconsidered.

The question thus remains: how should the government plan and provide for improvements in the public urban environment? If the threat that large-scale redevelopment posed to the historic city has been removed, what should be done about the threat posed by widespread, incremental demolition and densification by individual households? The Municipal Planning Bureau, the agency responsible for enforcing the city's plans and building regulations, has recognized that the answer to these questions must lie partly with individual households themselves, and with the community-level organizations that represent and communicate with residents directly. The financial strength of average households in Quanzhou is well known to city officials. Likewise, the willingness of residents to pool their resources to achieve communal goals has also not gone unnoticed. In the absence of a system of property taxation, how can these resources be drawn upon to improve the urban environment more generally? These questions, critical as they are for formulating the future approach to urban planning in Quanzhou, underscore the necessity of understanding the diverse patterns of urban change in Quanzhou today. In so doing, they provide a basic rationale for incorporating social research into the practice of urban planning.

Social Research and the Localization of Urban Planning

From our collaboration with planners from the Quanzhou Municipal Planning Bureau and other officials of local government, it is clear that localization of planning practice is now a high priority in Quanzhou. "Localization" here can mean a variety of things. Prominent on the city's agenda is the resolution of tensions between two separate sets of pressures coming down from above. The first, as previously discussed, are the nationally promulgated standards for urban upgrading and modernization, standards which are tending to produce a high degree of uniformity across the urban landscapes of China. Simultaneously, as a nationally designated historic city, Quanzhou is also under pressure to devise a heritage conservation approach to planning, an approach which of necessity emphasizes the historic uniqueness of place in the city.

But resolution of the conflicts between these two sets of directives from above must also be cognizant of the specific local processes of change. In Quanzhou, this means the conscious search for a balance between local household desires and broader collective visions of the future city, in that so many of the ongoing changes in the city are the aggregate results of initiatives by households and other non-state actors. As a result, one seeming oddity which has emerged in recent years (an oddity relative to the situations elsewhere in urban China) has been what can best be described as a preservationist local government, which is increasingly taking a hard line in the restriction of physical change in the built fabric of the Old City. Thus new tensions are emerging, forcing local planners to more carefully consider the diversity of urbanization processes ongoing in the city.

These pragmatic concerns provide the context for our research on neighborhood change in Quanzhou. In this work, we examined three sites in the city of Quanzhou, two in the historic urban core, including a previously redeveloped neighborhood, and one site on the rapidly changing periphery of the city. Our goal in undertaking this work was, first of all, to articulate the range of building typologies which now constitute the residential fabric of the city, and, second, to investigate the processes by which these different typologies have emerged. In all, we identified eleven different types of construction, which are distinguished as much by differing social processes as by distinct building forms (Abramson et al., 2000). The initial characterization of these processes was between what we termed "developer-built" and "self-built" construction. Our survey identified five different developer-built types, with three in the inner city and two on the periphery, three of which are exclusively residential, the other two with mixed uses; and six different types of self-built housing, one in the inner city, two on the periphery and three in both places, with all six exhibiting a mix of uses rather than being exclusively residential. Distinguishing characteristics of these six types may be seen in terms of the sources of capital for construction, intentions of use by those who built them, socioeconomic characteristics of the builders and residents, and the resulting environmental conditions.

This survey was useful as well in identifying the range of social actors in city-building, and explaining why different groups matter in different ways under different circumstances. Significant social actors identified in this work include the following:

- Local state agencies involved in the planning, administration, and infrastructure provision in the city. These agencies include not only municipal-level offices, but lower-level administrative structures, such as neighborhood committees and village committees on the periphery of the city's built-up area. In addition to the need to respond to local concerns, higher level agencies must also be cognizant of formal regulatory pressures from the central state.
- Local developers, who, although functioning in the newly emergent market economy of the city, nonetheless are not fully autonomous from the interests of the local state, as they are organized as essentially parastatal organizations, tied to one or another local state agency. The diversity of activities by developers, and how they intersect (or not) with the formal regulatory structures of the local state are indicative of the degree of fragmentation within local political structures.

- Other parastatal organizations, such as those groups organized for facilitating cooperation with overseas Chinese. The activities of such organizations may only be tangential to the overall development processes in the city, although they help to shape the climate for interactions between local citizens and their overseas relatives.
- Local citizens of longstanding, who tend to act autonomously or through individual negotiation with regulatory agencies in shaping their residential environments. The capability for autonomous action on the part of citizens derives largely from the continuing patterns of private ownership in the residential fabric of the city (and in its surrounding villages), and is conditioned in many instances by relations with overseas relatives, many of whom have contributed capital for upgrading or rebuilding of old houses. Capacity for local citizens to act collectively is conditioned to a large degree by local administrative structures, such as neighborhood committees and village committees.
- Other autonomous or quasi-autonomous groups of new residents who originate from outside of the immediate area. One example of this is the large number of rural migrants whose presence in the villages surrounding the city has transformed the local economic base of Quanzhou's peri-urban regions areas. Another smaller although still significant example is that of the rural elites who now have sufficient resources for purchasing newly built market housing in the urban core, thus putting new pressures on inner-city development.

How the interests of each of these groups intersect with local regulatory forms is a major factor in the continuing development of the city. Current practice tends to emphasize negotiated compliance (or in some cases, non-compliance) with the formal norms of development, thus creating a fair degree of unpredictability for the future planning of the city, despite the best intentions of local planners. Localization of planning practice thus argues for the development of more inclusive forms of planning, which can actively engage the various relevant interest groups in the normative process of shaping the future city. What makes this kind of survey and analysis significant from the perspective of conventional Chinese urban planning is that the social groups and processes identified in the survey were linked to specific types of built form. For planners who are trained to look at the city in primarily architectural terms, this provides a useful entry point into the application of social research well beyond the usual user needs analysis.

The most promising initial reaction to our work has been interest from the Planning Bureau in developing participatory neighborhood planning processes in the Old City, as they understand this to be a useful step toward articulating a compromise position between residents and municipal planners regarding future upgrading strategies. An initial exercise, consisting of a series of workshops with planners and residents, has since been carried out in one inner city neighborhood with support from the China office of the Ford Foundation. Our plans for further initiatives along these lines are to work with local planners on institutionalizing participatory planning practices at neighborhood levels and to carry out further research on the potential for local organizational capacity among residents.

The positive reactions to our work to date indicate an interest and willingness on the part of local planning practitioners to incorporate particular tools of social research into urban planning at local levels. In a small way, a new stream of thinking in Chinese city planning is perhaps being opened up. Whether this is the beginning of a significantly expanded approach to urban planning in China – something more akin to the two streams of planning thought in the West – is indeed a question for the long term. It is clear from our experience that what is needed is much more than just introducing the tools of social research to planning practitioners; an institutional context within which they will be relevant is also necessary. In this, we feel that there are distinct and pragmatic roles for Chinese social scientists to play.

Acknowledgments

This research was developed on the basis of a longstanding working relationship between the School of Community and Regional Planning at UBC, the Department of Urban Design and Planning of Tsinghua University, and the Quanzhou Municipal Planning Bureau. Initial work was carried out in 1994 in the form of a joint field studio project carried out by faculty and students from Tsinghua and UBC (see Leaf et al., 1995). This working relationship has also been bolstered over the years by a series of design projects undertaken by Tsinghua faculty in Quanzhou. We are grateful for support at various times by the Canadian International Development Agency, UBC Continuing Studies, and the Governance and Civil Society Unit of the Ford Foundation, China.

Part IV
Urban Impacts of Migration

12 Migrant Enclaves in Large Chinese Cities

Fan Jie and Wolfgang Taubmann

The economic reforms and internationalization of the Chinese economy are closely linked to processes of social change. A society which was split up into an urban and rural segment by the *hukou* system (household registration system) starts to differentiate itself, and at the same time the rural and urban inhabitants have to develop new forms of life and communication.

Today's rural–urban migrants are part of the urban everyday life, above all in the urban fringe. By taking migrant enclaves (*cun*) and mainly the "urban fringe" as examples, the processes of a radical social change with regard to local forms of life and economy can be analyzed in various aspects. It is of special interest how the migrants fare in the different worlds of labor and life. This chapter mainly concentrates on the development, spatial, and functional structure of migrant settlements, based on the migrants' strategies to survive on the basis of local economic traditions and behavior.

The new urban environment seems to be hostile to many migrants, because local governments erected a "labyrinthine system of permissions and fees through which rural migrants must pass" (Knight et al., 1999, p. 101). So far urban offices at different levels have tried to react to massive in-migration with the help of authoritarian forms of control (migration restrictions, restrictions concerning the issue of a *hukou*, expulsion, management of land use, etc.). But the relationship between local native inhabitants of the quarter and migrants is characterized by symbiosis as well as by frictions.

The network of relations between the migrants, the cities, and their places of origin is also of interest, though discussed only indirectly here. Frequently migration destinations are determined by group migrations or by the social network in the places of origin. This concerns compatriotic as well as family relationships. A permanent contact with their native areas enables a continuous crisscrossing between the traditional local sphere and the new forms of life in the big cities.

Rural to Urban Migration

Despite the vast array of publications on rural–urban migration in China, exact figures are understandably still hard to ascertain, since a consensus in the exact definition of migrants is missing and there is a lack of a consistent national survey. Though a great variety of sample surveys exist, in many cases their validity is hard to assess, since it is very difficult to obtain representative samples of rural migrants in urban areas of China. Nevertheless, some characteristic features of rural–urban migration can be presented with relative certainty.

First, most authors agree that the traditional urban institutional barriers which divided the urban and the rural sphere are no longer valid; however, the old separation between city and countryside is now replaced by new barriers which segregate urban migrants economically and socially from permanent residents within cities (Wang and Zuo, 1999). The background to this dividing line is still the dual *hukou* system, which denies migrants a permanent stay in the cities and, linked to this, access to housing, medical care, pensions, and more qualified and stable job opportunities.

Second, the number and destination of rural–urban migrants is at least roughly ascertainable. Most authors estimate the total number of migrant workers in China at between 60 and 80 million, about 50–60 million of them heading for cities (e.g. West, 1997; Li, 1998b; Gu et al., 1999; Rozelle et al., 1999; Solinger, 1999; Zhao, 1999b).

Third, the reasons for migration are now largely clarified, though the empirical figures given in different sample surveys and case studies still vary widely. Reasons for migration can be found at different levels, and they are obviously interrelated. At the macro-level, China's policy of opening up to the outside world and the location of foreign investment mainly in the coastal cities are important factors, since among other things they increased the large urban–rural income gap. The reintroduction of family farming has made redundant a large number of farmers and the accelerated growth of industry and commerce in the cities has created many centers of attraction (Chan, 1996a). At the meso-level the location of the migrants' places of residence is of importance within the regional context: typical places of origin are poor, fairly remote, but less rural villages in inland provinces. And at the micro-level there are numerous factors influencing migration (see e.g. Roberts, 1997; Yang, 1997; Gu et al., 1999; Wang and Zuo, 1999; Zhao, 1999c).

Of specific importance for migration seems to be the so-called chain effect: approximately 75 percent of China's first time migrants found jobs through relatives and friends, were reliant on their local fellow workers for information, or followed other rural workers from their village (State Council's Development Research Center, China Economic Monitoring Center, 1999b). Most migrant peasants are socially isolated because of their dialect, education, clothes, and eating habits. This social isolation is intensified by a spatial segregation, since many migrants not only live together in urban "villages," but also are together at their workplace, such as factory dorms, construction sites, restaurants, and workshops (Roberts, 1997; Wang and Zuo, 1999).

Migrants and Urban Bureaucracy

Since a considerable number of non-local people (*wailai renkou*) stay in big cities both as workers or employees and self-employed, numerous responsible authorities and administration offices are involved to administer the *wailai renkou*, including the job center, the office for industry and commerce, the tax office, the housing office, the office for family planning, and the town planning office. Coordinating authorities are the bureau for the administration of *wailai renkou* and the office to fight integratedly against crime (Hao et al., 1998).

Accordingly, the regulations for the temporary population are quite complex and complicated. For instance, in Beijing the city government has issued an "Instruction to administer non-local employees in Beijing." Nevertheless, many lower-level offices have problems in handling day-to-day business properly, because the superior authorities sometimes hesitate to give clear instructions, among other reasons to avoid conflicts with the temporary population (Arsilan et al., 1998).

Officially, migrants are only allowed to live and work in Beijing when they have obtained permission to reside and a permit to work. Additionally, women in their reproductive years need a certificate for marriage and reproduction, which is valid for three years. All these documents have to be renewed annually. The procedure for temporary residents to apply for documents – not only for those mentioned above, but also for a certificate of marital status, an ID card, and possibly documents regarding the right of ownership – is rather complicated. Further, any institution or person that wants to rent housing to non-local residents must obtain a house-leasing certificate from the district or county government and renew it annually. This certificate lays far-reaching obligations on the landlord, such as responsibility for preventing crime as well as for above-quota births (Zhao, 1999b, p. 782). Such a regulation clearly discriminates against temporary residents on the housing market. For those floating people who do not work, and for accompanying family members, exact legal provisions are missing. All in all, this situation seems to be adverse to temporary residents.

Thus, it is understandable that a substantial share – probably the majority – of the migrants live in the big cities without these permissions, especially without a work permit and a marriage certificate. In November 1995 only 40 percent of all temporary residents in Beijing possessed valid temporary residence permits (Chen, 1998). For the urban authorities it is impossible to carry out a tight permanent monitoring procedure, since most migrants are very mobile; many shift both lodgings and jobs several times per year. Circular migration is common; many migrant workers return home during the harvest or spring festival, and during their absence most landlords re-rent the rooms to others. And not a few local cadres are open to bribery and tolerate illegal practices.

On the other hand, officially registered temporary residents expect urban officials to give them assistance when they face such problems as high housing rents, housing shortages, personal security, and the lack of legal certainty (working overtime without payment, no work safety, problems regarding children's school attendance, too high fees, limited job opportunities, etc.). However, most migrant workers complain that they just have to pay a lot of money without receiving any service in return.

Offices concerned with the migrants have different goals and duties, e.g. law and order or revenue earning, to be carried out by the housing and taxation offices respectively. For instance, the city labor bureau wants full employment of city residents and therefore tries to keep down the number of outsiders or to prevent them to get certain jobs, while other offices such as the commercial and industrial bureau try to generate income also from the migrant workers (see also Zhang, 1998a, p. 90; Solinger, 1999, pp. 66ff).

When migrants live together in spontaneously created enclaves, in many cases the grassroots communities, such as village committees or township governments and their inhabitants, benefit significantly from floating people and therefore oppose the control policies carried out by the district or urban government. Many illegally erected buildings in Beijing's semi-rural suburbs have been tolerated silently by the village committees or township governments; many flats and rooms are leased to migrants without being reported to the responsible housing office (Chen, 1998).

A further problem is the fact that there is no straight line in the governmental policy facing the migrants. In the long run, the rather erratic official policy seems to be futile. The future policy toward migrants and the *hukou* system are widely discussed, though without much result. On the one hand it is argued that the strict implementation of the *hukou* system impedes normal economic growth, while other authors are of the opinion that abolition of the *hukou* system will cause chaos and disorder, since the big cities' infrastructure is already heavily overloaded. A comprehensive approach is needed to respond to the pressure, including administrative control in big cities, but also a more constructive and protective policy toward agricultural development and various kinds of service and training programs at all levels of administration to support migrant workers (Li, 1998b, pp. 54ff).

Migrant Enclaves: Development, and Spatial and Functional Structures

One of the major problems migrants have to face in the cities is accommodation, since much housing for the local residents is still provided by work units, though private ownership of housing has been re-established (Davin, 1999, p. 107). The housing opportunities for migrants are largely determined by the specific conditions of a particular city. However, according to the statistical data on temporary population published by the Administration Bureau of Household Registration in 1997, there are no significant deviations from the average figures in larger cities: about 39 percent of the temporary population stayed in rented flats or houses or with local households, while 17 percent lived on construction sites and 30 percent in company quarters (Shen, 1999). These data do not give any information on the spatial concentration of migrant workers in certain urban districts. Presumably, the major part of the about 40 percent of all migrants who lived in rented flats and houses or stayed as subtenants with local households is concentrated in informal settlements on the edges of many Chinese cities.

One of the reasons why migrants live close together in specific urban areas of big cities is to be seen in the above-mentioned chain migration. Settled migrants inform their fellow newcomers about job possibilities, introduce them to their own bosses, or offer them accommodation (Davin, 1999). This close social network, mainly based on kinship and same area of origin, creates migrant enclaves, often named after the sending province.

In the so-called "Zhejiang village" in Beijing, about 90 percent of the temporary residents stem from two counties (Leqing and Yongjia) in Zhejiang; most inhabitants of the "Anhui village" in the northern suburb of Beijing (Wudaokou) are from Wuwei county in Anhui province; in Shanghai most inhabitants of the "Hubei village" come from Xiaogang; the waste collectors in Changsha are mainly from the town Fenyan in the county of Jianli. Many other villages, such as "Xinjiang villages" in Beijing and Shanghai, "Henan villages" in Beijing, "Anhui village" in Shanghai, and "Hunan village," "Sichuan village," and "Jiangxi village" in Guangzhou bear similar features (Wang, 1995; Chen, 1998).

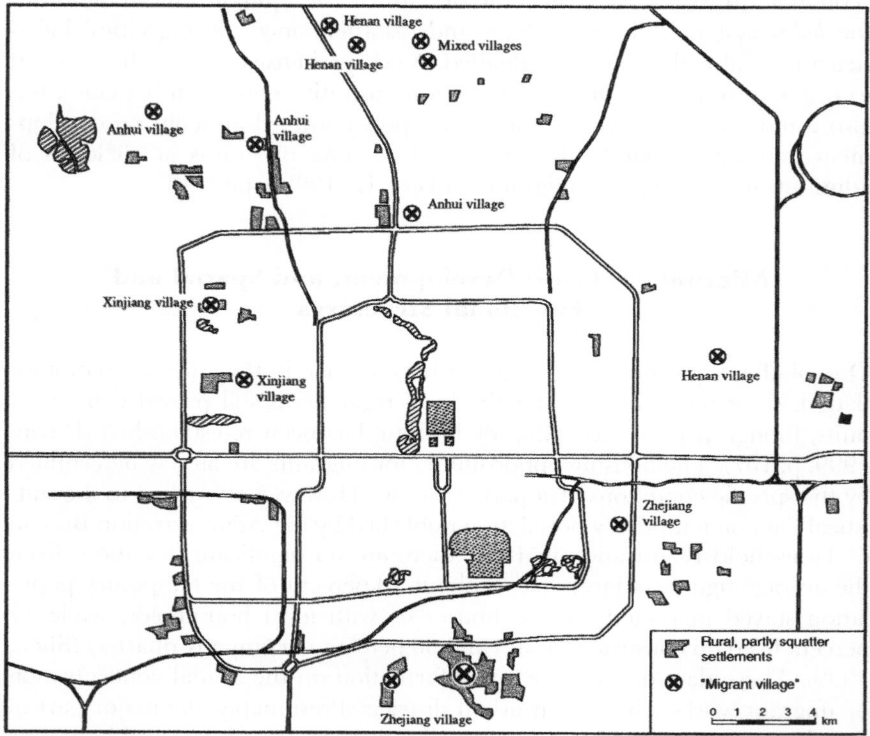

Figure 12.1 Migrant villages in Beijing (*Source*: Gu Chaolin, 1977; Xiang Bu, 1998; fieldwork, June 1998)

The term "village" is somewhat misleading, since it is not a natural village created by the migrants, but a conglomeration of dwellings mostly located in the urban–rural transitional zone. These "villages" of several thousands or even tens of thousands of temporary residents might expand over four to five existing natural villages (*ziran cun*) or even a number of administrative villages (*xingzheng cun*). In Beijing, approximately 57 percent of the migrant population stayed in the four suburban districts Chaoyang, Hadian, Fengtai, and Shijingshan, and another 18 percent in counties and districts further away, while only 25 percent lived in the four inner-urban districts, according to the sample survey of November 1994 (Song and Wu, 1997) (see figure 12.1).

At the edge of the city the informal economy provides sufficient opportunities for self-employment and jobs to be offered to co-migrants. Furthermore, ecologically harmful state and urban enterprises, having been relocated to the urban outer area, provide dirty and strenuous jobs for migrant workers.

Numerous township and village enterprises employ mostly non-local people to do the unpleasant jobs while the local residents work in administration and management. For instance, in a foundry located in the township of Datun, two-thirds of all workers are from other provinces, mainly from Henan and Shandong (Song and Wu, 1997). Additional reasons for migrants to settle down in the urban fringe are the availability of lodgings offered by the rural residents, sufficient open land, and a less strict governmental control (Liu and Liang, 1997).

Usually, village name-giving migrants related by blood, origin, and occupation are the minority in relation to the local residents and sometimes even to migrants from other areas. An exceptional case is the well known Zhejiang village, which is quite different from all the others in more than one respect. The migrants in Zhejiang village, but also in Beijing's Xinjiang villages, are often entrepreneurs investing money in businesses and creating employment, while migrants in the "Anhui villages" are typical surplus rural laborers, and people in "Henan village" are seasonal workers returning to their home villages during harvest time (Chen, 1998).

One illustrative example may show how such settlements develop. Some of the migrant enclaves (two Henan villages, one Anhui village and two mixed villages) are located in the northern suburb of Beijing clustering around the Institute of Geography, Academy of Sciences, comprising five administrative villages and four street committees near Datun Road, Beisihuan Zhong Road, and Anli Road. In November 1997 about 53,000 floating people lived in this area, approximately one-tenth of all floating people in Chaoyang district. Most (59 percent) of them stem from Henan province, 17 percent from Hebei, and 14 percent from Anhui, with the rest coming from Hubei, Jiangsu, Hunan, and north-eastern China (Chen and Zhao, 1998).

These migrant enclaves emerged within a relatively short period of time:

1 The germ cell was a couple from Anhui province who arrived in March 1991 to sell breakfast in the street. A few months later two other families arrived from the same province doing the same kind of business. The migrants were expelled in 1993, when the People's Congress held its meeting.
2 The years 1993–5 can be characterized as a zigzag phase: several markets and snack bars were established by migrants from Anhui to supply locals and migrant construction workers with breakfast, vegetables, and other food. The number of stalls increased quite quickly, until the city government drove the floating population away again when the International Women's Congress was held in Beijing in 1995.
3 Nevertheless, the year 1995 was quite favorable for the floating people in the northern part of Beijing, since the government's bid for the Olympic Games 2000 failed and consequently control over the floating people was

relaxed. The local village and township governments even supported the migrants to put up market stalls. The migrants' villages extended rapidly from the Datun to Wali township, clustering around the so-called Nangounihe village.

4 Since 1997 several larger settlements have developed, "villages" now known by their provincial origins (Anhui, Hebei, etc.). Furthermore, in the fairly large Henan villages a certain infrastructure and a range of services came into being, such as clinics, public baths, primary schools, hairdressers, and recreational facilities.

This example demonstrates not only the close interplay between shifting government interventions and the very flexible reactions of the migrant people, but also the local conditions for the development of migrant villages:

- The rapid increase in newly constructed residential and commercial buildings created various demands: the migrant construction workers needed food and clothing, the building trade material for construction and interior decoration.
- Many local – mostly former – peasants had rooms and business premises to let. Because of the expansion of the building area many farmers had lost their land and were no longer able to live on agriculture. For them it is difficult to find non-farm income, since they often reject low-paid and strenuous jobs. Therefore, income from letting rooms is essential. For instance, in the village Nangounihe, about 50 percent of the local workforce of 300 people are unemployed and stay at home, since their arable land is used for other purposes. However, the grain-tax still has to be paid in cash. To generate sufficient income, many former peasants enlarged their houses for rent and now earn between 1,000 and 2,000 yuan per month, sometimes even up to 10,000 and 20,000 yuan.
- Often, floating people have erected illegal structures because of the relaxed controls, openly or secretively supported by local governments, which earn considerable administration fees (about 6,000 to 7,000 yuan per year for a room in a business premise on a major street). Additionally, village and street committees built premises themselves to let to migrant entrepreneurs for 12,000 yuan a year.
- Even government and collective units in this area, including research institutions (such as the Institute of Geography) and schools, let premises and rooms to floating people to ease their own financial problems. Many *danweis* have literally pulled down the walls around their properties and built small business premises to let out to migrant entrepreneurs for on average 500 RMB per month. The incomes are shared between the *danwei* or several *danweis* and the responsible inhabitants' committee according to an exact plan.

- The example of the Academy and other institutions benefiting from the floating population is very interesting, since it is exemplary for the traditional dual structure of urban and rural land use. Since the 1950s and 1960s many state institutions and work units have been built as urban enclaves within the widely undeveloped rural areas, spatially separated from the central built-up core. These "leap-frogging" development structures remained more or less intact in the northern part of Beijing until the late 1980s, maintaining a separated rural and urban living pattern. In the Dahongmen area in the southern part of Beijing, where the "Zhejiang village" is located, a similar though much earlier development had taken place. Around a military airport many aviation- and aerospace-related factories, institutions, and warehouses had been erected as isolated urban enclaves surrounded by villages and agricultural land (see Liu and Liang, 1997). The present land-use conversion (to migrant settlements) is thus useful for the local landowners – mostly collectives rather than state enterprises – and land users such as villagers, township and village governments, local work units, institutions, and individual residents. They take advantage of a degree of administrative autonomy retained by the villages.

In detail, the single migrant-group villages vary in their structures and functions, because among other reasons each migrant group mainly covers a certain segment of the urban niche-economy. The migrants from Henan, for example, collect waste by cycling around in the city and picking up reusable waste. In one of the "Henan villages," located in the township of Wali in Chaoyang, waste (glass, paper, cardboard, scrap metal) is sorted and stored in huge rubbish heaps, each covering a floor area of about 2,000–5,000 square metres. The scrap dealers live in small huts in the immediate vicinity of the rubbish heaps. Since they have leased the plots from the local peasants who wanted to maximize their rent, this village has a very compact rectangular structure. Most of the scrap collectors and dealers earn only little money (Liu and Chen, 1998; own fieldwork, June 1998 and June 2000).

Among the several clusters of Henan villages, the largest can be found east of the Chaoyang Park in Liulituan and Dongfeng xiang, also located in the urban–rural transitional zone (Ma and Biao, 1998, p. 567). There, the migrant people work and live around a state-owned waste dump, which is subdivided and leased to garbage buyers mostly from Henan. Each of them hires two to three men – often migrant workers from Sichuan and Henan – who sort out the waste. A third group within this Henanese society consists of plain garbage collectors. Most of these scattered Henan villages lack not only infrastructure but also internal cohesion.

The "Anhui village," located in Wali township, is scattered, since migrants – predominantly from Anhui – stay with local residents in rented rooms or flats. Most of them work as small vendors, buying and selling vegetables and food in the nearby markets; others repair shoes, peddle small – partly illegal – items, or offer key services. They have business connections among each other. In these villages the infrastructure is badly developed, and only a few small shops exist.

Other migrant settlements have a ribbon structure. The so-called "Fujian village" in Haidian district, situated along a street (Jingli Street), has been established by migrants from Fujian and from Guangdong who sell building materials such as timber and aluminum. The traders work and live in small houses with a large floor space behind to store large amounts of construction materials. Though the government has repeatedly demolished the buildings, they always have been put up again.

The larger of the two "Xingjiang villages" has a similar ribbon structure. Uygur-minority migrants from Xinjiang rented houses from local residents along a street (Zengguang, Ganjiakou, in Haidian district) and rebuilt them to set up restaurants (Arsilan et al., 1998).

The "Zhejiang village," home to approximately 95,000 inhabitants mainly from two counties near Wenzhou in Zhejiang, and the largest and most influential migrant enclave in a Chinese city, is located in the southern part of Beijing centered on Dahongmen (Fengtai district). It comprises 26 natural villages, most inhabitants being concentrated in 12 of them. Administratively, the enclave is situated in the border area between eight street committees of the urban district and the rural township of Nanyan. Several "villages" are now exclusively inhabited by migrants from Zhejiang, who in many cases even stem from the same home village. The fate and structure of "Zhejiang cun" is well documented (see Wang, 1995; Liu and Liang, 1997; Meng and Cao, 1997; Zhang, 1998b; Biao, 1999).

Since about 1995 the cooperation between migrants and governments at different levels (township, district, city) has intensified and improved. The new commercial garment trade center (*Chengzhongcheng*), a complex of three large modern buildings, was jointly planned by the district government and the Beijing Industrial and Commercial Bureau, but investment came mainly from the traders, who on average spent 30,000 RMB per person. The main building alone accommodates about 4,500 trading stalls out of altogether 20,000 stalls in different markets. There are now some 20 different garment market places (Fieldwork June 1998 and June 2000; Ma and Biao, 1998, pp. 569ff; Zhang, 1998b, p. 347).

Today the "village" has a generally sufficient infrastructure, offering dispensaries, schools, nursery schools, doctors, restaurants, grocery stores, etc. Its size and economic power, its important garment industry, its well known commercial markets for textiles and garments, and its relatively close economic links with the state sector and bureaucracy obviously secure its further development. This extraordinary situation underlines its special position among all the migrant enclaves.

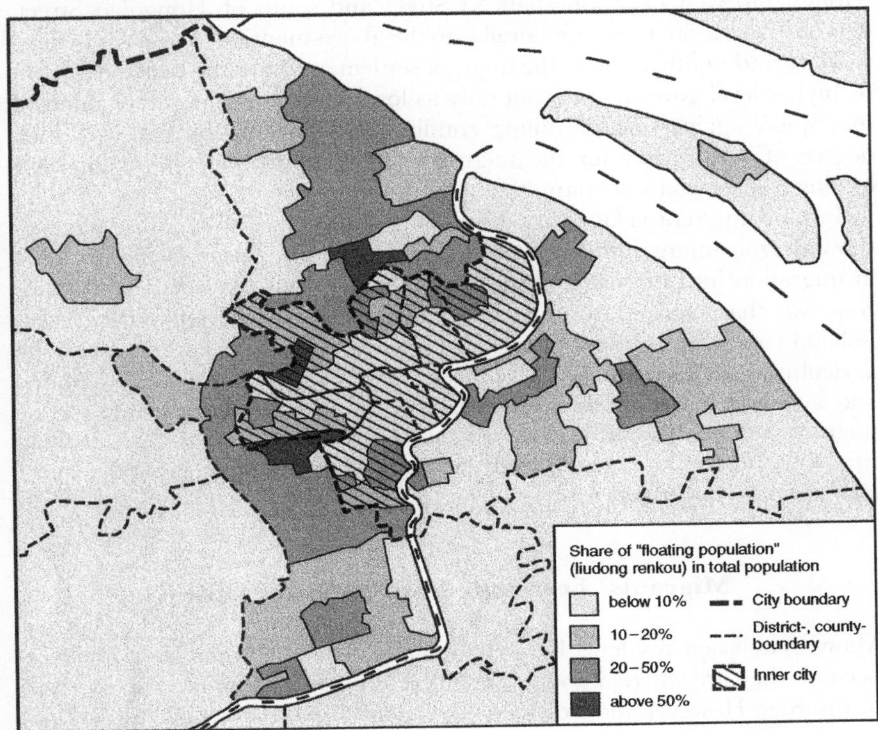

Figure 12.2 Location of the "floating population" in Shanghai, 1995 (*Source*: Bianzuan, 1997, p. 119)

Beijing is probably the city where the development and structure of migrant enclaves have been analyzed and documented better than elsewhere. There is no doubt, however, that there is similar development in many other big cities.

For example, in Shanghai about 12–15 migrant enclaves exist, mostly located in the fringe area of the city; for instance, in Pudong, Minhang, and Baoshan. Figure 12.2, presenting the distribution of the "floating population" in 1995, clearly indicates a high concentration of migrants (50 percent and more of the total population) along the boundary line of the inner city of Shanghai. The municipality has a long tradition of so-called shanty towns, since especially between the 1910s and 1940s many migrants from the country poured into Shanghai (Lu, 1995, pp. 563ff). After a break of several decades, we can now observe the revival of the rural exodus – naturally under changed social and economic conditions. A present-day example, the "Anhui village"

(Hongsicun) west of Zhongshan Xi Street and south of Hongqiao Street, demonstrates a situation quite similar to the above-mentioned cases in Beijing.

Here and in other places the migrant settlements have the tacit agreement of higher-level governments, but only as long as there are no other interests that speak against the prevailing conditions. This situation causes a high degree of uncertainty for the migrants and is partly the reason for their lacking a sense of local commitment.

In most migrant villages in both Beijing and Shanghai, land-use patterns show a highly unorganized and partly chaotic structure due to the fast increase in migration into the urban–rural fringe. While until the early eighties this zone was characterized by a mixture of agricultural land, traditional villages, isolated compounds of institutions, factories, and warehouses, nowadays the agricultural land is dramatically reduced and the villages have both expanded and acquired a densely built-up structure. A general characteristic of the migrant settlements is the highly unorganized use of all available land, leading to a dense mixture of housing, trade, manufacturing, and storage, and a severe lack of space for infrastructure.

Migrants' Economic Impacts in the Cities

Many established residents feel resentments toward the migrant population because they are worried about a strained infrastructure and a rise in crime or disorder. However, most of the reservations about the "outsiders" are not based on people's own experience but are caused by the negative image of the migrants presented in the Chinese media (Roberts, 1997; Ding and Stockman, 1999, p. 120).

As the examples above demonstrate, there are at least two types of positive impacts upon urban residents. First, the legal residents, who are living together with the migrants within one "village," benefit directly from the nonlocal population. Second, the urban labor market and especially the building industry and the service sector as a rule profit from the presence of migrant workers and self-employed households.

Many former local peasants and rural house owners are directly dependent on their income from renting out property to migrant workers. In many cases they are even exploiting the temporary residents. It is well known that most migrant workers have to pay rent which, in relation to the quality and size of housing, is much too high.

In "Zhejiang village," the usual relationship between "established locals" and "outsiders" is partly turned upside down. Today, in many cases the inmigrants from Wenzhou look down on the permanent residents, because the latter are dependent on them in many ways. Some are their landlords, others work as drivers or bodyguards for them. Even a few bankrupt state-owned enterprises rely on the Wenzhou people, since they would be unable to afford financial support to their laid-off workers without the migrants' rent payment (Fieldwork, June 1998 and June 2000).

Institutions and diverse administrative authorities also profit from the migrants. Many *danweis* tore down a part of the wall which had enclosed their buildings to erect small premises for letting to migrant entrepreneurs, and in many cases they also rent out rooms to migrants to balance their tight budgets. A large number of urban offices and bureaus regard migrants as a "golden goose" to be fleeced at any time. Last but not least, it has to be mentioned again that most of the village committees and township governments achieve considerable income by renting out land or premises to the temporary residents who live and/or work within their administrative areas.

Because of the specific structure of the Chinese economy, the urban labor market can be regarded as highly segmented (Taubmann, 1993; Nakagane, 1999). Despite increasing unemployment and serious underemployment in Chinese cities, so far the different segments of the labor market have only marginally overlapped each other. Fixed and qualified jobs in the formal urban labor market in both the state and non-state sectors (e.g. urban collectives or foreign–Chinese joint ventures) are usually reserved for permanent urban residents, while only temporary and unskilled jobs in the formal sector can be taken over by migrant workers. In the non-state formal sector foreign and joint-venture enterprises and – to a lesser extent – private enterprises are tapping the young rural migrant labor force, mainly in the Special Economic Zones and newly industrializing cities in Guangdong province (Wang, 1998, pp. 459ff; Davin, 1999, p. 115). In particular, young and unskilled female migrant workers are exploited as a cheap labor force for highly repetitive work in clothing, textiles, food processing, pharmaceuticals, electronics assembly, and consumer goods industries (Dai, 1998).

Hard or dirty jobs in the formal sector and jobs in the informal urban labor market are a domain of peasant migrants. In the latter segment there might arise competition between migrants and urban residents, since laid-off and unemployed urban workers from the formal segment might shift into this part of the labor market. A second job, so called moonlighting, is nowadays relatively common among state workers, who keep the safety net of their *danweis* and earn additional income in various informal sectors (Wang, 1998). So far, however, despite a high, though veiled, rate of structural unemployment in the cities, migrant workers are still needed. Since even laid-off workers from state-owned enterprises refuse to accept "dangerous, dirty, and hard" jobs in both the formal and informal sectors, temporary workers from the countryside have to take them on (Nakagane, 1999). Beside the fact that temporary residents, mostly small self-employed households, greatly enrich the service sector in the cities, the segmented urban labor market still offers complementary jobs to both permanent and temporary residents.

Conclusions

All available empirical data about the development and extent of rural–urban migration reveal that the previous migration movement will continue and probably increase. Most estimates conclude that about 20–30 percent of all rural laborers are underemployed (Wang, 1998, pp. 459ff; Nakagane, 1999, p. 16). If only 30 percent of the redundant rural workforce look for jobs outside their villages, a constant or even increasing potential source of at least 25–30 million additional rural–urban migrants remains. China's joining of the WTO will probably accelerate the process of restructuring and increase unemployment and underemployment. Beside a growing number of unemployed or laid-off employees in the cities, the city governments have to cope with an influx of migrants, which is irreversible and beyond the effectiveness of the traditional *hukou*-related set of actions. Nevertheless, it is to be expected that for the big cities the *hukou* system will not be abolished; for instance, Shanghai has reported a decreasing permanent population for several years – a fact that indicates a strict migration policy.

On the other hand, the central government has for the first time accepted rural–urban migration as a part of long-term development. According to recent news, Beijing is possibly intending to reverse the longstanding policy of limiting the number of residents in large cities. The State Development Planning Commission (SDPC) is proposing to resettle 85 million peasants into cities within the Tenth Five Year Plan (2001–5). Recently announced (though still tentative) plans call for the migration of 300 million peasants into urban areas over the next 15 years. However, the policy is still on the drawing board of the National Economy Research Institute under the China Reforms Foundation (*Business China*, October 25, 1999).

If this future migration stream is accepted by the authorities, only a very complex system of policies will be able to regulate migration and social and economic development in such a way that possible scenarios of "hundreds of millions of jobless peasants raiding the cities and the millions of urban underemployed workers starting a riot" (Wang, 1998, p. 464) remain a very unlikely nightmare scenario.

In the face of the enormous wave of migrant workers (*mingong chao*), most serious researchers suggest a set of possible strategies. To mention just one example, the "Research Group on the State of the Nation," Academy of Sciences, proposes the promotion of urbanization as the only solution (1996, pp. 82–6). Besides supporting agriculture, transferring investment into central and western regions, and encouraging the further expansion of township and village enterprises, a regionally differentiated foundation of thousands of new towns and cities is suggested. One of the key proposals to reduce the flow of rural laborers to major urban centers in the east is the development of medium-sized and large cities in poorer inland areas along major traffic routes, to initiate a diffusion effect in the rural areas and to offer sufficient job opportunities to keep some of the potential migrants in their home provinces.

In the big cities as destination areas, practiced regulation at the different administration levels is inefficient and inadequate as far as the organization and integration of migrants and migrant settlements are concerned. One important aspect is the lack of migrant security in the destination cities in terms of the legal right to reside for a longer period or even permanently. Therefore, a gradual reform of the *hukou* system seems to be inevitable. For instance, migrant workers should be allowed to settle with their families and become urbanized (see Knight et al., 1999). The reduction of the barriers for housing and school attendance will certainly increase social stability among migrant workers. These improvements to legal rights in the cities can be combined with a reorganization of the present land rights to ease the transfer and sale of family land in the place of origin (Zhao, 1999b, p. 779).

Another urgent problem is the chaotic management and usage of land on the urban–rural fringe. The conversion of agricultural land for urban use and the provision of some urban infrastructure create considerable speculation and intensive use of open land, since the value of land is changing rapidly (Liu and Liang, 1997, p. 107). Therefore, urban planning should be enabled to carry through a minimal land utilization plan. However, according to our own observations many town planners are still sketching green zones around the built-up area without having taken notice of the already existing intermixed land uses. They have to depart from their ideal concepts and recognize that this fast changing edge of the city urgently needs new planning ideas. Additionally, township governments and village committees, having gained most by the rapid development, should be urged to establish at least a certain level of infrastructure for the migrant population.

Acknowledgments

We would like to thank very much Professor Hu Zhaoliang of Peking University, Professor Chen Tian of Institute of Geographical Sciences and Natural Resources, Chinese Academy of Sciences, Beijing, Professor Zheng Gang of East China Normal University, Shanghai, and Dr Biao Xiang of Peking University for their kind assistance. Supported by the National Natural Science Foundation (no. 49971028) and the Innovation Project of the Institute of Geographical Science and Natural Resources, Chinese Academy of Sciences (CXIOG-B00-03).

13
Social Polarization and Segregation in Beijing

Chaolin Gu and Haiyong Liu

It is a popular belief that in socialist countries there is less sociospatial disparity than was present in the past or in comparison with Western countries (French and Hamilton, 1979). However, a new urban phenomenon – social polarization and spatial segregation – has taken place in Beijing since the implementation of the economic reforms and open-door policy in 1978, especially with the introduction of urban reforms in 1984. An enormous floating population began to migrate to urban areas from rural areas due to an erosion of the pillars of the migration controls, such as the state-run employment system, the resident registration (*hukou*) system, the grain rationing system, and the urban housing system. The original socialist equity of the urban classless society has been challenged by differential access to welfare benefits between registered urban residents and peasants living in the city. This difference has led to increased social polarization and spatial segregation in metropolitan areas as a consequence of the urban reform processes.

In the past three decades many researchers have argued the need for developing theories and approaches to the study of urban social structure (Rowthorn, 1974; Gregory, 1978; Johnston, 1983; Saunders and Williams, 1986). There have been two main directions of research: (a) urban social polarization (Russwurm, 1975; Bourne, 1982; Carter, 1982; Cook, 1988; Gregory and Urry, 1985); and (b) urban segregation (Pahl, 1975; Castells, 1976a, b). Works in traditional urban studies have, however, been unable to adequately address recent issues related to the rise of urban social polarization as a global phenomenon. Three major trends have been identified as important factors explaining this phenomenon. The first is the rise of post-Fordism since the 1980s (Albertsen, 1988; Gertler, 1988, 1992). The second is the development of a new international division of labor and related changes in urban social groups (Friedman and Wolff, 1982; Lash and Urry, 1994). The third is the growth of the new global economic system and the development of the world cities system (Sassen, 1991, 1994). With these developments and changes, urban social polarization and segregation are becoming an increasingly common phenomenon in many cities in developing countries.

The Social Polarization Phenomenon and Dynamics

The most general meaning of social polarization is the existence of a widening gap between the rich and the poor within a social entity. One of the most remarkable changes in Beijing during the past decade has been the appearance of such social polarization. In many Western countries, urban social polarization can be explained by the increasing gap in family income between the rich and the poor. This is partly the result of the growth in the urban migrant population and increases in the incomes of many in the professional working class (Lash and Urry, 1994). Immigration is at the root of social polarization in Western cities (Kesteloot, 1995). Beijing is experiencing a similar process: its rural migrants and well paid employees of foreign or joint-venture corporations have become two new social groups. One is the low-income group; the other is the high-income group. These two groups have created two new ends of the social ladder. The one end is composed of the floating population that is largely an unskilled and low-income social group. The other end consists of businesspeople and professionals working for foreign or joint-venture corporations who are making up a high-skilled and high-income social group.

Beijing's social polarization can be linked to two national-level policies: (a) successful rural and urban economic reforms that have created more opportunities for a floating population; (b) the open-door policy and increased international capital and technology flows, which have influenced the high-end professional working class. The growth of both social groups is also an interrelated process, paralleling the new international division of labor observed in many Western countries, where there has been a simultaneous growth of high-skilled and well paid jobs on the one hand, and unskilled, irregular, and low-paid jobs on the other hand (Friedman and Wolff, 1982; Sassen, 1991). In Beijing, social polarization dynamics can be explained by the following three main factors.

Transformation of the urban functional structure

Urban functional structural transformation from traditional manufacturing to service and high-tech industries is a driving force of urban social polarization. The growth of the service industry and economic internationalization are two basic dimensions of the changing environment in which urban social polarization has been occurring worldwide in recent decades. A new and specific form of urbanization is accompanying the new international divisions of labor and global economic restructuring (Sassen, 1994). These two processes are also resulting in a polarization of income distribution and occupational distribution. For this reason, social polarization has also been identified as a process related to the emergence of the new international divisions of labor and transformation of the urban functional structure.

The service and high-tech industries are playing important roles in Beijing's social and economic development. Although the secondary industry is still the dominant part of the urban economy, tertiary industries accounted for 47.0 percent of GDP in 1994. Employment increased about tenfold between 1949 and 1994, i.e. there was a net increase of 4,284,882 jobs in Beijing. Contributions to the increase came mainly from the sectors of tertiary industry (adding approximately 2,240,000 jobs or 52.34 percent); and then from manufacturing (adding 1,270,000 jobs or 29.69 percent). Within branches of the tertiary industries, employment in commerce and restaurant service increased fastest (addition of 400,000 jobs, 9.37 percent); culture and education sectors saw the second fastest growth (addition of 390,000 jobs, 9.02 percent); general services were third (addition of 330,000 jobs, 7.78 percent); and R&D and administration were about the same (addition of 260,000 and 244,000 jobs, 6.08 and 5.69 percent). It is notable that finance and insurance saw the fastest growth in the past decade. These increases in the service and high-tech industries, largely supported by global capital and technology, bring with them a growing wage differential between high-paid and low-paid jobs.

Foreign direct investment (FDI)

China has received a number of foreign direct investments since 1979. In Beijing, as the capital of China, the growth of FDI was faster than in other cities in China. Owing to the unbalanced distribution of FDI, some old manufacturing areas have decayed and some new service and high-tech industrial areas are booming in Beijing. In recent years, two inner suburb districts, Chaoyang and Haidian, have become main FDI areas, which has led to a sustained boom in their economies. Meanwhile, Chongwen and Xuanwu, two inner urban districts, have not drawn in as much FDI.

Since FDI brought a simultaneous growth of highly skilled and well paid jobs at management level, and unskilled, irregular, or low-paid jobs in the manufacturing industries in Chaoyang and Haidian, it is creating a new urban rich sector zone: East City district, West City district, Chaoyang district, and Haidian district. Another old residential and manufacturing area, Chongwen district, Xuanwu district, and Fengtai district, forms a sharp contrast: an old lagging sector zone.

Massive migration from rural areas

In Western cities, the migrants are the root of social polarization. Beijing is undergoing the biggest challenge of massive immigration from rural areas to the metropolitan areas. Labor migration may be coincident with capital growth, especially if FDI leads to a new concentration of labor-intensive manufacturing industries. Labor is also assumed to migrate in response to geographical variations in wages and job opportunities. Due to the introduction of market mechanisms and the flow of FDI, rural–urban migration has grown tremendously. Surveys of the floating population in both 1994 and 1998 estimated about 3.2 million such people in Beijing, accounting for nearly 30 percent of the total population.

New Urban Poverty and Its Causes

Compared with the distribution of wealth level among general urban population, migrants represent a new and disproportionately poor social group within cities. Due to the fact that the low-income and non-skilled migrants cause more conspicuous problems, considerable efforts have been made to explain what causes migrant poverty. A major characteristic of the occupation pattern of these poor migrants is that the floating population tends to depend on simple, unstable, temporary, and insecure unskilled and poorly paid jobs. In addition, they experience a shortage of social support and public infrastructure. We can also look for broader reasons to explain the economic stagnation of the migrant class through an analysis of the occupation structure, the lack of equal rights to live in cities, the family situation, and the education levels of the new migrants in Beijing.

Low-paid occupation structure

Most immigrants to Beijing are originally peasants. Their job typologies are mainly as follows. (a) *High labor intensity, low-income, but formal jobs.* Although the occupations of the floating population tend to concentrate on the secondary and tertiary industries, they get only half the salary of an urban resident, or less. Most of them replaced native Beijing workers in industrial sectors that contain low-paid jobs under the worse working conditions, such as spinner, caster, assembler, builder, and worker in heavily polluted chemical plants, or some office services, public service in catering industries, and private services that urban permanent inhabitants do not like to take up, such as professional typewriters, printing clerks, retailers, cashiers, and waitresses. (b) *Stable, contracting, but temporary jobs.* Another section of the immigrants are engaged in manual labor in small firms, such as family servants, housekeepers, babysitters, house decorators, furniture repairers, deliverers, street cleaners, family electrical equipment cleaners, movers, and porters. (c) *Unstable, temporary, and insecure jobs.* Others supply outdoor services, like street stand owners, peddlers, rickshaw boys, shoe menders, bicycle mechanics, locksmiths, watch repairers, seal engravers, knives sharpeners, and trash collectors. (d) *Jobs as either employees or employers in small firms.* Recently, some successful migrants have started to set up small firms, restaurants, and factories themselves. However, the traditional family structure of the immigrants does not provide sufficient conditions to allow for entrepreneurial success yet. The garments sector of Zhejiang immigrants in Beijing is a good example. Although the clothing and fashion industry became the main occupation of new immigrants in Zhejiang village, few were successful due to a shortage of management skills for operating a successful family workshop.

A very interesting phenomenon is the close relationship between the origins of migrants and their occupations in Beijing. From field surveys, we found the following. (a) Most male immigrants from Jiangsu, Shandong, and Hebei provinces work in construction sites as carpenters, bricklayers, and plumbers, while migrants from Henan collect waste or work as casters and street-cleaners, and those from Shandong are likely to be vegetable-mongers from Shandong to Beijing. (b) Most females from Jiangsu operate small businesses or become spinners and assemblers, while most from Anhui enter urban households as servants, babysitters, housekeepers, and so on. Migrants from Sichuan and Northeastern China work mainly in catering industries, such as restaurants, hotels, and other personal service sectors. (c) Migrants from richer provinces are likely to establish small firms, while those from poorer provinces open small local food restaurants or street stands. For example, the occupations of Zhejiang's immigrants are concentrated on clothing-making, shoe-making, locksmithing, watch repairing, and seal engraving, while most immigrants from Fujian and Guangdong set up small firms trading construction materials: firms specialized in wood or cement trading are mostly operated by Fujian people, and businesses engaged in aluminum alloy materials trading are run by people from Guangdong. Those from Xinjiang and Ningxia tend to open restaurants serving Muslim food, while migrants from Tibet or Qinghai are likely to vend their medicinal materials and herbs.

Restricted access to public services and opportunities in cities

According to a 1994 census, the average age of Beijing migrants was 27.7 years (28.5 for males; 26.4 for females). This was 6.6 years younger than the average age of the permanent urban residents. Migrants aged 15–59 years made up 87.9 percent of all migrants, while this age group made up only 60–70 percent of the permanent urban population. The youngest group (between 0 and 14 years) accounted for only 9.9 percent of the total migrant population, while the oldest group made up less than 2.2 percent. With fewer children and elderly, as a group, the migrant population has an advantage in terms of employment. However, the floating population from the rural areas, compared to the urban inhabitants, do not enjoy the same benefits as do urban residents, such as guaranteed education for children, access to low-cost health services and housing, and equal employment opportunities in state-owned enterprises or foreign and joint-venture companies.

Emphasis on savings

Marital status analysis of the female floating population showed that over 63 percent of them were married women with an average of 1.3 children. However, most of these are single-mother families given that there are only a small number of migrant families with husbands working and living in the same city. These women have to earn enough money to feed their families. In addition, for most males and the unmarried female migrants, their goal is to make more money to finance their weddings, to establish new families, or to rebuild their houses in their home towns. As a whole, the migrants live at a lower standard of living due to their high saving rate.

Low educational level

Only 3.1 percent of the Beijing's floating population had college degrees, while those with middle and primary school education accounted for 79.7 percent, and illiterate or almost illiterate migrants made up about 5.5 percent. The survey also showed that the educational level of female migrants was lower than that of male migrants. The proportion of migrants with higher than primary education was about 61 percent for males, but only 31 percent for females. As a social group with a lower education, it is impossible for migrants to succeed in the intense urban labor market. As a result, only low-paid, unskilled, or informal jobs, which urban residents are reluctant to take, are available for new migrants.

Table 13.1 Distribution of population density in Beijing, 1993 (number of streets)

	Population density (1,000 persons/sq km)										
	Over 40	*35–40*	*30–35*	*20–30*	*10–20*	*5–10*	*3–5*	*1–3*	*0.5–1*	*Less than 0.5*	*Total*
Xuanwu	2	2	1	2	1						8
Chongwen	2		1	2	2						7
East City		1	3	5	1						10
West City		1	2	3	4						10
Chaoyang		1		4	6	3	4	14	12	2	46
Haidian					9	3	1	2	5	7	27
Fengtai				1		2	2	5	3	2	15
Shijingshan					1	3	3	2	1		10
Total	4	5	7	17	24	11	10	23	21	11	134

Note: Street in China is similar to neighborhood in Western countries.

Social Segregation

In Western countries, changes in the housing market have been identified as a cause of social polarization (Forrest and Murie, 1988) and the process of urban social polarization has also resulted in urban spatial segregation (Lash and Urry, 1994). Similar urban problems are becoming more and more serious and common worldwide. Phenomena such as "underclass," "urban poverty," and "social polarization" bring with them sociospatial implications (Kempen, 1994). In Beijing, urban social segregation was greatly limited under the influence of the post-1957 socialist transformation, with the dominance of equity ideology in urban planning that put emphasis on the even development of new built-up areas. However, the social segregation of new poor rural migrants and high-income residents has led in turn to increased urban stratification and sociospatial divisions.

Table 13.1 shows that the spatial distribution of the population in Beijing in 1993 was very uneven. This spatial distribution of urban inhabitants serves as a frame of reference for examining the sociospatial division of the floating population. The census of the floating population in 1994 showed that 1.724 million people, or about 60 percent of the floating population, have found themselves permanent places to live. The survey also demonstrated that some working units that employed migrants were providing simple dwellings for them. Table 13.2 describes a relationship between employer units and shelters. As it shows, Beijing's floating population stayed mainly in construction sites, subordinate units, rural households, and cheap hotels.

According to the Beijing floating population census in 1994, new migrants from rural areas reached 2.877 million, but no information on their spatial

Table 13.2 Residencies and employer units of the floating population in Beijing, 1994

Type	*Immigrants*	*%*
Construction site	469,000	27.2
Office service	429,000	24.3
Rural families	256,000	14.8
Hotel	208,000	12.06
Small commerce and restaurant service	148,000	8.5
Training centers	93,000	5.4
Suburb agriculture bases	72,000	4.1
Offices from other provinces	54,000	3.1
Foreign offices	44,000	2.5
Hospital and sanatorium	25,000	1.4
Total	1,724,000	100.0

Source: Census of the floating population by the Beijing local government.

Table 13.3 Spatial distribution of the floating population in Beijing, 1994

	Total population (10,000 s)	*Inhabitants (10,000 s)*	*Immigrants (1,000 s)*	*Area (sq. km)*	*Ratio (Imm./Inh.)*	*Density of floating pop.*
West City	85.8	78.9	6.9	30.0	0.09	2,300
East City	72.0	64.3	7.7	24.7	0.12	3,117
Shuanwu	62.2	57.1	5.1	16.5	0.09	3,091
Congwen	46.5	43.3	3.2	15.9	0.07	2,013
Inner City	266.5	243.6	22.9	87.1	0.09	2,629
Haidian	157.5	140.3	17.2	426.0	0.12	404
Chaoyang	159.5	136.1	23.4	470.8	0.17	479
Fengtai	89.1	74.2	14.9	304.2	0.20	489
Shijinshan	35.8	30.9	4.9	81.8	0.16	599
Inner Suburb	441.9	381.5	60.4	1,282.8	0.16	471
Total	708.4	625.1	83.3	1,369.9	0.13	608

Source: *Beijing Statistics Yearbook* (1995).

distribution has been available until now. Table 13.3 shows the relative spatial distribution information from the 1995 *Statistical Yearbook*. As the table shows, about 66.6 percent of the floating population lived in three inner suburban districts: Chaoyang, Haidian, and Fengtai. It means that the ratio between immigrants and inhabitants reached 1 : 6 in the inner suburbs. The same ratio was 1 : 10 in inner-city areas with a higher density of inhabitants. East City and Xuanwu were two districts with a higher density of the floating population, while in Fengtai and Chaoyang the ratio between migrants and

Table 13.4 Change of spatial distribution of the floating population in Beijing, 1994

Region	*Immigrants*[a]	*%*	*Immigrants*[b]	*%*	*Immigrants*[c]	*%*
The inner city	229,000	26.17	NA		130,000	17.5
The inner suburbs	604,000	69.03	2,380,000	82.7	420,000	57.0
The outer suburbs	42,000	4.80	NA		188,000	25.5
Total	875,000	100.00	2,877,000	100.0	738,000	100.0

Note: NA, not available.
Source: [a] Beijing Statistic Yearbook 1995; [b] Census of the floating population by the Beijing local government; [c] Capital (Beijing) Planning Committee.

permanent urban residents was highest. Chaoyang saw the greatest concentration of migrants, in terms of both population count and density, owing to its booming economy in recent years (see table 13.3).

Comparing the spatial distributions of the floating population between 1988 and 1994, we found that the floating population tended to be living in the inner suburbs (*chengshi jiaoqu*) (see table 13.4). This change in spatial distribution is related to China's urban housing system. In the early 1950s, China had outlawed its real estate industry and privately owned housing was not encouraged, so the main urban housing market is the housing leasing market. Between the 1950s and 1980s, most urban public housing was constructed in newly built-up areas of the inner urban fringe. Private urban housing is distributed mainly in the old inner city and rural housing in the outer fringe or suburbs. Urban housing is in a supply shortage. Meanwhile, the rent in the unofficial (illegal) housing rental market is much higher than the standard rent in the open market. In the black market, the rent for public housing is higher than that for private housing, and the rent for private urban housing in the older inner city is higher than for rural private housing in the suburbs. For these reasons, the floating population is better able to find cheap shelters in the outer fringe or in the old inner city. However, due to the lower rents outside the city, the new rural migrants tend to concentrate in the urban fringe (Gu, 1995).

There are more than 100 peasant enclaves (migrant clusters) in Beijing. They are formed largely on the basis of geographic kinship (*diyuan*), especially relationships developed as a result of belonging to the same place of origin (*laoxiang guanxi*), which is rooted in the migrants' origins. Zhejiang village around Muxuyuan has become one of the biggest new slum areas, while there are some other peasant enclaves, such as Henan village, Xinjiang village, and Anhui village, around the urban fringe of Beijing, all of which are formed by peasants from the different respective provinces.

Zhejiang village

Zhejiang village is an outstanding example of peasant enclaves in Beijing. Compared with the above-mentioned villages, its population size is large enough to satisfy the threshold for grocery shops, medical services, and elementary education facilities, and the function of the village is relatively complete and advanced. The village typically assumes a pattern of polygons and a heavier residential density.

Residents of Zhejiang village are mainly composed of businessmen from Wenzhou, Zhejiang province. The geographical range includes the Dahongmen area of NanyuanXiang, where 24 naturally formed villages are involved. Up to mid-1998, an estimated 70,000–80,000 new migrants were living there, and these migrants have already completely replaced the original occupants, since most local owners moved out. Several successful Zhejiang businessmen even purchased old houses, and built more decent ones after bulldozing them. Most workers in the village are involved in garment making, services, and apparel retailing, while others are engaged in shoe fixing, locksmithing, and vending. Within the village, all kinds of facilities and markets, which mainly serve the garment producers and the villagers, have developed. They include wholesale and retail markets for dresses, cloth and silk, buttons, zippers, grocery stores, restaurants, clinics, and kindergartens. There are even Wenzhou's local specialities in most food markets and music cassettes of Wenzhou opera in some small stores. Zhejiang village is fairly large, while the family and original geographical linkages make its structure very clear in the sense that a specific part of the village is occupied by a clan from the corresponding sub-region of Wenzhou.

Anhui village

Anhui village is a type of migrant village characterized by scattered single migration households living in one large neighborhood. An Anhui peasant enclave in Beidingcun, WaliXiang, is representative of these. The major group of migrants residing in this village are from Anhui province. Beidingcun is a fairly large suburb village, where almost every owner has his or her leasing permit, although only a small number of these houses are occupied. Another feature of Anhui village is that it is not the usual case that landlords lease the whole house to their tenants, since their lessors tend to own small businesses without employees. In addition, the migrants in Anhui village keep their original lifestyle, following the scattered-spot pattern existing in southern Anhui. The migrant in Anhui village rarely has a stable job, with most people being involved in vegetable or traditional produce retailing. The lifestyles of individual migrants are fairly different and personal relationships among them are loose as well. The coming of these new "residents" failed to bring a considerable consumption augmentation and the threshold for several services has not been reached.

Henan village

Henan village is a special migrant village in Wali Xiang in Chaoyang district. The migrant clusters were created around several scattered landfills within a radius of one kilometer extending from the crossing of Datun Road and Zhongzhou Road. A floating population from Henan, Hebei, and the suburb of Tianjin comprises mainly garbage collectors, and more importantly most of them live around or within the landfills. These landfills (or trash storage plots) are leased to local villagers to manage. The managers of the plots split the whole court into several smaller plots and release these individual plots to senior migrants who have relatively sophisticated garbage management experience and adequate capital. These secondary managers then hire their own workers to collect, sort, weigh, and sell garbage in their plots. In turn, these workers live in shabby huts within the plots, with an accessory task – taking care of their "property" at the night. Typically the building materials of these cabins include boards and cardboard, which all come from the garbage. The cabins or huts in the plot make up the core of each migrant village, in which some independent garbage-men rent houses around the plot. Presumably, the resident density around the plot tends to become smaller as the distance to the plot becomes larger. In the neighborhood that is closest to the plot, usually, four or even more households share one house with a yard, where they can sort garbage and store materials temporarily. These garbage collectors and retailers outside the plots take advantage of the flexibility of retail prices and operation methods and attract lots of firms and persons that are involved in the recycling business. In turn, they occupy a considerable share of the recycled material market. There are hardly any grocery stores or medical facilities, even though the resident density of Henan village is fairly high, partly because the residents' income and consumption are too low.

Xinjiang village

Xinjiang village is one of the most distinctive of these peasant enclaves, since it was established by Uygurians, a minor nationality in China. Xinjiang village began to take shape in the later 1970s. Not all of the present residents in Xinjiang village migrated to Beijing directly, and some of them had gone through several cities or regions before they finally reached Beijing. At the beginning of their stay, they purchased silk scarves and cloth in bulk, then shipped the goods to their hometowns and sold them. From 1984, which was marked by the commencement of the nationwide urban reform, some Uygurians who saved money from the wholesale cloth business started to open their own restaurants, so as to avoid the intense competition in the reselling business.

There are two large Xinjiang villages, of which one is located in Zengguang Street, Ganjiakou, and the other at Weigongcun. Although the two villages are two kilometers apart, their structures are astonishingly similar. Both villages have a dual function – business and residency – and a typical business pattern involving Muslim foods, and, in addition, their expansion axes are similar downtown streets.

Owing to its preferable location, Zengguang Street, around the Ganjiakou Market, which is close to the agency of the Xinjiang Uygurian autonomous region in Beijing, bus stations, and post offices, became one of the largest Uygurian temporary settlements. Beishagou, where there are more cheap houses for rent, is adjacent to Ganjiakou Market, and accommodated more and more ambitious Uygurian migrants. According to the field survey, there are 27 Uygurian restaurants and nearly 1,000 residents.

The paths in the village connect the village residents with the city in terms of transferring people, goods, and information. The face of each single restaurant is on the side along the street. The basis of these restaurants is originally the old local flats, while the roof and front of each building are redecorated in a Muslim fashion. Behind each restaurant, one or two cabins are built as dormitories or operating rooms. The boss, his family, and employees live here. In Xinjiang village, due to the fairly high income of the restaurant bosses, they could rent a decent house (or apartment) with a yard to accommodate their family and employees. The landlords who lease houses to them have already moved into new houses outside of the current "village."

Even though there might be a couple of wealthy people in Xinjiang village, since the housing rent has been raised from 50–100 RMB per square meters per month in the early 1980s to 1,500–5,000 RMB per square meters per month now, and the heavy and discriminating administration fees are also a heavy burden for the Uygurian restaurant owners, the general economic status of the villagers remains poor and low. As far as the financial situations of the temporary employees are concerned, their monthly income is below half of that of the normal Beijing native citizens. Meanwhile, the landlords of the Uygurian restaurants gain a great deal of profit on the transactions and labor of these special rural migrants.

Due to the delicious, well favored, yet cheap food, and attractive Uygurian characteristics, Xinjiang village became a food-culture quarter, serving not only the Muslims in Beijing from all parts of China, but also the native citizens of Beijing and even foreign tourists and officials of diplomatic missions.

Fujian village

Fujian village is a type of peasant enclave, scattered by a bunch of construction materials trading companies expanding along Anli Highway in the northern suburb of Beijing. Since most businessmen here are originally from Fujian and Guangdong provinces, it is called "Fujian construction materials village."

The structure of Fujian village is fairly simple: the fence wall of a local factory makes up one side boundary and the highway takes the other side. Between the two boundaries there are temporary huts and warehouses, which are made of aluminum sheets. Each building has a dual function, i.e. including residency and business. Typically, the front part of the building is a yard, which is open to the highway. The emergence of Fujian village has been attributed to the real estate development in the northern suburb since the 1980s. Newly developed apartments, townhouses, and residential parks created a huge market for construction materials. Now, it attracts more and more construction material wholesalers, most from Fujian and Guangdong, and have sound capital pools and material sources. They come to build temporary buildings and locate their sale franchises. Even though the government seizes these illegal constructions again and again, they keep being rebuilt, since there exist markets and profits. The above-mentioned factory grasped this opportunity and accommodated these businessmen by building uniform shops and storage yards and leasing them. All the cabins are designed for the businesses of the clients, are connected with phone lines, and have open access to the highway. Due to the rich material storage and competent managing style these material wholesalers have gained the patronage of not only the suburb users but also the construction contractors and individuals from the inner city.

Conclusions

The social structure of Beijing has experienced great change during the past decade. Beijing's rural migrants and well paid employees who work in foreign and joint-venture companies are generating two new social groups: one is a low-income group, the other is a high-income group. These two groups have become two new poles on the social ladder. The poorer one is dominated by the so-called floating population: an unskilled and low-income social group. The wealthier one consists of businesspeople and employees who work in foreign or joint-venture corporations: a high-skilled and high-income social group. Beijing's social polarization is related to two factors: (a) the success of domestic rural and urban economic reforms, and their impacts on the movement of China's floating population; (b) the open door policy and international capital and technology flows which have influenced the growth of a new high-skilled and well paid group. Nowadays, new poor rural migrants and high-income earners are leading to greater urban stratification and sociospatial division by way of social segregation. The new rural migrants tend to concentrate in the urban fringe, since some surplus and cheap rental housing exists in this area. It is necessary to launch an effective policy in response to Beijing's floating population, which includes: (a) addressing urban growth through low-cost investment projects, and correct macroeconomic policy; (b) tackling three obstacles to eliminate the incidence of urban poverty, i.e. wages, prices, and public services; (c) coordinating the relationship between urban economic growth and environment management for sustainable development of Beijing's metropolitan fringe.

Acknowledgments

This chapter was written as part of a joint research project "Study on Urban Social Geography in Beijing" funded by the Chinese State Natural Sciences Fund (NSFC Grant 49871031) and Chinese Academy of Sciences' key research project (1995–2000): K8952-J-206. We would like to thank Alana Boland for her assistance on the first version of this work.

14
Temporary Migrants in Shanghai: Housing and Settlement Patterns

Weiping Wu

Since restrictions on temporary migration to cities were formally lifted in 1983, China has witnessed the largest tide of migration in its history – estimated at between 70 and 100 million migrants – and the dominant stream has been rural–urban migration. Officially recognized as temporary migrants, not permanent, and expected to return to their origins in the long run, most cannot obtain urban household registrations at the destination. Nevertheless, many temporary migrants stay in the cities for a prolonged period of time and often with their families in tow. For instance, Beijing's 1997 Floating Population Survey reports that close to half a million migrants have lived in the city for more than three years.

Migrant residential patterns have been a major influence on urban development in cities elsewhere in the world. For many migrants, urban life is precarious – lack of shelter, low and uncertain earnings, and increased threat of violence. The access to shelter, in particular, is worsening. Given the severe shortages of affordable housing in many developing cities, squatter settlements and urban slums have been the principal locations receiving migrants, many of whom are never fully integrated and become a permanent urban underclass. On the other hand, some migrants also bring with them informal channels for the flow of capital, skills, and social connections that can improve their economic opportunities and living experiences in cities.

This chapter examines migrant housing and settlement patterns in China's large cities, with a focus on Shanghai. The subjects of my study are temporary migrants who have moved to the city since the 1980s from outside of

Shanghai for economic reasons (these are only one portion of the entire "floating population," which also includes tourists, people on business, and other short-term visitors: Chan, 1996b). The temporary status refers to migration without official changes of registration from the origin to the destination. The chapter is motivated by two research questions: (a) how are migrant housing patterns affected by individual-level factors; and (b) what environmental factors influence migrant settlement locations in the city? Key findings are based on results drawn from the 1997 Shanghai Floating Population Survey as well as results from earlier surveys, and new fieldwork in Shanghai. Metropolitan-wide analyses are used to determine aggregate residential and settlement patterns of migrants. Individual-level analyses determine how housing choices correspond to personal and household characteristics.

Studying Migrants in the Context of China

Many of the prevailing theoretical inquiries on migrant settlement have evolved in a context in which private land ownership, housing, and rental markets are functional, and thus have largely focused on microanalyses. Turner's benchmark model (1968) suggests a two-stage process for rural–urban migrants in urbanizing countries: initial settlement in central city slum rental units and subsequent intraurban relocation to peripheral self-built or squatter settlements. Research on many developing countries suggests that migrant residential pattern is affected by a number of individual-level factors, including duration of residence in the city, employment status, and income level (Turner, 1968; Sudra, 1982; UNCHS, 1982; Conway, 1985; Gilbert and Varley, 1990; Selier and Klare, 1991; Klak and Holtzclaw, 1993). Specifically, there appears to be a direct relationship between housing choices (renting versus ownership) and the economic status of migrants. Often it is only after migrants reach the stage of a secure job with a reasonable income that they are able to become owners of a dwelling. Housing type is directly linked to the length of residence in the city. Over time migrants tend to move from rented rooms to squatter dwellings and then to houses. A number of studies also assert that squatter housing provides certain advantages over renting or buying on the formal market, serving the economic function of reducing or eliminating housing costs for migrants (Collier, 1976; Ulack, 1978; Costello et al., 1987).

Migrants are attracted to different parts of a city for different reasons. Proximity to existing or potential employment is a major determinant of their locational behavior. The formation and development of any informal settlement is often linked to changes in the economic activity of the surrounding area (Sudra, 1982; Conway, 1985; Gilbert and Varley, 1990; Selier and Klare, 1991; Klak and Holtzclaw, 1993). Others point out the importance of kinship and friendship ties, acting as social institutions (Abu-Lughod, 1961; Collier,

1976; UNCHS, 1982; Banerjee, 1983). Migrants' first place of residence in the city is largely predetermined by the location of kin or friends. A typical migrant gravitates to a small area of the city where people from his home place are already living and this results in the formation of "small enclaves of ex-villagers" (Abu-Lughod, 1961, p. 25).

Institutional factors, such as housing and land market dynamism, are also important in the migrant settlement process. In addition, any study of migrant residential patterns requires some understanding of how existing city residential areas are distributed geographically by socioeconomic status. In a number of developing countries with continuing urbanization, inner-city slums are no longer found to be the major receiving areas for new migrants due to the expansion and redevelopment of the commercial core and in turn the rapid rise of land costs. Large-scale squatting, mainly in the urban periphery, has occurred in cities where there are large areas of state-owned land around the city. Squatter settlements have also arisen as a result of the inability of government to meet the increasing demand for low-income housing, as well as speculative price levels in formal housing markets. Tenure or amenity considerations are often less important in driving migrants into peripheral settlements than the mere urge to escape continuously rising rents within the city (Collier, 1976; UNCHS, 1982). Hence, supply aspects of the housing market, rents and housing prices, are critical.

As China's economy undergoes the transition from plan to market, housing and land systems operate with a significant level of uncertainty and fluidity. There is not yet a well developed housing market and the secondary rental housing market is still in its infancy, with little regulatory oversight. Although housing is no longer a free public good to most people and rent has increased significantly, there is still a long way to go before the allocation of housing is controlled by the market (Tong and Hays, 1996; Zhou and Logan, 1996; Bian et al., 1997a). The rental market is further limited by the acute housing shortage in many large cities; for instance, per capita living space in Shanghai is currently about 11 square meters. Moreover, unlike some other former socialist states, China so far has not initiated a privatization program for land. It has chosen to preserve state ownership but permitted user rights (as distinct from ownership rights) of urban land to be leased out during urban land management reforms since the late 1980s. As a result, the security of obtaining housing and land tenure, shown as a chief factor for migrant residential mobility in many developing countries, may be irrelevant in China's context.

The tendency of migrants to cluster and congregate by areas of origin is relevant in China's context. Native place identity often is a critical component of personal identity in the ethnically homogeneous Chinese population (Roberts, 1997; Ma and Xiang, 1998). The function of social or kinship networks is often intensified if they are structuralized, with the emergence of migrant community elites and hierarchies. This structure may provide some protection to migrants in dealing with the outside world, offer assistance with information and housing, and reduce risks associated with migration and circulation (exemplified in the functions of *pondok* or community centers in Indonesia's urban migrant communities: see Jellinek, 1977). There has been some evidence that such structuralized social or kinship networks operate in emerging migrant communities in some Chinese cities (Ma and Xiang, 1998; Wang et al., 1998).

Migrant Housing Patterns

Housing in Shanghai, as elsewhere in China, was primarily provided through a system of welfare, low-rent housing distributed by either working units or municipal governments. A significant reform came in 1991, when a policy scheme was formulated that introduced a new mechanism of housing provision, one of the most comprehensive in the nation (Wu, 1999). The city, employers, and employees would all contribute through a newly established housing provident fund (*gong ji jin*), gradually shifting to a paid, self-supporting housing distribution system. The China Construction Bank was first authorized to supply mortgages to qualified home-buyers on behalf of the housing provident fund. Since 1998 all banks may cooperate with the fund reserve to offer various types of mortgages. In addition to new home purchases, many people have bought property rights to the homes they acquired under the old welfare housing system. Since early 1998 those with property rights can also put their homes on a secondary housing market and trade for better housing (Wu, 1998d).

Most migrants, however, cannot participate in this reformed housing distribution system. Without permanent residency in the city, they do not have access to urban public education, most municipal housing programs, and the pension system. As the housing market further liberalizes and a rental market develops, however, migrants may begin to have more options. For instance, Shanghai has begun granting a special type of residency to migrants. With cash purchase of housing units worth 100,000 yuan or more, depending on location, migrants can obtain the special residency that can become permanent after five years (Zhu, 1999). But this policy is only in favor of high-income migrants and is beyond the reach of most.

Housing choices and conditions

The operation of China's housing distribution system has relied on a vast number of state and collective working units, many of which provide basic housing and services to migrant workers. This arrangement is preferred by

Table 14.1 Migrant housing patterns in Shanghai (percentages)

	Hotels	*Dorms*	*Staying w. local residents*	*Renting public housing*	*Renting private housing*	*Renting self-built sheds*	*Self-built sheds*	*Purchased housing*	*Boats*	*Others*	*Total number of migrants*
Overall	1.1	33.1	8.6	13.9	**33.4**	5.2	2.0	0.9	0.2	1.7	22,558
Central downtown	3.0	15.3	**37.8**	26.8	10.1	3.1	0.3	0.2	0.0	3.5	1,591
Built-up districts	4.3	**42.5**	14.9	11.5	12.5	8.8	2.4	0.8	0.0	2.2	3,613
Peri-urban areas	0.1	31.3	4.6	13.4	**40.5**	5.6	1.9	0.8	0.0	1.7	13,270
Suburbs	0.6	37.7	5.0	12.3	**37.8**	1.5	2.4	1.3	1.1	0.3	4,084

Note: The category of location is based on both the 1993 and 1997 Shanghai Floating Population Survey. In the 1997 Survey, central downtown includes ten sub-districts in the very center of the city. Built-up districts refer to 16 sub-districts lying outside the downtown core but inside the ring road. Peri-urban areas consist of the rest of the sub-districts in the city proper, including those in the four districts that were recently upgraded from rural to urban status. Suburban/rural areas refer to the six outlying counties in Shanghai metropolitan area (today two of them have been upgraded to urban status). See Zhang et al. (1998).
Source: Based on a sample of 22,558 migrants coming from outside of Shanghai and for economic reasons in 1997.

government authorities, since it provides a better managed working and living environment in which matters related to temporary work and residence permits can be handled by the employer or enterprise. A Ministry of Labor survey of 120 enterprises in four cities (Beijing, Wuhan, Suzhou, and Shenzhen) shows that, on average, about 75 percent of labor migrants employed by the enterprises live in institutionally provided dormitories (based on own data analysis).

Private rental housing has become increasingly popular in Shanghai, and a variety of housing types is involved. Most is found in areas that used to be or still are agricultural within the Shanghai metropolitan area, where the owners were not eligible for urban public housing. Even with reforms, most of Shanghai's own residents with rural household registration do not have access to the municipal housing provident fund and related low-interest mortgages. In addition, urban residents who have purchased property rights to their public housing can rent it out upon obtaining permits, and some even rent out public housing that is prohibited from market transactions. There is also the rental of rooms built without proper permits or of rooms designated for institutional purposes. The rental market, however, is still in its infancy and operates without the necessary market rules.

Institutionally provided dormitories and private housing rental are the key housing choices for economic migrants, each accommodating about 33 percent (see table 14.1). These dorms are mainly provided by enterprises and businesses, but also include temporary housing on construction sites. Two other popular migrant housing choices are staying with local residents and renting public housing, which are particularly common in central downtown and other built-up districts. Most migrants staying with local residents are either relatives of or employed by the urban households. Other types of housing, including hotels, renting self-built sheds, purchased housing, and boats, accommodate only a limited number of migrants. In particular, housing ownership is minimal among migrants, at a mere 0.9 percent. Income level, in addition to restricted access, is likely the key factor. The mean monthly income for those migrants who own housing is almost twice that for an average migrant (1,002 versus 623 yuan).

Migrant housing patterns clearly differ among different geographical locations. Metropolitan Shanghai today consists of 17 urban districts and three suburban counties. These 20 units are then divided into street subdistricts and townships (a total of 312 in 1999: see Shanghai Statistical Bureau, 2000). In the central downtown area, where per capita housing area is small and industrial activities are limited, most migrants do not live in dorms or rent private housing, but instead stay with local residents or rent public housing. Outside of this central area but within the ring road, more migrants live in dorms than in any other types of housing. For migrants in both peripheral and suburban areas, private rental and dorms are the main choices. Such differences in housing patterns are likely to be related to the availability of housing and employment opportunities across different parts of the city.

Housing conditions for migrants do not compare favorably with those for local residents. Based on the results of a 1995 survey of over 3,000 economic migrants and 1,500 local residents, per capita usable area (including area used for bathroom, kitchen, and other auxiliary purposes) for migrants is only about half that for local residents (8.3 versus 15.5 square meters). The majority of migrants live in places where there are no kitchen and bathroom for their own use, although such basic utilities as water and electricity are available. Only about 18 percent of migrants have access to their own kitchens, as compared to 63 percent of local residents; about 11 percent of migrants live in housing equipped with private bathrooms, as compared to 51 percent of local residents (based on own analysis).

A new type of housing is becoming available in some areas of Shanghai – migrant housing complexes managed by subdistrict and township governments (the neighboring city of Hangzhou follows this practice as well: see *Liberation Daily*, July 14, 1999). Partially to reuse vacant housing once built to temporarily accommodate relocated local residents and partially to better manage the increasing migrant population, Taopu Township in the west of the city first began this practice. Pudong also began organizing similar facilities in 1999 and planned to open more, using a variety of management methods. Some reuse old temporary housing while some are new residential compounds built by large enterprises. One housing complex managed by Qinyang Township in Pudong has a capacity of 1,500–2,000 residents and is equipped with a community activity center, a small clinic, and a community security team of 29 people. The complex accepts migrants working in nearby enterprises or engaged in small businesses for a sustained period of time. Currently it is about two-thirds full due to its relatively low rents.

It appears that informal settlements are not a viable option for migrants, unlike in many other developing countries, largely due to the Shanghai authorities' control of migrant congregation and squatting. There are some small clusters of temporary housing that do not seem to belong to any enterprise or organization and that resemble squatter settlements. But the size of these clusters is no more than a handful of sheds on open farmland or areas undergoing development (field visits). However, a number of communities with concentrated migrant groups have been in existence in Beijing for over a decade (Ma and Xiang, 1998; Wang et al., 1998).

Individual-level determinants of migrant housing

Given the circulating nature of China's migrants and limited possibilities of settlement in destination cities, it is useful to understand how migrants make

Table 14.2 Migrant housing patterns by individual-level factors (percentages)

N = 22,558	*Dorms*	*Staying with local residents*	*Renting private housing*	*Renting other housing*	*Others*	*Total*	*Combined*
Type of employer							
State enterprises	**67.8**	5.5	12.6	10.4	3.7	100.0	17.3
Collective enterprises	**54.9**	4.4	21.3	14.1	5.2	100.0	13.4
Foreign enterprises	32.0	6.6	**52.2**	7.7	1.5	100.0	7.9
Private enterprises	28.5	11.4	**31.0**	24.3	4.8	100.0	6.0
Township & village enterprises	**57.8**	4.3	29.9	6.1	1.9	100.0	10.1
Self-employed	5.0	12.9	**45.2**	29.3	7.6	100.0	38.0
Others	28.2	7.3	30.2	20.8	13.4	100.0	7.3
Combined	33.1	8.6	33.4	19.0	5.8	100.0	100.0
Type of employment							
Construction	**72.1**	2.5	14.7	8.5	2.2	100.0	24.1
Industry & transportation	35.9	5.7	**40.9**	14.5	3.0	100.0	30.5
Agriculture	25.6	2.5	21.7	**32.3**	17.8	100.0	4.4
Trading	4.9	8.8	40.8	37.1	8.4	100.0	14.4
Services	7.7	23.3	35.5	26.1	7.4	100.0	15.0
Others	15.8	12.3	45.0	16.2	10.7	100.0	11.6
Combined	33.1	8.6	33.4	19.1	5.8	100.0	100.0
Length of residence in Shanghai							
Less than a month	**32.9**	9.4	28.1	19.5	10.1	100.0	9.8
A month to half a year	**45.5**	6.4	26.8	18.2	3.2	100.0	22.3
Half to one year	**37.7**	4.8	36.7	15.9	4.9	100.0	22.4
One to five years	25.7	9.5	**38.6**	20.9	5.3	100.0	35.3
More than five years	21.5	18.3	**27.9**	21.1	11.1	100.0	10.2
Combined	33.1	8.6	33.4	19.1	5.8	100.0	100.0
Type of household registration prior to migration							
Urban	18.7	25.2	17.8	**26.8**	11.6	100.0	10.1
Rural	34.7	6.8	**35.2**	18.2	5.1	100.0	89.9
Combined	33.1	8.6	33.4	19.1	5.8	100.0	100.0

Note: Differences by all five factors are statistically significant at 0.0001 (Pearson chi-square).
Source: Same as Table 14.1.

housing choices. Empirical analysis using a sample of 22,558 economic migrants from outside of Shanghai reveals some of the individual-level determinants (see table 14.2). There is less than a 0.1 percent chance that the distributions of key migrant housing choices would by chance differ as much as they do among types of employer and employment, length of residence in the city, and types of household registration prior to migration. Consequently, these differences are statistically significant. A conventional factor – income – appears to be affecting housing choices as well. But further analysis shows that income is correlated with types of employer, as migrants working in state and collective enterprises, on average, tend to have higher income levels than those self-employed (based on own data analysis). Therefore, the type of employer is a more important determinant and income plays only a small role.

Employment-related and migration-related factors significantly affect migrant housing patterns. Those working in state, collective, and township enterprises are mostly likely to be living in dorms, while self-employed migrants tend to rent private housing for accommodation. The majority of migrants working in the construction sector also live in dorms. Housing patterns for migrants involved in other employment activities are less clear-cut. Migrants who have lived in the city for a longer period of time are more likely to be living in rented housing than those in the city for less than a year. Another migration factor – entry method into the city – also appears to be affecting migrant housing patterns. When migrants come to Shanghai in an organized manner, such as recruited by Shanghai enterprises or "exported" by local governments, they tend to live in dorms. But additional analysis shows that the migration entry method is correlated with employment status. Migrants coming to Shanghai this way are more likely to work in state, collective, and foreign enterprises; whereas those who have migrated on their own tend to be self-employed in the city.

Migrants from rural origins show fairly different housing patterns from those from urban origins (see table 14.2). The former are more likely to be living in rented private housing and dorms, while the latter often stay with local residents or rent public housing. The distinction between rural and urban migrants is obvious among other attributes as well. Compared to rural migrants, urban migrants tend to be older (average age of 33 years compared to 29 years for rural migrants), with better education (42 percent with high school education compared to 8 percent), settling in more central areas of the city (47 percent compared to 20 percent), and working more frequently in trade-related jobs (47 percent compared to 28 percent).

Geographical Distribution of Migrants

In addition to economic factors, existing urban land-use patterns determine and in turn are affected by migrant settlements. More or less following a concentric pattern, Shanghai has a history of residential differentiation and migrant enclaves, dating back to the pre-1949 period. Shanty towns in the pre-1949 period were located along the boundaries of foreign concession areas and in areas designated for Chinese residents (Lu, 1995). Today, there are still signs of such shanty towns in several districts located immediately outside of the central downtown. But residential differentiation has been reduced markedly, with many years of building public housing and accelerated efforts to redevelop shanty areas. For instance, three extremely crowded slum neighborhoods in Putuo District lasted for more than half a century and were finally razed in 1999. Still, in many parts of the central city, the extreme

Table 14.3 Geographical distribution of Shanghai's floating population, 1986–1997 (percentages)

	Central downtown	*Built-up districts*	*Peri-urban areas*	*Suburban/rural areas*
1986	19.6	20.0	41.0	21.4
1988	12.3	13.8	51.9	22.0
1993	5.2	1.2	65.4	19.2
1997	7.7	16.3	58.4	17.6

Note: No detailed data are available for migrants coming to Shanghai for economic reasons (the focus of this chapter) for the 1986, 1988, and 1993 surveys. As a proxy, this table uses data for the entirety of the floating population surveyed in Shanghai's districts.
Source: Wang et al. (1995), Zhang et al. (1998).

conditions of high-density, rundown housing, aged infrastructure, and mixed land-use patterns are making the redevelopment effort a challenging one. As a way out, accelerated urban growth during the reform period has led to increasing concentration of functions on the outskirts of the built-up areas, in the form of high-tech development zones, office and industrial parks, and commercial subcenters.

Shanghai, therefore, may resemble a number of developing countries with continuing urbanization, where inner-city housing is becoming less attractive to migrants due to the redevelopment of the commercial core and in turn the rapid rise of housing costs. During the mid-1980s, comparable numbers of migrants lived in the urban center (combining the central downtown and built-up districts) and urban periphery (see table 14.3). But with continuing urban expansion and downtown redevelopment, Shanghai's urban periphery is now the primary receiving area for migrants (see table 14.3). The urban periphery today refers to outlying districts at the edge of the city property or built-up area, often acting as the intermediary between agricultural land in suburban counties and urban land use in the center. It is a similar concept to peri-urban areas. The urban periphery in Shanghai's 1997 survey, for instance, consisted of the subdistricts outside of the ring road and four districts that were upgraded to urban status (from suburban counties) only recently.

Environmental factors

Migrants are attracted to different parts of a city for a variety of reasons. One key factor likely to count for migrant concentration in the urban periphery is the availability of employment opportunities. In many large Chinese cities, accelerated urban development has intensified sprawl and led to a concentration of new construction on the outskirts of urban built-up areas. The urban periphery is often viewed by the authorities as a growth area for urban expansion. New functions, such as industrial parks, commercial subcenters, and technology development zones, are increasingly built there. Moreover, the urban periphery often houses a large number of wholesale markets for agricultural products because of its proximity to suburban farms.

Availability of rental housing is another important factor. In the urban periphery, private housing is more common because of the previous rural status of many peripheral districts. In addition, population density is significantly lower than in the urban center, and per capita living space is much larger. As a result, rental housing is more readily available and costs less in the urban periphery. Under less strict government supervision, local residents in these peripheral districts have reverted to building low-quality rental housing on vacant or farmland to make a quick profit. Evidence shows that even migrants in Beijing's large migrant communities in the urban periphery rent from local residents (Wang et al., 1998).

Peri-urban areas, where urban and rural land uses intersect, offer some unique attractions to migrants. The situation of a village in Baoshan district is a good case in point (interviews and field visits). Prior to 1984, the village occupied mostly agricultural land across an area that today belongs to three districts – Hongkou, Yangpu (both are now central city districts), and Baoshan. The wave of urban development as well as redistricting has since reshaped the village and left it with only about 0.15 square kilometers of agricultural land (within a total area of 4 square kilometers). The key sources of income for the village today are the nine enterprises and a nursery run by the village, as well as fees from land rental. Among the 750 or so village residents, only about 100 maintain agricultural household registrations and receive economic benefits directly from the village. The rest have been converted to urban status (*nong zhuan fei*), once their land has been acquired in exchange for jobs in state enterprises, and their ties with the village have been severed economically. But most of the converted urban residents in the village continue to live in old, privately owned farmhouses as development authorities have tended to avoid acquiring rural neighborhoods due to high costs of relocation.

Inexpensive rental housing is readily available in the village. Over half of the households or 188 households in the six village neighborhoods together rented out 783 rooms to migrants as of May 1999, at the rate of about 200 yuan for a room of 12 square meters (a price that could easily double in downtown neighborhoods). There are a number of reasons behind this. First, village residents have been allocated ample land to build private living quarters and an average household of four people tends to have at least eight to ten rooms (the average number of rooms rented out by a household was four rooms). Second, many of the newly "converted" urban residents have been assigned jobs in state enterprises that today are facing a great deal of pressure to restructure. Because of their severed economic ties with the village, these residents tend to fare worse than the remaining rural residents in the village. As a result, they have very strong incentives to rent out rooms for extra income. Third, four of the six neighborhoods are occupied by converted urban residents without residential committees and in turn have minimal levels of administrative oversight. Therefore private rentals are under few restrictions.

The village has a good location as well. It sits at the edge of the central city area and is connected to the downtown by a new elevated expressway. In the other direction, the expressway leads to the Wusong ferry that connects with Shanghai's rural hinterland – Chongming Island and Jiangsu Province. This location also has invited active real estate development backed by Baoshan District and Chongming County, which offer employment opportunities to migrants. In addition, many of the remaining rural residents in the village are no longer willing to farm themselves, as elsewhere in Shanghai's peri-urban areas, and instead lease land to migrants. The village enterprises also employ migrants and have built makeshift housing to accommodate them. Given all of these attractions, the village housed 1,050 migrants as of May 1999, far outnumbering its own residents. There is now a primary school operated by migrants in one of the village neighborhoods and the village committee has so far accommodated the school.

The case of this village is only a microcosm of Shanghai's periphery. The largest such area under tremendous growth is the Pudong New Area, designed to release spatial pressures on the old city center and accommodate new industrial and service development. Officially begun in 1990 on over 500 square kilometers of flat farmland, infrastructural works and construction have been under way to build a financial and trade zone, an export processing zone, a free trade zone, and numerous residential neighborhoods. This has created a huge demand for manual labor, which is increasingly satisfied by labor migrants. Between 1988 and 1998, the volume of the floating population in the Pudong New Area increased about tenfold, from around 40,000 to 395,000 (Pudong New Area Floating Population Office, 1998). The 1997 survey also shows that about 15 percent of Shanghai's floating population lived in Pudong, more than the 12 percent that Pudong's number of permanent residents (1.53 million) made up of the city's total in the same year (Shanghai Statistical Bureau, 1998).

In addition to employment opportunities, Pudong offers migrants abundant private as well as public housing for rental. Over 40 percent of the floating population coming from outside of Shanghai rent private housing for accommodation in Pudong, well above the rate for the city as a whole (about

27 percent). By May 1999, rentals of private housing totaled 54,700 rooms and those of public housing 12,500 rooms, together counting for about 5 percent of Pudong's housing stock of 1.5 million rooms (interview with the Pudong New Area Floating Population Office). In two of Pudong's townships – Qinyang and Yanqiao – migrants outnumbered local residents in 1998 and an even higher percentage of migrants rented private housing there (55 and 71 percent, respectively).

Pudong's situation again speaks to the attraction of peri-urban areas for migrants, based on field visits to the two townships and 18 villages in which migrants outnumbered local residents in 1998. The foremost factors are employment opportunities and the availability of inexpensive, private rental housing. In reality, there is already a large rental market operating in these areas, as rents tend to stabilize by location. The incentive on the supply side is particularly strong where farmland has been acquired for development, but old village neighborhoods still remain. Some of these neighborhoods are currently being vacated and have become concentrated living quarters for migrants. Administrative reorganization during the urbanization process and subsequent neglect or incapacity have also allowed the rental market to operate unregulated much more easily than in the city's established urban areas. This administrative fluidity is less prevalent in rural areas where traditional village communities are more intact.

It is clear that migrants by no means choose their settlement location in a random fashion. Since most economic migrants move to Shanghai in search of work to augment agricultural income, they tend to base their locational decisions on where the jobs are. Similar to circulating migrants in other developing countries, migrants who regard themselves as temporary members of the city often demonstrate different behaviors from permanent migrants (Nelson, 1976; Goldstein, 1993; Solinger, 1999). They tend to make different settlement choices, invest little income in housing, and demand fewer amenities and services. This is the case, for example, of an Anhui woman I have met. She works as a medical care worker in a major hospital located in a central downtown district, where she had slept on hospital chairs for three years until the hospital no longer allowed her to do so. Unable to afford the high rents in that central location by herself, she is renting a room of 10 square meters with four other co-workers. The relatively stable job she has in the hospital is the only factor that is keeping her where she is settling and even why she remains in Shanghai.

Conclusions

The main objective of this chapter has been to examine and explain migrant residential patterns in Shanghai. I have argued that interpretations of these patterns need to be linked with China's unique institutional factors, in particular the circulating nature of migration, the existing household registration system, and the transitional state of the urban housing market. Together they define constraints migrants face in making housing and settlement decisions. My analysis supports the argument that employment factors have significant impact on migrant settlement in the destination city, in terms of both housing patterns and geographical location. When migrants find jobs in state and collective enterprises, most of them also obtain the access to institutionally provided housing – a legacy of the welfare housing system. Otherwise, they have no access to the mainstream housing system. The best alternative they have is to rent private housing, which is more readily available in peri-urban areas.

Yet housing availability alone does not offer sufficient attraction for migrant settlement. Preliminary analysis shows that proximity to employment is by far the most important factor. The urban periphery is where such conditions are met, and therefore is the primary receiving area for migrants. Administrative reorganization during the urbanization process and subsequent lack of oversight have also eased restrictions on housing rental, as shown in the examples of the Pudong New Area and a village in Baoshan district.

Making settlement decisions, however, is only the first step for migrants when they begin a new life course in the city. Where and how they live and work are likely to affect their general level of satisfaction with urban living and the ease or difficulty of adapting to the new environment. Housing provides a context in which migrants make their adjustments to urban life, and residential patterns and outcomes are going to reflect their socioeconomic standing. Such housing characteristics as the type of structure, conditions of dwelling, access to facilities and services, and geographical location are all essential to migrants' quality of life. Attributes associated with urban living, including the higher density of urban housing and use of community facilities, may also have profound social impacts on the lifestyle of migrants. Addressing these additional inquiries is the ultimate goal of this research. New migrant housing surveys, in-depth interviews, and field visits have been completed for Shanghai and Beijing, and will be generating much richer analyses.

Beyond this research, studying the socioeconomic outcome of migration offers endless opportunities. Directly related to migrant residential and adaptation experience is how their educational and health needs are met through either existing urban institutions or the creation of new ones. Another direction points to the emergence of residential differentiation, which is not without precedent in Shanghai and several other Chinese cities. While some migrants gradually adjust to urban life or choose to preserve rural linkages, others may have no choice but to become the first of an emerging urban poor. This will have immediate implications for development policy.

Acknowledgments

Support from the National Science Foundation (SBR 97-09847) and the United States Department of Education (P019A80016) is deeply appreciated.

Part V
Urbanization of the Countryside

Part V
Urbanization of the Countryside

15

Return Migration, Entrepreneurship, and State-sponsored Urbanization in the Jiangxi Countryside

Rachel Murphy

This chapter examines the contribution of return migrant entrepreneurship to rural urbanization in Jiangxi province. Rural urbanization involves increasing interactions between rural and urban areas, with labor migration being both a cause and effect of these interactions. Rural urbanization is also characterized by an expansion in local off-farm earning opportunities and a diversification in local goods and services. Labor migration and rural enterprise creation are both recent phenomena in China.

Until the early 1980s the rural economy was arranged into the three-tiered system of production teams, brigades, and communes, with state directives on production being filtered down through the hierarchy. Collectivization operated in tandem with the household registration system: each household was allocated an occupational category, either agricultural or non-agricultural, and a place of residence (*hukou*). Food and other necessities were distributed at the place of residence through ration coupons. Private markets were eliminated, the collectives replaced market towns as the centre of rural activity, and state agencies dominated in the procurement and distribution of agricultural produce. Restrictions on mobility meant that counties had to rely upon their own stock of entrepreneurs in developing rural enterprises. Rural entrepreneurs were generally government officials and former cadres, supply and marketing personnel in township collectives, skilled workers in government enterprises, and some farmers. These entrepreneurs typically had strong local contacts, further compressing the geographical and social scope of information exchange. So localities poorly endowed with innovators and experienced managers failed to develop viable businesses (Byrd and Lin, 1990, p. 216).

Since the dismantling of the communes and the parcelling out of land farmers have been participating in both labor migration and local entrepreneurial activities. Households sign contracts to farm the household responsibility land and deliver grain quotas to their collectives. After they have paid the state agricultural tax, any surplus grain is either consumed or sold on free markets. The division of land and the rise of free markets have unveiled a critical problem of underemployment in the countryside, propelling labor migration to urban manufacturing zones and construction sites. Both rural households and governments have used savings accumulated from decollectivization productivity increases to invest in non-agricultural sectors of the rural economy that generate higher returns. Local rural leaders have played a dynamic role in rural urbanization by directly participating in rural entrepreneurship themselves and by facilitating the entrepreneurship of others. The local states promote rural urbanization in order to raise revenue for local development and to win popular support through job creation. Some scholars describe local state efforts to integrate rural entrepreneurs and their resources into its power base as "local state corporatism" (Oi, 1992).

This chapter argues that return migration is a potentially important component of the rural urbanization process because some migrants are entrepreneurial. The number of returnees in proportion to the volume of migrants is highest in the coastal provinces that have benefited most from the reforms (Zhang, 1997). For example, since the late 1990s the volume of return to north Jiangsu has been 25 percent greater than the out-migration from the region, and many of the returnees have set up businesses (Chen, 1997, p. 56). However, because the interior provinces are the key labor exporters, they boast the largest total volume of returning migrants (Zhang, 1997, p. 54). Figures from the China Rural Development Research Center suggest that one-third of migrants from Sichuan, Anhui, Hunan, and Jiangxi are now returning home (Ji, 1997; *Jiangxi qingnian bao*, February 18, 1997). Chinese policy-makers urge local states to ensure that returnee resources are used to enhance the effectiveness of rural towns and industries as population retainers (Song, 1997). However, as the following discussion reveals, the incorporation of returnees into the local state corporatism both stimulates and represses their entrepreneurship.

What follows is a case study of return migrant entrepreneurship in Xinfeng and Yudu, two counties in the hill country of south Jiangxi. The per capita GDP of both counties is below the provincial average. Since 1997, conditions in Xinfeng have improved with the opening of the Jing-Ju railway line that runs through the county seat, connecting it with Guangdong. In Yudu, main roads linking the county seat with highways heading north to Nanchang and southwest to Ganzhou have been covered with asphalt, but Yudu remains a state designated poverty county. One-third of the rural labor force from both counties are working in the cities, and each place has attracted nationwide media attention for the participation of returnees in business. The following discussion introduces the economic contribution of returnee entrepreneurs to their natal communities, then examines local state strategies for recruiting returnees in the task of rural urbanisation. Finally, the chapter considers instances of returnees negotiating and cooperating with the local state in reforming local policies and strengthening town infrastructure, thereby improving the rural business environment.

Returnee Businesses in Xinfeng and Yudu

Of the 85 returnee entrepreneurs that I interviewed in Xinfeng and Yudu, over 90 percent returned home to set up businesses that replicated the urban enterprises in which they had worked. Their manufacturing ventures include shoe, furniture, clothes, and toy workshops. Some returnees have cooperated with Cantonese bosses and overseas Chinese business people in setting up factories that part-process goods for coastal firms. In Xinfeng returnees are credited with advancing the local furniture industry by twenty years. Returnee industries are described by officials in both counties as "new points for growth in the rural economy" because they are generally more successful than other rural businesses (Zhang and Yang, 1996; Interview, June 9, 1997). Industries with the same types of products and production layouts did not exist in localities that I visited where the incidence of return migrant entrepreneurship was minimal. This is not to say that returnees are the only agents of enterprise creation, but in predominantly agricultural localities, they are important agents of information transfer and innovation. Returnee entrepreneurship in the tertiary sector is less spectacular than in manufacturing, with many enterprises replicating existing rural entities such as restaurants. However, some services – for example, a small roller-skating rink and a beauty salon – draw their inspiration from the cities.

Although the enterprises established by returned migrants do not represent a large number in either county, the incidence is significant enough for officials to target returnees as a new group of rural entrepreneur. The contributions of returnees to business creation in their natal counties are summarized in table 15.1. Of the 1,450 returnee manufacturing entities in Yudu, the three largest businesses have an annual product value of 100 million yuan. And in 1996, out of 109 new projects with annual product values of around one million yuan, 69 (63 percent) were either created or initiated by returnees. The higher product value of returnee enterprises as a proportion of the total industrial product value of industries in Yudu is partially because Yudu returnees have been successful in attracting Hong Kong merchants in setting

Table 15.1 Returnee business creation in Xinfeng and Yudu

	Xinfeng	*Yudu*
Getihu[a] service and manufacturing (1997)		
Total number of *getihu*	15,000 approx.	13,836[b]
Approx. proportion of returnee *getihu*	one-fifth[c]	one-third
% of total commercial tax from returnee *getihu*	Not available	14[d]
Getihu & Siying Qiye manufacturing (end of 1995)		
No. of returnee enterprises	153[e]	1,450[f]
Returnees working in these enterprises	1,349	4,000
Industrial product value of returnee enterprises as a proportion of 1995 total (nearest whole %)	13[g]	>46[h]

Notes: [a] In the early 1980s, "individual operators" (*getihu*) were forbidden to hire more than two employees and five apprentices, as more would constitute exploitation. Most *getihu* were traders or repairers. In 1987 a new term came into being, "private enterprise" or *siying qiye*, meaning those who employ over eight people. As the private sector has evolved, private businesses have differed from individual enterprises, not only in terms of size, but also in terms of their tendency to engage in industry and manufacturing.

[b] Total number of private and individual enterprises registered with the Bureau of Industry and Commerce.

[c] Interview, Ou Yangfeng, county head of Xinfeng, June 18, 1997.

[d] Interview, Deputy Director of the Yudu County Labour Export Bureau, 30 October 1997. Chen Puhua, pp. 35–6.

[e] Xinfeng County Association of Individual Enterprises, "Xinfeng County's statistical table for people who migrate to work then return to set up businesses during the period of 1995." The smallest business in the table has one employee, the largest business has 48 employees. The average number of employees is nine.

[f] Ji Enze, "Phoenix returns to the nest – a perspective on the return flow of migrant workers", *TPZF*, 1 (1997), p. 31; *Guanghua shibao* (Guanghua times), April 11, 1997, p. 3; *JQB*, February 18, 1997, p. 2; Chen Ru, "Analysis of the current phenomenon of returning rural youth," p. 26.

[g] Xinfeng County Association of Individual Enterprises, 1995. Total product value of these enterprises is 135,224,000 yuan. According to the 1996 Jiangxi Statistical Year Book, the total industrial product value for enterprises registered at the village level or above in Xinfeng county is 1,042,710,000 yuan. China Statistics Publishers, *1996 Jiangxi tongji nianjing* (1996 Jiangxi statistical year book), table 18-3, p. 566.

[h] See China Statistics Publishers, *1996 Jiangxi tongji nianjing*, table 18-3, p. 567. The total industrial product value of industries at the level of village and above is 797,060,000 yuan. Compare this against the total product value of the three enterprises with an annual product value of 100,000,000 yuan, plus the 69 enterprises with an annual product value of 1,000,000 yuan.

up large clothing factories. In contrast, small furniture workshops tend to predominate among the returnee enterprises in Xinfeng.

Some caution is required in reading the above figures on returnee entrepreneurship in Xinfeng and Yudu. The data for industrial product value shown in table 15.1 are drawn from different published sources that may have categorized industrial product value in different ways. Additionally, local governments tend to "add moisture" to their figures and newspapers frequently overstate economic successes. The data on returnee entrepreneurship and industrial product values in Xinfeng are based on surveys conducted by rural enterprise bureaus of various *xiang* and are at best a guide. Scholars of return migration commonly lament the difficulties in quantifying return flows, or plotting a known universe of returnee innovation (Cerase, 1970, p. 244; Connell et al., 1976, p. 121). In China, as in most countries, there is little in the way of official records of returnee entrepreneurship: return migration is a category of mobility which is normally omitted from census surveys, and those who register a business do not have to record whether or not they have ever migrated. The figures for return migrant entrepreneurship in Xinfeng and Yudu do not include a vast array of small stalls and specialized households that have never registered. Additionally, officials in both counties stress that the numbers of returned migrant entrepreneurs are in constant flux – many set up for a few months, fail, and are forced back out to the cities. Neither do these figures account for those workers in rural enterprises with migrant work experience. There are also cases where a migrant introduces an urban contact to local officials, who establish a project and invite others to contract the management of the business. Despite difficulties in obtaining accurate data, the available figures are consistent with the empirical evidence that the contribution of returnee entrepreneurs to the economies of Xinfeng and Yudu is "significant."

Local State Initiatives to Encourage Returnee Entrepreneurs

Whereas studies in other countries report the apathy of national governments toward returnees, and the resentment of local authorities toward innovators (Cerase, 1970, pp. 217–39; Laite, 1984), returnee entrepreneurship in China is sponsored by all levels of the state. At the Fifteenth National People's Congress, the then Premier Li Peng stated that migrant farmers who have obtained skills and managerial experience should be encouraged to return home and start businesses (*China Daily*, March 3, 1997, p. 4). Ganzhou prefecture has followed provincial recommendations and urged all counties under its jurisdiction to encourage return migrant entrepreneurship as a strategy for poverty alleviation (*Jiangxi ribao*, March 14, 1997). Government publications appeal to cadres by detailing the successes of particular counties where the government has been supportive of returnees. At the end of the chain, newspaper articles in Xinfeng and Yudu recommend active government support for returnee enterprises (*Xinfeng bao*, February 17, 1997, p. 1).

Local state measures to encourage returnee entrepreneurship include preferential policies, publicity campaigns, direct overtures to successful migrants, and the coordination of training, migration, and return. I discuss each measure in turn. Preferential policies for returnee entrepreneurs include temporary tax reductions, and assistance with access to factory space, credit, raw materials, water, and electricity. Local rural industry bureaus also provide information on viable projects. In Xinfeng administrative procedures for various business permits have been simplified and returnees are allowed a six month grace period before registering – "first get on the bus then buy a ticket" (Interview, June 9, 1997). In Yudu there has been a crackdown on unregistered enterprises, but officials are instructed to ensure that procedures for returnees are handled promptly (Interview, October 15, 1997).

In Xinfeng and Yudu public praise meetings reflect the capacity of the local government to confer "face" on returnees; that is, to offer visible political endorsement for their enhanced control over resources. Model returnee entrepreneurs exemplify ideals such as hard work, hometown loyalty, and persistence in the face of adversity. They also appeal to migrant youths by demonstrating possibilities for social mobility on home soil. Models inspire other migrants to return home, in part because the "demonstration effect" is an integral component of the migration process. Some returnees described to me the success of prominent returnees and their desire to emulate. Other migrants returned home after being contacted by former workmates who had returned home to establish businesses.

Ouyang Xiaofang, director of the Jinda Shiye Group Company in Yudu, is one example of a model returnee entrepreneur. In 1993 the All-China Federation of Industry and Commerce named him "All-China Outstanding Entrepreneur of the Private Economy" and in 1994 the Ministry of Agriculture awarded him the title of "All-China Rural Entrepreneur." The same year the Yudu County Government rewarded him with a Santana car and an imported jeep worth 280,000 yuan (US$31,000) (Xu, 1996). The Ouyang Complex, the tallest building in Yudu, incorporates a restaurant, shops, a hotel, and offices. It stands in the middle of the county town, metaphorically proclaiming the rise in the status of a lowly farmer: he earned his money as a labor contractor in Guangzhou and Xiamen, then invested in mines and factories at home.

Spring Festival is an ideal occasion for local officials to remind those migrants who have prospered not to forget the home soil that has nourished them. From January to March newspapers carry stories of migrants who have donated money to rural infrastructure projects, or who have prospered by setting up businesses. Banners at rural bus stations greet returnees: "Welcome Migrants to Come Home and Create Businesses." Letters are distributed to village households advising migrants of local business opportunities. Those who return for Spring Festival are invited to attend county and township conferences that have two purposes. One is to inform the migrants of local investment opportunities, and the other is for cadres to seek advice from migrants on the implications of urban business practices for local economic reforms.

The rural–urban information network created through migration is utilized by local governments for initiating contact with migrants in the cities. Postal remittance slips and hearsay from villagers enable cadres to identify high-earning migrants, or those who have reached white collar positions within a factory and are likely to have influential ties with bosses. Delegations of cadres visit urban destination areas persuading migrants to launch projects at home (Interviews, June 15 and October 15, 1997). The township labor management offices also contact rural households to obtain the city mail addresses and phone numbers of successful migrants (*Jiangxi ribao*, July 23, 1997). Direct government overtures have yielded results. In my study, 12 out of 27 large-scale manufacturing enterprises, four out of 26 small-scale manufacturing entities, and one out of five farming ventures were established as a result of official representation.

Finally, the local state is experimenting with projects that train migrants while they are in the cities so that on their return they can contribute to local economic development. Evening and weekend courses for migrants range from basic numeracy and literacy classes to vocational training in car repairs and electronics. The following comments on the cultural initiatives of the Yudu Labor Export Company at the Shanghai docks appear in *Jiangxi ribao* (July 23, 1997): "Using labor export as a means to relieve poverty . . . must use the radiation effect of the city to improve the quality of the peasants. This relates . . . to the role of return migrants in leading peasants to prosperity."

Returnees and the Local State: Negotiating for Change

Returnees participate in business at home in order to accumulate capital independently of an employer. On account of their urban work experience they are more committed to pursuing an independent livelihood than other peasant proprietors, a universal trait of returnees (Piore, 1979, pp. 117–19; Gmelch, 1980, p. 114; King et al., 1984, p. 117). The extent to which this translates into the pursuit of independence within the locality or in relation to the local state is an important question. However, given that return migrant entrepreneurship in Xinfeng and Yudu really only began in 1995, it is premature to assess these political implications. Returnees are only able to participate in rural urbanization with the support of the local state, and the local state courts them because they have obtained resources.

In contributing to rural urbanization, returnees push the boundaries of the local state corporatism by lobbying for change. County and township governments recognize that adjustments to the local policy environment are necessary to attract "phoenixes to the nest," and a Yudu Party Committee publicity brochure advises migrants, "we are going to further liberate our thought, become more open, formulate preferential policies" (January 18, 1995). The subtext is: "We are changing things so that you can make money at home!" The following section focuses on five areas of negotiation between returnees and the local state: returnees cooperate with the local state in developing towns, they introduce urban management practices to state and collective enterprises, they lobby for tax concessions, they improve the availability of loans, and they increase rural–urban market linkages.

Rural towns and enterprises

In Xinfeng and Yudu, the state-sponsored revival of rural industries and towns in the 1980s and 1990s has created market spaces to which migrants can transfer their urban acquired resources. Towns in Xinfeng and Yudu are single streets lined with shops and government offices and they are the place where farmers from surrounding villages trade goods on market days. The towns are known as *xiang* and *zhen*. The *xiang* or township is a rural administrative unit under the jurisdiction of the county that is subdivided into administrative villages. The *zhen* or town is the lowest unit in the urban hierarchy and also falls under the jurisdiction of the county.

Returnees prefer to build their houses in the towns because of the commercial advantage of location, with the ground floor reserved for some form of business activity such as a shop or repair booth. Throughout the countryside the visitor sees town roads lined with red brick constructions in various stages of completion. According to officials from township land management bureaus, migrant money funds over half of the construction activity. As my guide explained, "these houses are built by people who have money and most of those who have money do not earn it in the countryside of Yudu." In regions with low per capita allocations of land and a weak industrial base, brick factories are an attractive avenue of investment for returnees – especially given that migrant money now fuels a huge demand for bricks. The construction boom also generates a demand for the skills of returnee bricklayers, plasterers, and carpenters. Similar contributions by migrants to a rural construction boom have been noted in other developing countries (Fadayomi et al., 1992, p. 82).

Although the towns facilitate returnee contributions to rural urbanization, poor infrastructure and physical isolation create difficulties for the entrepreneurs with production and marketing. Production may be inconvenienced by an irregular electricity supply or poor roads. Sometimes enterprises can only manufacture for a few days a week, and with the onset of spring rains some township roads turn to sludge. These are serious obstacles for factories that engage in the contract manufacturing of export goods and must meet deadlines.

Problems in marketing stem from the fact that urban work experience rather than rural market conditions determines the type of business that returnees create. So entrepreneurs must overcome the incompatibility between urban consumer goods and the local market. Often they do this by modifying the urban product to suit rural consumers. For instance, shoe workshops produce cheap vinyl replicas of the stylish leather fashions of the city. If there are solid subcontracting arrangements with a coastal factory, then the entrepreneur does not face the dilemma of marketing the product. Yet the reliance of returnee subcontractors on specific coastal companies leaves them vulnerable to fluctuations in the Special Economic Zones, and susceptible to exploitation in their negotiation of prices and contracts. "They eat the meat, we chew on the bones," explained one boss (Interview, June 8, 1997). When city firms cancel orders, physical remoteness means that it is difficult for the entrepreneurs to find new clients.

Returnees in Xinfeng and Yudu lobby the local state for improvements to town infrastructure. In poor areas, planners have designated a special role for towns in eroding the urban and rural divide by becoming the central link in a three-tier system: the market town is a place from where fledgling rural industries can develop and a place where rural residents can be exposed to town culture (Zhou, 1995). During the 1980s, rural industrialization was guided by an idea that each village should develop its own industries. But the scattered location of the enterprises created inefficiencies and difficulties with supply and support services. Chinese demographers have argued that in tending to set up their new business ventures in the townships and county seats rather than the villages, returnee entrepreneurs promote the 1990s policy of integrating rural industrialization with the construction of small towns (Chen, 1996b). To this end, the local states in Xinfeng and Yudu have assumed an important role in channelling migrant resources toward the construction of town-based "returnee industry mini-zones." Although persons of any background may establish businesses in these mini-zones, publicity materials appeal directly to returnees. Take, for example, this extract from *Xinfeng News*:

> townships . . . have established "returnee migrant enterprise and industry mini-zones" which have attracted over one hundred returnee enterprises, and one Xiaohe returnee who has benefited greatly . . . sighed . . . "The preferential and supportive policies . . . [mean that] . . . entrepreneurs are even more able to raise a great sail among one hundred ships."

To address problems of poor infrastructure and physical isolation, township and county governments in Xinfeng have cooperated to facilitate the relocation of larger enterprises from the townships to the county seat. Township governments are unwilling for their enterprises to move further afield as this compromises their control over the resources that they generate. Thus, the county government has allowed the *xiang* or *zhen* to receive the tax revenues of these firms despite the change in location. Seven out of the twelve large manufacturing enterprises that I visited in Xinfeng had relocated from the towns to the county seat. This involved some negotiation between both levels of government and conforms with the recommendation of Chinese policy-makers that measures be taken to selectively relocate a portion of rural enterprises to county seats (Gu and Xinhua, 1994, p. 5). The overall policy is still one of developing rural market towns, but primacy is given to developing those towns higher up in the settlement hierarchy.

As an extension of the current role of returnee entrepreneurs in creating jobs and diffusing urban culture into the countryside, the state hopes that returnees will eventually promote a more complete urbanization of the countryside. In other words, planners see returnees as agents for promoting the *permanent transfer* of rural labor out of villages and into towns, and eventually into small cities (Zhou Yi, p. 319). However, some Chinese scholars complain that rural urbanization creates the undesirable situation of "all villages resembling towns, all towns resembling the countryside" (Zhao, 1999a). They argue that farmers who move into towns must end their semi-proletarian status by severing links with the land (Zhou, 1997, pp. 368–70). According to the demographer Chen Hao, returnees who lead in the establishment of rural enterprises not only transform their own social roles, they also help even more farmers realize a transition in status from farmer to worker by enabling more of the rural labor force to enter the industrial sector, and by enabling professional farmers to cultivate larger areas.

However, in Xinfeng and Yudu return migrant entrepreneurship does not promote the severing of ties with the land. Although most of the entrepreneurs have located their enterprises, and often their houses, in the towns and the county seat, they are generally reluctant to transfer their household registration from the villages to the towns, as this would mean relinquishing their hold on the land. Transferring the household registration (*hukou*) out of agriculture also involves a financial outlay. Many returnees feel that nowadays having money is more important than possessing an urban *hukou*. Returnees have been able to create enterprises at home precisely because they combine their savings from the urban labor markets with land in the village. In order to compete with the goods produced in the cities and in order to entice external bosses in establishing businesses in the hinterland, labor and subsistence costs must be lower than in urban areas. Agriculture contributes a sufficient portion of subsistence for the returnee entrepreneurs and their workforce to

Table 15.2 Job creation by the returnee enterprises visited by the author

Business category	*No. of enterprises*	*Total no. of employees in the category*	*Ave. no. of employees per enterprise*
Large manufacturing: Xinfeng	12	364	30
Large manufacturing: Yudu	14	808[a]	58[a]
Small manufacturing: Xinfeng	15	76	5
Small manufacturing: Yudu	10	48	5
Service sector: Xinfeng	11	44	4
Service sector: Yudu	11	30	3

Note: [a] This figure excludes the Yudu Woollen Sweater Company, which employs 860 people.

create a competitive basis for these industries by depressing labor costs. For some, the land is farmed by family members. For others, the land is rented for grain. Many interviewees state that although the sum of their earnings is less at home than in the cities, their economic situation in both locations is comparable: in the natal community, there is no rent to pay and grain does not have to be purchased. Moreover, land provides a security net should the enterprises fail.

Returnee enterprises and the creation of off-farm employment

The state views the participation of rural households in both farming and non-farm activities as a transitional phase, and advocates a role for returnee entrepreneurs in accelerating "permanent" urbanization; that is, the complete transfer of farm labor from fields and villages to factories and towns. This perspective differs from a position in the development studies literature that increasingly regards poverty alleviation through the diversification of household income sources, both cash and in-kind income, as an end goal in itself (Ellis, 1998).

Table 15.2 shows figures for job creation by returnee enterprises. These figures are respectable in light of limited empirical evidence from other developing countries, which finds that the majority of rural industries employ fewer than ten people (Chuta and Liedholm, 1984, p. 330). Yet the table does not tell the whole story. Rather than absorbing the non-migrants, most of the factories producing shoes, furniture, and clothes employ former migrants. In these factories, the skill requirements are high and the wages reflect this. Moreover, returnee bosses prefer former migrants because they are accustomed to the strict labor discipline of the coastal factories. However, in a few factories, in which most of the laborers have never migrated, tasks are simple, and the wages are low, the outflow of labor to the cities means that it is difficult to recruit suitable workers. Production often falls short of the quotas set by the parent company, so payment for the goods barely covers operating expenses.

Although returnee enterprises generate employment, they have not played a major role in providing livelihood opportunities for the local non-migrant laborers. Rather, by expanding the occupational structure of the natal community, returnee entrepreneurs have made it possible for other returned migrants with various kinds of urban work experience to earn a living at home. This helps to alleviate a shortage of skilled workers in economically depressed areas, and overtime may enhance the capacity of the industrial and tertiary sectors of the countryside to provide income generating opportunities for the non-migrant population.

Returnees and government enterprises

Although returnees create their own businesses, they are also enlisted by the local state to contribute to the salvaging of government enterprises. Local cadres benefit from the payment of contracting fees, and they hope that as emissaries of urban management, returnees can improve the fortunes of these enterprises. However, introducing "modern" management practices to the countryside may be to the detriment of the traditional welfare considerations that are reflected, for instance, by a reluctance to lay off workers and a relaxed working environment.

The case of Mr Yang illustrates the role of returnees in implementing efficient urban business practices. Mr Yang worked for ten years as a manager in a coastal factory before being contacted by local leaders and offered a position as a village leader, as well as the opportunity to contract out the Xinfeng Textile Factory. He recalls:

> The place was running at a loss before I took over. Two-fifths of the workers weren't skilled enough so I fired them. It is much better to hire the migrant girls who have come back from Guangdong, so I sent out word and got twenty returnee workers as replacements. . . . Since I came, the factory has started using clock-in cards and the workers know that if they are late then they pay a fine.

Mr Yang has also instituted a working day with ten hours. He has replaced the fabric used by the factory with a cheaper variety and he has negotiated a series of subcontracting arrangements with Pearl Delta factories (Interview,

June 12, 1997). His future plans include finding ways of dealing directly with Hong Kong.

Enlisting former migrants as managers and consultants in government enterprises may help to extend the leadership base of the state and collective sector beyond the network circles of the local state. For example, a returnee to a township in Yudu had been contacted by local authorities to oversee the establishment of a collective pottery factory. As he has been specifically recruited for his technical skill and management experience, he envisaged a high degree of autonomy in running the business (Interview, October 23, 1997).

Taxes

Returnees air dissatisfaction at the slow pace of reform in the countryside, the dominant presence of the local state in the distribution of resources, and its claims on rural incomes. They compare the developed urban economies with their hometowns, explaining the difference in terms of local policies and government behavior. One returnee reflects a common sentiment:

> My boss asked me why all the Jiangxi country cousins [*laobiao*] come to work in Guangzhou. I told him that it is all to do with the policies. Your policies are open and ours are backward. At home they tell us to run but tie our legs. If your policies were like ours and ours were like yours then Guangzhou people would be coming to work in Jiangxi. (Interview, June 17, 1997)

Although local state initiatives to encourage returnee participation in rural urbanization have been extensive, cadres make a variety of claims, both legitimate and otherwise, upon the resources of the entrepreneurs. Expectations are placed on the returnees by virtue of their status as both entrepreneurs and former migrants. The entrepreneurs contribute income to the local government and donate to politically important projects such as building village schools. For their part, cadres facilitate business activities by bestowing necessities such as business permits, permission to use an operating site, access to raw materials, and loans.

The predicament facing returnee entrepreneurs in Xinfeng and Yudu mirrors a nationwide situation whereby officials seek to appropriate the income generated by returnee entrepreneurs. For instance, government authorities in a prefecture in Hunan province have mounted signs outside large-scale returnee enterprises to protect them against the random appropriation of fees and fines by cadres. The purpose of the "sign protection system for key returnee enterprises" is to allow the entrepreneurs to feel at ease while operating their businesses in order to encourage the "flourishing development of the return project" (*Guangdong Labor News*, June 23, 1997).

Nonetheless, cadres allow the returnee businesses to survive as revenue-generating entities, and have instituted tax concessions in order to encourage the entrepreneurs. Moreover, operating within the local state corporatism, the operators of larger entities in particular townships or counties draw the attention of officials to the more liberal policies in the special economic zones. For instance, I heard an official ask a prominent returnee businessman, "Why don't you use spare space on the factory site to build another workshop, lay another egg?" He replied, "Then there are less eggs for you to break." The businessman then expounded on how the cadres in Guangdong have the right attitude in encouraging the creative potential of people, whereas in the interior, leaders tie up innovation with bureaucracy and exactions (Interview, October 5, 1997). He runs one of the largest businesses in Yudu and has introduced much investment from a Hong Kong boss, so is well positioned in his exchanges with the local state.

Loans

Returnees help to promote a market orientation in the lending practices of rural financial institutions, thereby broadening the social basis determining eligibility for loans. Returnees have been targeted by local states because of their potential to inject both their own savings and the funds of external business contacts into the local economy. Despite the fact that the 85 returnees that I interviewed brought home, on average, around half of their investment from the urban labor markets, 90 percent of the interviewees engaged in manufacturing cited insufficient capital as a major obstacle to expansion. An important part of the local government publicity campaign to attract returnees is the promise of help with obtaining credit. The linkage between deposits and loans, and the difficulties in obtaining loans from financial institutions in other localities, means that in poor areas the amount of credit available is highly restricted. In allocating loans, preference goes to those projects and persons supported by community leaders. Returnees who can demonstrate reliable access to a coastal market, substantial funds of their own, or the backing of a city partner are able to more effectively lobby for local state support. The larger-scale businesses in particular have obtained loans guaranteed by local governments and loans from credit rotation societies operating under the auspices of government institutions.

The local state has been most inventive in targeting migrant remittances, with important implications for expanding the amount of credit available for the development of rural industries within a particular locality. Rural financial institutions send representatives to destination areas and encourage migrants to entrust their remittances to these urban-based agents. Toward the end of 1997, electronic linkages were established between branches of the Agricultural Bank located in key migrant destination areas and branches in the townships of Yudu. The wages of Yudu migrant dock workers in Shanghai are paid directly into their accounts at a Shanghai branch of the Agricultural Bank. Migrants' relatives in Yudu villages explained to me that their husbands and children arrange transfers of money to the township branch of the Agricultural Bank within 24 hours (Interviews, October to November, 1997).

Chinese planners have acknowledged the potential for the injection of migrant remittance deposits to be channeled toward financial support for returnee business creation, though the idea awaits full transfer from policy documents to practice (Research Group of Yichun Prefecture, 1996; Interview, October 25, 1997). As more credit becomes available through remittance deposits and more returnees lobby community leaders for funding, some of the political criteria determining eligibility for loans may become more fluid.

Rural–urban market linkages

Returnees help in establishing rural–urban market and information networks that are semi-independent of the local state. This is significant because the local government still plays a dominant role in resource distribution and sales in both the agricultural and industrial sectors. The return of successful migrants to Xinfeng and Yudu offers possibilities not only for the direct injection of capital and equipment, but also for an infusion of entrepreneurs who have access to external networks. Even though external networks dilute the control of the local state, these networks are established with local official support, as indicated by policies targeting both successful migrants and investors from outside of the county. Through welcoming returnees into the corporatism, local states expand their horizontal linkages into the developed coast to reach the business contacts of the returnees, some of whom have connections with coastal and overseas Chinese bosses. This idea is expressed in the following extract from an open letter to Yudu migrants:

> We hope that you can use all the skills and capital you acquired outside to return to the townships and take the lead in setting up businesses. . . . [P]lease use all channels and contacts to introduce Hong Kong, Macao, and Taiwan members of the business community to invest and set up factories and develop tertiary industries in your home towns.

The original impetus for establishing representative offices in key coastal cities was to coordinate labor export from the counties, and provide services for migrants. However, these offices have since expanded their function to include advertising local products and promoting both government and private businesses. Xinfeng and Yudu have offices in Dongguan city, Guangdong province, and there is a Yudu office in Shanghai.

Conclusions

The local states in Xinfeng and Yudu have been inventive in harnessing resources generated by return migration and directing them toward rural urbanization. Their efforts form part of a broader attempt to increase local government revenue for social expenditure, generate local off-farm employment opportunities, and diversify the range of goods and services available in the rural market place. Although Chinese planners designate a role for returnees in promoting urbanization through the permanent transfer of labor out of agriculture, the returned migrant bosses and their employees are reluctant to lose their links with the land because farming forms a crucial basis for household livelihood diversification. Moreover, although returnee enterprises expand the occupational structure of the natal economy and attract the return of skilled migrants, their role in providing off-farm jobs for non-migrant labor is limited.

Operating within the local state corporatism, returnees are able to pursue their own goals, namely accumulating capital through independent means. Yet, in rural areas, problems with town infrastructure and government policy inhibit the realization of this goal. Through negotiation with the local state, returnees help to make the natal environment more conducive to business. This is illustrated by the actions of returnees and migrants in improving town infrastructure, salvaging ailing government enterprises, contesting the claims of officials on business resources, injecting capital into the local economy, expanding credit supplies, integrating the local markets into the national economy, and fostering rural–urban market linkages.

Acknowledgments

This chapter presents material from Rachel Murphy (1999) Return migrants and economic diversification in two counties in South Jiangxi, China. *Journal of International Development*, 11, 661–72 (© 1999 John Wiley & Sons Ltd, reproduced with permission); and Rachel Murphy (2000) Return migration, entrepreneurship and local state corporatism. *Journal of Contemporary China*, 9 (24), 231–48 (© 2000 Taylor & Francis Ltd, reproduced with permission: web site http://www.tandf.co.uk).

16
Region-based Urbanization in Post-reform China: Spatial Restructuring in the Pearl River Delta

George C. S. Lin

The ongoing process of globalization, defined as the functional integration of economic activities at the global scale, has altered significantly the processes and spatial patterns of urban change in at least three important respects. First, there is the emergence of "world cities" or "global cities," which no longer function as simply centers of the national economy but have become command and control centers within the world system and home to a complex of financial firms and corporate headquarters (Sassen, 1991; Friedmann, 1995b; Knox and Taylor, 1995). Second, there are the deepened processes of spatial restructuring taking place in many American and European metropolitan regions consequent on the increased mobility of capital and labor at the global scale (Scott, 1988; Soja, 1995; Knox, 1996; Harris, 1997). Such processes are evident not only in the (re)agglomeration of selective metropolitan centers but also in the greater segmentation and segregation of the intraurban space based on occupation, race, ethnicity, immigrant status, income, and other socioeconomic identities. Finally, there is the proliferation of a "metrocentric global culture" or "global metropolitanism" (Knox, 1996, p. 116) which is rooted in (post)modern materialistic consumerism and often radiated from major metropolitan centers in the West. Attention to these consequences, rather than others, underscores the existing paradigm of urban transition. This paradigm postulates an urbanization process centered on the city and driven primarily by the forces of agglomeration economies (Friedmann and Wulff, 1975; Timberlake, 1985; Scott, 1986; Lin, 1994; Ingram, 1998).

This study of rural industrialization and urbanization in the rapidly growing Chinese Pearl River Delta region (PRD hereafter) reveals a different process and spatial pattern. Despite the dramatic growth and restructuring of this regional economy, the level of urbanization (defined as the proportion of the urban or non-agricultural population in the total population) in most places has remained moderate, and population concentration in large cities has been limited. Instead of a high concentration of population in the cities, particularly large cities where agglomeration economies operate, what is more remarkable in the PRD has been a spontaneous industrialization and urbanization of the countryside. This rural and region-based urbanization, described as "urban–rural integration" (*cheng xiang yitifa*) by the local Chinese or "*kotadesasi*" by McGee (1989) and Gingsburg (1990), is the complex outcome of the interaction between various local and global forces. These include the reconfiguration of the power and capacity of the socialist state, inflow of foreign capital not simply into large cities but also into suburban areas on the basis of pre-existing social ties, and marketization and industrialization of the local agricultural economy.

This chapter examines the process of economic and spatial restructuring of the PRD region since the 1980s when China started to actively (re)articulate itself into the world economy. Located on the southern coast of China's mainland (see figure 16.1), the PRD has been one of the most populous and productive economic regions in the country. Its geographic proximity to and extensive social connections with the newly industrializing economies of Hong Kong and Taiwan have enabled the delta region to be chosen by the post-Mao pragmatic regime to practice flexible economic policies. Two of China's Special Economic Zones were established in the delta in 1979 and the entire delta was subsequently designated as an Open Economic Region where local governments, individual enterprises, and farm households enjoy great autonomy in economic decision-making. Table 16.1 lists key economic indicators of the PRD in comparison with the national and provincial situations. Viewed in a political economy perspective, the PRD has served as not only a testing site for the post-Mao regime to develop an open market economy within the socialist territory but also a valuable laboratory for investigating how local and global forces have interacted in the Chinese context and what spatial economy has been (re)produced by these forces.

The development experience of the PRD is not typical of the situation of the entire country. Nevertheless, the PRD has been one of the first regions selected by the Chinese government to develop an open economy and practice free market forces. As other Chinese regions are opened to foreign investment, it is likely that the PRD may no longer be able to maintain its leading economic position in the nation and its development experience will gradually lose much of its uniqueness. If this is the case, then this study of economic and spatial restructuring of a "pioneer" region will provide important

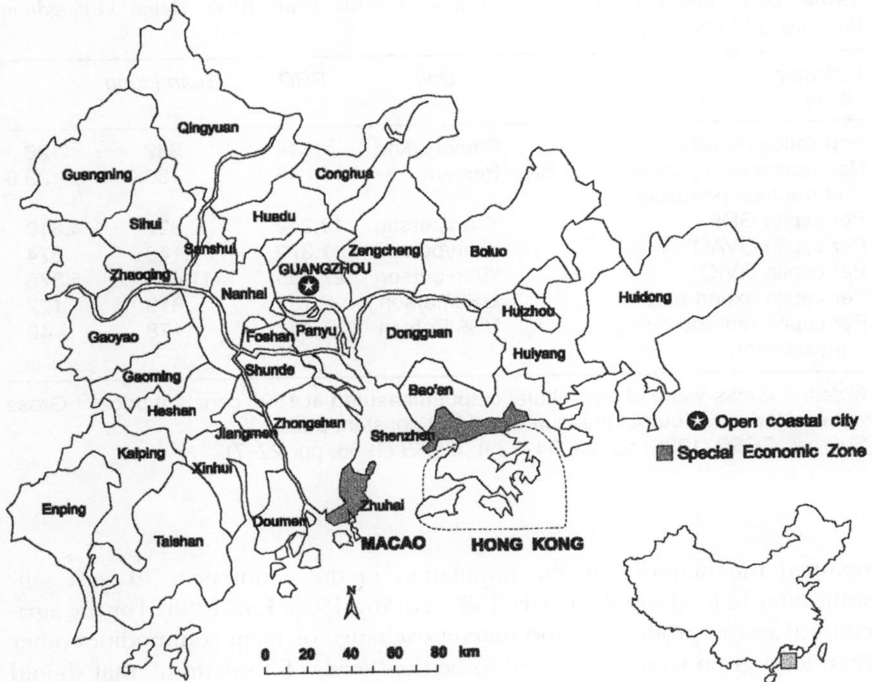

Figure 16.1 The Pearl River Delta open economic region

lessons for other developing Chinese regions which have more recently been exposed to forces of globalization and market reform.

Market Reform and Economic Restructuring

When economic reforms were initiated in the late 1970s, the regional economy of the PRD was predominantly agricultural in the nature, with over 75 percent of its total population engaged in agricultural production. Within the agricultural sector, the mainstay was food grain production, which accounted for over 75 percent of the total output value (GPSB, 1991, pp. 14–407; 1992, pp. 65–6). Rural industry, defined by the provincial authorities as industry located at and below the village level, only contributed a tiny portion to the total industrial output. This picture very much represented the legacy of socialist development under Mao. To maintain urban manageability in a shortage socialist economy, the Maoist regime adopted a strategy that

Table 16.1 Selected economic indicators for the Pearl River Delta, Guangdong Province, and China, 1995

Indicator	*Unit*	*PRD*	*Guangdong*	*China*
Population density	Persons/km^2	514	382	126
Non-agricultural population as % of the total population	Percent	43.9	30.0	23.6
Per capita GDP	Yuan/person	18,242	7,927	4,810
Per capita GVAO[a]	Yuan/person	1,379	1,148	874
Per capita GVIO[b]	Yuan/person	27,495	11,446	5,376
Per capita export output	US$/person	2,157	819	122
Per capita realized foreign investment	US$/Person	401	178	40

Notes: [a] Gross value of agricultural output measured at 1990 constant price. [b] Gross value of industrial output measured at 1990 constant price.
Source: *GPSB* (1996, pp. 93, 54–129); *CSSB* (1996, pp. 22–7).

retained the majority of the population in the countryside to seek self-sufficiency in food supply (Lardy, 1983; Kirkby, 1985; Lin, 1998). For the agricultural sector, production and market exchange of farm commodities other than food grain were considered to be the "seeds of capitalism" that should be and were indeed severely oppressed. For strategic and ideological reasons, the regional economy of the PRD was divided by the Maoist regime into two parts: an agrarian economy in the countryside that involved the great majority of the population who were denied the benefits of commercialization, industrialization, and urbanization, versus a protected industrial urban economy that accommodated only a limited number of people.

The agrarian economy articulated by the Maoist regime was under tremendous pressure from continued population growth. While cultivable land remained limited, the population of the province grew from 27.8 million in 1949 to 50.64 million in 1978. Population density increased from 156 to 285 persons per square kilometer, whereas per capita cultivated land dropped from 1.46 to 0.82 mu per person for the same period (GPSB, 1990, pp. 103, 147). Consequently, there was a great and growing demand among peasants in the countryside for increasing the intensity of cultivation, which is limited after centuries of farming, and/or finding a non-farm outlet that could generate income and employment more efficiently and effectively. Such a demand had never been satisfied until state control was relaxed in 1978.

The Chinese practice of economic reforms and the open door policy have been extensively documented (Ash, 1988; Lo, 1989; Fan, 1995b; Lin, 1999; Wu, 1999d). The reforms essentially represent an important trade-off the socialist regime has made: to decentralize economic decision-making so as to arouse local initiatives and individual production enthusiasm. This pragmatic and flexible attitude has been conducive to the growth and restructuring of the regional economy in the PRD. Once the state constraints were removed, local governments and individuals took initiatives to reorganize the regional economy to satisfy their demand for generating income and employment effectively outside the traditional agricultural sector. This has given rise to a remarkable process of economic restructuring. The general picture of structural change has been a large proportional increase in industrial production and a simultaneous decline in the share held by the agricultural sector. Within the agricultural sector, paddy-rice cultivation dropped proportionally from 75 to only 49 percent and the balance was picked up by market farming activities such as forestry, livestock husbandry, sideline business, and fisheries, whose share of the total output rose from 25 percent in 1980 to 50 percent in 1990 (GPSB, 1991, pp. 14–407; 1992, pp. 65–6). The regional economy has thus become increasingly industrialized and the agricultural sector has experienced a significant process of commercialization and diversification.

The industrialization of the delta's regional economy has been fueled primarily by the dramatic expansion of rural industry. The relative standing of heavy industry, which refers to the manufacturing of modern machinery or capital goods, has declined since 1980. It is rural industry that has recorded not only the highest growth rate but also the biggest proportional increase in total industrial production. This industry is mostly low-tech, small-scale and labor-intensive (Lo, 1989; Byrd and Lin, 1990; Ho, 1994; Lin, 1997c). It is now widely scattered all over the countryside and functions as the most important absorber of surplus rural laborers who have been released from agricultural production because of increased productivity.

Spatial Restructuring and Urbanization

Market reform and the sectoral reorganization of the regional economy have effectively reshaped the spatial distribution of economic activities and population. The general picture of spatial transformation was a relative decline of Guangzhou City as a dominant metropolitan center, the accelerated growth of the counties and cities located in the areas outside and between metropolitan centers, and the persistent stagnancy of locales in the periphery of the region. The two newly established Special Economic Zones (Shenzhen and Zhuhai) took the lead in the growth of industrial and agricultural production. Next to the SEZs were the newly developing counties and cities, mostly located in the Guangzhou–Hong Kong–Macao corridors. Medium-sized cities such as Huizhou, Foshan, and Zhaoqing have also continued to grow. By comparison, Guangzhou, the traditional primate city and chief economic center of the region, recorded a low growth rate. Among the 31 counties and municipalities of the region, Guangzhou's production growth during the 1980s was the second lowest, higher only than that of Qingyuan, a mountainous underdeveloped municipality. The weakening of Guangzhou's dominant economic position in the region is clearly shown not only by its slower pace of economic growth but also by its share of the total regional production value, which dropped from 44 percent in 1980 to 22 percent in 1990 (GPSB, 1992, pp. 83–206).

Does the declining dominance of Guangzhou as the primate city in the regional economy result in a reduction of spatial inequality for the whole region? An analysis of the coefficient of variation for key economic indices such as per capita gross value of industrial and agricultural output and per capita income reveals that this has not been the case. Despite the reduction of urban primacy and accelerated growth of an extended metropolitan zone outside of the primate city, resulting in a declining coefficient of variation in urban (non-agricultural) population, regional inequality in terms of productivity and income for the PRD widened further during the 1980s, possibly because of the persistence of a backward economy in the peripheral area of the region (Lin, 2001). This finding is consistent with that of several recent studies which show that regional inequality in China since the reforms has been reduced at the interprovincial level but increased at the intraprovincial level (Lo, 1990; Fan, 1995b; Wei and Ma, 1996).

How and to what extent has the sectoral and spatial restructuring of the regional economy reshaped the geographic distribution of population? First, overall population density for the region increased from 370 to 437 persons per square kilometer during the 1980s. As the natural increase in population was low because of the effective national campaign of family planning, any significant increase in population density must be primarily the result of in-migration from other areas. In general, higher population density in 1980 was found mostly in the central delta, with the designated cities of Guangzhou, Foshan, Jiangmen, and Zhaoqing being the most populous places. This pattern carried on into the 1990s. The only thing that changed was that the SEZs (Shenzhen and Zhuhai) became much more populated than anywhere else in the delta due to their economic appeal. The pattern of population distribution has remained one of high concentration. The degree of spatial variation measured by the coefficient of variation of population density increased from 1.25 in 1980 to 1.28 in 1990 (Lin, 2001). Clearly, the spatial pattern of population distribution, which concentrated in the central delta at the expense of the periphery, was maintained and reinforced during the 1980s.

While the overall pattern of population concentration has remained virtually unchanged, except for a slight increase in regional variation, the mobility of the population has significantly increased as a result of both the process of economic restructuring and the relaxation of state control over population movement. As indicated, economic restructuring in the PRD was characterized by a relative decline in traditional farming and the rapid surge of the rural industry. This process of economic restructuring significantly increased the potential mobility of the population in the region. On the one hand, the demise of traditional food-grain production released a sizable number of rural laborers from the field. On the other hand, the flourishing of numerous rural industries, and the revitalized commercial activities in small towns, created phenomenal employment opportunities for the rural exodus. The combined effect of these push-and-pull forces has been a movement of people from farming to non-farming activities, and from rural to urban settlements. Such a movement has been facilitated since the mid-1980s by the state's deregulation of rural–urban migration.

One of the most important indicators of rural–urban migration in the Chinese statistics is what is termed the "temporary population" (*zanju renkou*), which refers to migrants who have lived in a locale for longer than one year without holding a permanent household registration in that locale. Data show that between the two national census years of 1982 and 1990, the "temporary population," essentially migrants moving to and within the PRD, increased by 42 percent, or an average of 350,000 persons per year. This growth rate was much higher than the provincial average of 29 percent per year. The total number of the "temporary population" rose from 184,000 in 1982 to 2.98 million in 1990. Almost 80 percent of the temporary population found in Guangdong province in 1990 ended up in the PRD (GPPCO, 1991, pp. 30–44). It is obvious that the PRD has become the chief destination for migrants moving to and within the province.

When analyzed at the intraregional level, the growth and distribution of migration exhibits a spatial pattern similar to the one associated with industrial and agricultural production. The most dramatic growth of migration occurred in the two SEZs of Shenzhen and Zhuhai, both of which recorded an extraordinary annual growth rate of over 75 percent. Their share of the regional total of temporary population rose significantly from a mere 2.4 percent to 21 percent during the eight years between 1982 and 1990 (GPPCO, 1991, pp. 40–4). The primate city of Guangzhou and other existing designated cities, such as Jiangmen, Zhaoqing, and Huizhou, did not receive many in-migrants during this period. The growth rates of migration to these cities were all lower than the regional average.

The most remarkable increase in temporary population occurred in the newly developing counties within the Guangzhou–Hong Kong–Macao triangle. These counties, especially Baoan and Dongguan, have experienced not only a much faster growth rate of in-migration than other parts of the region, but also a dramatic increase in their share of the regional total of the temporary population. As a group, they tripled their share of the regional total in eight years, accounting for a disproportionate 45 percent of all of the temporary population in 1990 (GPPCO, 1991, pp. 40–4).

While the SEZs and the newly developing counties were receiving an increasing and disproportionate number of in-migrants, cities and counties on the periphery were left far behind. These peripheral cities and counties accounted for 72.97 percent of the delta's land area and 47.88 percent of its total population, but received only 31 percent of the total in-migrants in 1982. That disproportionately low percentage dropped even further to 11 percent in 1990 (GPPCO, 1991, pp. 40–4). This spatial pattern of migration, characterized by a high concentration in the extended metropolitan zone bordered by Hong Kong, Guangzhou, and Macao, by a metropolitan center whose primacy has declined, and by a relatively backward periphery, is consistent with the spatial distribution of production facilities revealed in the previous section.

That the suburban zone of the PRD has accepted a large number of in-migrants as a result of economic restructuring may not be unique to the Chinese case. It took place in North America and Western Europe in the 1960s when highway development greatly facilitated the suburbanization of the urban population. What, then, are the distinct features of population redistribution in this Chinese region? Who are the migrants? Do they originate from the central cities? Why do they move into the suburban zone outside and between metropolitan centers? According to a 1 percent sample survey of migrants conducted by the provincial census authorities in 1988, increased migration since the reforms has been predominately intraprovincial. Migrants who originated from areas outside of the province accounted for only 11 percent (GPPCO, 1988, pp. 546–53; Ma and Lin, 1993; Fan, 1996, p. 35). The majority of migrants (57 percent) were female. In terms of their origins, most migrants (72 percent) came from villages in the countryside. Over 70 percent ended up in towns. As for the motive of migration, seeking employment, including job transfer, job assignment, and entering business or doing factoring work, was reported by most migrants (70 percent) as the main reason to change their residence (Ma and Lin, 1993, p. 595). When the results of this survey are pieced together, it becomes clear that migration in the PRD since the reforms has involved primarily an internal movement of surplus rural laborers from the countryside to towns in the quickly developing corridor between metropolitan centers for the purpose of seeking a factory job or for other more profitable non-agricultural pursuits. This pattern stands in sharp contrast with the earlier American experience of suburbanization, which primarily involved the relocation of urban residents from the central cities to the suburbs for greater open space. Most Chinese migrants have not moved into large cities, partly because of continued government regulation and partly because of high living costs there (Xu and Li, 1990, pp. 55–6; Zhou and Ma, 2000, p. 227). They have tended to move into towns located in the suburban zone outside and between the metropolitan centers of Hong Kong and Guangzhou primarily because, as revealed in the previous section, this zone has been the area of fastest economic growth where more job opportunities can be found.

It is clear from the above analysis that market reform and the opening up of the local economy have not resulted in an excessive concentration of population in large cities. Instead, expansion of non-agricultural activities and urbanization have taken place on a regional basis, particularly in the areas adjacent to and between such major metropolitan centers as Hong Kong, Guangzhou, and Shenzhen. The process and spatial pattern of region-based urbanization did not preclude the formation of new cities and towns. On the contrary, it is the rapid growth of cities and towns widely scattered in the region, particularly in the Hong Kong–Shenzhen–Guangzhou corridor, that helped accommodate the rural exodus and relieve the pressure on the metropolitan centers. On the surface, the formation of new cities such as Shenzhen, Zhongshan, and Dongguan seems to provide evidence to support the city-based urbanization model. A close examination of the demographic structure and functioning of these new cities suggests that they are distinct settlements with very special characteristics. These cities are characterized by the hypermobility of their population. Of the 3.8 million population in Shenzhen in 1997, for instance, 2.7 million or over two-thirds of the total lived and worked there on a temporary basis. The average age of these people was 25.19, making Shenzhen one of the youngest cities in the country and possibly in the world. In Dongguan, the number of temporary residents (1.42 million) was almost identical to the number of local residents (1.43 million). More importantly, these "cities" are home to people who are engaged in both agricultural and non-agricultural activities. A large proportion of the people who live in towns continue with their agricultural pursuits. There are also people who live in the countryside within these "cities," but are actually working in the non-agricultural sectors. Of the total population of the "city" of Dongguan in 1995, for instance, only 24.6 percent were classified as non-agricultural people. Similarly, only 28.3 percent of the population in the "city" of Zhongshan were in the non-agricultural category in 1995. Consequently, these newly emerged "cities" are actually a distinct form of settlement in which industry and agriculture or urban and rural activities are intensively mixed. They are neither "urban" nor "rural" in the classic terms but they demonstrate features of both types (McGee, 1989; Ginsburg, 1990).

To a great extent, the process and spatial pattern of region-based urbanization identified above has been shaped by forces of globalization, particularly the inflow of capital and industry from Hong Kong across the border. As a number of previous studies have documented (Smart and Smart, 1991; Leung, 1993; Lin, 1997d; Sit and Yang, 1997; Hsing, 1998), the export processing industry in the PRD has been set up primarily by Hong Kong entrepreneurs on the basis of social capital or pre-existing personal connections. Such industry is small-scale, low-tech, and labor-intensive, and is not always environmentally friendly. It needs a considerable amount of land and labor but does not necessarily require the educated professionals and high-class legal and financial services that are available only in large cities. The location of this industry is therefore not limited to only the large metropolitan centers of the region. Instead, rural townships and villages in the suburban areas of the Hong Kong–Shenzhen–Guangzhou corridor have become the loci of the export processing industry because of their pre-existing personal kinship ties, an abundant supply of cheap surplus rural laborers and land, an improved transportation infrastructure, and a less regulated environment. This situation is significantly different from the process of spatial restructuring in many American and European metropolitan areas, where the location and operation of multinational corporations remain based on large metropolitan centers because of the availability of financial institutions and producer services.

Conclusions

In recent years one of the most fervent topics for urban research has been the emerging processes and spatial patterns of urban change in the proclaimed era of globalization. Although the exact nature and extent of globalization remain highly controversial (Cox, 1997; Dicken, 1998, p. 4; Yeung, 1998), it has been generally recognized that, as perhaps both causes and consequences of globalization, distinct processes of flexible production and spatial reagglomeration are under way in selective American and European metropolitan regions. With few exceptions (McGee and Robinson, 1995; Yeung and Lo, 1996; Yusuf and Wu, 1997; Wu and Yeh, 1999; Wu, 2000), most of the documentation of globalization and urban change has concentrated on the situation in North America and Western Europe (Dogan and Kasarda, 1988; Scott, 1988; Knox, 1991; Sassen, 1991; Soja, 1995). Relatively little has been written on the processes and consequences of spatial restructuring in metropolitan regions of "the other world," particularly in those embedded in a transitional socialist economy. Without a good knowledge of what has been taking place in other parts of the interdependent world, however, any attempt to understand and theorize the logic of globalization and its spatial implications must be necessarily limited and incomplete.

This study of metropolitan development in socialist China focuses on the case of the PRD, where dramatic economic and spatial transformation has taken place since major institutional changes were made in 1978. An analysis of data at the regional level has suggested that the PRD has undergone profound changes of economic restructuring, through which agricultural production has become diversified and commercialized and rural industry has expanded dramatically. This process of change is distinct from what has taken place in North America and Western Europe, where economic restructuring has been centered on the growth of the service sector and high-tech industry. While the growing importance of the service economy and high-tech industry has brought about massive though selective reagglomeration of production activities in major American metropolitan regions, the process of agricultural diversification and rural industrialization in China has resulted in a shifting focus of economic development and urbanization, from central cities of the region to a zone outside and between major metropolitan centers. The emergence of the extended metropolitan zone has not been the result of urban sprawl, such as took place in North America several decades ago. Instead, most of the increased population (in-migrants) and expanded production facilities originated in the countryside. What has taken place in the PRD since the reforms is, therefore, an "urbanization of the countryside," in which peasants of the region "leave the soil but not the village" (*litu bulixiang*) and "enter the factory but not the city" (*jinchang bujincheng*). A derived outcome of this process has been an intensive mixture of industrial/agricultural or urban/rural activities therein, making it a zone of what the Chinese have called "urban–rural integration" or "urban–rural interlocking."

The driving forces that have shaped the distinct pattern of metropolitan development in the Chinese context are complex. They include a dense and growing population which has created tremendous pressure for agricultural diversification and industrialization, the relaxation of state control over the regional economy which allows local people to seek profitable non-agricultural pursuits and urbanize their life, the determined action taken by local governments to create a transactional environment conducive to external capital investment, and the intrusion of global capitalism in the form of not only capital but also information and technology. It is the interaction of these local and global forces that has given rise to the distinct, if not unique, features of metropolitan development that are found in the Chinese region.

What can we learn from the experience of the PRD? How can we relate this empirical study to the broader context of theoretical inquiry into the operating mechanism of urbanization? From a theoretical standpoint, at least three important issues require further research and reassessment in view of the changes taking place in this dynamic Chinese region. First, the relationship between industrialization and urbanization embedded in different political economies appears to be more sophisticated than has been generally believed. In the context of a free market economy, the transition of the society from pre-industrial to industrial has often resulted in a concentration of population in cities, especially large cities, where manufacturing and infrastructure facilities are clustered to generate and utilize agglomeration economies. The subsequent transition from industrial to post-industrial society has brought about flexible specialization of production, suburbanization, and the formation of "world cities" (Friedmann, 1995b). The scale of urbanization has expanded and the function of cities has changed from production bases to control centers. But the intertwined industrialization and urbanization logic remains constant. Cities are "centers of production and work in modern capitalist society" and "industrialization as a generalized process of economic organization and social integration is the basis of modern urban development" (Scott, 1986, pp. 25, 35). Urbanization is thus believed to be a process necessarily based on cities and driven by forces of industrialization.

The relationship between industrialization and urbanization becomes complicated when it is embedded in a transitional socialist society in which a market economy is yet to "grow out of the plan" (Naughton, 1995). While the city-based planned economy remains under the tight control of the state, restraints on the rural economy have been relaxed. The result has been twofold. Economically, the emphasis of growth has shifted from cities, where the planned economy is based, to the countryside, where peasants are relatively free to arrange production activities in their own way for a maximal generation of employment and income. Geographically, a dual-track pattern of urbanization has taken shape, consisting of a city-based urbanization manipulated by the state and a region-based urbanization emerging spontaneously from the grassroots of the countryside. This has given rise to an "anomaly" to the prevailing urban paradigm: urbanization and industrialization are not necessarily city-based. Industrialization may not necessarily result in increased urbanization if that is defined as a growing concentration of population and economic activities in cities.

Second, the utility of the arbitrary urban–rural dichotomy, which has been fundamental to the theory of urban transition and development studies, requires systematic reassessment. The importance of urban–rural interaction has received scholarly attention since the 1980s (Gould, 1982; Potter and Unwin, 1989; Douglass, 1998). However, the spatial manifestation of urban–rural interaction and the underlying forces that bring the two classified sectors together remain elusive. This study clearly identifies a zone surrounding and between metropolitan centers as the loci of urban–rural interaction. It is in this zone that the growth of industrial and agricultural production takes place side by side, where most of the rural footloose find their factory jobs, and where much of the cultivated land is converted into non-agricultural uses. This zone has been able to grow at a pace faster than both central cities and the periphery of the region primarily because of its high population density, improved transportation infrastructure, loosened state regulation, and pre-existing social capital. Will this zone of urban–rural integration continue to exist as the transition of the socialist economy moves further ahead? Has it taken place elsewhere in China and in Asia? Does it represent a new form of spatial organization in addition to town and country? Further studies are required to answer these questions.

Finally, the reconfiguration of state power in a transitional socialist economy and its peculiar interaction with the forces of global capitalism appear to be another fascinating topic for further investigation. Prophets of the globalization discourse have often cited the recent development in the HK-PRD region as a prime example to illustrate the breakdown of territorial boundaries, "the end of the nation-state," and the emergence of "region-states" (O'Brien, 1992; Guehenno, 1995; Ohmae, 1995, pp. 79–85). The "end of the nation-state" assertion has been criticized by others as "overtly simplistic" (Cox, 1997; Yeung, 1998, p. 292). A recent study of Chinese suburbanization has identified state policies as the most powerful driving force behind suburbanization, despite globalization and market reform (Zhou and Ma, 2000). This study suggests that it is the reconfiguration of the socialist state and its articulation with global market forces that explain the distinct process and spatial pattern of region-based urbanization. Rural industrialization of the PRD since the reforms has been a direct outcome of the state's reorganization of its central–local relation, which gave rise to the flourishing of the township and village enterprises in the vast countryside. The rapid growth of in-migrants in the suburban zone of the PRD is inseparable from the state's new approach toward internal migration, which continues to block population movement into large cities but allows rural–town migration. The capability of the PRD to maintain its growth momentum and narrowly escape the devastating effect of the Asian financial turmoil in 1997–8 was also a result of the foreign economic policy adjustments made by the state in 1987 after the Mexican financial turmoil (Lin, 2000, p. 463). The continued reconfiguration of the socialist state, its changing articulation with the forces of global capitalism, and the subsequent transformation of the transitional socialist space economy in the era of volatile globalization will remain intriguing topics for further investigations.

Bibliography

Abramson, Daniel (1997a) "Marketization" and institutions in Chinese inner-city neighborhood redevelopment: a commentary on "Beijing's old and dilapidated housing renewal" by Lu Junhua. *Cities*, 14(2), 71–5.

Abramson, Daniel (1997b) Neighborhood redevelopment as a cultural problem: a Western perspective on current plans for the old city of Beijing. Doctoral thesis, Tsinghua University.

Abramson, Daniel, Leaf, Michael, and Students of Plan 545 (2000) Urban development and redevelopment in quanzhou, china: a field studio report. Asian Urban Research Network, Working Paper no. 26, UBC Center for Human Settlements, Vancouver.

Abu-Lughod, Janet (1961) Migrant adjustment to city life: the Egyptian case. *American Journal of Sociology*, 67(1), 22–32.

Aglietta, Michael (1998) Capitalism at the turn of the century: regulation theory and the challenge of social change. *New Left Review*, 232, 41–90.

Albertsen, N. (1988) Postmodernism, post-Fordism, and critical social theory. *Environment and Planning D*, 6, 339–65.

Altvater, Elmar (1993) *The Future of the Market*. London: Verso.

Andrusz, G. D. (1984) *Housing and Urban Development in the USSR*. Albany, NY: State University of New York Press.

Andrusz, Gregory, Harloe, Michael, and Szelenyi, Ivan (1996) *Cities after Socialism: Urban and Regional Change and Conflict in Post-socialist Societies*. Cambridge, MA: Blackwell Publishers.

Arsilan, Mamut (1997) Determinants of the origin and development of the Xinjiang village in Beijing (Beijing shi Xinjiang cun de xingcheng jizhi yu fazhan fangxiang yanjiu). Unpublished BA thesis, Department of Geography, Peking University.

Arsilan, Mamut, Chen, Tian, and Liu, Erxiang (1998) Situation, problems and countermeasures in the Xinjiang village, Ganjiakou, Beijing (Beijing Ganjiakou Xingjiangcun, Wenti yu duice). Unpublished manuscript, Beijing.

Ash, R. F. (1988) The evolution of agricultural policy. *China Quarterly*, 116, 529–55.

Banerjee, Biswajit (1983) Social networks in the migration process: empirical evidence on chain migration in India. *Journal of Developing Areas*, 17(2), 185–96.

Barnes, T. (1996) *Logics of Dislocation: Models, Metaphors, and Meanings of Economic Space.* New York: Guilford.

Bello, W. and Rosenfeld, S. (1990) *Dragons in Distress: Asia's Miracle Economies in Crisis.* San Francisco: Institute of Food Development Policy.

Berger, Suzanne and Lester, Richard K. (1997) *Made by Hong Kong.* Hong Kong: Oxford University Press.

Bergere, M. (1981) "The other China": Shanghai from 1919 to 1949. In C. Howe (ed.), *Shanghai: Revolution and Development in an Asian Metropolis.* Cambridge: Cambridge University Press.

Bertaud, A. and Renaud, B. (1997) Socialist cities without land markets. *Journal of Urban Economics*, 41, 137–51.

Bian, Yanjie and Logan, John R. (1996) Market transition and the persistence of power: the changing stratification system in urban China. *American Sociological Review*, 61, 739–58.

Bian, Yanjie, Logan, John R., Hanlong Lu, Yunkang Pan, and Ying Guan (1997a) Work units and the commodification of housing: observations on the transition to a market economy with Chinese characteristics. *Social Science in China*, 18(4), 28–35.

Bian, Yanjie, Logan, John R., Hanlong Lu, Yunkang Pan, and Ying Guan (1997b) Work units and housing reform in two Chinese cities. In Elizabeth Perry and Xiabo Lu (eds), *The Danwei: The Changing Chinese Workplace in Historical and Comparative Perspective.* New York: M. E. Sharpe.

Bianzuan, Weiyuanhui (1997) *Shanghai shi ditu ji.* Shanghai: Shanghai kexue jishu chuban she.

Biao, Xiang (1999) Zhejiang village in Beijing: creating a visible non-state space through migration and marketized networks. In Frank N. Pieke and Hein Mallee (eds), *Internal and International Migration: Chinese Perspectives.* Surrey: Curzon.

Bourne, Larry S. (1982) Urban spatial structure: an introduction essay on concepts and criteria. In *Internal Structure of the City*, 2nd edn. New York: Oxford University Press.

Boyer, Robert (1990) *The Regulation School: A Critical Introduction.* New York: Columbia University Press.

Brenner, Neil (1999) Globalization as reterritorialization: the re-scaling of urban governance in the European Union. *Urban Studies*, 36(3), 431–51.

Browning, H. L. (1958) Recent trends in Latin American urbanization. *Annals of the American Academy of Political and Social Sciences*, 316, 111–20.

Byrd, William A. and Lin Qingsong (1990) *China's Rural Industry.* Oxford: Oxford University Press.

Cai, Fang (1997) The characteristics of the organization of rural migrant workers. *Social Sciences of China*, 6(4), 127–38 (in Chinese).

Cao, Guangzhong and Yanwei Chai (1998) The transition of internal regional structure and suburbanization in Dalian. *Geography Science*, 18(3), 234–41.

Carter, H. (1982) *The Study of Urban Geography*. London: Edward Arnold.

Castells, M. (1976a) Is there an urban sociology? In C. G. Pickvance (ed.), *Urban Sociology: Critical Essays*. London: Tavistock.

Castells, M. (1976b) Theory and ideology in urban sociology. In C. G. Pickvance (ed.), *Urban Sociology: Critical Essays*. London: Tavistock.

Cerase, F. (1970) Nostalgia or disenchantment: considerations on return migration. In H. Bernstein, B. Crow, and H. Johnson (eds), *The Italian Experience in the United States*. New York: Center for Migration Studies.

Chan, D. (1999) Suzhou handover in 2001. *Singapore Straits Times*, June 29, p. 1.

Chan, Kam Wing (1994) *Cities with Invisible Walls*. Hong Kong: Oxford University Press.

Chan, Kam Wing (1996a) Internal migration in China: an introductory overview. *Chinese Environment and Development*, 7, 3–13.

Chan, Kam Wing (1996b) Post-Mao China: a two-class urban society in the making. *International Journal of Urban and Regional Research*, 20(1), 134–50.

Chan, R. C. K. (1995) The urban migrants – the challenge to urban policy. In L. Wong and S. MacPherson (eds), *Social Change and Social Policy in Contemporary China*. London: Avebury.

Chen, Demei (1997a) Rising and falling wave: a look at migrant workers returning to the countryside and starting businesses. *Chinese Peasantry*, 3, 56–7.

Chen, Hanxin (1999) The research on the patterns of high-tech development zone and construction distribution in China. *Economic Geography*, 16(2), 6–10.

Chen, Hao (1996a) The outflow of China's rural labour and rural development. *Population Research*, 20(4), 1–11 (in Chinese).

Chen, Lingsheng (1997b) 1990s: great changes in Shanghai urban construction. *China Construction Newspaper (East China News)*, September 8, p. 1.

Chen, Ru (1996b) Analysis of the current phenomenon of returning rural youth. *Problems in Agricultural Economics*, 10, 26–30 (in Chinese).

Chen, Tian (1998) Long-term policy for a well ordered administration of non-local settlements (Wailai renkou jujuqu guifanhua guanli de changqi duice). Unpublished manuscript, Institute of Geography, Chinese Academy of Sciences, Beijing.

Chen, Tian and Zhao, Xiaobin (1998) Micro-analysis of the development of the floating people's settlement – empirical investigation of the development of Liudong Renkou's enclaves in Beijing (Liudong renkou jujuqu xingcheng yu yanhua jizhi de weiguan toushi – yi Beijing wailai renkou jujuqu yanhua guocheng de shizheng fenxi weili). Unpublished paper, Institute of Geography, Chinese Academy of Sciences, Beijing.

Chen, Wenjuan and Cai Renqun (1996) The process and dynamic of suburbanization of Guangzhou. *Tropics Geography*, 16(2), 122–9.

Chen, Xiangming and Parish, William (1996) Urbanization in China: reassessing an evolving model. In Josef Gugler (ed.), *The Urban Transformation of the Developing World*. New York: Oxford University Press.

Chen, Xiangming (1995) The evolution of free economic zones and the recent development of cross-national growth zones. *International Journal of Urban and Regional Research*, 19(4), 593–616.

China Economic Monitoring Center (1999a) *Consumers: A Stronger Demand for Social Security*. report.drc.gov.cn, November 24.

China Economic Monitoring Center (1999b) *Continuous Increase of Migrant Laborers.* report.drc.gov.cn, November 24.

China Financial Society (1998) *China Financial Yearbook 1998.* Beijing Editorial Department of China Financial Yearbook.

China–Singapore Suzhou Development (CSSD) (1999) *China–Singapore Suzhou Industrial Park Prospectus.* Suzhou: CSSD.

China State Statistical Bureau (1993) *Statistical Yearbook of China.* Beijing: China Statistics Publishing House.

China State Statistical Bureau (1996) *Statistical Yearbook of China:* Beijing: China Statistics Publishing House.

Chiu, Stephen W. K. (1996) Unraveling Hong Kong's exceptionalism: the politics of laissez-faire in the industrial takeoff. *Political Power and Social Theory*, 10, 229–56.

Chiu, Youliang and Tian Chen (1998) Land utilization in the in-migration areas of Beijing (Beijing shi wailai renkou jujiqu tudi liyong tezheng yu xingcheng jizhi yanjin). Unpublished manuscript, Institute of Geography, Chinese Academy of Science, Beijing.

Christerson, Brad and Lever-Tracy, Constance (1997) The third China? Emerging industrial districts in rural China. *International Journal of Urban and Regional Research*, 21(4), 569–88.

Chu, D. K. Y. (1986) The special economic zones and the problem of territorial containment. In Y. C. Jao and C. K. Leung (eds), *China's Special Economic Zones: Policies, Problems and Prospects.* Hong Kong: Oxford University Press.

Chuta, E. and Liedholm, C. (1984) Rural small-scale industry: empirical evidence and policy issues. In Calvin Goldscheider (ed.), *Agricultural Development in the Third World.* London: Johns Hopkins University Press.

Clark, D. (1996) *Urban World/Global City.* London: Routledge.

Clark, G. H. and Gertler, Meric (1983) Migration and capital. *Annals of the Association of American Geographers*, 73(1), 18–34.

Clarke, Susan and Gaile, G. (1998) *The Work of Cities.* Minneapolis: University of Minnesota Press.

Clemens, W. C. (1999) China: alternative futures. *Communist and Post-Communist Studies*, 32, 1–21.

Collier, David (1976) *Squatter Settlements and the Incorporation of Migrants into Urban Life: The Case of Lima.* Cambridge, MA: Center for International Studies, MIT.

Commerce and Industry Bureau (2000) *Competitiveness and Knowledge-based Industries: Policy Objective Booklet 2000.* Hong Kong Special Administration Region.

Connell, John, Dasgupta, Biblab, Laishley, Roy, and Lipton, Michael (1976) *Migration from Rural Areas: The Evidence from Village Studies.* Oxford: Oxford University Press.

Conway, Dennis (1985) Changing perspectives on squatter settlements, intraurban mobility, and constraints on housing choice of the Third World urban poor. *Urban Geography*, 6(2), 170–92.

Cook, P. (1988) Flexible integration, scope economics, and strategic alliances: social and spatial mediations. *Environment and Planning D*, 6(3), 281–300.

Costello, Michael A., Leinbach, Thomas R., and Ulack, Richard (1987) *Mobility and Employment in Urban Southeast Asia: Examples from Indonesia and the Philippines.* Boulder, CO: Westview Press.

Cox, Kevin (1981) Capitalism and conflict around the communal living space. In Michael Dear and Allen J. Scott (eds), *Urbanization and Urban Planning in Capitalist Society*. New York: Methuen.

Cox, Kevin (1997) *Spaces of Globalization: Reasserting the Power of the Local*. New York: Guilford.

Dai, Fan (1998) The feminization of migration in the Pearl River Delta. *Journal of Chinese Geography*, 8(2), 101–15.

Dai, Yifeng (1996) Overseas migration and the economic modernization of Xiamen City during the twentieth century. In Leo Douw and Peter Post (eds), *South China: State, Culture, and Social Change During the Twentieth Century*. Amsterdam: North-Holland.

Davin, Delia (1999) *Internal Migration in Contemporary China*. Basingstoke: Macmillan.

Davis, Deborah S., Kraus, R., Naughton, Barry, and Perry, Elizabeth J. (1995) *Urban Spaces in Contemporary China*. New York: Cambridge University Press.

Deng, N. and Jiang, L. (1998) Study on the strategic problems of the development of China's international cities. *Urban Planning Forum*, 2, 13–16 (in Chinese).

Deng, Qing (1998) Housing reform and China's property market. *Warburg Dillon Read*, July, 34–42.

Deng, Wei (1997) Constructing modern saving-land city. *City Development and Land Use*, 3, 15–18.

Dicken, Peter (1998) *Global Shift: Transforming the World Economy*, 2nd edn. London: Paul Chapman.

Ding, Jinhong and Stockman, Norman (1999) The floating population and the integration of the city community: a survey on the attitudes of Shanghai residents to recent migrants. In Frank N. Pieke and Hein Mallee (eds), *Internal and International Migration: Chinese Perspectives*. Surrey: Curzon.

Dobson, Wendy (1997) East Asian integration: synergies between firm strategies and government policies. In W. Dobson and S. Y. Chia (eds), *Multinationals and East Asian Integration*. Ottawa and Singapore: IRDC and ISEAS.

Dogan, Mattei and Kasarda, John D. (1988) *The Metropolis Era: A World of Giant Cities*. Newbury Park, CA: Sage.

Dong, Wei (1997) Research on the land-use problem in the old and dilapidated area renewal of Beijing: the case of Xicheng District. Postdoctoral report, Tsinghua University.

Douglass, M. (1998) A regional network strategy for reciprocal rural–urban linkages. *Third World Planning Review*, 20(1), 1–33.

Dowall, David E. (1993) Establishing urban land markets in the People's Republic of China. *Journal of the American Planning Association*, 59(2), 182–92.

Dowall, David E. (1994) Urban residential redevelopment in the People's Republic of China. *Urban Studies*, 31, 1497–516.

Dunning, John H. (1997) Governments and the macro-organization of economic activity: an historical and spatial perspective. *Review of International Political Economy*, 4(1), 42–86.

Editorial Department (1997) The external population: advantaged or disadvantaged? *Population Study*, 4, 44–8.

Economist (1998) The trouble with Singapore's clone. *The Economist*, January 3, p. 39.

Economist (1999) Undesirable, maybe, but vital. The big cities don't like China's migrants from the countryside, but they cannot cope without them. *The Economist*, October 16, p. 41.

Economist Intelligence Unit (1999) Business China. *The Economist*, October 25, pp. 11–12.

Eisinger, Peter K. (1988) *The Rise of the Entrepreneurial State: State and Local Economic Development Policy in the United States*. Madison: Wisconsin University Press.

Ellis, Frank (1998) Household strategies and rural livelihood diversification. *Journal of Development Studies*, 35, 1–38.

Eng, Irene (1997) The rise of manufacturing towns: externally driven industrialization and urban development in the Pearl River Delta of China. *International Journal of Urban and Regional Research*, 21(4), 554–68.

Enright, Michael (1998) Transcript, Public Conference on Hong Kong's Competitiveness. Hong Kong Special Administration Region: Central Policy Unit, www.info.gov.hk/cpu/english/hon.htm, April, accessed on October 26, 2000.

Enright, M., Scott, E., and Dodwell, D. (1997) *The Hong Kong Advantage*. Hong Kong: Oxford University Press.

Evans, Peter B. (1996) Government action, social capital and development: reviewing the evidence on synergy. *World Development*, 24(6), 1119–32.

Fadayomi, T. O., Titilola, S. O., Oni, B., and Fapohunda, O. J. (1992) Migrations and development policies in Nigeria. In Moriba Toure and T. O. Fadoyomi (eds), *Migrations, Development and Urbanization Policies in Sub-Saharan Africa*. London: Codesria Book Series.

Fagan, Robert H. and Le Heron, Richard B. (1994) Reinterpreting the geography of accumulation: the global shift and local restructuring. *Environment and Planning D: Society and Space*, 12(3), 265–86.

Fainstein, Susan (1994) *The City Builders: Property, Politics, and Planning in London and New York*. Oxford: Blackwell.

Fainstein, Susan, Fainstein, Norman I., and Armistead, P. Jefferson (1983) San Francisco: urban transformation and the local state. In Susan Fainstein, Norman I. Fainstein, Richard Child Hill, Dennis Judd, and Michael Peter Smith (eds), *Restructuring the City: The Political Economy of Urban Redevelopment*. New York and London: Longman.

Fan, C. Cindy (1995a) Developments from above, below and outside: spatial impacts of China's economic reforms in Jiangsu and Guangdong provinces. *Chinese Environment and Development*, 6, 85–116.

Fan, C. Cindy (1995b) Of belts and ladders: state policy and uneven regional development in post-Mao China. *Annals of the Association of American Geographers*, 85(3), 421–49.

Fan, C. Cindy (1996) Economic opportunities and internal migration: a case study of Guangdong province. China *Professional Geographer*, 48(1), 28–45.

Fan, Lie, Zhang Zhemin and Bo Jiancheng (1999) First migrant apartment in Hangzhou completed and opened. *Liberation Daily*, July 14.

Forrest, Ray and Murie, Alan (1988) *Selling the Welfare State: The Privatization of Public Housing*. London: Routledge.

French, R. A. and Hamilton, F. E. I. (1979) *The Socialist City*. Chichester: John Wiley and Sons.

Friedman, B. S. (1983) Public housing in china: policies and practices. *Journal of Housing*, 40(3), 82–5.

Friedmann, John (1978) The spatial organization of power in the development of urban systems. In L. S. Bourne and J. W. Simmons (eds), *System of Cities*. New York: Oxford University Press.

Friedmann, John (1986) The world city hypothesis. *Development and Change*, 17(1), 69–83.

Friedmann, John (1995a) Where we stand: a decade of world city research.In Paul L. Knox and Peter J. Taylor (eds), *World Cities in a World-System*. Cambridge: Cambridge University Press.

Friedmann, John (1995b) The world city hypothesis. In Paul L. Knox and Peter J. Taylor (eds), *World Cities in a World-System*. Cambridge: Cambridge University Press.

Friedmann, John (1998) World city futures: the role of urban and regional policies in the Asia-Pacific region. In Yue Man Yeung (ed.), *Urban Development in Asia: Retrospect and Prospect*. Hong Kong: The Chinese University of Hong Kong.

Friedmann, John and Wolff, Goetz (1982) World city formation: an agenda for research and action. *International Journal of Urban and Regional Research*, 6, 309–43.

Friedmann, John and Wulff, R. (1975) *The Urban Transition: Comparative Studies of Newly Industrialising Societies*. London: Edward Arnold.

Gaubatz, Piper (1999) China's urban transformation: patterns and processes of morphological change in Beijing, Shanghai and Guangzhou. *Urban Studies*, 36, 1495–521.

Geddes, Patrick (1915) *Cities in Evolution* (1947 reprint edited by J. Tyrwhitt). London: Williams & Norgate.

Gertler, M. S. (1988) The limits to flexibility: comments on the Post-Fordist vision of production and its geography. *Transactions Institute of British Geography NS*, 13, 419–32.

Gertler, M. S. (1992) Flexibility revisited: districts, nation-states, and the forces of production *Transactions Institute of British Geography NS*, 17, 259–78.

Gilbert, Alan and Varley, Ann (1990) Renting a home in a Third World City: choice or constraint? *International Journal of Urban and Regional Research*, 14(1), 89–108.

Ginsburg, N. (1990) *The Urban Transition: Reflections on the American and Asian Experiences*. Hong Kong: The Chinese University Press.

Gmelch, George (1980) Return migration. *Annual Review of Anthropology*, 9, 135–59.

Goldstein, Alice and Shenyang Guo (1992) Temporary migration in Shanghai and Beijing. *Studies in Comparative International Development*, 27(2), 39–56.

Goldstein, Sidney (1993) The impact of temporary migration on urban places: Thailand and China as case studies. In John D. Kasarda and Allan M. Parnell (eds), *Third World Cities: Problems, Policies, and Prospects*. Newbury Park, CA: Sage Publications.

Gore, Lance L. P. (1999) The communist legacy in post-Mao economic growth. *The China Journal*, 41, 25–54.

Gould, W. T. S. (1982) Rural–urban interaction in the Third World. *Area*, 14, 334.

Gregory, D. (1978) *Ideology, Science and Human Geography*. London: Routledge.

Gregory, D. and Urry, J. (1985) *Social Relations and Spatial Structure*. Hong Kong: Macmillan.

Gu, Chaolin (1995) China's urban housing system in transition. *Journal of Chinese Geography*, 6(2), 16–38.

Gu, Chaolin (1999) Social polarization and segregation phenomenon in Beijing. In Adrian Guillermo Aguilar and Irma Escamilla (eds), *Problems of Megacities: Social Inequalities, Environmental Risk and Urban Governance.* Mexico City: Institute of Geography.

Gu, Chaolin and Qin Zhang (1997) The planning theory and method of town system in the new period. *Journal of Urban Planning,* 4(2), 14–17.

Gu, Chaolin et al. (1999) A study of the pattern of migration in Chinese large and medium-sized cities *Acta Geographica Sinica,* 54(3), 204–11 (in Chinese).

Gu, Shengzu and Xinhua Jian (1994) *Population Mobility and Urbanization in Contemporary China.* Wuhan: Wuhan daxue chubanshe (in Chinese).

Guangdong Province Population Census Office (GPPCO) (1988) *Tabulation of China's One Percent Population Sample Survey of 1987: Guangdong Volume.* Beijing: Zhongguo tongji chubance.

Guangdong Province Population Census Office (GPPCO) (1991) *Manual Processed Data for the Fourth Population Census for Guangdong Province.* Guangzhou: Internal Publication.

Guangdong Province Statistical Bureau (GPSB) (1990) *1990 Statistical Yearbook of Guangdong Province.* Changsa: Zhongguo tongji chubance.

Guangdong Province Statistical Bureau (GPSB) (1991) *National Economic Statistical Data for Cities and Counties in Guangdong Province.* Guangzhou: Internal Publication.

Guangdong Province Statistical Bureau (GPSB) (1992) *National Economic Statistical Data for the Zhujiang Delta, 1980–1991.* Guangzhou: Internal Publication.

Guangdong Province Statistical Bureau (GPSB) (1996) *Statistical Yearbook of Guangdong Province.* Beijing: Zhongguo tongji chubance.

Guehenno, J. M. (1995) *The End of the Nation-state.* Minneapolis: University of Minnesota Press.

Guldin, Gregory E. (1996) Desakotas and beyond: urbanization in southern China. *Ethnology,* 35, 265–83.

Guldin, Gregory E. (1997) *Farewell to Peasant China: Rural Urbanization and Social Change in the Late Twentieth Century.* Armonk, NY: M. E. Sharpe.

Guthrie, Douglas (1996) Organizational action and institutional reforms in China's Economic transition: a comparison of two industries. *Research in the Sociology of Organizations,* 14, 181–221.

Hall, Peter (1966) *The World Cities.* London: Weidenfeld and Nicolson.

Hall, Peter (1998) Globalization and the world cities. In Fu Chen Lo and Yue Man Yeung (eds), *Globalization and the World of Large Cities.* Tokyo: United Nations University Press.

Hao, Hongsheng et al. (1998) Management problems and preventive measures regarding "non-local" population in big cities – case study in Hadian district, Beijing. *Renkou Yanjiu (Population Research),* 21(1), 13–20 (in Chinese).

Harloe, Michael (1996) Cities in the transition. In G. Andrusz, M. Harloe, and I. Szelenyi (eds) *Cities after Socialism: Urban and Regional Change and Conflict in Post-socialist Societies.* Oxford: Blackwell Publishers.

Harris, C. D. (1997) "The nature of cities" and urban geography in the last half century. *Urban Geography,* 18(1), 15–35.

Harvey, David (1989) From managerialism to entrepreneurialism: the transformation in urban governance in late capitalism. Paper delivered to the Vega symposium, Stockholm, April.

Heberer, Thomas and Taubmann, Wolfgang (1998) *Chinas laendliche Gesellschaft im Umbruch. Urbanisierung und sozio-oekonomischer Wandel auf dem Lande*. Wiesbaden: Westdeutscher Verlag.

Hegedus, J. (1987) Reconsidering the roles of the state and the market in socialist housing systems. *International Journal of Urban and Regional Research*, 11, 79–97.

Henderson, J. (1989) *The Globalization of High Technology Production: Society, Space and Semi-conductors in the Restructuring of the Modern World*. London: Routledge.

Henderson, J. (1999) Uneven crisis: institutional foundations of East Asian economic turmoil. *Economy and Society*, 28(3), 327–67.

Heyman, Josiah M. and Smart, Alan (1999) States and illegal practices: an overview. In Josiah M. Heyman (ed.), *States and Illegal Practices*. Oxford: Berg.

Ho, S. P. S. (1994) *Rural China in Transition*. Oxford: Clarendon Press.

Holland, Lorien (1999) Poor and poorer. *Far Eastern Economic Review*, 11(19), 26–7.

Hong Kong General Chamber of Commerce (1999a) *Industry and Technology – A Constructive Role for the Chamber*. www.chamber.org.hk, March 16, accessed on October 26, 2000.

Hong Kong General Chamber of Commerce (1999b) *Chamber Urges Industrial Policy on Innovation and Technology*. www.chamber.org.hk, March 22, accessed on October 26, 2000.

Hong Kong Special Administration Region (1998a) *Chief Executive's Commission on Innovation and Technology: First Report*. September.

Hong Kong Special Administration Region (1998b) *From Adversity to Opportunity*. Address by the Chief Executive, the Honorable Tung Chee Hwa, at the Legislative Council Meeting on October 7.

Hong Kong Special Administration Region (1999a) *Chief Executive's Commission on Innovation and Technology: Second and Final Report*. June.

Hong Kong Special Administration Region (1999b) *Quality People, Quality Home: Positioning Hong Kong for the Twenty-first Century*. Address by the Chief Executive, the Honorable Tung Chee Hwa, at the Legislative Council Meeting, October 6.

Hong Kong Special Administrative Region (2000a) *Bringing the Vision to Life: Hong Kong's Long-term Development Needs and Goals*. Central Policy Unit Commission on Strategic Development, February.

Hong Kong Special Administration Region (2000b) *The 2000–2001 Budget: "Scaling New Heights."* Speech by the Financial Secretary, moving the Second Reading of the Appropriation Bill 2000, March 8.

Hong Kong Trade Development Council (1999) *Hong Kong's Competitiveness Beyond the Asian Crisis*. Research Department, February.

Honig, Emily (1992) *Creating Chinese Ethnicity: Subei People in Shanghai, 1850–1980*. New Haven, CT: Yale University Press.

Hsing, You-tien (1998) *Making Capitalism in China: The Taiwan Connection*. Oxford: Oxford University Press.

Hu, Xuwei (1998) The study of spatial gathering and spreading in the coast region where towns concentrated. *Urban Planning*, 22(6), 22–8.

Hu, Xuwei, Yixing Zhou, and Chaolin Gu (2000) *Studies on Agglomeration and Dispersion in China's Coastal City-and-town Concentrated Area*. Beijing: Science Press (in Chinese).

Hu, Zhaoliang (1987) The study of the internal dynamic of Chinese metropolitan development. *Urban Problems*, 2, 2–4.

Huang, Meiyu (1997) Jiucheng Gaizao de Huimou yu Qianzhan (A glance back and a look ahead at the redevelopment of the Old City). *Quanzhou Wanbao (Quanzhou Evening News)*, November 11.

Huang, Yasheng (1998) *FDI China: An Asian Perspective*. Singapore: Institute of Southeast Asian Studies and Chinese University Press.

Huff, W. G. (1994) *The Economic Growth of Singapore: Trade and Development in the Twentieth Century*. Cambridge: Cambridge University Press.

Ingram, G. K. (1998) Patterns of metropolitan development: what have we learned? *Urban Studies*, 35(7), 1019–35.

Innes, Judith (1995) Planning theory's emerging paradigm: communicative action and interactive practice. *Journal of Planning Education and Research*, 14(3), 183–90.

Institute of Geography (1998) Department of Urban and Human Geography, Academy of Science, Beijing, material from field studies (Bufen gean fangwen diaocha shilu). Unpublished material (in Chinese).

Jankowiak, William (1999) Research trends in the study of Chinese cities: a review essay. *City and Society*, 13, 369–95.

Jellinek, Lea (1977) The Pondok of Jakarta. *Bulletin of Indonesian Economic Studies*, 13, 67–71.

Jessop, Bob (1997) The entrepreneurial city: re-imaging localities, redesigning economic governance. In Nick Jewson and Suzanne MacGregor (eds), *Realizing Cities: New Spatial Divisions and Social Transformation*. London: Routledge.

Jessop, Bob (1998a) The enterprise of narrative and the narrative of enterprise: place marketing and the entrepreneurial city. In T. Hall and P. Hubbard (eds), *The Entrepreneurial City*. Chichester: Wiley.

Jessop, Bob (1998b) The rise of governance and the risks of failure: the case of economic development. *International Social Science Journal*, 155, 29–47.

Jessop, Bob and Sum, Ngai-Ling (2000) An entrepreneurial city in action: Hong Kong's emerging strategies in and for (inter-)urban competition. *Urban Studies*, 37(12), 2290–315.

Jessop, Bob and Sum, Ngai-Ling (2001) Pre-disciplinary and post-disciplinary perspectives on new political economy. *New Political Economy*, 6(1), 89–102.

Ji, Enze (1997) The stealthy return of migrants, *Country Tribune*, 1, 13 (in Chinese).

Ji, Wen (1998) Shanghai: clarifying the city construction goal in the coming three years. *City Star*, July 25, p. 1.

Jian, C. (1989) *Zhongshan: A Photographic Introduction*. Hong Kong: Tianyi Publishing House.

Jiang, D., Chen, J. J., and Isaac, D. (1998) The effect of foreign investment on the real estate industry in China. *Urban Studies*, 35, 2101–10.

Jin, Dengjian and Haynes, Kingsley E. (1997) Economic transition at the edge of order and chaos: China's dualism and leading sectoral approach. *Journal of Economic Issues*, 31(1), 79–101.

Johnston, R. J. (1983) *Philosophy and Human Geography: An Introduction to Contemporary Approaches*. London: Edward Arnold.

Kempen, E. T. (1994) The dual city and the poor: social polarization, social segregation and life chances. *Urban Studies*, 31(7), 995–1015.

Kesteloot, Christian (1992) Some spatial implications of socialist planned economies. *Acta Geographic Lovaniewsia*, 33, 277–81.

Kesteloot, Christian (1995) Three levels of socio-spatial polarization in Brussels. *Built Environment*, 20(3), 204–17.

King, Russell, Mortimer, J., and Strachan, A. (1984) Return migration and tertiary development: a Calabrian case study. *Anthropological Quarterly*, 57, 112–23.

King, Russell (1985) *Return Migration and Regional Economic Problems*. London: Croom Helm.

Kirkby, R. J. R. (1985) *Urbanization in China*. New York: Columbia University Press.

Klak, Thomas and Holtzclaw, Michael (1993) The housing, geography, and mobility of Latin American urban poor: the prevailing model and the case of Quito, Ecuador. *Growth and Change*, 24(2), 247–76.

Knight, John, Lina Song, and Huabin Jia (1999) Chinese rural migrants in urban enterprises: three perspectives. *Journal of Development Studies*, 35(3), 73–104.

Knox, P. L. (1991) The restless urban landscape: economic and sociocultural change and the transformation of Washington, DC. *Annals of the Association of American Geographers*, 81(2), 181–209.

Knox, P. L. (1996) Globalization and urban change. *Urban Geography*, 17(1), 115–17.

Knox, P. L. and Taylor, P. J. (eds) (1995) *World Cities in a World-system*. Cambridge: Cambridge University Press.

Koh, B. S. (1996) Suzhou Park: S'pore steps up officials' training. *Singapore Straits Times*, April 16, p. 1.

Krause, Lawrence B. (1987) Thinking about Singapore. In Lawrence B. Krause, Ai Tee Koh, and Tsao Yuan Lee (eds), *The Singapore Economy Reconsidered*. Singapore: ISEAS.

Kwang, M. (1998) Why Suzhou Park gets priority. *Singapore Straits Times*, March 3, p. 25.

Lague, D. (1998) China "shenanigans" over $30bn plan for clone city miffs Lee. *International Herald Tribune*, March 21, p. 21.

Laite, Julian (1984) Circulatory migration and social differentiation in the Andes. In Guy Standing (ed.), *Labor Circulation and the Labor Process*. London: Croom Helm.

Lakuiyin, A. (1996) Facing the city's future of sustainable development. *Urban Planning*, 4, 28–31.

Lardy, N. P. (1983) *Agriculture in China's Modern Economic Development*. Cambridge: Cambridge University Press.

Lardy, N. R. (1996) The role of foreign trade and investment in China's economic transformation. In Andrew G. Walder (ed.), *China's Transitional Economy*. Oxford: Oxford University Press.

Lash, Scott and Urry, John (1994) *Economies of Signs and Space*. London: Sage.

Leaf, Michael L. (1998) Urban planning and urban reality under chinese economic reforms. *Journal of Planning Education and Research*, 18, 145–53.

Leaf, Michael L. et al. (1995) Planning for urban redevelopment in Quanzhou, Fujian, China. Asian Urban Research Network, Working Paper no. 5, UBC Centre for Human Settlements, Vancouver.

Leung, Chi K. (1993) Personal contacts, subcontracting linkages, and development in the Hong Kong–Zhujiang Delta region. *Annals of the Association of American Geographers*, 83, 272–302.

Lever-Tracy, Constance, Ip, David, and Tracy, Noel (1996) *The Chinese Diaspora and Mainland China: An Emerging Economic Strategy*. London: Macmillian Press.

Li, Cheng (1998a) Surplus rural laborers and internal migration in China. Current status and future prospects. In Børge Bakken (ed.), *Migration in China*. Copenhagen: Nordic Institute of Asian Studies, NIAS Report Series 31.

Li, Fen (1998b) To divide Shanghai downtown area into six comprehensive districts, *City Star*, December 22, p. 1.

Li, L. X. and Xu, X. Q. (1994) A preliminary thinking on Guangzhou becoming international city. *Economic Geography*, 14(2), 32–7 (in Chinese).

Li, Mengbai (1999) The urban development and urban modernization. *Study of Urban Development*, 2, 56–8.

Li, Zhibin (1997a) The change of socioeconomic spatial structure in Chinese suburbs. *Human Geography*, 13(2), 18–22.

Li, Zhibin (1997b) Urban problems and urban sustainable development. *Urban Study*, 4, 8–11.

Liang, Fang (1995) The new urban center in Guangzhou – the new city of Zhu River. *Zhu River Economy*, 6, 15–16.

Lim, Chong Yah et al. (1988) *Policy Options for the Singapore Economy*. Singapore: McGraw-Hill.

Lin, Dongcai (1997a) Quanzhou Shi Guchengqu Tumen Jie, Dong Jie Pianqu Baohu Jianshe de Guihua yu Shixian (Planning and implementation of conservation and construction in the Tumen Street and East Street parcels of Quanzhou's Old City District). *Haixia Chengshi (Strait Cities)*, 10, 45–6.

Lin, G. C. S. (1994) Changing theoretical perspectives on urbanization in Asian developing countries. *Third World Planning Review*, 16(1), 1–23.

Lin, G. C. S. (1997b) *Red Capitalism in South China: Growth and Development of the Pearl River Delta*. Vancouver: University of British Columbia Press.

Lin, G. C. S. (1997c) Transformation of a rural economy in the Zhujiang Delta. *China Quarterly*, 149, 56–80.

Lin, G. C. S. (1997d) Intrusion of global forces and transformation of a local Chinese economy: the experience of Dongguan. In R. F. Watters and T. G. McGee (eds), *Asia Pacific: New Geographies of the Pacific Rim*. London: Hurst.

Lin, G. C. S. (1998) China's industrialization with controlled urbanization: anti-urbanism or urban-biased? *Issues and Studies*, 34(6), 98–116.

Lin, G. C. S. (1999) State policy and spatial restructuring in post-reform China, 1978–95. *International Journal of Urban and Regional Research*, 23(4), 670–96.

Lin, G. C. S. (2000) State, capital, and space in China in an age of volatile globalization. *Environment and Planning A*, 32(3), 455–71.

Lin, G. C. S. (2001) Evolving spatial form of urban–rural interaction in the Pearl River Delta, China. *Professional Geographer*, 53.

Liu, Guiting (1997a) Shilun ba Quanzhou Jiancheng Yatai Diqu de Guojixing Luyou Chengshi (An attempt to discuss the making of Quanzhou into an Asian-Pacific Regional international tourist city). Masters thesis, Fujian Normal University, Fuzhou.

Liu, Haiyong and Chen Tian (1998) Beijing liudong renkou juluo de jegou xingtai he xingcheng jizhi (Structure and development of floating people's settlements in Beijing). Unpublished manuscript, Institute of Geography, Chinese Academy of Sciences, Beijing (Chinese).

Liu, Xiaoli and Liang Wei (1997) Zhejiangcun: social and spatial implications of informal urbanization on the periphery of Beijing. *Cities*, 14(2), 95–108.

Liu, Yang (1997b) Research on artificial environment benefit and residential mobility of housing area renewal in the old city of Beijing. Doctoral Thesis, Tsinghua University.

Liu, Ying Qiu (1999) Macroeconomic policy choices during second-high increase stage. *Economic Information Daily*, April 28, p. 2 (in Chinese).

Lo, C. P. (1989) Recent spatial restructuring in Zhujiang Delta, South China: a study of socialist regional development strategy. *Annals of the Association of American Geographers*, 79(2), 293–308.

Lo, C. P. (1990) The geography of rural regional inequality in Mainland China. *Transactions of the Institute of British Geographers*, 15, 466–86.

Lo, F. C. and Yeung Yue Man (1996) *Emerging World Cities in Pacific Asia*. Tokyo: United Nations University Press.

Logan, John R. and Molotch, Harvey L. (1987) *Urban Fortunes: The Political Economy of Place*. Berkeley: University of California Press.

Logan, John R., Yanjie Bian, and Fuqin Bian (1999) Housing inequality in urban China in the 1990s. *International Journal of Urban and Regional Research*, 23, 7–25.

Loh, H. Y. (1999) Singapore to finish only portion of Suzhou park. *Singapore Straits Times*, June 10, p. 1.

Lovering, J. (1990) Fordism's unknown successor: a comment on Scott's theory of flexible accumulation. *International Journal of Urban and Regional Research*, 14, 159–74.

Lu, Hanchao (1995) Creating urban outcasts: shantytowns in Shanghai, 1920–1950. *Journal of Urban History*, 21(5), 563–96.

Lu, Junhua (1997) Beijing's old and dilapidated housing renewal. *Cities*, 14(2), 59–69.

Luo, Yadong (1998) *International Investment Strategies in the People's Republic of China*. Aldershot: Ashgate.

Ma, Laurence J. C. and Lin, C. (1993) Development of towns in China: a case study of Guangdong province. *Population and Development Review*, 19(3), 583–606.

Ma, Laurence J. C. and Xiang Biao (1998) Native place, migration and the emergence of peasant enclaves in Beijing. *The China Quarterly*, 155, 546–81.

Ma, T. (1993) Housing investment and housing finance. *Housing and Real Estate*, 4, 58–9.

Ma, Wuding (1998) The cultural function of the twenty-first century city. *Journal of Urban Planning*, 5(1), 1–2.

McGee, T. G. (1989) Urbanisasi or Kotadesasi? Evolving patterns of urbanization in Asia. In F. J. Costa, A. K. Dutt, L. J. C. Ma, and A. G. Noble (eds), *Urbanization in Asia*. Honolulu: University of Hawaii Press.

McGee, T. G. (1991) The emergence of Desakota regions in Asia: expanding a hypothesis. In N. Ginsburg, B. Koppel, and T. G. McGee (eds), *The Extended Metropolis: Settlement Transition in Asia*. Honolulu: University of Hawaii Press.

McGee, T. G. and Robinson, I. M. (1995) *The Mega-urban Regions of Southeast Asia*. Vancouver: UBC Press.

McMillan, J. and Naughton, Barry (1992) How to reform a planned economy: lessons from China. *Oxford Review of Economic Policy*, 8(1), 130–43.

Massey, D. (1993) Power-geometry and a progressive sense of place. In J. Bird et al. (eds), *Mapping the Future: Local Culture, Global Change*. London: Routledge.

Meng, Yanchun and Guangzhong Cao (1997) Analysis of the structure, position and characteristics of the "Zhejiang cun" in the South of Beijing. *Journal for Urban and Environmental Research*, Spring, 15–21 (in Chinese).

Meyer, D. (2000) *Hong Kong as a Global Metropolis*. Cambridge: Cambridge University Press.

Mirza, Hafiz (1986) *Multinationals and the Growth of the Singapore Economy*. London: Croom Helm.

Mollenkopf, John (1983) *The Contested City*. Princeton, NJ: Princeton University Press.

Moore, Sally F. (1978) *Law as Process: An Anthropological Approach*. London: Routledge and Kegan Paul.

Nakagane, Katsuji (1999) The workings of unemployment in China. *China Perspectives*, 25, 14–21.

Naughton, Barry (1995) *Growing Out of the Plan: Chinese Economic Reform, 1978–1993*. Cambridge: Cambridge University Press.

Nee, Victor (1989) A theory of market transition: from redistributive to markets in state socialism. *American Sociological Review*, 54, 663–81.

Nee, Victor (1991) Socialist inequalities in reforming state socialism: between redistribution and markets in China. *American Sociological Review*, 56, 267–82.

Nee, Victor (1992) Organizational dynamics of market transition: hybrid forms, property rights, and mixed economy in China. *Administrative Science Quarterly*, 37, 1–27.

Nee, Victor (1996) The emergence of a market society: changing mechanisms of stratification in China. *American Journal of Sociology*, 101, 908–49.

Nelson, Joan M. (1976) Sojourners versus new urbanities: causes and consequences of temporary versus permanent city-ward migration in developing countries. *Economic Development and Cultural Change*, 24(4), 721–57.

Ng, Mee Kam and Wing-shing Tang (1997) *The Pearl River Delta Urban System Plan*. Hong Kong: Hong Kong Institute of Asia-Pacific Studies.

Ning, Yueming and Tang Wing-shing (1996) Studies on suburbanization in Shanghai. In S. M. Li, W. S. Tang, L. H. Chiang, and S. Q. Zhou (eds), *Regional Economic Development in China*. Taipei and Hong Kong: National Taiwan University and Hong Kong Baptist University.

Nyaw, Mee-kau (1996) Investment environment: perceptions of overseas investors of foreign-funded industrial firms. In Yue Man Yeung and Y. W. Sung (eds), *Shanghai: Transformation and Modernization under China's Open Policy*. Hong Kong: The Chinese University Press.

O'Brien, R. (1992) *Global Financial Integration: The End of Geography*. New York: Council on Foreign Relations Press.

Ohmae, K. (1995) *The End of the Nation State: The Rise of Regional Economies*. London: HarperCollins.

Oi, Jean C. (1992) Fiscal reforms and the economic foundations of local state corporatism in China. *World Politics*, 45(1), 99–126.

Olds, Kris (1995) Pacific rim mega-projects and the global cultural economy: tales from Vancouver and Shanghai. Doctoral thesis, Department of Geography, University of Bristol.

Pacific Century (1999) What is Cyber-port? www.cyber-port.com/whatis.html, accessed on September 6, 1999.

Pahl, Ray E. (1975) *Whose City?*, 2nd edn. Harmondsworth: Penguin.

Pang, X. M. (1996) A preliminary study on the conditions and prospects for China to develop world cities. *Geographical Research*, 15(2), 67–73 (in Chinese).

Pannell, C. W. and Veeck, G. (1991) China's urbanization in an Asian context: forces for metropolitanization. In N. Ginsburg et al. (eds), *Extended Metropolis*. Honolulu: University of Hawaii Press.

Park, Jung Dong (1997) *The Special Economic Zones of China and Their Impact on Its Economic Development*. Westport: Praeger.

Peebles, Gavin and Wilson, Peter (1996) *The Singapore Economy*. Cheltenham: Edward Elgar.

Pereira, Alexius A. (2000) State collaboration with transnational corporations: the case of Singapore's industrial policies (1965–1999). *Competition and Change*, 4(4), 1–29.

Perry, Elizabeth (1993) *Shanghai on Strike: The Politics of Chinese Labor*. Stanford, CA: Stanford University Press.

Perry, Martin and Yeoh, C. (2000) Singapore's overseas industrial parks. *Regional Studies*, 34(2), 199–206.

Philips, David R. (1989) Special Economic Zones. In D. Goodman (ed.), *China's Regional Development*. London: Routledge.

Piore, Michael (1979) *Birds of Passage*. Cambridge: Cambridge University Press.

Planning Department of China Civil Aviation Bureau (1998) *Statistical Data on Civil Aviation of China 1998*. Beijing: China Civil Aviation Press (in Chinese).

Polanyi, Karl (1957) The economy as instituted process. In K. Polanyi, C. Arensberg, and H. Pearson (eds), *Trade and Market in Early Empires*. Glencoe, IL: Free Press.

Porter, Michael (1990) *Competitive Advantage*. Basingstoke: Macmillan.

Potter, R. and Unwin, T. (1989) *The Geography of Urban–Rural Interaction in Developing Countries*. London: Routledge.

Project Group of Shanghai (1995) *Shanghai City toward the Twenty-first Century*. Shanghai: Shanghai People's Press (in Chinese).

Pudong New Area Floating Population Office (1998) *Floating Population in Shanghai Pudong New Area – Statistical Data*. Processed.

Qu, R. X. (1997) New research on the indexes of degree of economic openness. *Economist*, 5, 77–83 (in Chinese).

Quanzhou Municipal Construction Commission Gazetteer Editorial Office (1995) *Quanzhou Municipal Architectural Gazetteer*. Beijing: Zhongguo Chengshi Chubanshe.

Quanzhou Municipal Government (1992) *Quanzhou Municipality Old City District Plan*.

Quanzhou Municipal Government (1995) *Quanzhou Municipal Urban Master Plan, 1995–2020*.

Quanzhou Municipal Statistical Bureau (1998) *Quanzhou Statistical Handbook*.

Rawski, Thomas G. (1999) Reforming China's economy: what have we learned? *The China Journal*, 41, 139–56.

Research Group of Yichun Prefecture Agricultural Bank Planning Research Group and Zhangshu City Agricultural Bank Planning and Science Federation (1996) The impact of labor export on rural financial markets. *Journal for the Study of Rural Society and Economy*, 3, 40–3 (in Chinese).

Research Group on the State of the Nation, Academy of Sciences (1996) *City and Countryside. Studies on Urban–Rural Conflicts and a Harmonious Development*. Beijing: Kexue Chubanshe (in Chinese).

Rittel, Horst and Webber, Melvin (1973) Dilemmas in a general theory of planning. *Policy Sciences*, 4, 155–69.

Roberts, Kenneth D. (1997) China's "tidal wave" of migrant labor: what can we learn from Mexican undocumented migration to the United States? *International Migration Review*, 31(2), 249–93.

Rosenthal, Elisabeth (1999) 100 million restless Chinese go far from home for jobs. *New York Times*, February 24, p. A1.

Rowthorn, R. E. (1974) Neo-classicism, neo-Ricardianism and Marxism. *New Left Review*, 86, 63–87.

Rozelle, Scott et al. (1999) Leaving China's farms: survey results of new paths and remaining hurdles to rural migration. *The China Quarterly*, 158, 367–93.

Russwurm, L. H. (1975) Urban fringe and urban shadow. In R. C. Bryfogle and R. R. Krueger (eds), *Urban Problems*, rev. edn. Toronto: Holt, Rinehart and Winston.

Sassen, Saskia (1991) *The Global City: New York, London, Tokyo*. Princeton, NJ: Princeton University Press.

Sassen, Saskia (1994) *Cities in a World Economy*. London: Pine Forge Press.

Saunders, Peter and Williams, P. R. (1986) The new conservatism: some thoughts on recent and future development in urban studies. *Environment and Planning D: Society and Space*, 4, 393–9.

Saxenian, A. (1994) *Regional Advantage*. Cambridge, MA: Harvard University Press.

Schein, Edgar (1996) *Strategic Pragmatism: The Culture of Singapore's Economic Development Board*. Cambridge, MA: MIT Press.

Schinz, Alfred (1989) *Cities in China*. Berlin: Gebrüder Borntraeger.

Scott, A. J. (1986) Industrialization and urbanization: a geographical agenda. *Annals of the Association of American Geographers*, 76(1), 25–37.

Scott, A. J. (1988) *Metropolis: From the Division of Labor to Urban Form*. Berkeley: University of California Press.

Seidlitz, P. (1998) Letter from Suzhou: an oasis for foreign investors. *Singapore Business Times*, April 1, p. 8.

Selier, Frits and Klare, Ivo (1991) Are thresholds of migrant-consolidation changing? Family and low-income housing in Karachi. In Jan van der Linden and Frits Selier (eds), *Karachi: Migrants, Housing and Housing Policy*. Lahore: Vanguard.

Services Promotion Strategy Group (1998) *Tripartite Forum 1999: Report for the Services Promotion Strategy Group October 1998*, www.info.gov.hk/bspu, accessed on October 26, 2000.

Shachar, A. (1994) Randstad Holland: a world city? *Urban Studies*, 31(3), 381–400.

Shanghai Municipal People's Bureau of Civil Affairs (1999) *The Report of Shanghai Civil Administration Development*.

Shanghai Statistical Bureau (1990) *Shanghai Statistics Almanac, 1990*. Beijing: China Statistical Publishing Housing.

Shanghai Statistical Bureau (1997) *Statistical Yearbook of Shanghai 1997*. Beijing: China Statistical Publishing Housing.

Shanghai Statistical Bureau (1998a) *Shanghai Statistics Almanac, 1998*. Beijing: China Statistical Publishing Housing.

Shanghai Statistical Bureau (1998b) *Shanghai Economic Yearbook, 1998*. Beijing: China Statistical Publishing Housing.

Shanghai Statistical Bureau (2000) *Shanghai Statistics Almanac, 2000*. Beijing: China Statistical Publishing Housing.

Shen, Jianfa (1999) Housing temporary population in Chinese cities. Paper presented to the International Conference on Urban Development in China, Zhongshan, Guangdong, December.

Shirk, Susan (1993) *The Political Logic of Economic Reform in China*. Berkeley: University of California Press.

Short, J. R., Benton, M., and Walton, John (1993) Reconstructing the image of an industrial city. *Annals of the Association of American Geographers*, 83, 207–24.

Short, J. R. and Kim, Y.-H. (1999) *Globalization and the City*. London: Longman.

Shuai, Jiangping (1997) The population problem and policy in global metropolises in China. *Study of Urban Development*, 5, 10–13.

Singapore Economic Development Board (1995) *EDB Yearbook 1995*. Singapore: EDB.

Sit, Victor F. S. and Yang, C. (1997) Foreign-investment-induced exo-urbanization in the Pearl River Delta. China *Urban Studies*, 34, 647–77.

Sklair, Leslie (1993) *Assembling for Development: The Maquila Industry in Mexico and the USA*. London: Routledge.

Sklair, Leslie (1998) Globalization and the corporations: the case of the California Fortune 500. *International Journal of Urban and Regional Research*, 22(2), 195–215.

Smart, Alan (1992) *Making Room: Squatter Clearance in Hong Kong*. Hong Kong: Center of Asian Studies.

Smart, Alan (1998) Economic transformation in China: property regimes and social relations. In John Pickles and Adrian Smith (eds), *Theorising Transition: The Political Economy of Post-Communist Transformations*. London: Routledge.

Smart, Alan (1999a) Flexible accumulation across the Hong Kong border: petty capitalists as pioneers of globalized accumulation. *Urban Anthropology*, 28(3/4), 1–34.

Smart, Alan (1999b) Economic culture in theory and practice: getting things done across the Hong Kong border. In L. M. Douw, C. Huang, and M. R. Godley (eds), *Qiaoxiang Ties: Interdisciplinary Approaches to "Cultural Capitalism" in South China*. London: Kegan Paul International.

Smart, Alan (2000) The emergence of local capitalisms in China: overseas Chinese investment and patterns of development. In Si-ming Li and Wing-shing Tang (eds), *China's Regions, Polity and Economy: A Study of Spatial Transformation in the Post-reform Era*. Hong Kong: Chinese University Press.

Smart, Alan and Smart, Josephine (1998) Transnational social networks and negotiated identities in interactions between Hong Kong and China. In Michael P. Smith and Luis E. Guarnizo (eds), *Transnationalism from Below*. New Brunswick, NJ: Transaction Publishers.

Smart, Josephine and Smart, Alan (1991) Personal relations and divergent economies: a case study of Hong Kong investment in China. *International Journal of Urban and Regional Research*, 15(2), 216–33.

Smart, Josephine and Smart, Alan (1993) Obligation and control: employment of kin in capitalist labor management in China. *Critique of Anthropology*, 13(1), 7–31.

Smith, Adrian (1998) *Reconstructing the Regional Economy: Industrial Transformation and Regional Development in Slovakia*. Cheltenham: Edward Elgar.

Smith, Adrian and Swain, Adam (1998) Regulating and institutionalizing capitalisms: the micro-foundations of transformation in Eastern and Central Europe. In John Pickles and Adrian Smith (eds), *Theorizing Transition: The Political Economy of Post-Communist Transformation.* London: Routledge.

Smith, David (1996) The socialist city. In Gregory Andrusz, Michael Harloe, and Ivan Szelenyi (eds), *Cities after Socialism: Urban and Regional Change and Conflict in Post-Socialist Societies.* Cambridge, MA: Blackwell.

Smith, Michael P. (1999) Transnationalism and the city. In Sophie Body-Gendrot and Robert Beauregard (eds), *The Urban Moment.* Newbury Park, CA: Sage.

SND (1999) *Suzhou New District Investors Guide.* Suzhou: SND.

Soja, Edward W. (1995) Postmodern urbanization: the six restructurings of Los Angeles. In S. Watson and K. Gibson (eds), *Postmodern Cities and Spaces.* Oxford: Blackwell.

Solinger, Dorothy J. (1999) *Contesting Citizenship in Urban China: Peasant Migrants, the State, and the Logic of the Market.* Berkeley: University of California Press.

Song, Linfei (1995) The formation, trend and countermeasures concerning the tide of migrant workers. *China Social Sciences*, 4, 78–91 (in Chinese).

Song, Yinchang and Wei Wu (1997) On the characteristics of spatial agglomeration mechanism of formation and governing measures for the floating population in Beijing. *Economic Geography*, 17(4), 60–4 (in Chinese).

State Statistical Bureau, PR China (1996) *China Statistical Yearbook 1996.* Beijing: China Statistical Publishing House.

State Statistical Bureau, PR China (1997) *Urban Statistical Yearbook of China 1997.* Beijing: China Statistical Publishing House.

State Statistical Bureau, PR China (1998) *China Statistical Yearbook 1998.* Beijing: China Statistical Publishing House.

Storper, Michael (1997) The city: the centre of economic reflexivity. *Service Industries Journal*, 17(1), 1–27.

Sudra, Tomasz (1982) Mexican shanty towns: costs, benefits, and policy options. *Habitat International*, 6, 189–96.

Sum, Ngai-Ling (1997) Time-space embeddedness and geo-governance of cross-border regional modes of growth: their nature and dynamics in East Asian cases. In Ash Amin and Jerzy Hausner (eds), *Beyond Market and Hierarchy.* Cheltenham: Edward Elgar.

Sum, Ngai-Ling (1999) Rethinking globalization: re-articulating the spatial scales and temporal horizons of trans-border spaces. In Kris Olds et al. (eds), *Globalization and the Asia-Pacific.* London: Routledge.

Sum, Ngai-Ling (2001a) An integral approach to the Asian crisis: the (dis)articulation of the production and financial (dis-)orders. *Capital and Class*, 139–64.

Sum, Ngai-Ling (2001b) Varieties of capitalism in time and space: "embedded exportism" of East Asian newly-industrializing countries and their governance. In H. Beynon et al. (eds), *Varieties of Capitalisms.* Manchester: Manchester University Press.

Sum, Ngai-Ling (2001c) Material-discursive approach to the asian crisis: the breaking and re-making of the production and financial orders In P. Preston (ed.), *Asia–Europe Linkages.* Aldershot: Edward Elgar.

Sun, Yishe (1994) The spreading transformation of urban spatial structure: theory and experiments. *Urban Planning*, 5, 16–20.

Suzhou Municipal Statistical Bureau (1999) *Suzhou Statistical Yearbook 1998*. Beijing: China Statistical Press.

Szelenyi, Ivan (1978) Social inequalities in state socialist redistributive economies. *International Journal of Comparative Sociology*, 19, 63–87.

Szelenyi, Ivan (1983) *Urban Inequalities Under State Socialism*. New York: Oxford University Press.

Szelenyi, Ivan (1996) Cities under socialism – and after. In Gregory Andrusz, Michael Harloe, and Ivan Szelenyi (eds), *Cities after Socialism: Urban and Regional Change and Conflict in Post-Socialist Societies*. Cambridge, MA: Blackwell.

Szelenyi, Ivan and Manchin, R. (1987) Social policy under state socialism: market, redistribution, and social inequalities in East European socialist societies. In G. Esping-Andersen, M. Rein, and L. Rainwater (eds), *Stagnation and Renewal in Social Policy*. Armonk, NY: M. E. Sharpe.

Tan, T. H. (1994a) 14 investors sign up for Suzhou township. *Singapore Straits Times*, September 14, p. 1.

Tan, Ying (1994b) Social aspects of Beijing's old and dilapidated housing renewal. *China City Planning Review*, 10(4), 45–55.

Tan, Ying (1997) Redevelopment practices of housing area renewal in the old city of Beijing: a study from the residents' perspective. Doctoral thesis, Tsinghua University.

Tang, W. (1994) Urban land development under socialism: China between 1949 and 1977. *International Journal of Urban and Regional Development*, 18, 392–415.

Tanzer, A. (1997) Stepping-stones to a new China? *Forbes*, January 27, pp. 78–83.

Tao, Tao (1995) Problems in the implementation of Quanzhou's old city redevelopment plan. In *Proceedings of Renewal and Development in Housing Areas of Traditional Chinese and European Cities, An International Conference, July 6–18, Xi'an, Quanzhou and Beijing*. Beijing: Tsinghua University.

Taubmann, Wolfgang (1993) Socio-economic development and rural–urban-migration in China since the beginning of the 1980s. In Kok Chiang Tan, Wolfgang Taubmann, and Ye Shunzan (eds), *Urban Development in China and South-East Asia*. Bremen: Bremer Beiträge zur Geographie und Raumplanung.

Taubmann, Wolfgang (1997) Migration into rural towns (Zhen) – some results of a research project on rural urbanization in China. In Thomas Scharping (ed.), *Floating Population and Migration in China*. Hamburg: Mitt. des Instituts für Asienkunde.

Thielbeer, Siegfried (2000) Unzufriedenheit auf dem Land. *Frankfurter Allgemeine Zeitung*, October 23, p. 246.

Tickell, Adam and Peck, Jamie A. (1992) Accumulation, regulation and the geographies of post-Fordism: missing links in regulationist research. *Progress in Human Geography*, 16(2), 190–218.

Timberlake, Michael (1985) *Urbanization and the World Economy*. Orlando, FL: Academic Press.

Tolley, George (1991) Urban housing reform in China: an economic analysis. World Bank Discussion Paper 123.

Tong, Ming (1997) The change of industrial structure and the trend of urban development. *Journal of Urban Planning*, 4, 12–18.

Tong, Zhongyi and Hays, R. Allen (1996) The transformation of the urban housing system in China. *Urban Affairs Review*, 31(5), 625–58.

Turner, John F. C. (1968) Housing patterns, settlement patterns, and urban development in modernizing countries. *Journal of the American Planning Association*, 34(6), 354–63.

Ulack, Richard (1978) The role of urban squatter settlements. *Annals of the Association of American Geographers*, 68(4), 535–50.

United Nations Center for Human Settlements (1982) *Survey of Slum and Squatter Settlements*. Dublin: Tycooly.

van Ekland, Rachel (1995) Singapore's development strategy. In Kenneth Bercuson (ed.), *Singapore: A Case Study in Rapid Development*. Washington, DC: IMF.

Verdery, Katherine (1993) What was socialism and why did it fall? *Contention*, 3(1), 1–23.

Verdery, Katherine (1996) *What Was Socialism, and What Comes Next?* Princeton, NJ: Princeton University Press.

Wade, Robert (1998) The Asian debt-and-development crisis of 1997–?: causes and consequences. *World Development*, 26(8), 1535–53.

Walder, Andrew G. (1986) *Communist Neo-traditionalism: Work and Authority in Chinese Industry*. Berkeley: University of California Press.

Walder, Andrew G. (1992) Property rights and stratification in socialist redistributive economies. *American Sociological Review*, 57, 524–39.

Walder, Andrew G. (1995) Local governments as industrial firms: an organizational analysis of China's transitional economy. *American Journal of Sociology*, 101(2), 263–301.

Walder, Andrew G. (1996) Markets and inequality in transitional economies: toward testable theories. *American Journal of Sociology*, 101, 1060–73.

Wan, Yanhua (1998) The modernization of Chinese cities across the century. *Study of Urban Development*, 1, 4–6.

Wang, Chunguang (1995) *Social Mobility and Social Restructuring: Studies of the Zhejiang Village in Beijing*. Hangzhou: Zhejiang Renmin Chubanshe (in Chinese).

Wang, Fei-ling (1998) Floaters, moonlighters, and the underemployed: a national labor market with Chinese characteristics. *Journal of Contemporary China*, 7(19), 459–76.

Wang, Feng and Xuejin Zuo (1999) Inside China's cities: institutional barriers and opportunities for urban migrants. *American Economic Review*, 89(2), 276–80.

Wang, Hansheng et al. (1998) Zheijiang village: a unique way for Chinese peasants to move into the cities. *Social Sciences in China*, 19(1), 22–37.

Wang, Wuding et al. (1995) *Shanghai's Floating Population in the 1990s*. Shanghai: Eastern China Normal University Press.

Wang, Ya Ping (1990) Private sector housing in urban China since 1949: the case of Xian. *Housing Studies*, 7(2), 119–37.

Wang, Ya Ping and Murie, Alan (1996) The process of commercialization of urban housing in China. *Urban Studies*, 33, 971–89.

Wang, Ya Ping and Murie, Alan (2000) Social and spatial implications of housing reform in China. *International Journal of Urban and Regional Research*.

Webb, D. M. (1999) *Pacific Century CyberWork*. May 5, webb-site.com/articles, accessed on June 10, 2000.

Wei, Y. (1999) Regional inequality in China. *Progress in Human Geography*, 23(1), 49–59.

Wei, Y. and Ma, Laurence J. C. (1996) Changing patterns of spatial inequality in China, 1952–1990. *Third World Planning Review*, 18(2), 177–91.

West, Loraine A. (1997) Shifting boundaries. The lure of the city reshaping rural China. *China Business Review*, 24(5), 15–19.

White, G. (1993) *Riding the Tiger: The Politics of Reform in Post-Mao China*. London: Macmillan.

Whyte, M. K. and Parish, W. L. (1984) *Urban Life in Contemporary China*. Chicago: University of Chicago Press.

Wong, John (1999) China's fascination with the development of Singapore. *Asia-Pacific Review*, 5(3), 51–63.

Wong, Linda and Wai-Po Huen (1998) Reforming the household registration system: a preliminary glimpse of the blue chop household registration system in Shanghai and Shenzhen. *International Migration Review*, 32(4), 974–94.

Wong, P. K. and Ng, C. Y. (1997) Singapore's industrial policy to the year 2000. In S. Masuyama, D. Vandenbrink, and S. Y. Chia (eds), *Industrial Policies in East Asia*. Singapore: ISEAS and Nomura Research Institute.

Woo, Wing T. (1999) The real reasons for China's growth. *The China Journal*, 41, 115–37.

World Bank (1992) *China: Implementation Options for Urban Housing Reform. A World Bank Country Study*. Washington, DC: The World Bank.

World Bank (1999) *World Development Report 1998/99*. Beijing: China Financial and Economic Publishing House (in Chinese).

Wrnzhong, Wang, Jie Zhang, and Yiping Bu (1999) The change of Shanghai's housing twenty years later. *Shanghai Housing*, 2, 39 (in Chinese).

Wu, Fulong (1992) The types and characteristics of urban communities in China. *Urban Problems*, 5, 24–7 (in Chinese).

Wu, Fulong (1995) Urban processes in the face of China's transition to a socialist market economy. *Environment and Planning C*, 13, 159–77.

Wu, Fulong (1996) Changes in the structure of public housing provision in urban China. *Urban Studies*, 33, 1601–27.

Wu, Fulong (1997a) Urban restructuring in China's emerging market economy. *International Journal of Urban and Regional Research*, 21, 640–63.

Wu, Fulong (1998a) Polycentric urban development and land use change in a transitional economy: the case of Guangzhou, PRC. *Environment and Planning A*, 30, 1077–100.

Wu, Fulong (1998b) An empirical model of intrametropolitan land use changes in a Chinese city. *Environment and Planning B*, 25, 245–63.

Wu, Fulong (1998c) The new structure of building provision and the transformation of the urban landscape in metropolitan Guangzhou, China. *Urban Studies*, 35, 259–83.

Wu, Fulong (1999a) Intrametropolitan FDI firm location in Guangzhou, China: a Poisson and negative binomial analysis. *Annals of Regional Science*, 33, 535–55.

Wu, Fulong (1999b) The "game" of landed property production and capital circulation in China's transitional economy, with reference to Shanghai. *Environment and Planning A*, 31, 1751–71.

Wu, Fulong (2000) The global and local dimensions of place-making: the remaking of Shanghai as a world city. *Urban Studies*, 37, 1359–77.

Wu, Fulong and Yeh, Anthony Gar-On (1997) Changing spatial distribution and determinants of land development in Chinese cities in the transition from a centrally planned economy to a socialist market economy: a case study of Guangzhou. *Urban Studies*, 34, 1851–79.

Wu, Fulong and Yeh, Anthony Gar-On (1999) Urban spatial structure in a transitional economy: the case of Guangzhou, China. *Journal of the American Planning Association*, 65, 377–94.

Wu, Harry Xiaoying (1994) Rural to urban migration in the People's Republic of China. *The China Quarterly*, 139, 669.

Wu, Liangyong (1999c) *Rehabilitating the Old City of Beijing: A Project in the Ju'er Hutong Neighborhood*. Vancouver: UBC Press.

Wu, Lin and Minhong Xu (1999) To solve the difficulty from 1987. *China Construction Newspaper*, January 7, p. 1.

Wu, Weiping (1997b) The case of China. In Üner Kirdar (ed.), *Cities Fit for People*. New York: United Nations.

Wu, Weiping (1999d) *Pioneering Economic Reform in China's Special Economic Zones*. Brookfield: Ashgate.

Wu, Weiping (1999e) City profile: Shanghai. *Cities: The International Journal of Urban Policy and Planning*, 16(3), 207–16.

Wu, Xuelin (1999f) The educational level of Shanghai people increasing continuously. *WenHui Newspaper*, June 5.

Wu, Zheng (1998d) Shanghai to supply $843m in mortgages to help mart. *China Daily*, May 25, p. 7.

Xu, Juzhou (1993) Thoughts on the development of China's international cities. *Urban Planning*, 3, 20–3 (in Chinese).

Xu, Juzhou (1995) About the development space of China's international cities. *Urban Planning Review*, 19(3), 23–5 (in Chinese).

Xu, Juzhou (1998) Rational view on Chinese urban development in twenty-first century. *Urban Planning*, 2, 17–21.

Xu, Weina (1997) The distribution of Shanghai population going to be rationalized. *City Star*, November 4, p. 1.

Xu, Xiaogan (1996) Work and then return to set up big business. *Jiangxi Pictorial*, 3(14), 18–19 (in Chinese).

Xu, X. Q. and Li, S. M. (1990) China's open door policy and urbanization in the Pearl River Delta region. *International Journal of Urban and Regional Research*, 14(1), 49–69.

Yan, Xiaopei (1994) The effect of the information industry on the development of Guangzhou. *Economic Geography*, 14(3), 58–64.

Yan, Xiaopei (1995) The information industry and the urban system of the world. *Economic Geography*, 15(3), 18–24.

Yan, Xiaopei (1996a) The analysis of regional factors of the information industry. *Economic Geography*, 16(2), 1–7.

Yan, Xiaopei (1996b) The effect of the information network on the spatial organization of enterprises. *Economic Geography*, 16(3), 1–4.

Yan, Xiaopei (1998a) The analysis of the benefits of industrial structure and the trend of change in Guangzhou. *Study of Geography and National Land*, 8, 28–31.

Yan, Xiaopei (1998b) The analysis of the highly new technical industry developmental zone and change of regional structure. *Pearl River Delta Economy*, 4, 15–18.

Yan, Xiaopei (1999a) The good condition, restrictive factors and policy advice about the development of the knowledge economy in Guangzhou. *Study and Development of Region*, 2, 4–8.

Yan, Xiaopei (1999b) The study on change of social structure in Guangzhou since reform. *Journal of Zhong Shan University*, 39(2), 70–8.

Yan, Xiaopei and Yimin Yao (1997) Analysis of the development of the service sector and the characteristics of spatial distribution in Guangzhou. *Economic Geography*, 17(2), 41–7.

Yang, Dali (1999) *Beyond Beijing: Liberalization and the Regions in China*. London: Routledge.

Yang, Dennis Tao (1997) China's land arrangements and rural labor mobility. *China Economic Review*, 8(2), 101–15.

Yang, L. and Wang, Y. (1992) *Housing Reform: Theoretical Rethinking and Practical Choices*. Tianjin: People's Press of Tianjin.

Yang Rongnan and Zhang Xuelian (1997) The study on dynamic and model of urban spatial expansion. *Regional Study and Development*, 2, 1–4.

Yao, Shimo (1995) The background to and opportunities for building international cities. *Urban Planning Forum*, 3, 25–7 (in Chinese).

Yao, Shimo (1997a) Analysis on the spatial level of continued urban development. *Urban Development Study*, 5, 37–9.

Yao, Shimo (1997b) Some suggestions on the construction of Greater Shanghai international city. *Collection of Urban Planning*, 1, 21–3 (in Chinese).

Yao, Shimo (1998) *The Spatial Expansion of Chinese Metropolises*. Hefei: Chinese Science and Technology Press.

Yeh, Anthony G. O. and Fulong Wu (1996) The new land development process and urban development in Chinese cities. *International Journal of Urban and Regional Research*, 20, 330–53.

Yeh, Anthony G. O., Xu, X. Q., and Hu, H. Y. (1995) The social space of Guangzhou city, China. *Urban Geography*, 16, 595–621.

Yeung, Henry Wai-Chung (1998) Capital, state and space: contesting the borderless world. *Transactions of the Institute of British Geographers*, 23(3), 291–309.

Yeung, Wai-Chung Henry (2000) Neoliberalism, *laissez-faire* capitalism and economic crisis: the political economy of deindustrialization in Hong Kong. *Competition and Change*, 4, 1–49.

Yeung, Yue Man (1996) Introduction. In Yue Man Yeung and Y. W. Sung (eds), *Shanghai: Transformation and Modernization under China's Open Policy*. Hong Kong: The Chinese University Press.

Yeung, Yue Man and Lo, F. (1996) Global restructuring and emerging urban corridors in Pacific Asia. In F. C. Lo and Yue Man Yeung (eds), *Emerging World Cities in Pacific Asia*. Tokyo: United Nations University Press.

Yu, Tony F. (1997) Entrepreneurial state: the role of government in the economic development of the Asian newly industrialising economies. *Development Policy Review*, 15(1), 47–64.

Yusuf, S. and Weiping Wu (1997) *The Dynamics of Urban Growth in Three Chinese Cities*. New York: Oxford University Press.

Zhang, Kangqing (1998a) Some findings from the 1993 survey of Shanghai's floating population. In Børge Bakken (ed.), *Migration in China*. Copenhagen: Nordic Institute of Asian Studies.

Zhang, Li (1998b) Strangers in the city: space, power, and identity in China's floating population. PhD thesis, Cornell University.

Zhang, Maolin (1997) Theoretical thoughts on the phenomenon of the return wave of the migrant workers' wave. *Economic Research*, 7, 54–6 (in Chinese).

Zhang, Shanyu and Yang Shaoyong (1996) The tide of migrant workers will bring forth a tide of return. *Population and Economy*, 1, 43–7 (in Chinese).

Zhang, Shenghua et al. (1998) *The Current Status and Future of Shanghai's Floating Population.* Shanghai: East China Normal University Press.

Zhang, Xinsheng and He Jianbang (1996) The estimate of urban spatial growth and pattern change. *Geography and National Land Study*, 8, 12–15.

Zhao, Min (1999a) Urbanization, population mobility and China's road to urbanization in the twenty-first century. Paper presented at the Conference on the Future of Chinese Cities, Shanghai, July 30 (in Chinese).

Zhao, Yaohui (1999b) Labor migration and earnings differences: the case of rural China. *Economic Development and Cultural Change*, 47(4), 767–82.

Zhao, Yaohui (1999c) Leaving the countryside: rural-to-urban migration decisions in China. *American Economic Review*, 89(2), 281–6.

Zhongshan Planning Bureau (1993) *Comprehensive Municipal Planning.* Zhongshan.

Zhou, G. (1993) Current situation in real estate development. A report to the national conference of the construction industry. In *Briefing on Real Estate Development in Guangdong.* Guangzhou: Guangdong Yearbook Committee Printing Office.

Zhou, Lanchun et al. (1996) *Floating Population in Beijing.* Beijing: China Population Press.

Zhou, Min and Logan, John R. (1996) Market transition and the commodification of housing in urban China. *International Journal of Urban and Regional Research*, 20(3), 400–21.

Zhou, Pei (1995) Building a tripartite social structure is the strategic choice for the orderly flow of the migrant worker tide. *Nanjing Social Science*, 10, 117–24 (in Chinese).

Zhou, Xueguang (2000) Economic transformation and income inequality in urban China: evidence from panel data. *American Journal of Sociology*, 105, 1135–74.

Zhou, Yi (1997) *The Chinese Population and Resources, Environment and the Sustainable Development of Agriculture.* Taiyuan: Shanxi jingji chubanshe.

Zhou, Yixing (1986) Some suggestions on the definitions of urban place and the statistical standard for the urban population. *Urban Planning Review*, 3, 10–15 (in Chinese).

Zhou, Yixing (1991a) The metropolitan interlocking region in China: a preliminary hypothesis. In N. Ginsburg, B. Koppel, and T. G. McGee (eds), *The Extended Metropolis: Settlement Transition in Asia.* Honolulu: University of Hawaii Press.

Zhou, Yixing (1991b) *Introduction to Sociology of Housing.* Hefei: Anhui People's Publishing.

Zhou, Yixing (1998) Major directions of economic linkages: Some theoretical considerations. *Urban Planning Review*, 2, 22–5 (in Chinese).

Zhou, Yixing and Meng Yan Chuen (1998) The trend of suburbanization in Chinese large cities. *Journal of Urban Planning*, 3, 22–7.

Zhou, Yixing and Laurence J. C. Ma. (2000) Economic Restructuring and Suburbanization in China *Urban Geography* 21: 205–36.

Zhou, Z., Chen, C., and Zou, Z. (1992) *Eye on the Real Estate Industry in China.* Guangzhou: Guangdong Educational Publishing.

Zhu, Bin and Ni Guohe (1999) Bidding adieu to "poor street" with smile. *Wenhui Newspaper*, June 4, p. 1.

Zhu, Jieming (1994) Changing land policy and its impact on local growth: the experience of the Shenzhen Special Economic Zone, China, in the 1980s. *Urban Studies*, 31, 1611–23.

Zhu, Jieming (1996) Denationalization of urban physical development: the experiment in the Shenzhen Special Economic Zone, China. *Cities*, 13, 187–94.

Zhu, Jieming (2000) Urban physical development in transition to market: the case of China as a transitional economy. *Urban Affairs Review*, 36, 178–96.

Zhu, Liting (1999) How I can apply for the blue-chop household registration by following the new criteria. *Xinmin Evening News*, January 22.

Zhuang, Guotu (1996) The social impact on their home town of Jinjiang emigrants' activities during the 1930s. In Leo Douw and Peter Post (eds), *South China: State, Culture and Social Change during the Twentieth Century*. Amsterdam: North-Holland.

Zhuang, Yancheng et al. (1991) *A Comprehensive Review of Investment Environments in China's Coastal Cities: Quanzhou Volume.* Shanghai: East China Teacher's University Press.

Zong, Yueguang (1998) The corridor efficiency and landscape of metropolitan spatial expansion – the example of Beijing. *Geography Study*, 17(2), 119–24.

Index

Note: page references to figures and tables are in italics.

Printed and bound by CPI Group (UK) Ltd, Croydon, CR0 4YY

23/04/2025

14660945-0001